At War's End

All fourteen major peacebuilding missions launched between 1989 and 1999 shared a common strategy for consolidating peace after internal conflicts: immediate democratization and marketization. This volume argues that transforming war-shattered states into market democracies is a basically sound idea, but that pushing the process too quickly can have damaging and destabilizing effects. A more sensible approach would first establish a system of domestic institutions capable of managing the disruptive effects of democratization and marketization, and only then phase in political and economic reforms as conditions warrant. Avoiding the problems that marred many peacebuilding missions in the 1990s will require longer-lasting, better-planned, and ultimately more intrusive forms of intervention in the domestic affairs of war-torn states.

Roland Paris is Assistant Professor of Political Science and International Affairs at the University of Colorado at Boulder. He is an award-winning scholar and teacher, and a regular commentator on international affairs in national and local media.

At War's End

Building Peace After Civil Conflict

ROLAND PARIS
University of Colorado, Boulder

CAMBRIDGE
UNIVERSITY PRESS

PUBLISHED BY THE PRESS SYNDICATE OF THE UNIVERSITY OF CAMBRIDGE
The Pitt Building, Trumpington Street, Cambridge, United Kingdom

CAMBRIDGE UNIVERSITY PRESS
The Edinburgh Building, Cambridge CB2 2RU, UK
40 West 20th Street, New York, NY 10011-4211, USA
477 Williamstown Road, Port Melbourne, VIC 3207, Australia
Ruiz de Alarcón 13, 28014 Madrid, Spain
Dock House, The Waterfront, Cape Town 8001, South Africa

http://www.cambridge.org

First published 2004

Printed in the United States of America

Publication of this volume is supported in part by a grant from the Eugene M. Kayden Endowment through the Faculty Manuscript Award, University of Colorado at Boulder.

Typeface Sabon 10/12 pt.   *System* LATEX 2$_\varepsilon$ [TB]

A catalog record for this book is available from the British Library.

Library of Congress Cataloging in Publication Data
Paris, Roland, 1967–
At war's end : building peace after civil conflict / Roland Paris.
     p.   cm.
Includes bibliographical references and index.
ISBN 0-521-83412-0 (hardback) – ISBN 0-521-54197-2 (pbk.)
1. Peace-building.   2. Democracy.   3. Capitalism.   I. Title.
JZ5538.P37   2004
327.1′72 – dc22

2003065621

ISBN 0 521 83412 0 hardback
ISBN 0 521 54197 2 paperback

For Katie

Il est plus facile de faire la guerre que de faire la paix.
– Georges Clemenceau, 1918

Contents

Figures

Preface

This book examines every major peacebuilding mission launched between 1989 and 1999. There were fourteen in total; all were deployed to countries in which a civil war had just ended. Despite many differences, these missions shared a common strategy for consolidating peace after internal conflicts: immediate democratization and marketization. What can we learn from the peacebuilding record about the effectiveness of this strategy as a means of preventing the recurrence of fighting in postconflict situations? This volume argues that the idea of transforming war-shattered states into stable market democracies is basically sound, but that pushing this process too quickly can have damaging and destabilizing effects. Market democracy is not the miracle cure for internal conflict. On the contrary, the process of political and economic liberalization is inherently tumultuous: It can exacerbate social tensions and undermine the prospects for stable peace in the fragile conditions that typically exist in countries just emerging from civil war.

A more sensible approach to postconflict peacebuilding would seek, first, to establish a system of domestic institutions that are capable of managing the destabilizing effects of democratization and marketization within peaceful bounds and, second, to phase in political and economic reforms slowly over time, as conditions warrant. To do this effectively, international peacebuilders will have to abandon the notion that war-shattered states can be hurriedly rehabilitated. One set of elections, without creating stable political and economic institutions, does not produce durable peace in most cases. Avoiding the problems that marred many peacebuilding operations in the 1990s will require longer-lasting and ultimately more intrusive forms of intervention in the domestic affairs of these states, because more gradual and controlled approaches to postconflict liberalization are more likely to achieve the central goal of peacebuilding: the establishment of a peace that endures long after the departure of the peacebuilders themselves.

I developed this argument over several years. During this time, I was blessed with sharp-eyed and thoughtful colleagues and friends, many of whom offered their reactions to this project in its various stages of completion, and whose critiques prompted me to rethink and refine my analysis. They include Pamela Aall, Steven Brooks, Christopher Cavoli, Chester Crocker, Robert Dahl, Charles Hill, William Hitchcock, Alan James, Paul Kennedy, Jeffrey Kopstein, Ingrid Lehmann, Dan Lindley, Kimberly Zisk Marten, Mark Peceny, Kenneth Rodman, Bruce Russett, Jack Snyder, Steven John Stedman, James Sutterlin, Thomas Weiss, Alexander Wendt, and H. Bradford Westerfield. In addition, seven colleagues read and commented on the entire manuscript: Michael Barnett, Ian Cooper, Fen Osler Hampsen, Ian Hurd, Michael Ignatieff, Peter Viggo Jakobsen, and Michael Pugh. I thank all these people for their helpful criticism and advice, although I remain solely responsible for any errors of fact or interpretation.

I gratefully acknowledge financial assistance from the Overbrook Foundation, the Academic Council on the United Nations System, Yale University, the Council on Research and Creative Work of the University of Colorado, the Fulbright Foundation, the Eugene M. Kayden Endowment, the Social Sciences and Humanities Research Council of Canada, and the Canadian Department of National Defence. This project would not have been completed without their generous support.

In addition, I owe a debt of gratitude to the publishers and editors who allowed me to reproduce portions of previous works in which I tested out earlier renditions of my argument. Thanks in particular to Owen Coté, Sean Lynn-Jones, Michael Brown, and the MIT Press for permission to reproduce passages from Roland Paris, "Peacebuilding and the Limits of Liberal Internationalism," *International Security* 22:2 (Fall 1997), pp. 54–89; to Chester A. Crocker, Fen Osler Hampson, Pamela Aall, and the United States Institute of Peace for permission to reproduce passages from Roland Paris, "Wilson's Ghost: The Faulty Assumptions of Post-Conflict Peacebuilding," in *Turbulent Peace: The Challenges of Managing International Conflict* (Washington, D.C.: United States Institute of Peace Press, 2001), pp. 765–784; and to Michael Pugh and Frank Cass Publishers for permission to reproduce passages from Roland Paris, "Peacebuilding in Central America: Reproducing the Sources of Conflict?" *International Peacekeeping* 9:4 (Winter 2002), pp. 39–68. Some of the ideas presented in these writings survived the criticism of colleagues and my own rethinking; many others did not.

I would also like to thank Christopher Coleman of the United Nations Department of Peacekeeping Operations for allowing me to spend several weeks at UN headquarters; Elizabeth Olsen for research assistance on Guatemala; Richard Holbrooke for answering my queries about Bosnia; and the many Cambodians and foreigners in Phnom Penh who shared their thoughts about peacebuilding with me.

Finally, several members of my family contributed to this project, both directly and indirectly. My mother, Erna Paris, an award-winning journalist and author, sparked my interest in politics and offered invaluable editorial advice on this book. Both she and my stepfather, Tom Robinson, gave me the privilege of growing up in a home that was full of books, discussion, and love – and, for that, I am deeply grateful. My sister and brother, Michelle Paris and Robert Paris, have been steadfast supporters throughout. My father, Jacques Paris, made two trips to a library in Montreal to track down the quotation from Georges Clemenceau that became the epigraph of this book.[1] I thank him and my stepmother, Régine Guérin, for their affection and encouragement and not least for all the wonderful meals we have shared – and will share in the future. But my greatest appreciation goes to my wife and two children: Katie, Julia, and Simon Paris. Katie lived with this project from its inception, through highs and lows. Somehow, despite her own busy job of protecting wilderness and open spaces in Colorado, the arrival of Julia and Simon, and the tango of diaper changing and bottle filling that we have happily danced for the last three years, Katie found the time to pore through this volume in its many drafts, and I benefited immensely from her editorial talents. For her love and friendship, the book is dedicated to her.

[1] The source of the quotation is Alexandre Ribot, *Journal d'Alexandre Ribot et Correspondances Inédites, 1914–1922* (Paris: Plon et Nourrit, 1936), p. 255.

Introduction

In the early 1990s, a new threat to global security and human welfare caught the attention of political analysts and policymakers around the world, a threat that few observers had anticipated: pervasive and pernicious internal violence. They were right to be concerned. Civil wars (which take place primarily within the borders of a single state and among belligerents who normally reside in that state) accounted for 94 percent of all armed conflicts fought in the 1990s.[1] From Africa to Central Asia, internecine violence and collapsing states became an unfortunate but familiar feature of the post–Cold War political landscape.[2]

The nature of the threat posed by these conflicts was both humanitarian and strategic. From a humanitarian standpoint, this violence inflicted appalling losses on civilian noncombatants. At the beginning of the twentieth century, approximately 90 percent of war victims were soldiers; during the 1990s, by contrast, an estimated 90 percent of those killed in armed conflicts were civilians.[3] Attacks and atrocities against noncombatants became widely employed as deliberate strategies of warfare – including such tactics as systematic rape, mass executions, ethnic cleansing, and even genocide – prompting some commentators to lament the revival of "premodern" forms of fighting that dispensed with customary constraints on the waging of war.[4] Internal conflicts were also the principal source of mass

[1] Wallensteen and Sollenberg 2001, p. 632. From 1989 to 2000 (inclusive), there were 111 armed conflicts in the world, of which 104 were intrastate conflicts.
[2] For vivid though somewhat apocalyptic description of these conflict zones, see Kaplan 1996.
[3] UNDP 2002, p. 85; and Collier et al. 2003, p. 17. Also striking is the fact that the ratio of civilian-to-military deaths nearly tripled from the 1980s to the 1990s alone (Kaldor 1999, p. 9).
[4] For example, Snow 1996; and Ignatieff 1997.

refugee movements in the 1990s, which often gave rise to further humanitarian emergencies.[5]

In addition, chronic civil unrest represented a threat to regional, and even global, stability. Several internal conflicts spilled over international borders and undermined the security of adjacent states – as the Rwandan conflict did when it spread to neighboring Zaire in the mid-1990s, causing the collapse of the Zaire government and triggering a regional war that continued for the rest of the decade. Even when fighting remained geographically contained, the flight of refugees from war-torn states endangered the political stability of nearby countries – as in the case of Macedonia, which became the reluctant host to millions of refugees from Kosovo in 1999. Terrorist and criminal networks, operating with relative impunity in states riven by civil war, also posed security threats to other countries.[6] The September 2001 attacks on New York and Washington, D.C., reportedly perpetrated by a terrorist group based in war-ravaged Afghanistan, dramatically illustrated the danger of allowing civil conflicts to fester. As British Foreign Secretary Jack Straw observed in light of these attacks, "When we allow governments to fail, warlords, drug barons, or terrorists fill the vacuum.... Terrorists are strongest where states are weakest."[7]

In response to these challenges, the international community experimented with a number of new techniques for managing the problem of civil unrest and state failure. This task fell largely to the United Nations (UN) and several other leading governmental and nongovernmental organizations, which launched a succession of major operations in countries plagued by internal violence. A few of these missions sought to deliver humanitarian assistance and protect civilian populations in the midst of ongoing conflicts. Most, however, were deployed in the immediate aftermath of civil wars with the goal of preventing a recurrence of violence. These postconflict missions became known as "peacebuilding" operations.[8]

The aim of peacebuilding, in the words of UN Secretary-General Kofi Annan, was "to create the conditions necessary for a sustainable peace in war-torn societies" – that is, a peace that would endure long after the departure of the peacebuilders themselves.[9] Annan's predecessor, Boutros Boutros-Ghali, similarly defined the purpose of peacebuilding as the attempt "to identify and support structures which will tend to strengthen and solidify peace

[5] Of the twenty countries that were the largest sources of refugees in the world in 1995, no fewer than nineteen were embroiled in intrastate conflicts at the time (Kane 1995, p. 18; and Kane 1996, p. 96).
[6] Takeyh and Gvosdev 2002.   [7] Quoted in Chege 2002, p. 147.
[8] Some commentators define peacebuilding more broadly – as efforts to avert conflict either before or after war. This volume adopts the more common designation of peacebuilding as a *postconflict* activity, as I shall explain in Chapter 1.
[9] Annan 1999b, para. 101.

in order to avoid a relapse into conflict."[10] The rationale for this kind of mission was straightforward and compelling: Without effective techniques for preventing the recurrence of violence in war-shattered states, large-scale conflict might resume after the initial termination of hostilities, thereby undermining and squandering international efforts to stop the fighting in the first place. But creating the conditions for a stable and lasting peace in the immediate aftermath of a civil war would not be an easy task, because it entailed much more than just monitoring a ceasefire. As both Annan and Boutros-Ghali pointed out, peacebuilding involved identifying and alleviating the underlying sources of conflict within a war-shattered state, which required a thorough understanding of local conditions.[11]

To complicate matters, many states emerging from civil conflicts were teetering on the brink between peace and war, with their inhabitants divided by mutual animosities, resentments, and fears, and with large numbers of readily available weapons and ex-combatants proficient in using them. In addition, conditions of general economic distress, weak or nonexistent governmental institutions, few social services for the needy (including those displaced or dispossessed during the war), and damaged physical infrastructure combined to exacerbate local instability. Yet these volatile conditions were precisely what made postconflict peacebuilding so indispensable. The very fragility of war-shattered states – and the fact that countries with a recent history of civil violence had an almost 50 percent chance of slipping back into violence – created the need.[12]

Postconflict peacebuilding developed into something of a growth industry in the 1990s. The first major operation was deployed to Namibia in 1989, followed by missions to Nicaragua (1989), Angola (1991), Cambodia (1991), El Salvador (1991), Mozambique (1992), Liberia (1993), Rwanda (1993), Bosnia (1995), Croatia (1995), Guatemala (1997), East Timor (1999), Kosovo (1999), and Sierra Leone (1999). In total, fourteen major peacebuilding operations were deployed between 1989 and 1999 to territories that had recently experienced civil conflicts.[13] These operations involved a diverse array of international actors performing a wide range of functions – from

---

[10] Boutros-Ghali 1992, p. 11.
[11] Boutros-Ghali 1992, p. 32; Boutros-Ghali 1995, para. 49; and Annan 1998, para. 63.
[12] Collier et al. (2003, p. 83) report that the typical country emerging from a civil war has a 44% chance of sliding back into conflict within the first five years of peace. They base this finding on a study of seventy-eight large civil conflicts between 1960 and 1999. See also Collier and Sambanis 2002, p. 5.
[13] This excludes missions that did not follow a civil war (such as the one deployed to Haiti) and missions that took place in the midst of an ongoing conflict (such as the operation in Somalia). For a full explanation of why I define certain missions, and not others, as "major postconflict peacebuilding operations," see Chapter 3. Bosnia-Herzegovina is referred to as "Bosnia" throughout this book.

writing and rewriting national constitutions to drafting criminal laws, organizing and administering elections, tutoring policemen, lawyers, and judges, formulating economic policies, and temporarily taking over the administration of entire territories – all in the hope of establishing the conditions for stable and lasting peace. Some missions, such as the operations in Bosnia and Kosovo, attracted close attention from the international news media, while others labored away in relative obscurity. But taken together, these fourteen peacebuilding operations represented the most ambitious and concerted international effort to rehabilitate war-shattered states since the Allied reconstruction of Germany and Japan following World War II. Peacebuilding was nothing less than an enormous experiment in social engineering, aimed at creating the domestic conditions for durable peace within countries just emerging from civil wars.

What principles and assumptions guided this experiment? Which models or theories of conflict management, if any, did international peacebuilders apply in their efforts to rehabilitate war-shattered states? While the literature on peacebuilding has burgeoned since the end of the Cold War, few writers have scrutinized the assumptions that underpin the design and conduct of these operations.[14] Observers have dissected the strengths and weaknesses of many missions, but paid relatively little attention to the conceptual foundations of peacebuilding itself, or the basic premises upon which these operations are based.[15] Such questions are important, however, because they allow us to investigate whether the prevailing approach is, or is not, well suited to the task of consolidating peace in war-shattered states, and whether alternative means might be more appropriate. Given the importance of peacebuilding as a means of managing civil violence in the post–Cold War world and the threats that uncontrolled internal conflicts pose to regional and global security and to human welfare, any opportunity to improve the effectiveness of future operations should be vigorously pursued.

Indeed, there is no sign that the demand for new peacebuilding missions will decline in the coming years. Although this book focuses on postconflict operations launched between 1989 and 1999, the early years of the twenty-first century have already witnessed the deployment of new missions to places such as Afghanistan (2002), Ivory Coast (2003), and Liberia

---

[14] I elaborate this critique in Paris 2000. Recent works on peacebuilding that pay little attention to the underlying assumptions of peacebuilding include Doyle and Sambanis 2000; Cousens and Kumar 2001; Reychler and Paffenholz 2001; Stedman, Rothchild, and Cousens 2002; Fortna 2002; Howard 2002; and Caplan 2002. Many of these works offer important insights into the challenges that peacebuilders have encountered in the field, but they do not "problematize" the theoretical underpinnings of these operations. For a comprehensive bibliography of pre-2000 publications on peacebuilding, see Clerc 2000.

[15] Works that *do* consider the underlying assumptions of peacebuilding include Barnett 1995 and 1997; Debrix 1999; Pugh 2000b; Stanley and Peceny 2001; Lipson 2002; and Jakobsen 2002.

(2003)[16] – and at this writing, the United States is seeking to rebuild Iraq, a country that it occupied in the late spring of 2003. This volume does not investigate these latter operations, not only because they were launched after 1999, the cut-off date for this study, but also because the Afghanistan and Iraq missions followed foreign invasions of these countries. The challenges of peacebuilding after foreign conquest are quite different from those in post–civil war missions, particularly when the peacebuilders are the conquering powers themselves. So while it is essential to apply the lessons of the 1990s to new and future operations, this book focuses on a particular category of peacebuilding missions – those deployed in the aftermath of internal wars – and the lessons of these missions do not apply automatically, or directly, to other types of operations.[17]

The Argument of This Book

My thesis is straightforward. Peacebuilding missions in the 1990s were guided by a generally unstated but widely accepted theory of conflict management: the notion that promoting "liberalization" in countries that had recently experienced civil war would help to create the conditions for a stable and lasting peace. In the political realm, liberalization means democratization, or the promotion of periodic and genuine elections, constitutional limitations on the exercise of governmental power, and respect for basic civil liberties, including freedom of speech, assembly, and conscience. In the economic realm, liberalization means marketization, or movement toward a market-oriented economic model, including measures aimed at minimizing government intrusion in the economy, and maximizing the freedom for private investors, producers, and consumers to pursue their respective economic interests. Although the fourteen peacebuilding operations launched between 1989 and 1999 varied in many respects, their most striking similarity is that they all sought to transform war-shattered states into "liberal market democracies" as quickly as possible.

Underlying the design and practice of these operations was the hope and expectation that democratization would shift societal conflicts away from the battlefield and into the peaceful arena of electoral politics, thereby replacing the breaking of heads with the counting of heads; and that marketization would promote sustainable economic growth, which would also help to reduce tensions. Peacebuilding, in this sense, was a specific *kind* of social

---

[16] The 2003 mission to Liberia (the United Nations Mission in Liberia, or UNMIL) should not be confused with the operation that was launched in 1993 (the United Nations Observer Mission in Liberia, or UNOMIL), which ended in 1997 and is analyzed in Chapter 5.

[17] Because Afghanistan had been suffering from its own civil war prior to the U.S. intervention, I shall briefly discuss the early results of peacebuilding in that country in Chapter 11.

engineering, based on a particular set of assumptions about how best to establish durable domestic peace.

However, this approach turned out to be more problematic than anticipated. If the test of "successful" peacebuilding is simply whether large-scale conflict resumed in the aftermath of a peacebuilding mission, then most of the operations conducted in the 1990s were successful, because in all but three cases (Angola, Rwanda, and Liberia), large-scale hostilities have not resumed. But if we use instead the standard of success articulated by Kofi Annan and Boutros Boutros-Ghali – namely, the establishment of a "sustainable" peace, or a peace that will endure long after the peacebuilders depart from the country – then the picture becomes less favorable.[18] As we shall see, international efforts to transform war-shattered states have, in a number of cases, inadvertently exacerbated societal tensions or reproduced conditions that historically fueled violence in these countries. The very strategy that peacebuilders have employed to consolidate peace – political and economic liberalization – seems, paradoxically, to have increased the likelihood of renewed violence in several of these states.

Peacebuilders apparently believed that democratization and marketization would foster domestic peace; and, as it happens, there is a large body of empirical scholarship that partially supports this belief. Students of the "liberal peace thesis," from John Locke to the present day, have argued that liberally constituted states tend to be more peaceful both domestically and in their dealings with other countries, and recent evidence has shown that well-established market democracies are, indeed, less subject to internal violence than other types of states.[19] But it also appears that the *transition* from civil conflict to a well-established market democracy is full of pitfalls: Promoting democratization and marketization has the potential to stimulate higher levels of societal competition at the very moment (immediately following the conflict) when states are least equipped to contain such tensions within peaceful bounds. Peacebuilders in the 1990s seemed to underestimate the destabilizing effects of the liberalization process in the fragile circumstances of countries just emerging from civil wars. Their desire to turn war-torn states into stable market democracies was not the problem; rather, the *methods* they used to effect this change, including their failure to anticipate and forestall the destabilizing effects of liberalization, proved to be the Achilles' heel of peacebuilding.

I call the belief that democratization and marketization will foster peace in war-shattered states "Wilsonianism" – after Woodrow Wilson, the twenty-eighth president of the United States, who believed that liberalism was the key to peace and security in both international and domestic politics. Democracy, he wrote, promotes the "ascendancy of reason over passion" and promises

[18] See Chapter 3 for a discussion of standards for evaluating peacebuilding.
[19] For example, Rummel 1997. See Chapter 2 for more references to this literature.

"the supreme and peaceful rule of counsel," or rational debate, which is a recipe for "peace and progress" in political life.[20] Drawing on these ideas, Wilson insisted that the only way to establish a durable peace in Europe after the First World War was to emancipate the various nationalities that lived under authoritarian rule and to open the conduct of international relations to public scrutiny. Until the nationalities, or "peoples," of Eastern and Central Europe were permitted to exercise their right to self-government, he argued, unrequited grievances would continue to foment new conflicts. Any attempt to build peace that did not "recognize and accept the principle that governments derive all their just powers from the consent of the governed" was bound to fail.[21] Only a peace "planted on the tested foundations of political liberty" would be likely to endure.[22]

Peacebuilding missions in the 1990s reproduced Wilson's faith in the peace-producing powers of liberalization. This faith proved to be overly optimistic in Central and Eastern Europe after World War I, where tensions remained and fighting resumed, and also seems to be an overly optimistic formula for peacebuilding in the post–Cold War era. The purpose of this book, however, is not to reject the Wilsonian peacebuilding strategy in its entirety, but to expose the weaknesses of the naive version of Wilsonianism that informed the missions of the 1990s. Indeed, I shall argue that peacebuilders should preserve the broad goal of converting war-shattered states into liberal market democracies, because well-established liberal market democracies tend to be peaceful in both their domestic affairs and their relations with other states. The challenge, however, is to devise methods of achieving this Wilsonian goal without endangering the very peace that the liberalization process is supposed to consolidate. To this end, I shall propose a new peacebuilding strategy called "Institutionalization Before Liberalization," which begins from the premise that democratization and marketization are inherently tumultuous transformations that have the potential to undermine a fragile peace.

The new strategy would seek to minimize the destabilizing effects of liberalization in several ways. First, peacebuilders should delay the introduction of democratic and market-oriented reforms until a rudimentary network of domestic institutions, capable of managing the strains of liberalization, have been established. Second, once these institutions are in place, peacebuilders should manage the democratization and marketization process as a series of incremental and deliberate steps, rather than immediately unleashing political and economic competition. The strategy contains many other elements, but its core principle is this: What is needed in the immediate postconflict period is not quick elections, democratic ferment, or economic "shock therapy" but a more controlled and gradual approach to liberalization, combined with

[20] Wilson 1968, p. 90.   [21] Quoted in Knock 1992, p. 121.
[22] Quoted in Pomerance 1976, p. 2.

the immediate building of governmental institutions that can manage these political and economic reforms.

Institutionalization Before Liberalization may, at first glance, seem more costly and time-consuming than the "quick and dirty" approach to liberalization that predominated in the 1990s. However, the potentially higher expense and longer duration of such operations must be weighed against the costs, both in human lives and material resources, that would follow a recurrence of large-scale violence. This strategy may also appear to be contrary to the goal of promoting market democracy, because it calls upon peacebuilders to delay the liberalization of political and economic life during the first, fragile period of postwar reconstruction. The objective of this approach, however, is ultimately to achieve more successful transitions to market democracy in countries that are vulnerable to the destabilizing effects of rapid liberalization, and thus to establish a more durable peace. If, as I argue, pervasive civil conflict poses one of the principal threats to human welfare and global security in the post–Cold War era, and the prevailing approach to peacebuilding is flawed, then new policies for more effective peacebuilding are warranted.

Bridging Theory and Practice

The book speaks simultaneously to scholars and practitioners of peacebuilding, and to others interested in the challenges of managing civil violence. The central finding – that implementing liberalization too quickly and in the absence of effective institutions can counteract efforts to consolidate peace – has immediate implications for policymakers in national governments and international organizations who have the primary responsibility for designing peacebuilding operations. Yet this is not simply a work of policy analysis or policy prescription, for it raises questions that scholars of international relations and comparative politics have yet to explore in depth. In what ways, for example, might the transition to market democracy *imperil* domestic peace, particularly in the immediate aftermath of civil conflict? The liberalization process itself, I shall argue, can give rise to several different "pathologies" that may occur in any state undergoing such a transition. Peacebuilding host states are particularly susceptible to these problems because of the distinctive characteristics of societies that have recently experienced internecine violence – characteristics that will be described in Chapter 9 – and, as we shall see, the Institutionalization Before Liberalization strategy is specifically designed to anticipate and avert these pathologies.

This volume also contributes to ongoing debates over the liberal peace thesis. As noted, supporters of this thesis have long argued that liberal states tend to be more peaceful than other kinds of states. Unlike their Enlightenment-era predecessors, however, contemporary contributors to this literature have tended to "bracket" or ignore the question of how to *build* market democracies in conditions where governmental institutions do not exist or are only fragmentary.[23] As a result, we have learned a great deal from this literature about the benefits of market democracy once it is established, but very little about the war-proneness of states undergoing this transition, particularly in the immediate aftermath of internal violence. This book uses the record of peacebuilding to investigate this little-explored branch of the liberal peace thesis: the relationship between liberalization, institution building, and peace in countries that are just emerging from civil conflict.

In addition to addressing the specific concerns of both practitioners and theorists of conflict management, this book seeks to break down the artificial separation between those who study "theory" and those who focus on the "real world" problems of policy analysis and implementation. Too often, the practitioners of peacebuilding dismiss academic theorizing as overly abstract and detached from the practical challenges of running field operations. At the same time, many theorists of international relations and comparative politics make too little effort to translate their findings into recommendations for policymakers. This volume, by contrast, aims to set out and scrutinize the theoretical foundations of peacebuilding, and in so doing, to diagnose problems in the design and practice of these operations that might otherwise go undetected.

Organization of the Book

At War's End is divided into three parts. Part I ("Foundations") examines the political and ideological origins of peacebuilding, and investigates the assumptions that underpin these operations. Chapter 1 traces the history of peacebuilding and the resurgence of Wilsonian approaches to conflict management at the end of the Cold War. Chapter 2 examines historical and contemporary scholarship on the liberal peace thesis, arguing that many important questions remain unanswered, including the question of whether marketization and democratization offer a reliable remedy for civil conflict.

Part II ("The Peacebuilding Record") evaluates the effects of internationally sponsored liberalization efforts in eleven peacebuilding missions deployed between 1989 and 1998. Chapter 3 explains the methodology and scope of the case studies. Chapters 4 through 8 examine the effects of democratization and marketization in Namibia, Nicaragua, Angola, Cambodia, El Salvador, Mozambique, Liberia, Rwanda, Bosnia, Croatia, and Guatemala. Three post-1998 operations – in Kosovo, East Timor, and Sierra Leone – are discussed later in the book and in more provisional terms, because of their relative recentness.

Part III ("Problems and Solutions") describes the shortcomings of rapid liberalization as a peacebuilding strategy during the 1990s and recommends a new approach for future operations. Chapter 9 summarizes the findings of

[23] See Chapter 2.

the case studies and explains why liberalization has sometimes had destabilizing effects on peacebuilding host states. Chapter 10 elaborates the "Institutionalization Before Liberalization" strategy and responds to several possible critiques of this approach. Chapter 11 examines the record of missions launched after 1998, and explores the logistical and political challenges to reforming peacebuilding in the future.

PART I

FOUNDATIONS

I

The Origins of Peacebuilding

As the Cold War was coming to a close in 1989, the United Nations launched its first major peacebuilding mission in Namibia, following the negotiation of a peace settlement in that country's decades-long civil war. At that time, few observers predicted that postconflict peacebuilding would become an international growth industry, but over the next decade, operations were deployed to no fewer than thirteen other territories that were just emerging from internal conflicts.

Ostensibly, these missions provided "technical assistance" to local actors in war-torn countries – assistance aimed at preventing the recurrence of violence and establishing a stable and lasting peace. In practice, however, these operations were more than merely technical (or ideologically neutral) exercises in conflict management. As we shall see, they all promoted a particular model of political and economic organization: liberal market democracy. Why did peacebuilders embrace democratization and marketization as strategies for preventing renewed violence? And why did this brand of peacebuilding proliferate so rapidly in the 1990s? Answers to both of these questions can be found in the peculiar political and ideological conditions that prevailed at the end of the Cold War, when peacebuilding came into being.

The Cold War's End and the Rise of Peacebuilding

During the Cold War, the UN's main security activity was "peacekeeping," which typically involved the deployment of a lightly armed military force to monitor a cease-fire or patrol neutral buffer zones between former combatants.[1] The first major peacekeeping operation was deployed to Egypt in 1956, following the invasion of that country by Britain, France, and Israel. With the agreement of all of the parties, including Egypt and the

---

[1] See the Appendix of this chapter for a glossary of key terms, including "peacekeeping" and "peacebuilding."

invading countries, the United Nations Emergency Force (UNEF) oversaw
the departure of foreign forces from Egyptian territory, and then took up
positions along the Egypt-Israel border. UNEF was prohibited from using
force (except in self-defense) and from interfering in the domestic politics
of Egypt. The mission's mandate clearly stated that UNEF should "refrain
from any activity of a political character in a Host State" and in no way
"influence the military balance in the present conflict and, thereby, the political balance affecting efforts to settle the conflict."[2] An "after action" report
written two years later by then–UN Secretary-General Dag Hammarskjöld
reiterated the importance of these principles to the mission's success: Any
future peacekeeping operations, he argued, "must be separate and distinct from activities by national authorities," and must limit their role
to addressing the "external [that is, international] aspects of the political
situation," or else "United Nations units might run the risk of getting
involved in differences with local authorities or [the] public or in internal conflicts which would be highly detrimental to the effectiveness of the
operation."[3]

   The principles that guided UNEF in Egypt provided a template for future
peacekeeping operations conducted during the Cold War, including missions
in Cyprus and Lebanon and on the India-Pakistan border. Most of these
operations involved lightly armed contingents deployed to monitor cease-
fires and prohibited from intruding in the domestic affairs of the host states.
The mandate of the UN Interim Force in Lebanon (UNIFIL), for instance,
stated bluntly that "UNIFIL, like any other United Nations peacekeeping
operation, cannot and must not take on responsibilities which fall under the
Government of the country in which it is operating."[4]

   Before 1989, only two UN operations deviated from these "traditional"
principles of peacekeeping. The first was an ill-fated mission to the former
Belgian Congo in the early 1960s, which set out to provide the government
of the newly independent Republic of Congo with limited security assistance, but got caught in a power struggle between the president and prime
minister, and ultimately took over many of the functions of the Congolese
government, including the task of forcibly suppressing a revolt in one of
the country's provinces. The second was the United Nations Security Force

[2] "Regulations for the United Nations Emergency Force" (February 20, 1957) and "Second
and Final Report of the Secretary-General on the Plan for an Emergency International United
Nations Force," November 6, 1956 (UN doc. A/3302), reprinted in Siekmann 1989, pp. 40
and 4.
[3] "Report of the Secretary General: Summary Study of the Experience Derived from the Establishment and Operation of the Force," October 9, 1958 (UN doc. A/3943), reprinted in
Siekmann 1989, p. 52.
[4] "Report of the Secretary-General on the Implementation of Security Council Resolution 425,"
March 19, 1978 (UN doc. S/12611), reprinted in Siekmann 1989, p. 216.

in western New Guinea, which governed the territory from October 1962 to April 1963, between the end of Dutch colonial rule and the territory's transfer to Indonesian sovereignty.[5]

Apart from these two exceptions, peacekeepers went to great lengths to stay out of domestic politics, for several reasons. First, the United Nations Charter – the legal basis for UN peacekeeping – expressly prohibited the organization from intervening in matters "essentially within the domestic jurisdiction of any state."[6] Second, expanding the role of peacekeepers beyond the relatively limited task of monitoring a cease-fire would have required a more intrusive role for international personnel than the parties to a conflict were normally willing to accept. Third, the permanent members of the Security Council – including the Cold War enemies, the United States and the Soviet Union – were generally opposed to UN involvement in the domestic affairs of their respective allies and client states. Both the Soviets and Americans were concerned with maintaining the integrity of their own spheres of influence and did so partly by insulating these spheres from outside meddling. Achieving Security Council agreement for the deployment of a new peacekeeping mission was therefore possible only when both veto-wielding "superpowers" believed that their strategic interests were not threatened. In cases where civil unrest endangered the stability of a client state, the superpowers typically preferred to deal with these situations directly, rather than through the United Nations, in order to maintain greater control over the outcome.

Fourth and finally, even if the Soviets and Americans saw little threat to their strategic interests, Cold War ideological differences made it impossible for the United Nations to promote any particular model of domestic governance within the borders of individual states. The United States and most of its allies promoted liberal democracy and market-oriented economics, whereas the Soviet bloc championed a different version of democracy – communist "people's democracy" – which emphasized public rather than private ownership of the means of production and control of the state by a vanguard communist party on behalf of the working class. Some developing countries espoused their own brand of "guided" or "developmental" democracy, which rejected both the competitiveness of liberal market democracy and the class orientation of communist people's democracy, and instead advocated single-party rule as a means of carrying out the "general will" and of promoting national unity and economic development. So while support for democracy was nearly universally shared among UN members during the Cold War, there was fundamental and heated disagreement over the

---

[5] The administrative arm of the operation was known as the Temporary Executive Authority (UNTEA).
[6] Article 2(7) of the UN Charter.

meaning of democracy itself, which in practice prevented the organization from promoting any particular model of democracy as the "proper" model and reinforced the tendency of UN officials to distance themselves from questions of domestic politics.

"As a universal organization neutral in big Power struggles over ideology and influence," wrote Hammarskjöld in 1960, the UN's impartiality on matters of ideology and domestic governance allows the organization to "render service which can be received without suspicion."[7] In all of these ways, the political and ideological conditions of the Cold War era helped to restrict the functional scope of peacekeeping to narrowly defined and predominantly military tasks, such as cease-fire observation, and worked to limit the involvement of these operations in domestic affairs.

Many of these conditions changed suddenly when the Cold War ended in the late 1980s and early 1990s. With the decline in East-West tensions, neither the Soviet Union (later Russia) nor the United States was willing to maintain Cold War levels of military and economic assistance to their respective allies, particularly in parts of the world that were now perceived to be strategically inconsequential, such as sub-Saharan Africa. This allowed international organizations, including the UN, to become more directly involved in efforts to bring an end to several long-standing conflicts. The erstwhile rival superpowers, seeking to disengage themselves from costly foreign commitments, were now quite happy to have international agencies assume responsibility for these tasks.

The end of the Cold War not only created new opportunities for mediation in countries that had been proxy battlegrounds for the superpowers; it also sparked new civil conflicts in several other countries. Some regimes, such as those of Zaire and Somalia, had depended on foreign aid in order to monopolize political power in their countries by doling out patronage and ruling with an iron fist. When the flow of external aid diminished, their ability to squelch internal dissent slipped away and long-suppressed resentments came to the fore, sometimes violently. Perhaps the most vivid example of this phenomenon was Somalia, where the government of Said Barre was driven from office by its political enemies, who ultimately fought among themselves in what became an enduring and brutal civil conflict that blurred the boundaries between warfare and criminal violence. Meanwhile, dormant ethnic tensions reasserted themselves and sparked internecine violence across a band of formerly communist states stretching from Yugoslavia through the Caucasus to Central Asia. With Russia and the United States no longer willing to devote the resources and energy that would be needed to rehabilitate these "failed states," such international organizations as the United Nations were increasingly called upon to take action, particularly when

[7] Quoted in Urquhart 1972, pp. 458–459.

humanitarian crises in these states drew the attention of the international media.[8]

For all of these reasons, the "demand" for new multilateral peace operations swelled at the end of the Cold War. Simultaneously, the United Nations and other international organizations were more willing and able to "supply" these new missions, and a new collegiality in the UN Security Council raised the possibility of reaching consensus (or at least avoiding vetoes) on proposals to deploy new operations to countries that were experiencing, or just recovering from, civil conflicts. The result of this combined growth in demand and supply was a sharp rise in the number of multilateral missions launched in the years immediately following the Cold War. In the decade from 1989 to 1999, the United Nations deployed thirty-three peace operations, more than double the fifteen missions that the organization conducted in the four preceding decades.

Some of the UN's new operations undertook tasks that resembled the traditional peacekeeping missions of the Cold War. In 1988, for example, the organization deployed fifty military observers to oversee the withdrawal of Soviet troops from Afghanistan. Although this was the first time that a UN operation had monitored Russian forces, the nature of the assignment itself – verifying a cease-fire and troop movements – was something that the world body had done several times before.

Other operations, however, required the United Nations to perform more complex and less familiar tasks. In 1989, for instance, the UN was called upon to monitor the conduct of local police and to disarm former fighters in Namibia, while preparing the country for its first democratic election and assisting in the preparation of a new national constitution. These functions went well beyond the constraints that had traditionally been imposed on peacekeepers, including the prohibition on involvement in the domestic affairs of host countries. In 1991, new missions were also launched in Angola, El Salvador, Western Sahara, and Cambodia, which involved the organization of elections, human rights training and monitoring, and even (in Cambodia) temporarily taking over the administration of an entire country. In 1992, the UN deployed personnel to Bosnia and Somalia in the midst of ongoing civil conflicts, with the formal Security Council authorization to use armed force for purposes other than simply self-defense – which contrasted with the traditional practice of deploying peacekeepers only after the cessation of hostilities. Also in 1992, a new mission was sent to Mozambique with wide-ranging responsibilities that paralleled the operations in Angola, El Salvador, and Cambodia, including the preparation and supervision of democratic elections.

---

[8] On "failed states," see Helman and Ratner 1992/93. On the role of the international media in the creation of new peace operations, see Jakobsen 1996.

The term "peace operations" emerged as a generic label for the wide variety of missions that the UN began to conduct at this time, since many of these interventions no longer seemed to fit the traditional mold of peacekeeping. In 1992, Secretary-General Boutros Boutros-Ghali issued a policy statement entitled *An Agenda for Peace* that offered a new taxonomy of peace operations for the post–Cold War era.[9] Among other things, Boutros-Ghali differentiated between peacekeeping, peace enforcement, and postconflict peacebuilding. Peacekeeping involved the deployment of UN military personnel to the field with mandates that largely complied with "the established principles and practices" of traditional peacekeeping.[10] Peace enforcement referred to something relatively new: the deployment of missions that resembled peacekeeping operations in many respects, but that were more heavily armed and authorized to use armed force for purposes other than self-defense.[11] The operations in Bosnia and Somalia, both of which were authorized to use armed force to accomplish their goals, represented early applications of the peace-enforcement concept. The third category of peace operation – postconflict peacebuilding – sought "to identify and support structures which will tend to strengthen and solidify peace" in the aftermath of "civil strife."[12] Boutros-Ghali offered examples of particular tasks that peacebuilding might entail: "disarming the previously warring parties and the restoration of order, the custody and possible destruction of weapons, repatriating refugees, advisory and training support for security personnel, monitoring elections, advancing efforts to protect human rights, reforming or strengthening governmental institutions and promoting formal and informal processes of political participation."[13]

As it turned out, most of the UN's peace operations after 1988 focused on the task of postconflict peacebuilding. These missions differed from traditional peacekeeping not only in their functional complexity but also in their composition. The United Nations had virtually monopolized the practice of peacekeeping in the preceding decades, in part because the relatively straightforward tasks of traditional peacekeeping – such as cease-fire monitoring – could be performed by military personnel acting largely alone. But the more expansive and diverse functions of postconflict peacebuilding lent themselves to a new division of labor between the UN and other international agencies. In some missions, for example, military tasks were delegated to the North Atlantic Treaty Organization (NATO), while various specialized agencies of the United Nations, including the UN Development Program (UNDP), increasingly shared authority with regional organizations, such as the Organization of American States (OAS), the European Union (EU), and the Organization for Security and Cooperation in Europe (OSCE). In the realm

---

[9] Boutros-Ghali 1992.   [10] Ibid., p. 29.

[11] I say "relatively" new because UN peacekeepers in the Congo operation during the Cold War were given extraordinary enforcement powers as well. See Abi-Saab 1978.

[12] Boutros-Ghali 1992, pp. 11 and 32.   [13] Ibid., p. 32. See also United Nations 1996a.

of economic reconstruction, important responsibilities were delegated to international financial institutions – the International Monetary Fund (IMF), the World Bank, and regional development banks – along with the EU, national development agencies, and a host of international nongovernmental organizations (NGOs).

The precise constellation of international actors varied from one mission to the next. Some organizations were regular participants – in particular, the United Nations and its specialized agencies – while other actors made rarer appearances, so that a distinct alphabet soup of organizational acronyms constituted each mission. The peacebuilding operations of the 1990s, in other words, were not "run" by the United Nations – or by any other single organization. Although "lead agencies" were designated for some missions and for certain tasks, there was typically little central coordination of each agency's activities in the field; there was always considerable room for individual peacebuilders to define their own objectives and initiatives.

Given the multiplicity of peacebuilding agencies and the absence of a centralized peacebuilding authority, perhaps the most remarkable feature of the peacebuilding operations in the 1990s was that they all pursued the same general strategy for promoting stable and lasting peace in war-shattered states: democratization and marketization. The typical formula for peacebuilding included promoting civil and political rights, such as the right to free speech and a free press, as well as freedom of association and movement; preparing and administering democratic elections; drafting national constitutions that codified civil and political rights; training or retraining police and justice officials in the appropriate behavior for state functionaries in a liberal democracy; promoting the development of independent "civil society" organizations and the transformation of formerly warring groups into democratic political parties; encouraging the development of free-market economies by eliminating barriers to the free flow of capital and goods within and across a country's borders; and stimulating the growth of private enterprise while reducing the state's role in the economy. Another recurrent feature of these operations was their emphasis on *rapid* democratization and marketization. Planning for elections began immediately in every mission. Although in a few cases violence reignited before elections could be held, in all the remaining cases, elections took place within three years of the beginning of the operation. The same was true of economic reform: Comprehensive marketization programs were usually initiated right away.

The fact that these agencies tended to promote liberalization as a remedy for civil conflict reflected another major change that occurred in world politics at the end of the Cold War: the perceived triumph of liberal market democracy as the prevailing standard of enlightened governance across much of the world, including places where it had been anathema only a few years earlier. Few commentators had predicted the sudden collapse of liberalism's principal ideological competitor, Soviet-style communism. As recently as the mid-1970s, one prominent American political observer, the late Daniel Patrick Moynihan, had expressed pessimistic thoughts about the long-term prospects of liberal democracy. "Liberal democracy on the American model," he wrote despondently, "increasingly tends to the condition of monarchy in the nineteenth century: a holdover form of government, one which persists in isolated or peculiar places here and there, and may even serve well enough for special circumstances, but which has simply no relevance to the future. It is where the world was, not where it is going."[14] Moynihan listed the symptoms of liberal democracy's alleged decline, including the seeming strength of communist ideology in many parts of the world, and the failure of liberal democratic experiments in several developing countries, such as India, the "largest and most important experiment of all," which temporarily abandoned democracy for dictatorship in 1975. These developments, he argued, gave liberal democracy "a fateful air of a transitional arrangement."[15]

As it turned out, however, Moynihan's pessimism about the future of market democracy soon gave way to heady optimism as the Soviet bloc began to disintegrate in the late 1980s and formerly communist countries instituted elections. From 1990 to 1996, more than three dozen countries adopted liberal democratic constitutions for the first time, raising the total number of liberal democracies in the world from 76 to 118.[16] By the mid-1990s, 61 percent of the world's countries were holding competitive, multiparty elections for major public office, as compared with only 41 percent a decade earlier.[17] These developments prompted several commentators to declare that a "democratic revolution in global politics" had taken place,[18] or, in the even loftier words of one pundit, "Democracy's won!"[19] In a much-discussed article, U.S. State Department official Francis Fukuyama proclaimed the "end point in mankind's ideological evolution and the universalization of Western liberal democracy as the final form of human governance."[20] Although Fukuyama seemed to overstate both the finality and the extent of liberalism's new ascendancy,[21] the Western liberal conception of democracy did seem to have emerged as the "the only model of government with any broad legitimacy and ideological appeal in the world."[22]

---

[14] Moynihan 1975, p. 6.   [15] Ibid.

[16] Diamond and Plattner 1996, p. ix; and Diamond 1997, p. xvi.

[17] Diamond and Plattner 1996, p. ix.

[18] Roberts 1990, p. ix; Gershman 1990; and Ledeen 1996.

[19] Krauthammer 1989.   [20] Fukuyama 1989, p. 4.

[21] If history is any guide, new political and economic ideologies periodically sweep across human societies, displacing contemporary orthodoxies. On this historical tendency, see Lasswell 1935.

[22] Diamond, Linz, and Lipset 1990, p. x. In the words of Manuel Pastor (1998, p. 154): "With the Cold War's end, the norm of free elections as the legitimate basis of governing has become almost universal."

To be sure, the principles of political liberalism were not observed universally – there continued to be significant pockets of resistance, both within the Western liberal democracies (among certain groups of commentators, who believed that "democracy" connoted not only elections and civil liberties but also social and economic rights)[23] and from the governments of a few resolutely antidemocratic countries (such as in China, Iran, and Cuba). Furthermore, some states that formally adopted democratic constitutions and conducted elections continued to behave "illiberally" by refusing to grant their citizens basic civil and political rights.[24] But what was striking about the post–Cold War period was the relative absence of disagreement in world politics over the definition and desirability of "democracy" itself. Whereas during the Cold War the meaning of democracy had itself been a lightning rod for ideological conflict, there now seemed to be widespread agreement – even in the former Soviet bloc and in much of the developing world – that the liberal definition of democracy (emphasizing elections and political liberties) was the "correct" definition.[25]

The global shift to liberal democracy took place along with an equally impressive movement toward market-oriented economics. "By the mid-1990s," observed the Harvard economist Jeffrey Sachs, "almost the entire world had adopted the fundamental elements of a market economy, including private ownership at the core of the economy, a currency convertible for international trade, shared standards of commercial transactions..., and market-based transactions for the bulk of the productive sectors of the economy."[26] Even such putatively socialist countries as China and Vietnam moved away from central planning and toward marketization in the aftermath of the Cold War.

One indication of this economic revolution emerges from the *Economic Freedom of the World* report for the year 2000.[27] The report, sponsored by fifty-five economic research institutions, annually rates the economic openness of most countries in the world on a scale from 1 to 10, with 10 being the most open. Every country (for which data was available) is assigned a score, based on the composite index of economic openness, for each year from 1970 to 1997. According to these figures, economic openness declined by an average of 9.9 percent in 1970–1975, increased at just over 2 percent in 1975–1980 and 1980–1985, and rose by 4 percent in 1985–1990, reflecting the trend toward market-oriented economic reform in many parts of the world during this period. But in 1990–1995, the increase in economic openness was striking, with average scores climbing by over 16 percent. In the words of Claude Ake, market-oriented economics quickly became "something

---

[23] For example, Hyland 1995; Robinson 1996; and Peeler 1998. See also Gould 1988.
[24] On the phenomenon of "illiberal democracies," see Zakaria 1997 and 2003.
[25] Schmitter and Karl 1991, p. 75; Armijo, Biersteker, and Lowenthal 1994, p. 161; and Held 1998, p. 11.
[26] Sachs 1999, p. 98. See also Gilpin 2000, p. 15.   [27] Gwartney and Lawson 2000.

close to a global theology" in the immediate aftermath of the Cold War.[28] This was the political and ideological milieu in which the first flurry of peace-building operations were launched at the very end of the Cold War – and it was the context that shaped the design and conduct of these operations in fundamental ways, as we shall see.

The Agents of Peacebuilding

When faced with the task of postconflict peacebuilding, the world's leading international organizations seemed almost predisposed to adopt strategies promoting liberal market democracy as a remedy for conflict. Many of these organizations had, in fact, become active and vocal proponents of liberal democracy, market-oriented economics, or both, at the end of the Cold War. This ideological reorientation took place not only in the United Nations but also in other major organizations – including the UN's specialized agencies, the OSCE, the EU, NATO, the OAS, the IMF and World Bank, national development agencies, and many international NGOs engaged in relief and development tasks – in short, the principal practitioners of peacebuilding.

United Nations
The UN had been nominally committed to upholding the principles of representative democracy since the Universal Declaration of Human Rights was adopted by the General Assembly in 1948, stating that "everyone has the right to take part in the government of his country, directly or through freely chosen representatives" and that the "will of the people . . . expressed in periodic and genuine elections . . . shall be the basis of the authority of government."[29] In practice, however, Cold War disagreements effectively turned the organization into a "battleground between two opposing ideologies and power blocs,"[30] which prevented the UN from emphasizing its commitment to the principles of representative democracy and civil rights.[31] But a remarkable change took place within the organization at the end of the Cold War. "Suddenly," writes Carl Gershman, the provisions of the Universal Declaration of Human Rights relating to democracy were "dusted off and presented to the international community as the foundation for a new world order."[32]

The turning point came in 1989, with the launching of a UN mission to Namibia that set a number of precedents for the world body: For the first time, a UN field operation not only observed a cease-fire but also actively assisted in the creation of democratic political institutions within a sovereign

---

[28] Ake 1997, p. 287.
[29] Article 21. A similar passage also appears in Article 25 of the International Covenant on Civil and Political Rights.
[30] Jakobson 1993, p. 23.   [31] Forsythe 1996, p. 111.   [32] Gershman 1993, p. 9.

state. Shortly thereafter, the organization created a permanent Electoral Assistance Division to provide countries making the transition to democracy with technical advice and outside observers for the holding of elections.[33] The General Assembly underscored the organization's more active support for representative democracy by passing a resolution in December 1991 declaring that "periodic and genuine elections" are a "crucial factor in the effective enjoyment ... of a wide range of other human rights."[34] The UN High Commissioner for Human Rights also began to provide states with advice on electoral laws and other election-related legislation, and helped to train public officials filling key roles in the administration of national elections.[35] Further, in April 1999, the United Nations Commission on Human Rights, which had been one of the principal ideological battlegrounds of the Cold War, adopted a resolution affirming that "democracy fosters the full realization of all human rights" and defining democracy in clearly Western-liberal terms, emphasizing elections and civil liberties in particular.[36] The resolution passed by a vote of 51–0 with two abstentions: China and Cuba.

The UN Development Program, the world's largest multilateral grant-making agency, also embraced the goal of democratization after the Cold War. Although the UNDP's mandate was to promote "sustainable human development," primarily through measures aimed at eradicating poverty,[37] in the early 1990s the agency began to argue that the promotion of "good governance" in developing countries could help to achieve this goal. According

---

[33] As of July 2002, the Unit had received formal requests from a total of 103 member states for electoral support. ("Member States' Requests for Electoral Assistance to the United Nations System," http://www.un.org/Depts/dpa/ead/assistance_by_country/ea_assistance.htm, accessed in May 2003.)

[34] UN General Assembly Resolution 46/137 of December 17, 1991, "Enhancing the Effectiveness of the Principle of Periodic and Genuine Elections," reprinted in United Nations 1992, pp. 588–589.

[35] "Support by the United Nations System of the Efforts of Governments to Promote and Consolidate New or Restored Democracies," UN document A/53/554, October 29, 1998, para. 37.

[36] UN Commission on Human Rights Resolution 1999/57 (April 27, 1999). According to the resolution, democratic rights include: "(a) The rights to freedom of opinion and expression, of thought, conscience and religion, and of peaceful association and assembly; (b) The right to freedom to seek, receive and impart information and ideas through any media; (c) The rule of law, including legal protection of citizens' rights, interests and personal security, and fairness in the administration of justice and independence of the judiciary; (d) The right of universal and equal suffrage, as well as free voting procedures and periodic and free elections; (e) The right of political participation, including equal opportunity for all citizens to become candidates; (f) Transparent and accountable government institutions; (g) The right of citizens to choose their governmental system through constitutional or other democratic means; [and] (h) The right to equal access to public service in one's own country."

[37] United Nations Development Program, "Mission Statement," http://www.undp.org/info/discover/mission.html, accessed in March 2002.

to the UNDP, good governance meant "the exercise of economic, political and administrative authority" in ways that are "participatory, transparent and accountable."[38] In practice, this definition included support for democratic elections, which the agency views as "a major mechanism to promote accountability."[39] The promotion of good governance could also include efforts to help "establish and operate" national executive, legislative and judicial institutions in developing countries, on the grounds that

[s]ound national and local legislatures and judiciaries are critical for creating and maintaining enabling environments for eradicating poverty. Legislatures mediate differing interests and debate and establish policies, laws and resources priorities that directly affect people-centered development. Electoral bodies and processes ensure independent and transparent elections for legislatures. Judiciaries uphold the rule of law, bringing security and predictability to social, political and economic relations.[40]

For these reasons – and because the UNDP believes that "democracy, human rights, and good governance are indivisible" – the agency came to view the promotion of good governance as one of its central goals.[41] In the period 1997–2000, for example, the UNDP devoted 46 percent of its regular budgetary resources to good-governance programs, such as training election personnel in the Philippines and helping elected officials in Gambia to implement the administrative and legislative provisions of their country's new democratic constitution.[42]

If there were any doubts that the UN had, in fact, embraced a distinctly Western-liberal conception of democracy, the organization's post–Cold War secretaries-general – Boutros Boutros-Ghali and Kofi Annan – dispelled these doubts in their public statements. In 1996, Boutros-Ghali defined a democracy as a state that observed the following principles:

that the will of the people is the basis of governmental authority; that all individuals have a right to take part in government; that there shall be periodic and genuine elections; that power changes hands through popular suffrage rather than intimidation or force; that political opponents and minorities have the right to express their views; and that there can be loyal and legal opposition to the Government in power.[43]

In 2000, Kofi Annan similarly described the "principle of democracy" as "the right of all people to take part in the government of their country through free and regular elections."[44] Such endorsements of liberal democracy by the UN secretary-general would have been virtually unthinkable during the

---

[38] UNDP 1997, pp. 2–3.   [39] UNDP 2000c, chap. 5.   [40] UNDP 1997, p. 14.
[41] Cheema 1999.
[42] UNDP 2000a. For an overview of the UNDP's role in promoting democracy in peacebuilding operations, see Santiso 2002.
[43] Boutros-Ghali 1996, para. 21. See also Boutros-Ghali 1994.   [44] Annan 2000.

Cold War. Yet, as Annan characterized the UN's new values and priorities: "Support for democratization has become one of our major concerns."[45]

Organization for Security and Cooperation in Europe

A similar evolution took place in the Organization for Security and Cooperation in Europe. Prior to 1990, members of the OSCE (which was then known as the Conference on Security and Cooperation in Europe, or CSCE) operated on the principle of "respecting each other's right freely to choose and develop its political, social, economic and cultural systems as well as its right to determine its laws and regulations."[46] This meant that all forms of government – both democratic and nondemocratic – enjoyed equal legitimacy within the organization. But after popular revolutions swept across Eastern Europe in 1989, the organization passed a resolution in June 1990 declaring that "the development of societies based on pluralistic democracy and the rule of law are prerequisites for progress in setting up the lasting order of peace, security, justice, and cooperation that they seek to establish in Europe."[47] To minimize ambiguity, the resolution included a list of specific governmental structures and processes that the organization would promote, including representative government in which the executive is accountable to the voters, either directly or through the elected legislature; the duty of government to act in compliance with the constitution and laws; a clear separation between the state and political parties; a commitment to consider and adopt legislation through regular public procedures; publication of regulations as a condition of their validity; effective means of redress against administrative decisions and the provision to the person affected of information about the remedies available; an independent judiciary; and various requirements in the area of criminal procedure.[48]

The OSCE's democracy-promoting functions were concentrated in a new Office for Democratic Institutions and Human Rights (ODIHR), based in Warsaw, with a mandate to help OSCE-participating states "to ensure full respect for human rights and fundamental freedoms, to abide by the rule of law, to promote principles of democracy and...to build, strengthen and protect democratic institutions as well as promote democracy throughout society."[49] In its field missions, ODIHR drafted rules and regulations for democratic elections (primarily in the countries of the former Soviet bloc), trained election observers and administrators, conducted voter education programs, and encouraged grassroots political organization in states undergoing

---

[45] Annan 1997.
[46] This is one of the ten "guiding principles" set out in the Helsinki Final Act, which was signed by members of the CSCE in August 1975. Cited in Kritz 1993, p. 19.
[47] CSCE 1990, p. 1307.   [48] This summary is drawn from Kritz 1993, pp. 19–20.
[49] ODIHR website, http://www.osce.org/odihr/about.htm, accessed in August 2000.

the transition to democracy.[50] In 1999 alone, ODIHR conducted more than fifty projects in twenty countries, and sent more than nineteen hundred observers to monitor elections in eleven states.[51]

European Union

During the Cold War, the European Union's efforts to promote democracy beyond its borders were limited and haphazard,[52] but since the early 1990s, the organization has been actively engaged in fostering democracy in other parts of Europe and overseas. First, in Europe, negotiations aimed at inducting new states into the EU have included express requirements for candidate countries in Eastern Europe to consolidate their transitions to democracy and institutionalize civil liberties and the rule of law, among other things.[53] Economic liberalism is also a condition of joining the EU, with candidate states being required to have a "functioning market economy."[54] It appears, in fact, that these conditions have strongly reinforced the consolidation of transitional democracies in Eastern Europe that are seeking to demonstrate their suitability for membership in the Union.[55]

Second, in the Balkans, the EU has been deeply engaged in the peacebuilding operations in Bosnia and Kosovo. In Bosnia, one of the organization's primary goals has been "to establish functioning institutions and a viable democracy, based on the rule of law and respect for human rights."[56] It has pursued this goal by funding independent local media, helping to draft new laws for Bosnia that are compatible with European Union standards, and supporting a commission whose tasks include enforcing the human rights provisions of the Bosnian constitution.[57] In Kosovo, where the EU is by far the largest external donor agency, the organization has focused on developing a "modern market economy" in the territory, a task that it shares with the World Bank and International Monetary Fund.[58]

Third, in its relations with countries beyond Europe, the EU has not only funded democracy-promotion programs but also imposed increasingly

---

[50] Diamond 1995, p. 35; Franck 2000, p. 38; and the following ODIHR websites: http://www.osce.org/odihr/democratization.htm, and http://www.osce.org/odihr/unit-eassistance.htm, accessed in August 2000.

[51] ODIHR website, http://www.osce.org/odihr/elections.htm, accessed in August 2000.

[52] Youngs 2001b, p. 2.

[53] These criteria were determined at the EU's Copenhagen European Council in June 1993, reproduced in the website of the European Parliament, http://www.europarl.eu.int/enlargement/ec/cop_en.htm, accessed in May 2003.

[54] Ibid.   [55] Kopstein and Reilly 2000.   [56] European Union 2001.

[57] European Union 2000a.

[58] European Union 2000b. For more on the division of institutional responsibilities in the Kosovo operation, see Chapter 10. Since 1999, the EU's activities in the Balkans have been guided in part by the provisions of the Stability Pact for South East Europe, which include the goals of democratization and marketization in Bosnia and Kosovo (see Bartlett and Samardžija 2000).

stringent conditions on states with which it negotiates commercial agreements. Revisions in 1989 were made in the Lomé Convention – an agreement between the EU and developing countries in Africa, Asia, and the Caribbean – requiring these states to respect human rights as a condition of the agreement. A further revision in 1995 provided for the suspension of agreements with states that failed to "respect ... democratic principles and fundamental human rights."[59] Under these arrangements, the EU suspended trade and aid relations with several countries in the 1990s, including Lesotho in 1994, Niger and Sierra Leone in 1996, and Cameroon in 1997.[60] Although some commentators have accused the EU of failing to implement these provisions fully and consistently across all states with which it has trade and aid relationships,[61] the European Union nevertheless emerged as one of the world's most vigorous promoters of democracy in the 1990s.

North Atlantic Treaty Organization

The North Atlantic Treaty, signed in 1949, formally committed NATO to upholding "the principles of democracy, individual liberty, and the rule of law."[62] During the Cold War, the organization's pursuit of this goal was limited to the defense of liberal democracies of Western Europe against the threat of hostilities with the Soviet Union and its Warsaw Pact allies. NATO did not, in other words, actively promote democracy in states outside the area of the alliance itself. The demise of the Soviet Union, however, profoundly altered the strategic landscape of Europe. The likelihood of a military attack upon NATO suddenly seemed very remote, but at the same time a new problem emerged: Long-suppressed tensions threatened to erupt into violence in parts of the former communist bloc, including in nearby Yugoslavia, which collapsed into civil war in 1991. In response to these shifting circumstances, NATO began to reorient its activities. In June 1992, NATO foreign ministers decided that the alliance could make available its resources and expertise in support of the OSCE's conflict-resolution efforts in the former communist bloc.[63]

Since then, NATO has accepted primary responsibility for implementing the military aspects of the Bosnian and Kosovo peace accords, missions that aim, among other things, to establish functioning democratic institutions in these war-shattered Balkan territories. Furthermore, when NATO established the Partnership for Peace program in 1994 – a framework for cooperation between NATO and the members of the former Warsaw Pact organization, along with other states – the alliance imposed the condition that any state joining the program had to commit itself "to the preservation

---

[59] Quoted in Youngs 2001b, p. 35.   [60] Youngs 2001a, p. 19.
[61] For example, Olsen 2002; and Kubicek 2002.   [62] North Atlantic Treaty, preamble.
[63] Barrett 1996, p. 145. For an overview of changes in NATO's mission since the end of the Cold War, see Rader 1996; and Kaufman 2002.

of democratic societies."[64] Democracy is also a condition for gaining full membership in the organization.[65] In these various ways, NATO became directly involved in the promotion of democracy in countries outside its membership.

Organization of American States

Like the UN, the Organization of American States has always been constitutionally committed to upholding representative democracy,[66] but until the 1990s, the organization's efforts to enforce this commitment were, in the words of one commentator, "modest and episodic at best."[67] In June 1991, however, the OAS membership passed a resolution calling for "the immediate convocation of a meeting ... in the event of any occurrences giving rise to the sudden or irregular interruption of the democratic political institutional process or the legitimate exercise of power by the democratically elected government of any of the Organization's member states."[68] The adoption of this resolution signaled the start of a new period of activism in the promotion and defense of democratic governance by the OAS.[69] The organization has since monitored elections in Haiti, Nicaragua, El Salvador, Paraguay, and Surinam, and imposed sanctions following antidemocratic coups in Haiti and Peru.[70]

At the same time, the OAS also established a new Unit for the Promotion of Democracy to "provide guidance and support to the member states to strengthen their democratic institutions and procedures."[71] The unit's many projects have included educational courses for national politicians and officials on the workings of democracy, the coordination of OAS electoral assistance, and local-level projects to promote dialogues between ordinary citizens and their elected leaders in OAS member states.[72] In September 2001, members of the organization signed the Inter-American Democratic Charter, reaffirming their commitment to promote democracy in the Americas and to suspend the membership of any state in which an "unconstitutional interruption of the democratic order" has occurred.[73]

---

[64] NATO 1994.   [65] NATO 1999.

[66] In the preamble to the OAS Charter, member states express their conviction that "representative democracy is an indispensable condition for the stability, peace and development of the region." See also Articles 3(d) and 2(b).

[67] Diamond 1995, p. 36. See also Acevedo and Grossman 1996, p. 137; and Boniface 2002, p. 365.

[68] Resolution AG/Res. 1080 (XXI-0/91), cited in Franck 1992, pp. 65–66.

[69] For an overview, see Parish and Peceny 2002.

[70] See Schnably 2000; and Boniface 2002, pp. 365–367.

[71] Unit for the Promotion of Democracy website, http://www.upd.oas.org/Introduction/aboutus.htm, accessed in March 2002.

[72] OAS 2000.

[73] Article 21 of the Inter-American Democratic Charter, signed at Lima on September 11, 2001.

Bretton Woods Institutions

The International Monetary Fund and the World Bank are known collectively as the Bretton Woods institutions, with the World Bank itself comprised of two main constituent units: the International Bank for Reconstruction and Development and the International Development Association.[74] Before the 1980s, the Bretton Woods institutions had clearly different roles: The IMF provided short-term "stabilization" loans aimed at helping countries overcome temporary balance-of-payments problems, while the World Bank concentrated on lending for large-scale development projects. During this period, the International Monetary Fund frequently attached strings to its loans; the World Bank generally did not. In particular, the IMF typically required recipient states to implement fiscal and monetary austerity measures – such as reductions in public spending, limits on the provision of credit, and devaluation of the local currency – in order to lower the rate of inflation and restore macroeconomic balance.[75]

In the 1980s, however, the distinction between the respective roles of the IMF and World Bank gradually eroded as IMF lending packages became longer term, and as the World Bank began to impose policy conditionalities on its loans that were similar to those advocated by the IMF.[76] There was also a partial convergence in their conception of what was required in order to promote economic growth in the developing world – sometimes described as the "Washington consensus" – which held that international donors should encourage recipient states to implement economic liberalization policies, on the grounds that deregulation and privatization of these states' economies would create the most propitious conditions for sustained growth.[77] Specifically, both organizations began promoting "structural adjustment" programs in developing states, which included provisions for fiscal austerity and deflationary policies, privatization of state-owned enterprises, trade liberalization, currency devaluation, and deregulation of financial and labor markets.[78] John Walton and David Seddon explain the reasoning behind these policies:

Currency devaluations make Third World exports more competitive in international trade; reduced public spending curbs inflation and saves money for debt repayment; privatization of state-owned corporations generates more productive investment and reduces public payrolls; elimination of protectionism and other restraints on foreign investment lures more efficient export firms; cuts in public subsidies for food and basic necessities help to "get the prices right," benefiting domestic producers; wage

---

[74] The other major units of the World Bank are the International Finance Corporation (IFC), the Multilateral Investment Guarantee Agency (MIGA), and the International Centre for Settlement of Investment Disputes (ICSID).

[75] Taylor 1993, pp. 41–42.   [76] Feinberg 1988; Polak 1997, pp. 473–493; and Krueger 1998.

[77] Williamson 1989. See also Taylor 1997.

[78] Rapley 1996. See Weaver 1995 for a general description of structural adjustment, including an overview of the main elements of the "typical" structural adjustment program.

restraints and higher interest rates reduce inflation and enhance competitiveness; and import restrictions conserve foreign exchange for debt servicing.[79]

Since the end of the Cold War, structural adjustment programs sponsored by the Bretton Woods institutions have routinely demanded that developing states undertake not only economic liberalization but political liberalization as well – a policy shift that has been more evident in the World Bank than in the IMF.[80] In theory, the Bank is prohibited by its own Articles of Agreement from interfering in "the political affairs of any member" state, and Bank officials are required to make lending decisions only on the basis of "economic considerations."[81] From 1990 onward, however, the World Bank has effectively linked its lending to a requirement for "good governance" in recipient states, which includes "holding those in positions of authority responsible for their actions through the rule of law and due process rather than by administrative fiat" and "giving citizens a voice in governmental decisions and activities – not only through voting and representation but also through direct involvement in shaping and implementing programs that affect their lives and well-being."[82]

Although the Bank claims that it does not seek to impose any particular form of government on developing states, its conception of "good governance" (like that of the UN Development Program) nevertheless implies support for the principles of limited government and popular accountability through elections, which are central elements in the Western notion of liberal democracy.[83] In the words of Wolfgang Reinicke: "It is difficult to imagine how an independent judiciary, freedom of organization, speech, the media, and even elections, all of which are preconditions for good governance but also elements of democracy, could be operated only with reference to economic efficiency and effectiveness criteria."[84] Nevertheless, they are. For better or worse, the good-governance agenda pursued by the Bank (and to a lesser extent by the IMF)[85] has sought to remedy "two undesirable characteristics that had been prevalent earlier, the unrepresentative character of governments and the inefficiency of non-market systems."[86] Thus, the

[79] Walton and Seddon 1994, p. 41.
[80] Williams and Young 1994, pp. 85–86; and Shaw 1996, p. 41.
[81] Article IV, Section 10 of the World Bank's Articles of Agreement, cited in Skogly 1993, p. 760.
[82] World Bank 1995, pp. 5–6. See also World Bank 1992 and 1994.
[83] Jeffries 1993, p. 26; Islam and Morrison 1996, p. 11; and Gillies 1996. For an overview of the various ways in which "good governance" has been defined, see Moore and Robinson 1995.
[84] Reinicke 1996, p. 293.
[85] The IMF's global governance efforts focus primarily on "the rule of law, improving the efficiency and accountability of the public sector, and tackling corruption." See IMF 1997. For analysis of IMF "good governance" activities, see James 1998; and Phillips 1999.
[86] Weiss 2000. See also Abrahamsen 1997, pp. 145–146.

lending practices of the Bretton Woods institutions in the 1990s seemed to presuppose that Western models of economic and political organization were optimal, and that market-oriented economies and political democracies were mutually reinforcing.[87]

National Development Agencies

The national development agencies of the wealthy industrialized democracies, which are among the most prominent players in the world of international aid, have also shifted toward democracy promotion since the end of the Cold War, reflecting the broader trend toward "political conditionality" in development lending.[88] The United States Agency for International Development (USAID), for example, the world's largest aid donor, historically focused on social and economic development in poor countries, especially in the areas of health, population, and the environment, and until recently placed relatively little emphasis on democracy and human rights.[89] This focus began to change under the Reagan administration in the 1980s, when USAID initiated several programs to assist in the administration of justice and the conduct of democratic elections, particularly in Latin America.[90] In 1990, the agency identified the promotion of democracy as one of its central goals, announcing that "allocations of USAID funds to individual countries will take into account their progress toward democratization," with the objective of placing "democracy on a comparable footing with progress in economic reforms and the establishment of a market-oriented economy, key factors which are already used as criteria for allocating funds."[91] USAID subsequently launched a series of new programs aimed at assisting developing states in the areas of free and fair elections, constitution drafting, legislatures, judicial systems, local government, anticorruption efforts, regulatory reform, civic education, and independent organizations and media in civil society (including human rights, legal aid, and women's, professional, and church groups).[92]

Comparable changes have also taken place in the national aid agencies of other industrialized states, as virtually all major donor governments have placed more emphasis on democracy and human rights in their allocations of development aid since the end of the Cold War, including Canada, the Nordic countries, Holland, Britain, Belgium, France, Germany, Switzerland, and the European Union.[93] Further, the Development Assistance Committee of the

---

[87] Harbeson 1994, p. 7. See also Hibou 2002.   [88] Stokke 1995.
[89] Diamond 1995, p. 13.   [90] Ibid. See, in particular, n. 13 on p. 71.
[91] Cited in Nelson and Eglinton 1992, p. 16. See also Nelson and Eglinton 1996, pp. 170–172.
[92] Diamond 1995, p. 13.
[93] See Uvin 1993; Robinson 1993; Leftwich 1993; Baylies 1995; Islam and Morrison 1996; Forsythe 1996; Selbervik 1997; Commins 1997; and Blair 1997.

Organization for Economic Cooperation and Development (OECD), which coordinates policy among the world's preeminent aid donors, has endorsed the objective of using development assistance to promote "democratic and accountable governance."[94] Even Japan, which has traditionally been reluctant to link aid to the policies of recipient governments, announced in 1992 that it would include progress toward democracy among the principles that would guide the future apportionment of aid.[95]

International Nongovernmental Organizations

The number and variety of international nongovernmental organizations has increased rapidly in recent decades, making it difficult to generalize about the activities or ideological orientation of the international NGO sector as a whole.[96] In the final years of the twentieth century, however, a new class of international nongovernmental actors gained prominence – the so-called democracy NGOs – based primarily in the United States and in other Western democracies. Ronald Reagan's decision to emphasize democracy promotion in the early 1980s led to the creation of the National Endowment for Democracy (NED), modeled on Germany's *Stiftungen,* which had subsidized democratic groups in the developing world since the 1950s.[97] The NED, a publicly funded but privately run grant-making agency, has transferred funds directly to foreign organizations and democracy movements and has also channeled grants through four other U.S.-based international NGOs: the National Democratic Institute for International Affairs, the International Republican Institute, the Free Trade Union Institute, and the Center for International Private Enterprise.[98]

The British government founded the independent Westminster Foundation for Democracy, fashioned after the NED, in 1992; and the Canadian government established the International Centre for Human Rights and Democratic Development in 1989, with a mandate to "encourage and support the universal values of human rights and the promotion of democratic institutions and practices around the world."[99] Several private NGOs, such as the International Foundation for Electoral Systems, the Institute for Democracy in Eastern Europe, and George Soros's Open Society Institute, were also created around this time in order to support democratic transitions and elections in developing countries and the states of the former Soviet bloc.[100]

---

[94] OECD 1996; and Kondo 1999.   [95] Nelson and Eglinton 1996, p. 175.
[96] Rosenau 1995.   [97] Carothers 1999, pp. 30–31.   [98] Diamond 1995, p. 16.
[99] International Centre for Human Rights and Democratic Development 2000, p. 1.
[100] The proliferation of these international democracy-promoting organizations was, in part, the result of the shifting priorities of the industrialized democracies, which began to "contract out" the delivery of development assistance in the 1980s to NGOs. See de Wall 1997; and Barkan 1997.

To be sure, a number of NGOs were critical of the new prominence of political and economic liberalization as development goals. Some organizations in the human rights field – such as Amnesty International, the Lawyers Committee for Human Rights, and the International League for Human Rights – contended that too much emphasis was being placed on elections and too little on civil liberties. As the former director of Human Rights Watch, Aryeh Neier, wrote in 1993: "By and large the human rights movement would prefer not to be associated with the global crusade to promote democracy."[101] Others claimed that aid donors should do more to foster popular "grassroots" forms of political participation, instead of focusing so narrowly on elections.[102] Still others criticized the allegedly disruptive and damaging effects of market-oriented adjustment policies on developing countries.[103]

Yet these criticisms were less fundamental than they appear at first glance. Few international NGOs ever went so far as to endorse antiliberal political or economic policies – say, dictatorships or command economies. When international human rights organizations argued, for instance, that more attention should be paid to civil and political rights, they were still advocating principles that derived from liberal democratic ideology.[104] As David Williams and Tom Young note, most development NGOs share a "common vision of what development means which is rooted in Western notions of the state, 'civil society' and the self. The most radical part of the NGO discourse ... is their emphasis on 'grass roots' participation. ... But this terminology is always to be understood entirely within Western preconceptions."[105] This is not to say that these organizations' criticisms were insignificant but, rather, that they tend to remain committed to promoting liberal political or economic goals, albeit by different means. Put differently, most international NGOs (in the fields of human rights, development, and emergency relief) seemed to accept the view that free and fair elections, respect for civil liberties, and market-oriented economics are desirable objectives for developing states.[106]

For many of these governmental and nongovernmental organizations, liberalization was an uncontroversial solution for reconstituting war-torn societies. No great ideological debates were required to reach this consensus; it emerged almost automatically and without much questioning or comment, reflecting the newfound enthusiasm for liberal democracy and market-oriented economics in the world's leading international organizations, which in turn mirrored the ascendancy of liberal political and economic ideas in world politics at the end of the Cold War. "It is clear," wrote David Chandler in 1999, "that we have witnessed a major transformation in the language

[101] Neier 1993, p. 47.   [102] For example, VeneKlasen 1996.
[103] For example, Oxfam 1995.   [104] Carothers 1994, p. 112.
[105] Williams and Young 1994, p. 98.   [106] Fernando and Heston 1997, p. 14.

and themes of international relations. The international policy agenda today is dominated by issues such as the consolidation of democracy and the protection of rights."[107] This observation applies directly to the international organizations described here, which exhibited a newfound and "unprecedented commitment ... to the promotion of liberal pluralist arrangements" after the Cold War.[108] As three commentators put it in 1994, "the primary debate now taking place within governments and many international organizations centers not around whether democracy and market-oriented reforms are desirable, but rather around how they can be supported most effectively by external actors, and how best to secure and target the necessary resources."[109] Given all of the changes that occurred at the end of the Cold War – the increased demand for postconflict peacebuilding, the ability of the United Nations and other international agencies to respond to this demand, and the turn toward liberalism both in world politics and in the commitments of the world's leading international organizations – it comes as little surprise that peacebuilding operations would emerge as a growth industry in the post–Cold War era, and that these operations would tend to promote political and economic liberalization.

Indeed, it appears that it was a combination of changes in the power structure of international affairs at the end of the Cold War and a concurrent and related shift in the "cultural" environment of world politics that led the agents of peacebuilding to adopt the strategy of promoting liberalization as a means of consolidating peace in war-shattered states. One could argue that both the Soviet Union and the United States had been conducting their own versions of peacebuilding during the Cold War, within their respective spheres of influence. For the United States, that meant managing internal conflicts by propping up friendly regimes that were often touted as democratic (even if the real character of the regimes was different). For the Soviet Union, dealing with civil conflict within its client states meant building up socialist regimes on the Soviet model. When the Cold War ended, the power structure of world politics changed, and the American version of peacebuilding "won" and was largely adopted by international agencies for the peacebuilding operations of the 1990s. This model was, in a manner of speaking, internationalized.

But changes in the power conditions of world politics tell only part of the story, because there was a related shift in what might be called the international norms of legitimate statehood. The "world polity" school of sociology offers one set of analytical tools for examining this normative change.[110] Like other sociologists, members of this school study the norms,

[107] Chandler 1999a, p. 18.   [108] Taylor 1999, p. 555.
[109] Armijo, Biersteker, and Lowenthal 1994, p. 161.
[110] Examples of this school's work include Meyer and Hannan 1979; Meyer 1980 and 1999; Thomas, Meyer, Ramirez, and Boli 1987; Boli and Thomas 1997 and 1999; and Meyer, Boli, Thomas, and Ramirez 1997.

customs, and widely held beliefs – or the "culture" – of human societies, but rather than focusing on the culture of a particular national or religious group, they examine the formal and informal rules of the *international* system, or what they call the "global culture." Among other things, global culture defines who the principal actors in world politics should be, how these actors should organize themselves internally, and how they should behave. From this perspective, the modern state is itself a cultural form that is continuously reproduced because it is widely viewed as the most appropriate model for organizing human societies. At a given moment in history, some states may be considered as more legitimate than others; and it appears that the end of the Cold War gave rise to a historic shift in global culture in which liberal democracy came to be generally perceived as the most legitimate form of the state. This cultural revolution cannot be separated from the power changes that occurred at the end of the Cold War, as noted, but the global culture perspective does help to explain why international organizations seem to have willingly embraced liberalization as the "natural" solution to civil conflict and strategy for peacebuilding.[111]

Liberalization as an All-Purpose Elixir

Decades from now, historians may look back on the immediate post–Cold War years as a period of remarkable faith in the powers of liberalization to remedy a broad range of social ills, from internal and international violence to poverty, famine, corruption, and even environmental destruction. In the statements of government policymakers and the writings of academics, especially in the first half of the 1990s, market democracy took on the qualities of a universal antidote to misery and conflict, "almost mystically endowed with an array of characteristics that are supposed to assure both domestic and international peace and prosperity."[112] Writing in 1995, for example, Stanford University's Larry Diamond, coeditor of the *Journal of Democracy,* offered this paean to liberal democracy as a panacea for so many of the world's problems:

The experience of this century offers important lessons. Countries that govern themselves in a truly democratic fashion do not go to war with one another. They do not aggress against their neighbors to aggrandize themselves or glorify their leaders. Democratic governments do not ethnically "cleanse" their own populations, and they are much less likely to face ethnic insurgency. Democracies do not sponsor terrorism against one another. They do not build weapons of mass destruction to use on or to threaten one another. Democratic countries form more reliable, open, and enduring trading partnerships. In the long run they offer better and more stable climates for investment. They are more environmentally responsible because they must answer to their own citizens, who organize to protest the destruction of their environments. They are better bets to honor international treaties since they value legal obligations

---

[111] For an elaboration of this argument, see Paris 2003c.   [112] Slaughter 1998, p. 129.

and because their openness makes it much more difficult to breach agreements in secret. Precisely because, within their own borders, they respect competition, civil liberties, property rights, and the rule of law, democracies are the only reliable foundation on which a new world order of international security and prosperity can be built.[113]

At the same time that Diamond was writing these words, UN Secretary-General Boutros Boutros-Ghali was drafting a major policy statement that later became known as the *Agenda for Democratization*.[114] In the report, Boutros-Ghali expressed a similar missionary-like faith in the many benefits of liberal democracy. Given the importance of the UN as a peacebuilding agency and symbol of the international community, and the fact that the organization had been so riven by ideological disputes during the Cold War, the *Agenda for Democratization* is worth quoting at length. According to the secretary-general, "the practice of democracy is increasingly regarded as essential to progress on a wide range of human concerns and to the protection of human rights." These "human concerns," he went on to explain, include interstate and intrastate peace, economic development, cultural enrichment, control of crime and corruption, and protection of the environment:

Because democratic Governments are freely chosen by their citizens and held accountable through periodic and genuine elections and other mechanisms, they are more likely to promote and respect the rule of law, respect individual and minority rights, cope effectively with social conflict, absorb migrant populations and respond to the needs of marginalized groups. . . . Democracy within States thus fosters the evolution of the social contract upon which lasting peace can be built. . . . Democratic institutions and processes within States may likewise be conducive to peace among States. . . . The legitimacy conferred on democratically elected Governments commands the respect of the peoples of other democratic States and fosters expectations of negotiation, compromise and the rule of law in international relations. When States sharing a culture of democracy are involved in a dispute, the transparency of their regimes may help to prevent accidents, avoid reactions based on emotion or fear and reduce the likelihood of surprise attack. . . .

In today's world, freedom of thought, the impetus to creativity and the will to involvement are all critical to economic, social and cultural progress, and they are best fostered and protected within democratic systems. In this sense, the economic act of privatization can be as well a political act, enabling greater human creativity and participation. The best way to cultivate a citizen's readiness to participate in the development of his or her country, to arouse that person's energy, imagination and commitment, is by recognizing and respecting human dignity and human rights. The material means of progress can be acquired, but human resources – skilled, spirited and inventive workers – are indispensable, as is the enrichment found through mutual dialogue and the free interchange of ideas. In this way, a culture of democracy, marked by communication, dialogue and openness to the ideas and activities of the world, helps to foster a culture of development. . . .

[113] Diamond 1995, pp. 6–7.   [114] Boutros-Ghali 1996.

By providing legitimacy for government and encouraging people's participation in decision-making on the issues that affect their lives, democratic processes contribute to the effectiveness of state policies and development strategies. Democratic institutions and practices foster the governmental accountability and transparency necessary to deter national and transnational crime and corruption and encourage increased responsiveness to popular concerns. In development, they increase the likelihood that state goals reflect broad societal concerns and that government is sensitive to the societal and environmental costs of its development policies.[115]

Boutros-Ghali concluded that the promotion of democracy was essential because "peace, development and democracy are inextricably linked."[116]

Given all these claims, it would have been surprising if the UN had *not* embraced liberalization as the grand strategy for postconflict peacebuilding, particularly since one of the core arguments in favor of liberalization is that it promotes peace. In fact, as we shall see in the next chapter, the proposition that liberalization fosters peace – sometimes called the "liberal peace thesis" – is a very old idea, dating back to the writings of eighteenth-century Enlightenment philosophers. Scholars "rediscovered" this idea in the 1980s. It became a major area of social scientific research in the early 1990s, providing timely ammunition to policymakers in national governments and international organizations who were already inclined to believe that democratization and marketization represents the surest route to lasting peace in countries that are just emerging from civil wars.

But to what extent was the peace-through-liberalization proposition based on demonstrated fact? Did democratization and marketization actually create conditions for stable and lasting peace in the countries that hosted peacebuilding operations after the Cold War? These are questions that the remainder of this book will address, after we take a closer look at the liberal peace thesis itself.

[115] Ibid., paras. 17, 18, 22, 24.   [116] Ibid., para. 118.

Appendix to Chapter 1

The Terminology of Peace Operations

The terminology of peace operations is notoriously slippery. Some commentators use "peacekeeping" as a label for all types of military operations that do not involve outright war fighting, whereas others assign specific labels to different kinds of missions. Following is a short glossary of terms used in this book, including a definition of peacebuilding itself:

- *Preventive diplomacy* is action to prevent conflicts from starting in the first place or spreading to neighboring territories.
- *Peacekeeping* is the deployment of a lightly armed, multinational contingent of military personnel for nonenforcement purposes, such as the observation of a cease-fire.
- *Peacemaking* is the attempt to resolve an ongoing conflict, either by peaceful means such as mediation and negotiation, or, if necessary, by the authorizion of an international military force to impose a settlement to the conflict.
- *Peace enforcement* is the threat or use of nondefensive military force to impose, maintain, or restore a cease-fire.
- *Peacebuilding* is action undertaken at the end of a civil conflict to consolidate peace and prevent a recurrence of fighting. A *peacebuilding mission* involves the deployment of military and civilian personnel from several international agencies, with a mandate to conduct peacebuilding in a country that is just emerging from a civil war.
- Finally, the generic phrases *peace operations* and *peace missions* refer to any international peacemaking, peacekeeping, peace-enforcement, peacebuilding, or preventive diplomacy operations that include a multinational military force aimed at restoring or preserving peace.

These terms are not mutually exclusive. Peacebuilding, for instance, can involve the deployment of lightly armed, multinational contingents for nonenforcement purposes, and can therefore incorporate elements of peacekeeping. Alternatively, peacebuilding missions may include troops with enforcement rather than peacekeeping duties and powers. Confusion sometimes arises from the fact that peacebuilding operations seek to prevent a recurrence of violence, which is, in effect, a type of preventive diplomacy. Furthermore, peacebuilders can become involved in peacemaking if fighting reignites during a mission.

While it is easy to become entangled in these definitions, two distinguishing features of peacebuilding are worth highlighting. First, peacekeeping and peacebuilding are not synonymous. Peacekeeping is a primarily military activity that typically concentrates on cease-fire monitoring, whereas peacebuilding involves a wide variety of both military and nonmilitary functions, including the administration of elections; the retraining of judges, lawyers, and police officers; the nurturing of indigenous political parties and nongovernmental organizations; the design and implementation of economic reforms; the reorganization of governmental institutions; the promotion of free media; and the delivery of emergency humanitarian and financial assistance. The military component of a peacebuilding operation therefore represents only one element in a larger effort to establish the conditions for stable and lasting peace. Second, peacebuilding begins when the fighting has stopped. It is, by definition, a postconflict enterprise. Some commentators use the term more broadly to encompass other types of interventions, including those aimed at preventing violence from erupting in the first place, or what I have labeled preventive diplomacy. However, I have adopted the more common usage: Peacebuilding operations are deployed to consolidate peace in countries that have recently experienced civil conflict, and where hostilities have already ended.[117]

---

[117] For example, the U.S. Army field manual on peace operations (United States Army 1994) has defined peacebuilding as "postconflict actions...that strengthen and rebuild civil infrastructures and institutions in order to avoid a return to conflict."

2

The Liberal Peace Thesis

> Democracy contributes to safety and prosperity – both in national life and in
> international life – it's that simple.
> – Strobe Talbott, U.S. Deputy Secretary of State, 1997[1]

As noted in the Introduction, the idea that liberalization is a remedy for
violent conflict is not new; in fact, it was one of the central principles of
U.S. President Woodrow Wilson's foreign policy at the end of World War I.
Wilson viewed the American model of market democracy as the apogee
of political development, and believed that the spread of this model would
promote peace in both domestic and international affairs. "Democracy," he
proclaimed, "is unquestionably the most wholesome and livable form of
government the world has yet tried. It supplies as no other system could the
frank and universal criticism, the free play of individual thought, the open
conduct of public affairs, the spirit . . . of community and cooperation, which
make governments just and public spirited."[2] Governments that rest "not
upon the armed strength of the governors, but upon the free consent of the
governed," he added, "seldom coerce their subjects" and use force only as a
"last . . . resort."[3]

When Wilson traveled to France for the Versailles peace conference,
he envisaged the creation of a world order based on the democratic self-
determination of peoples, constitutional protections of minority rights, free
trade and commerce, the opening up of diplomacy to public scrutiny, and
the creation of a League of Nations to keep the peace.[4] "What we seek," he
stated, "is the reign of law, based upon the consent of the governed and
sustained by the organized opinion of mankind."[5] His peace proposals
focused primarily on the problem of interstate conflict, but he also believed
that these principles were essential to domestic or civil peace as well, because

---

[1] Talbott 1997. [2] Quoted in Notter 1965, p. 109. [3] Wilson 1901, pp. 572–573.
[4] Wilson 1965, pp. 406–414, 420–422, and 442. [5] Quoted in Hofstadter 1948, p. 247.

people denied justice and freedom would be prone to disaffection and unrest: "The world can be at peace only if its life is stable, and there can be no stability where the will is in rebellion, where there is not tranquility of spirit and a sense of justice, of freedom, and of right."[6] A precondition for international peace, then, was political stability within states, which in turn depended on securing the rights of ordinary people and small nations to democratic self-determination. "If you leave a rankling sense of injustice anywhere," he argued, "it will... produce a running sore presently which will result in trouble and probably war."[7] World peace "must be planted on the tested foundations of political liberty."[8]

By applying these ideas to the Versailles settlement, Wilson became the first statesman to articulate what is now called the liberal peace thesis, or the notion that democratic forms of government are more peaceful – both in their internal politics and in their international relations – than other forms of government. These ideas dated back at least to the writings of such Enlightenment philosophers as John Locke and Adam Smith. But only when Wilson, a scholar of liberal political theory, became the leader of a rising great power did these principles gain their first politically powerful patron. Today, the president is often remembered for wanting to "make the world safe for democracy," but it would be more accurate to say that he arrived at Versailles wanting to make the world safe *through* democracy.

Revisiting Wilson's beliefs about conflict management is a natural starting point for an investigation of contemporary peacebuilding operations, which have been based on a similar set of beliefs, including the assumption that democratization and marketization foster peace in countries just emerging from civil wars. There is, in fact, an interesting parallel between the period immediately following World War I and the post–Cold War years. In both eras, the international community faced a security threat to which it responded with a Wilsonian remedy. For the leaders who gathered at the Palace of Versailles in 1919, the principal challenge was to prevent the recurrence of general war in Europe. At the end of the Cold War, it was the "apparently remorseless rise of ethnic and communal conflict" that became a major challenge for the international community.[9] There was no grand Versailles-like conference to define the principles for conflict management in the post–Cold War era, but once again Wilson's ideas about war and peace assumed a leading role, and international peacebuilding operations took on a decidedly Wilsonian cast.

At first glance, there are good reasons to expect democratization and marketization to foster peace in war-shattered states. Since the mid-1980s, one of the most extensively studied questions in political science has been

---

[6] Wilson 1965, pp. 411–412.   [7] Ibid., p. 437.
[8] Quoted in Knock 1992, p. 121.   [9] Roberts 1994, p. 6.

the relationship between liberal forms of government and the incidence of both civil and international conflict.[10] The bulk of the recent research is focused on the international dimension of the liberal peace thesis – that is, the relationship between liberalism and *inter*state conflict – and a general consensus has emerged around the finding that market democracies rarely go to war against one another. Several analyses of civil violence have similarly concluded that market democracies are generally less prone to *intra*state disturbances. Given these findings, political and economic liberalization would appear to be a sensible and promising strategy for consolidating domestic peace in states that are just emerging from civil wars.

At least, this is how UN Secretary-General Kofi Annan, the chief administrator of the world's most prominent peacebuilding agency, seems to have interpreted this scholarship. "There are many good reasons for promoting democracy," he proclaimed in 2000, "not the least – in the eyes of the United Nations – is that, when sustained over time, it is a highly effective means of preventing conflict, both within and between states."[11] What is more, the secretary-general referred directly to the academic literature to back up this claim, noting that "a number of studies do show that democracies have very low levels of internal violence compared with non-democracies."[12] Annan's predecessor, Boutros Boutros-Ghali, made similar arguments about the benefits of promoting democracy in war-torn countries, including the assertion that democracy "fosters the evolution of the social contract upon which lasting peace can be built [and] is the only long-term means of both arbitrating and regulating many political, social, economic and ethnic tensions that constantly threaten to tear apart societies and destroy states."[13]

Policymakers in national governments have also subscribed to this position. As U.S. Deputy Secretary of State Strobe Talbott declared in 1997, "Democracy contributes to safety and prosperity – both in national life and in international life – it's that simple."[14] Indeed, one of the central tenets of the Clinton administration's foreign policy was that of "democratic enlargement," or the spread of liberal democracy and market-oriented economics, on the grounds that market democracies are less hostile in their international relations and less prone to internal violence.[15]

But how much do we really know about the pacifying effects of political and economic liberalization, particularly in countries that have recently experienced civil conflict? In fact, as I will argue in the remainder of this chapter, we know very little. Widespread support for the Wilsonian approach to peacebuilding has, to put it simply, rested on little more than hopeful assumptions.

[10] Chan 1997, Ray 1998, and Russett and Starr 2000 review this literature in detail.
[11] Annan 2000.   [12] Annan 1999a. See also Annan 2001.
[13] Boutros-Ghali 1996, paras. 17 and 122.   [14] Talbott 1997.   [15] See Carothers 2000.

Unanswered Questions

Few subjects have attracted more attention from students of political science in recent years than the questions that surround the liberal peace thesis. Are liberal democracies especially peaceful in their international relations or in their domestic politics? If so, under what circumstances, and why? Will efforts to promote market democracy enhance domestic or international peace? Scholars have examined all of these questions since the 1980s and early 1990s, when the liberal peace thesis returned to prominence after decades of neglect.

In 1983, Michael Doyle published an influential article contending that democratic states had seldom engaged in wars with other democracies and had thereby created a "separate peace."[16] Since then, a flurry of studies has scrutinized and elaborated the relationship between liberal democracy and interstate violence.[17] Most of these works have reached conclusions that broadly support Doyle's findings, prompting one scholar to note that "the absence of war between democracies comes as close as anything to an empirical law in international relations."[18] This research continued to develop and grow in new directions during the 1990s and beyond. For example, Bruce Russett and several of his collaborators produced analyses in the late 1990s and early 2000s showing that liberal economic policies also contribute to peaceful relations among democracies.[19]

In the meantime, a smaller group of researchers was examining the relationship between market democracy and *intra*state, or civil, violence. Foremost among them was R. J. Rummel, who found that democracies are considerably less likely than nondemocracies to experience a broad range of domestic disturbances, including "revolutions, bloody coups d'état, political assassinations, antigovernment terrorist bombings, guerrilla warfare, insurgencies, civil wars, mutinies, and rebellions."[20] In democratic countries, Rummel wrote,

social conflicts that might become violent are resolved through voting, negotiation, compromise, and mediation. The success of these procedures is enhanced and supported by the restraints on decision makers of competitive elections, the cross-pressures resulting from the natural pluralism of democratic...societies, and the development of a democratic culture and norms that emphasize rational debate, toleration, negotiation of differences, conciliation, and conflict resolution.[21]

---

[16] Doyle 1983. See also Doyle 1986. Similar findings had already been published by Babst 1972 and Rummel 1979.

[17] See n. 10. [18] Levy 1988, pp. 661–662.

[19] Oneal and Russett 1997; Bliss and Russett 1998; Russett, Oneal, and Davis 1998; Oneal and Russett 1999a, 1999b, and 1999c; Russett and Starr 2000; Oneal and Russett 2001. These arguments are examined in depth in Russett and Oneal 2001.

[20] Rummel 1997, p. 85. See also Rummel 1995. [21] Rummel 1995, p. 4.

Several subsequent studies reached similar conclusions. In 2001, for example, a group of scholars affiliated with the International Peace Research Institute in Norway published the most comprehensive examination to date of democracy and internal violence, finding strong evidence that well-established liberal democracies are considerably less likely than any other kind of state to experience civil war.[22]

Policymakers, commentators, and academics have cited these findings as evidence that international and domestic peace can be enhanced by "exporting" the institutions and practices of market democracy to nondemocratic states, echoing the arguments made by Kofi Annan and Boutros Boutros-Ghali. Morton Halperin, for instance, has contended that "the United States should take the lead in promoting the trend toward democracy" because democratic governments "are more peaceful and less given to provoking war or inciting violence."[23] According to R. J. Rummel, "just reforming regimes in the direction of greater civil rights and political liberties will promote less violence."[24] Joshua Muravchik maintains that spreading democracy is not only "conducive to peace among states, but it can be the key to resolving bloody battles within them,"[25] and Larry Diamond has called for democracy promotion because democratic governments "do not ethnically 'cleanse' their own populations and they are much less likely to face ethnic insurgency," among other reasons.[26]

Unfortunately, these arguments tend to gloss over an important distinction: Although well-established market democracies may be more peaceful in their internal and international affairs than nondemocracies, the policy of promoting democracy necessarily involves *transforming* a state into a market democracy. Most scholarship on the liberal peace focuses on states that have already made this transition, and therefore offers little insight into the war-proneness of countries that are in the process of becoming market democracies. So while we have learned a great deal in recent years from debates about the relative peacefulness of liberal states, these debates have largely skirted the relationship between *liberalization* and conflict. Those who use the existing liberal peace scholarship to assert that the promotion of democracy will foster peace, either within or between states, typically address only part of the story – the likelihood of the state experiencing civil conflict, or engaging in international conflict, once the transition is complete. Yet any careful analysis of peace-through-liberalization policies must consider both

---

[22] Hegre et al. 2001. See also Krain and Myers 1997. These results appeared to lend support to commentators who claimed that democracy "transfers conflict from the violent to the political arena" (Zartman 1993, p. 327), "inhibits communal rebellion" (Gurr 1993, p. 138), and "encourages marginalized communities to seek justice by nonviolent political means" (Riggs 1995, p. 397).

[23] Halperin 1993, p. 105. See also Smith 1994.   [24] Rummel 1997, p. 52.

[25] Muravchik 1996, p. 576.   [26] Diamond 1995, pp. 6–7.

the end result of a successful transition to market democracy and the effects of the transition itself.

There is, moreover, reason to doubt that liberalization fosters peace. Although most liberal peace scholars have ignored this issue, a few have not, and their findings suggest that transitional countries may be prone to internal and international conflict. Edward Mansfield and Jack Snyder, for example, argue that states undergoing a transition from authoritarian to democratic rule are more likely than either established democracies or nondemocracies to be involved in an international war, because political opportunists in such states often employ belligerent nationalism as a means of building domestic political support.[27] Others have reached similar, though more narrowly targeted, conclusions: that transitional states are particularly warlike only in the earliest phases of a transition to democracy,[28] or that the greatest danger of international conflict arises from "uneven" transitions (where the state effectively swings back and forth from democracy to autocracy).[29] The war-proneness of democratizing states remains a matter of disagreement among scholars, but there is sufficient evidence to be at least skeptical of the notion that the promotion of democracy necessarily enhances international peace.

There is also little agreement on the precise relationship between liberalization and *internal* conflict – a relationship that needs to be clarified, given the international community's propensity to prescribe political and economic liberalization as a remedy for internal violence. Some studies suggest that democratization enhances domestic peace, whereas others find the opposite. One major research project, for example, concludes that substantial changes of "regime type" – including a movement from autocracy to democracy – are often accompanied by increased civil violence.[30] Several other studies highlight the apparently conflict-inducing effects of political liberalization efforts in specific countries, including Yugoslavia and Sri Lanka,[31] Algeria,[32] Sudan,[33] Burundi,[34] Ethiopia,[35] and Nigeria, Uganda, Chad and Pakistan.[36] These works offer prima facie evidence that democratization may not always be a dependable means of fostering domestic peace and that the transition to democracy may be more destabilizing than the supporters of Wilsonianism contend – although this debate, too, continues.[37]

We also know relatively little about the connections between marketization and internal violence. While it is plausible that a well-established market economy is particularly conducive to domestic peace,[38] some evidence

---

[27] Mansfield and Snyder 1995a and 1995b. See also Snyder 2000.
[28] Gleditsch and Hegre 1997.   [29] Gleditsch and Ward 2000.
[30] Hegre et al. 2001. See also Fearon and Laitin 2003.   [31] Snyder 2000.
[32] Arfi 1998.   [33] Salih 1991; and Deng 1995.
[34] Dravis 2000.   [35] Ottaway 1994 and 1995.
[36] Horowitz 1991.   [37] See Sambanis 2002 for a summary of findings.
[38] For example, scholars investigating the causes of civil wars have examined the relationship between a country's level of wealth and economic growth rate on the one hand, and the

suggests that marketization has increased, not decreased, civil unrest in a number of countries. After examining the incidence of food riots in several developing countries, John Walton and David Seddon conclude that there is a clear "relationship between widespread popular unrest in the cities of the developing world... and the process of economic and social transformation... associated with a renewed emphasis on liberalization and the promotion of 'free markets.'"[39] Other scholars have also described the apparently destabilizing effects of liberal economic adjustment policies in Egypt, Jordan, Nigeria, Burundi, Tanzania, Tunisia, Venezuela, Zambia, and Mali, among other places.[40]

In sum, many questions relating to the liberal peace thesis remain unanswered, including the precise relationship between the process of economic and political liberalization and the propensity of states undergoing these transitions to engage in international war or experience internal violence. We know even less about the effects of liberalization in the particular circumstances of states recovering from civil war. Until these questions are answered, the strategy of promoting liberalization as a means of fostering peace will remain an uncertain one. Yet this fact is rarely acknowledged by proponents of Wilsonian approaches to conflict resolution, including those who present democratization and marketization as a generalized formula for peace. Perhaps the prevailing enthusiasm for liberalization as a recipe for peace will ultimately prove warranted, but at present there is little hard evidence to support such a belief.

The Disappearing Leviathan

There is a more fundamental problem with the liberal peace literature as it relates to peacebuilding: It tends to take the existence of *functioning states* as a given. Contributors to the literature have used this assumption to determine whether states with certain types of political regimes (democratic, authoritarian, etc.) or economic systems (market-oriented, state-directed, mixed, etc.) are more peaceful than others. But this methodology offers few insights into the challenges of peacebuilding, because war-shattered states typically lack even the most rudimentary governmental institutions. By taking the existence of a working government for granted, many authors have effectively "assumed away" one of the most difficult and important problems that peacebuilders confront in their field operations: namely, how to establish

incidence of civil conflict on the other, finding (as one might expect) that richer states and states experiencing economic growth are considerably less likely than poorer or recessionary states to experience large-scale internal violence. See *Journal of Conflict Resolution* 2002.

[39] Walton and Seddon 1994, p. 3.
[40] See Haggard and Kaufman 1992, p. 337; Skogly 1993, pp. 751–778; Adekanye 1995, p. 368; Ake 1996, p. 118; Ihonvbere 1996a, pp. 196–197; Jeong 1996, pp. 155 167; Kaiser 1996, pp. 227–237; Wright 1997, p. 27; and van de Walle 1997, pp. 26–29.

functioning governments and stable nonviolent politics in conditions of virtual anarchy.

It is interesting to note that the earliest writers on the liberal peace thesis – the classical liberal philosophers of the Enlightenment – were more attuned to the challenges facing modern peacebuilders. Their starting point was typically some form of "natural state" in which a common government did not exist, and their aim was to describe the circumstances in which a society characterized by justice, peace, and prosperity might emerge. John Locke argued that the state of nature would be so "full of fears and continual dangers" – including the peril of being "constantly exposed to the Invasion of others" – that people living in this condition would be compelled to "joyn in Society with others" and create a common government.[41] According to Locke, only one type of government would be compatible with a secure and just peace: a law-based regime operating under constitutional rules and established by popular consent. The creation of a government that ignored such limitations and violated individual liberties would effectively return society to a state of nature, with all of the insecurities this entailed, including fear of physical attack and lawless violence.[42]

Locke and many of his intellectual successors were consciously responding to Thomas Hobbes's major work, *Leviathan*.[43] Hobbes vigorously opposed many of the cardinal principles of liberalism, including constitutional constraints on the power of government, but he pioneered the technique of considering the conditions necessary for transforming a state of nature into a peaceful, stable society – a technique that several classical liberals adopted in their own work. The answer, Hobbes argued, was to confer sovereign authority upon one individual or group of individuals: the Leviathan. Hobbes argued that the powers of the sovereign should not be limited, and that members of society should pledge "not to resist the commands of that man or council that they have recognized as their sovereign."[44] By contrast, Locke and later liberal theorists rejected the necessity and desirability of authoritarian rule, arguing not only that it unduly threatens individual liberties but also that it stifles the human spirit, violates natural rights, and spawns rebellion and civil unrest – whereas constitutionally limited government provides the basis for durable domestic peace.

However, Hobbes and Locke did have one important thing in common, beyond their shared use of the state of nature as a heuristic device. Both men believed that domestic peace presupposed the existence of governmental institutions capable of defending society against internal and external threats. Locke, for example, argued that rulers should be given sufficient

---

[41] Locke 1963 [1698], book II, para. 123, p. 395.
[42] Although Locke's version of the state of nature did not necessarily imply a Hobbesian state of war, he left little doubt that violence and conflict are more prevalent in the state of nature than under "civil" (that is, constitutionally limited) government. See Goldwin 1987, p. 485.
[43] Hobbes 1968 [1651].   [44] Berns 1987, p. 402.

"prerogative" or freedom of action to respond quickly and forcefully to national emergencies.[45] The "good of the Society," he argued, requires "that several things should be left to the discretion" of the executive power, "since in some Governments the Law-Making Power is not always in being, and is usually too numerous, and so too slow, for the dispatch requisite to Execution: and because also it is impossible to foresee, and so by laws to provide for, all Accidents and Necessities, that may concern the publick."[46] He even wrote that the government should be permitted to act above the law in cases of emergency, provided the actions taken are for the "publick good," rather than for private gain.[47] How Locke reconciled these extraordinary powers with his conception of law-governed rule remains unclear; he seemed to believe, paradoxically, that the last line of defense for constitutional government was to permit leaders to behave as Hobbesian Leviathans – outside of constitutional restraints – in order to preserve the "lives, liberty, and property" of the governed. "In this sense," writes one commentator, "Hobbes makes his presence felt in Locke's Second Treatise."[48]

For Locke, then, limited government was not synonymous with weak government. On the contrary, maintaining a free society required constitutionally constrained – but effective and functioning – governmental institutions. Other classical liberal thinkers shared this view. Adam Smith is remembered for having sought to limit the role of government in economic affairs, believing that the "invisible hand" of the market would promote prosperity and peace, and that allowing people to pursue their interests in relative freedom would foster the "harmonious interplay of very different kinds of human beings living very different kinds of lives without the social whole dissolving into chaos."[49] But Smith also insisted that government had an essential, if limited, role to play in a well-ordered society. First, it needed to protect against foreign invasion; second, government was necessary for the administration of justice, including the enforcement of contracts; and third, it was needed to build and maintain public works.[50] In particular, Smith believed that the state had a vital responsibility to establish and maintain the rule of law, without which the benefits of the free market would be lost. "Commerce and manufactures," he declared,

can seldom flourish long in any state which does not enjoy a regular administration of justice, in which the people do not feel themselves secure in the possession of their property, in which the faith in contracts is not supported by law, and in which

[45] Locke 1963 [1698], book II, chap. 14, p. 422.   [46] Ibid., pp. 421–422.
[47] Locke: "[T]he Laws themselves should in some Cases give way to the Executive Power." Ibid., p. 421.
[48] McClelland 1996, p. 239. On Locke's conception of executive "prerogative" in times of emergency, see Seliger 1968, pp. 59–62.
[49] McClelland 1996, p. 433.
[50] Smith 1976 [1776], book IV, chap. 9, pp. 687–688 and 723.

the authority of the state is not supposed to be regularly employed in enforcing the payment of debts from all those who are able to pay.[51]

In *Wealth of Nations,* Smith went on to discuss the importance of a "well-regulated standing army," which was essential not only for national defense but also for domestic order.[52] Sovereigns who could not depend on a loyal and effective army, he asserted, would be more likely to suppress liberty than rulers backed by a steadfast military, because leaders with the support of the army would feel secure enough to permit expressions of public dissent. Consequently, the "degree of liberty which approaches to licentiousness can be tolerated only in countries where the sovereign is secured by a well-regulated standing army."[53] Smith's view of a good society thus presupposed the existence of a limited yet functioning state, ultimately backed by the presence of a military force.[54]

Immanuel Kant echoed this sentiment. For him, the ultimate purpose of social life is to permit individuals to develop all of their "natural capacities," which is possible only if human beings are permitted the exercise of their "freedom of will based upon reason."[55] But Kant also warned of the dangers of unrestricted liberty, or "wild freedom."[56] In the absence of the rule of law enforced by a central authority, he argued, peaceful coexistence among completely free individuals would be impossible, and would collapse into a "lawless state of savagery."[57] Peace therefore requires a powerful sovereign – a "supreme authority" – but one whose powers are limited to what is necessary in order to preserve the rule of law, because only by constraining individual liberty through the consistent (and, if necessary, coercive) application of law is it possible to preserve the security and freedom of all.[58]

A final example of the dual emphasis that early liberals placed on limited and effective government comes from *The Federalist Papers,* the classic American statement of liberal political philosophy, principally written by James Madison and Alexander Hamilton in the 1780s. Both men railed against "tyranny," by which they meant the invasion of personal liberties by government, and believed that the combination of individual freedom,

[51] Ibid., book V, chap. 3, p. 910. On another occasion he wrote: "The first and chief design of every system of government is to maintain justice; to prevent the members of a society from encroaching on one another's property, or seizing what is not their own" (Smith 1976 [1776], p. 689, n. 1).

[52] Ibid., book II, chap. 3, p. 342; and book V, chap. 1, p. 707.

[53] Ibid., book V, chap. 1, p. 707.

[54] As Joseph Cropsey (1957) writes, "The freedom implicit in the Smithian principle is accompanied by restraint, and the authoritative restraint implicit in the Hobbesian formula is the necessary condition of freedom," although "Smith's principle was intended to, and did, lead to a liberal society, while that of Hobbes need not have done so" (p. 72).

[55] Kant 1991 [1784], pp. 45 and 43.   [56] Ibid., p. 46.

[57] Ibid., pp. 44–47.   [58] Ibid., pp. 46 and 45.

representative government, and institutional checks on the exercise of power would produce a just and peaceful society. But Hamilton also emphasized the need for government to maintain domestic and external security in moments of crisis. "A firm Union," he wrote, "will be of the utmost moment to the peace and liberty of the states, as a barrier against domestic faction and insurrection," and as a guarantor of "internal tranquility."[59] He argued that a strong executive branch was especially important to public security and for the administration of law, including the protection of individual rights:[60] "A feeble Executive is but another phrase for a bad execution; and a government ill executed, whatever it may be in theory, must be, in practice, a bad government."[61] Although Madison's contributions to *The Federalist Papers* focused more on constraining than on bolstering governmental power, he echoed Hamilton's view that government was needed as "a bulwark against foreign danger" and a "conservator of peace among ourselves."[62]

According to these and other classical liberal thinkers – including the French essayist Baron Charles-Louis de Montesquieu, and the British theorist James Mill – successful state building called for a careful balancing of two competing imperatives: limiting the power of the state in order to preserve individual liberty, and endowing government with sufficient means to uphold the rule of law and to protect the constitutional order itself against foreign and domestic threats. These writers rejected Hobbes's argument that an all-powerful ruler was needed to maintain domestic order and social life, but they did not entirely dispense with the Leviathan. They domesticated it. Lasting peace required *both* the protection of individual freedom and the existence of effective governmental institutions, since the alternative to effective government was untenable: the insecure state of nature.

Modern students of the liberal peace have taken a different approach. As noted earlier, they have tended to "bracket" or ignore the question of whether functioning governments exist. While classical liberal theorists recognized the vital role of effective state institutions as a necessary condition for domestic stability, this concern has virtually disappeared from the contemporary liberal peace literature. The Leviathan no longer lurks in the shadows of the liberal state; it is nowhere to be found.

The new character of the liberal peace scholarship limits its application to peacebuilding. For countries just emerging from civil wars, the relevant starting point is something closer to the "state of nature" of early liberal theory, in which government is largely, or entirely, absent. By taking the existence of effective states for granted, the contemporary scholarship offers scant guidance to those engaged in peacebuilding, who face the challenge of *making* governments in the immediate aftermath of civil conflict. This literature

[59] Hamilton, Madison, and Jay 1992 [1788] (*Federalist No. 9*), pp. 36 and 38.
[60] Ibid. (*Federalist No. 70*), p. 359.   [61] Ibid., p. 360.
[62] Ibid. (*Federalist No. 14*), p. 62

has taught us a great deal about the war-proneness of different types of government, but has shed little light on the potential effectiveness of democratization and marketization as strategies for building peace in war-shattered states. Those who cite this literature to support the Wilsonian approach to peacebuilding – including the two most recent secretaries-general of the UN – have tended to blur the distinction between liberal*ism* and liberal*ization*. Well-established market democracies may, indeed, be more internally and internationally peaceful than other kinds of states, but we still know little about the precise relationship between liberalization and violence, and even less about the effects of democratization and marketization in the specific circumstances of postconflict countries.

Have modern peacebuilders operated on a faulty set of assumptions? Can peacebuilders learn anything from classical versions of the liberal peace thesis, which paid more attention to the problem of constructing stable societies out of conditions of nongovernment? By examining the record of peacebuilding, we can begin to answer these questions.

PART II

THE PEACEBUILDING RECORD

3

Introduction to the Case Studies

Has the Wilsonian assumption of peacebuilding – that rapid liberalization would foster a stable and lasting peace in countries that are just emerging from civil wars – been borne out in practice? How should we go about answering this question? This chapter sets out the investigative framework for the case studies that follow. Specifically, I shall address three issues: First, what are the specific causal hypotheses that will be evaluated against the record of peacebuilding? Second, how will the case studies of peacebuilding missions be structured in order to evaluate these hypotheses? Third, which particular peacebuilding missions will be studied?

Most studies of peacebuilding outcomes begin by establishing a standard of effectiveness or success and then proceed to evaluate the record of one or more operations against this standard.[1] My aim is slightly different: to examine whether the strategy of peace-through-liberalization, in particular, has enhanced the prospects for stable and lasting peace in countries that have hosted peacebuilding missions. Put differently, the "independent variable" that I am interested in studying is political liberalization (including the establishment of political and civil freedoms, and preparations for and the holding of elections) and economic liberalization (including the movement toward market-oriented economic policies and practices), while the "dependent variable" is the likelihood of stable and lasting peace within the host country.

I use this dependent variable for two reasons. First, it corresponds with the view that the United Nations – the world's most active peacebuilding agency – has articulated with regard to the purposes of postconflict peacebuilding. In his landmark 1992 policy statement, *An Agenda for Peace*, former UN Secretary-General Boutros-Ghali defined peacebuilding as "action to identify and support structures which will tend to strengthen and solidify peace" in the aftermath of "civil strife," with the ultimate goal of preventing

---

[1] For example, Hampson 1996; Doyle and Sambanis 2000; Cousens and Kumar 2001; and Stedman, Rothchild, and Cousens 2002.

"a relapse into conflict."[2] Three years later, Boutros-Ghali described the "essential goal" of peacebuilding as "the creation of structures for the institutionalization of peace."[3] Similarly, Boutros-Ghali's successor, Kofi Annan, wrote in 1998 that postconflict peacebuilding refers to "actions undertaken at the end of a conflict to consolidate peace and prevent a recurrence of armed confrontation."[4] The fundamental purpose of peacebuilding, according to these statements, is to establish the conditions for stable and lasting peace in countries that are just emerging from civil wars. The second reason to use this dependent variable is that it allows us to evaluate a dimension of the liberal peace thesis about which we know relatively little: whether liberalization is a reliable remedy for civil violence.

Is the achievement of a stable and lasting peace too high a standard for peacebuilding operations, given the difficult task they face in pacifying war-shattered states? Some commentators argue that it is, and propose more modest measures of effectiveness in peacebuilding. George Downs and Stephen Stedman, for example, suggest that a more reasonable gauge of success is whether peace prevails in the host countries at the moment when peacebuilding agencies depart.[5] However, there are at least two problems with this reduced standard of effective peacebuilding. First, it departs from the central goal that practitioners of peacebuilding have themselves identified for these operations – namely, to establish conditions that will prevent the recurrence of violence in the foreseeable future, or what some scholars and UN officials call a "self-sustaining" peace – as opposed to a peace that lasts only for as long as international peacebuilders remain in the host country.[6] Second, by focusing solely on whether fighting recurs in the short run, the Downs-Stedman formula deflects attention from the question of whether or not peacebuilders successfully address the underlying sources of conflict, which the UN also views as essential to the establishment of a self-sustaining peace. If the conditions that gave rise to civil conflict in the first place are left in place, conflict may simply rekindle after foreign peacebuilders have departed. Given that the declared purpose of peacebuilding is to "identify and support structures" that minimize the likelihood of renewed fighting, any serious evaluation of the effectiveness of peacebuilding should include a consideration of why civil violence erupted in the first place, and whether the conditions that gave rise to this violence have been ameliorated through

---

[2] Boutros-Ghali 1992, pp. 11 and 32.   [3] Boutros-Ghali 1995, para. 49.
[4] Annan 1998, para. 63.   [5] Downs and Stedman 2002. See also Stedman 2002, pp. 18–19.
[6] See statements by Annan in W. H. Reilly 2001a and 2001b; by Carlos Westendorp, the UN-appointed High Representative in Bosnia, in Lederer 1999; the text of the Brahimi Report (Panel on United Nations Peace Operations 2000, para. 28); and Elisabeth Cousens's use of "self-enforcing peace" as the appropriate measure for peacebuilding success (in Cousens 2001, pp. 11–12). Annan has also used the term "stable and lasting peace" to describe the fundamental goal of peacebuilding (in UN document SG/SM/8023, November 13, 2001).

peacebuilding. For the same reason, a full assessment of the peacebuilding record should consider the possibility that international peacebuilders, themselves, might inadvertently create *new* conditions that endanger peace.

All of this raises difficult issues of analysis and evidence, particularly for peacebuilding cases in which outright fighting has not resumed. Yet even in these latter cases, judgments about the durability of the peace and the effects of peacebuilding operations on the likelihood of renewed conflict must still be made. The prospective nature of these judgments necessarily limits our ability to reach definitive conclusions about the effectiveness of peacebuilding in the post–Cold War era, and it will be decades before a full retrospective analysis of the effects of these operations on the host states will be feasible. Yet these difficulties should not lead us down the path of expediently adopting a reduced standard of successful peacebuilding that focuses solely on the short term effects of these operations, rather than considering whether these missions have fostered conditions for a more durable peace, which is the stated goal of peacebuilding.[7] Given that a number of these missions have already been completed – in some cases several years ago – a provisional assessment of the peacebuilding record *is* possible now, particularly if we focus on specific aspects of these operations.

With these provisos in mind, I will use the record of peacebuilding to evaluate the Wilsonian hypothesis that attempting to transform a war-shattered state into a liberal market democracy fosters a stable and lasting peace, and the more general belief that liberalization offers a remedy for civil conflict. If these two hypotheses are sound, the efforts of peacebuilding agencies to promote political and economic liberalization should at the very least: 1) not cause fighting to resume; 2) not exacerbate preexisting conditions that previously led to civil violence within the host state; and 3) not create new conditions within the host state that are likely to spark a resurgence of fighting. If the record of peacebuilding shows that these expectations have not been borne out in practice – in other words, if internationally sponsored liberalization efforts in war-shattered states have diminished, rather than enhanced, the likelihood of stable and lasting peace – this finding will cast doubt on the central assumptions of peacebuilding.

Other analysts argue that peacebuilding missions should be held to a much higher standard. Followers of John Galtung, for instance, contend that peacebuilding should aim to produce "positive peace" that liberates ordinary people from various forms of "structural violence" within their societies.[8] Structural violence refers to any kind of harm caused by "poverty

---

[7] By adopting a reduced standard for evaluating peacebuilding, we would repeat the mistake that Downs and Stedman (2002) and others have made: allowing the demands of methodological neatness to determine what the goals of peacebuilding should be.

[8] Galtung 1969. For an application of these concepts to contemporary peacebuilding operations, see Cockell 2000.

and unjust social, political, and economic institutions, systems, or structures."[9] Although the alleviation of harmful conditions is certainly a worthy
goal, there are two problems in using this concept to evaluate the effectiveness of peacebuilding missions. First, the notion of "structural violence" itself
is so broad, and potentially encompasses so many things, that it verges on
meaninglessness. Galtung writes, for example, that structural violence occurs
"when human beings are being influenced so that their actual somatic and
mental realizations are below their potential realizations."[10] The challenge
of determining precisely whether people are "realizing their mental potential" would be difficult enough, but the broader problem with this concept is
that it lacks definitional boundaries: Virtually anything could be considered
a form of "violence."[11] The second problem is that alleviating structural violence represents a considerably more ambitious goal for peacebuilding than
the secretaries-general of the United Nations and other sponsors of these
missions have articulated.

    This book, therefore, charts a middle course between those who claim that
peacebuilding should aim only to police cease-fires, and those who believe
that peacebuilding should solve all the social ills of a country. I investigate,
instead, the relationship between liberalization and the prospects for renewed
fighting in states hosting these operations, which is both analytically tractable
and more faithful to the declared purposes of peacebuilding.

Case Study Guidelines

I examine each major peacebuilding operation launched between 1989 and
1998 (see the next section for a discussion of case selection) by using an
investigative approach that Alexander George has called "controlled comparison."[12] This methodology is designed for circumstances in which the
total number of cases of a given phenomenon is too small to permit effective statistical analysis, or when researchers wish to examine specific causal
mechanisms in greater detail than is possible simply through the study of statistical correlations. Both conditions apply to the present study: The number
of peacebuilding operations is limited, and the complexity of the subject
matter (the effects of political and economic liberalization on war-shattered
states) demands individual attention to the details of each case. But if our
goal is to investigate specific causal hypotheses across several cases, we must
be conscious of the need to treat each case in a focused manner – by defining

---

[9] Köhler and Alcock 1976, p. 343.   [10] Galtung 1969, p. 168.
[11] This problem of definitional boundaries also applies to most formulations of "human secu-
    rity," another concept that some commentators have used to evaluate the success of peace-
    building. See Paris 2001.
[12] George 1979.

in advance a set of questions that we will seek to answer. This is the essence of controlled comparison: ensuring that the information derived from each case study is directly relevant to the question under investigation.

To this end, I use the following analytical steps to examine each operation. My central question, as noted, is whether democratization and marketization fostered conditions for a stable and lasting peace in the states that hosted peacebuilding missions. I define "peace" as the absence of large-scale violence,[13] and "stable and lasting peace" as a peace that is likely to endure beyond the departure of the peacebuilders themselves and into the foreseeable future. Peacebuilding cases are divided into two groups: first, those in which large-scale violence *did* recur after the start of a peacebuilding mission (either during the mission or thereafter); and second, those in which large-scale violence *did not* recur during the peacebuilding mission and has not recurred since the termination of the mission.

The rationale for separating the cases in this manner is straightforward. If fighting recurred, the conditions for a stable and lasting peace were clearly not established, and the key question is, What role did the internationally sponsored process of political and economic liberalization play in either deterring or inciting renewed violence? If fighting did *not* recur, the main question becomes whether or not the liberalization process helped to create conditions for a stable and lasting peace. This is a difficult question to answer, for the reasons I described above. However, if the Wilsonian hypothesis is correct, democratization and marketization should not be responsible for any of the following: the re-creation or exacerbation of domestic conditions that previously caused civil conflict in the host state; the deepening of divisions and antagonism among the formerly warring parties; or the creation of new conditions that endanger the peace. Any of these outcomes would appear to contradict – or, at least, challenge – the notion that liberalization fosters the conditions for stable and lasting peace in war-shattered states (see Figure 3.1).

If the case studies indicate that internationally sponsored liberalization efforts appear to have sparked renewed fighting – or to have created conditions that make resurgent violence more, not less, likely – then the Wilsonian assumptions of peacebuilding would, as I have suggested, be called into question. Furthermore, the case studies should also allow us to develop a more detailed and accurate understanding of *why* the political and economic liberalization process has had certain effects in countries that host peacebuilding missions. The empirical analysis that follows, therefore, represents an intermediate step in a larger project: one that involves both an initial assessment of the Wilsonian hypothesis and the development of new hypotheses and

---

[13] I define "large-scale violence" as at least 1,000 battle-related deaths in a single year. This is the most common cut-off figure for students of war. See Wallensteen and Sollenberg 2001.

Regarding cases in which violence recurred, I pose the following question:

   • Did political liberalization (i.e., the holding of elections, the
     liberalization of rules governing political expression, efforts to
     enhance respect for civil and political rights, the freeing up of the
     media) or economic liberalization (i.e., the introduction of market-
     oriented reforms) contribute in any discernible way to the resur-
     gence of fighting?

Regarding cases in which violence *did not* recur, I ask these questions:

   • Did the process of political or economic liberalization ameliorate
     domestic societal conditions that had previously fueled violent
     conflict?

   • Did the process foster a movement toward peaceful reconciliation
     among the formerly warring parties?

   • Did the process exacerbate tensions within the society in a manner
     that endangered the prospects for a stable and lasting peace?

FIGURE 3.1. Case Study Questions

theory from the evidence collected, or what some scholars call the "discovery of theory from data."[14]

Case Selection

Between 1989 and 1999, there were fourteen major international peacebuilding operations deployed to countries that were just emerging from civil wars
(see Figure 3.2).[15] By "major" operations I mean missions that included at
least two hundred international military personnel – anything smaller would
constitute a very small operation by the historical standards of peacekeeping
and peacebuilding. By "international" I mean that the deployment of these
personnel was formally approved by the UN Security Council. By "countries
that were just emerging from civil wars" I mean states where armed conflicts were fought for at least one year (which helps to differentiate "wars"
from more transitory disturbances) and where these conflicts were mainly
within the borders of a single state and among parties who normally reside in
that state (thereby distinguishing "civil" from "international" wars). These
are not arbitrary definitions: Because our goal is to examine the effects of
Wilsonian peacebuilding policies in countries that have recently experienced
civil wars, we stand to learn little – or, worse, we risk drawing distorted

[14] Glaser and Strauss 1967, p. 14.
[15] I treat instances in which there was technically more than one operation created for the same
     territory – for example, in Croatia – as a single mission for the purposes of the case studies.

Location	Duration*
Namibia	1989–1990
Nicaragua	1989–1992
Angola	1991–1997
Cambodia	1991–1993
El Salvador	1991–1995
Mozambique	1992–1994
Liberia	1993–1997
Rwanda	1993–1996
Bosnia	1995–present
Croatia	1995–1998
Guatemala	1997
East Timor	1999–present
Kosovo	1999–present
Sierra Leone	1999–present

* Military component.

FIGURE 3.2. Major Peacebuilding Operations Deployed in 1989–1999

conclusions – if we consider peace missions that either did not follow an armed conflict or that followed an international rather than a civil war.

Several peace operations launched after the Cold War fall outside the above definition. The international mission in Haiti, for example, which was launched in 1994, followed a political crisis, not an armed conflict. The now-infamous Somalia operation also falls outside the scope of this work, because fighting in that country effectively never ended and the operation sheds little light on the subject of *post*conflict peacebuilding. I also exclude the mission to the Central African Republic in 1998 for different reasons: Although the mission did follow internal violence in that country, the preceding period of unrest was very brief (lasting only a few weeks) and less of a civil war than a mutiny among certain elements of the country's military. Since the early 1990s, another peacebuilding mission has been planned for the territory of the Western Sahara (between Morocco and Mauritania), but at the time of writing, local parties have still not agreed on the details – so it, too, has been left out of this work. Two further operations were deployed to the former Soviet republics of Tajikistan and Georgia in the early 1990s, but in both cases, fighting had been taking place for considerably less than a year, and both missions included a very small number of international military personnel (81 and 103, respectively). The only other peace operation approved by the UN Security Council during the 1989–1999 period was a tiny mission that comprised nine military observers, who were sent to a strip of land between Chad and Libya in order to oversee the termination of Libyan administration in the territory, a mission that neither followed a civil conflict nor came close to meeting the definition of a "major" operation.

Figure 3.2 lists three major peacebuilding operations that were deployed in 1999 to East Timor, Kosovo, and Sierra Leone.[16] I offer some preliminary observations on these three missions in later chapters of the book, but I do not include them as in-depth case studies because, at the time of writing, all three were still too new to judge their effects with the same degree of confidence. The eleven remaining missions in Figure 3.2 – Angola, Rwanda, Liberia, Cambodia, Bosnia, Croatia, El Salvador, Nicaragua, Guatemala, Namibia, and Mozambique – represent a rich and diverse set of cases. Five of these missions took place in Africa, three in Latin America, two in Europe, and one in Asia. They concern some of the most prominent and distressing international events of the 1990s, including the war in the former Yugoslavia and the genocide of ethnic Tutsis in Rwanda. Some of these missions have been viewed as great successes, such as the operations in El Salvador and Mozambique; others, like the mission in Angola, have been branded failures. Given the diversity of these eleven cases – and the fact that they include all of the major international postconflict peacebuilding operations launched between 1989 and 1998 – it should be possible to draw general conclusions about postconflict peacebuilding.

---

[16] Another mission – to the Democratic Republic of Congo – was formally authorized in 1999 but did not deploy (more than 200 troops) until summer 2001.

4

Angola and Rwanda

The Perils of Political Liberalization

No peacebuilding operations have failed more miserably than the missions in Angola and Rwanda: Both countries slipped back into violence before peacebuilders could accomplish their tasks. The war in Angola continued for several years at varying degrees of intensity, while Rwanda experienced not only resurgent war but genocide. The question under consideration, however, is not how these missions turned out in general but, rather, how effective the peacebuilders' liberalization efforts were as a remedy for civil violence. Let us examine each of the cases in turn.

Angola

Angola, located on the southwestern coast of Africa, was ruled by Portugal until 1975. As many as eleven national liberation movements sprang up during the 1960s to fight against the colonial government.[1] By the early 1970s, three of these organizations had emerged as the strongest indigenous groups: the Movimento Popular de Libertação de Angola (MPLA), the Frente Nacional de Libertação de Angola (FNLA), and the União Nacional para a Independência Total de Angola (UNITA).[2] These organizations not only waged a guerrilla war against the Portuguese colonial authorities but also battled among themselves for predominance.[3] After the departure of the Portuguese, the MPLA gained control of the Angolan capital, Luanda, and decisively defeated the FNLA in 1976, leaving UNITA as its only major rival. Fighting in Angola between UNITA and the MPLA continued for more than fifteen years, sustained in part by foreign military aid for both sides. UNITA received support from South Africa and later the United States, while the MPLA enjoyed the backing of the Soviet Union and its allies, including Cuba,

---

[1] Papp 1993, p. 162.   [2] Hampson 1996, p. 87.   [3] Fortna 1993a, pp. 376–377.

which deployed up to fifty thousand combat troops alongside MPLA forces in Angola.[4]

During the early 1980s, international efforts to negotiate a peaceful settlement of the conflict repeatedly failed.[5] The first major progress came in December 1988, with the signing of the agreement that ended the war in neighboring Namibia.[6] Among other things, this agreement provided for a cease-fire in Angola, the withdrawal of Cuban troops from the country, and the termination of South African support for UNITA.[7] The United Nations subsequently deployed seventy military observers to monitor the phased departure of Cuban troops.[8] It soon became clear, however, that these measures were insufficient to stop the war between the MPLA and UNITA, in part because both parties continued to receive external support.[9] Negotiations toward a final resolution of the Angolan conflict resumed in 1989 and continued through to the spring of 1991, in the presence of a Portuguese mediator along with American and Soviet observers.[10]

On May 2, 1991, the parties initialed a comprehensive peace accord in Bicesse, Portugal, which included provisions for a full and permanent cease-fire, "free and fair" multiparty elections, respect for civil liberties including freedom of association, and the integration of the two armies into a single national army.[11] These provisions were to be implemented by the Angolan parties under the supervision of the United Nations and other international observers. Soon after, the Security Council approved the creation of a new UN verification mission in Angola (UNAVEM II) to ensure that the parties carried out their responsibilities under the Bicesse accord.[12] The primary responsibility for monitoring the implementation of the accords was assigned to two commissions consisting of representatives from UNITA and the MPLA, along with observers from Portugal, the United States, and the Soviet Union. The mandate of UNAVEM II was to ensure that these joint commissions carried out their monitoring responsibilities – in other words, to monitor the monitors. Several other public and private international agencies provided humanitarian and logistical aid to the local parties, including the International Committee of the Red Cross, the UNDP, and the UN High Commissioner for Refugees.[13]

In November, the MPLA and UNITA settled on the details of the electoral arrangements: The president of Angola would be elected by direct and secret suffrage through a majority system "with recourse to a second round, if necessary," while the National Assembly would be elected through

[4] Krška 1997, p. 79.   [5] Papp 1993, pp. 175–180; and Hampson 1996, pp. 89–91.
[6] See Chapter 8 for a discussion of the operation in Namibia.
[7] United Nations 1996b, pp. 234–235.   [8] Malaquias 1996, p. 92.   [9] Papp 1993, p. 186.
[10] For an account of these negotiations, see Rothchild 1997, pp. 120–135.
[11] "Peace Accords for Angola [*Acordos de la Paz para Angola*]," UN Security Council document S/22609 (May 17, 1991), annex.
[12] UN Security Council Resolution 696 (May 30, 1991).   [13] Hampson 1996, p. 124.

proportional representation.[14] UNAVEM II's mandate was subsequently expanded to oversee the preparations and conduct of the elections, which were scheduled for the fall of 1992.[15]

The agreement to hold elections and to transform the Angolan polity into a "multiparty democracy," as the Bicesse accord promised, represented a significant shift in the MPLA's traditional preference for one-party government on the Soviet model.[16] The leader of the MPLA government of Angola, José Eduardo dos Santos, had insisted as recently as early 1990 that "only the one-party system realistically serves our country."[17] It was not until peace talks shifted to Portugal in the spring of 1990, and the United States (together with the Soviet Union) started applying pressure on both parties for a settlement that included multiparty elections, that dos Santos accepted the principle of holding an open election as part of a broader peacebuilding process.[18]

Soon after, dos Santos also agreed to liberalize the Angolan economy.[19] Like the shift to liberal democracy, official support for market-oriented economic reforms contrasted with the MPLA's long-standing espousal of Marxist-Leninist economic policies (dating back to at least 1964), which included central economic planning and state-run cooperative farms and industries.[20] The Angolan government's endorsement of market democratic principles reflected the many pressures it faced in the early 1990s. Its principal foreign patron, the Soviet Union, was collapsing at a time when the war with UNITA had reached a stalemate. The MPLA's only realistic prospect of gaining external investment and financial aid for Angola was to negotiate a rapprochement with the United States and the international financial institutions, which in turn required settling the conflict with UNITA and implementing democratic and market-oriented reforms.[21]

It would, therefore, be misleading to suggest that the ensuing peacebuilding operation simply monitored the implementation of a peace agreement that the Angolan parties had themselves devised, since central components of the agreement, including the commitment to multiparty democracy, had been urged upon the parties by Western states involved in the negotiations (the United States and Portugal) and by the very international agencies that later undertook key peacebuilding tasks (the UN, the IMF, and the World Bank). The peacebuilding operation was not merely an exercise in conflict management, but part of a broader international effort to transform Angola

[14] United Nations 1996b, p. 239.
[15] UN Security Council Resolution 747 (March 24, 1992).
[16] Krška 1997, p. 77; and Rothchild 1997, p. 113.
[17] Cited in McCormick 1991, p. 5   [18] Walter 1994, p. 144.   [19] Hampson 1996, p. 111.
[20] Lodico 1996, p. 105; Ciment 1997, p. 16; and Rothchild 1997, p. 113. The notable exception was the oil sector, which remained open to Western corporations.
[21] Papp 1993, p. 188; and Ciment 1997, pp. 16 and 169.

from a warring one-party state into – it was hoped – a peaceful and prosperous market democracy.

The peace process suffered from many delays. Such problems as lack of office space and housing in Luanda, and UNITA's initial refusal to admit UN reconnaissance teams into its territory, slowed the initial deployment of international observers.[22] The original timetable called for UNITA and the MPLA to transport their troops to designated "assembly areas" by August 1, 1991, and for the demobilization process and the formation of a new national army to be completed before the holding of national elections in the fall of 1992. Both deadlines were missed. The arrival of troops in the assembly areas was delayed for a number of reasons, including the lack of adequate transportation, the shortage of food and medicine at assembly areas, and the apparent reluctance of both parties to relinquish control over their best military forces and equipment.[23] In April 1992, the Angolan parliament scheduled the elections for September 29 and 30, but by the end of September, demobilization was still far from complete: Only 65 percent of the MPLA and 26 percent of UNITA forces had been processed to return to civilian life, while only eight thousand (of a planned fifty thousand) soldiers had been integrated into the new Angolan army.[24]

Meanwhile, preparations for the elections moved forward under the supervision of international monitors, and with the advice of experts from the United Nations Development Program. Registration of voters took place between May 20 and August 10, 1992, and the electoral campaign extended from August 29 to the eve of the election, September 28. Despite increased reports of political violence as the voting neared, including several clashes between UNITA and MPLA supporters,[25] there were no major violations of the cease-fire.[26] An estimated 92 percent of eligible voters cast ballots during the two days of polling, which took place without serious incidents of violence, under the supervision of approximately eight hundred international observers.[27] Although some polling irregularities were noted, the special representative of the UN secretary-general, Margaret Joan Anstee, reported that there was "no conclusive evidence of major, systematic or widespread fraud, or that the irregularities were of a magnitude to have significant effect on the results" – a view that was echoed by most other international observers.[28]

On October 3, while the ballots were still being counted, UNITA officials

---

[22] Fortna 1993b, pp. 398–399; and Fortna 1995, pp. 290–291.
[23] Fortna 1993b, pp. 399–400; Malaquias 1996, p. 95; United Nations 1996b, p. 242; and Krška 1997, pp. 87–88.
[24] Anstee 1996, p. 48; Lodico 1996, p. 111; and Krška 1997, p. 87.
[25] Hampson 1996, p. 113.
[26] United Nations 1996b, p. 240. There were, however, several reported skirmishes between UNITA and MPLA forces between January and September 1992 (Stedman 1997, p. 37).
[27] Krška 1997, p. 88.   [28] Anstee 1996, p. 205. See also *Economist* 1992, p. 51.

complained that the election had been fraudulent.[29] In an apparent effort to counter rumors that the MPLA was leading in the vote count, the head of UNITA, Jonas Savimbi, declared that the MPLA "is not winning and cannot win" and insisted that, "in all provinces, UNITA is ahead both in the presidential and the parliamentary results."[30] In fact, Savimbi and his UNITA party were trailing in both the presidential and parliamentary races. Final results were announced on October 17. The MPLA won 54 percent of the seats in the legislature versus UNITA's 34 percent, while dos Santos took 49.6 percent of the presidential vote compared to 40.1 percent for Savimbi.[31] Neither candidate had received the minimum 50 percent support required for a first-round victory, but instead of waiting for a second round of elections to be held, as required under the Bicesse accord, Savimbi denounced the results and launched UNITA on a nationwide campaign to occupy municipalities and take over the MPLA government's administrative structures. Fighting first broke out in areas of Huambo province and soon spread to other parts of the country, including Luanda, in spite of international efforts to broker a new cease-fire. In the first week of November, MPLA forces had regained control of Luanda and hunted down UNITA officials and supporters who were attempting to flee the capital city. UNITA fared better in the countryside, where its forces surrounded key provincial capitals and ports. By the start of 1993, UNITA was estimated to control 50 of Angola's 164 municipalities and 75 percent of the country's territory, including virtually all of the roads and Angola's major diamond-producing region.[32]

Fighting continued for the next two years, killing approximately three hundred thousand people, or about 3 percent of the country's population, which exceeded the estimated number of Angolans killed in the eighteen years of civil war leading up to the signing of the Bicesse accord in 1991.[33] In November 1994, after the MPLA had reversed UNITA's territorial gains, the parties signed a new cease-fire and peace agreement in Lusaka, Zambia, which provided for the reintegration of the two armies and the formation of a government of national unity with representation from both the MPLA and UNITA, as well as a second round of presidential elections.[34] But the Lusaka agreement did not hold, and the Angolan civil war continued. Frustrated with the recalcitrance of the local parties and fearing for the safety of its

---

[29] United Nations 1996b, p. 244.

[30] Anstee 1996, p. 201. Officials from the National Electoral Commission, along with UNAVEM II observers, investigated UNITA's complaints and found no evidence of systematic fraud or fraud that would have significantly affected the outcome of the election (United Nations 1996b, p. 244).

[31] Pereira 1994, pp. 16–17.   [32] Meldrum 1993b, p. 45; and Anstee 1996, pp. 329–330.

[33] USIP 1996; and Tvedten 1997, p. 111.

[34] "Lusaka Protocol," November 15, 1994. For a description of the negotiations leading up to the signing of the Lusaka Protocol, see Hare 1998. With the signing of the Protocol, the UN transformed UNAVEM II into UNAVEM III.

personnel, the United Nations finally decided in February 1999 to terminate its peace mission in Angola.[35] Hostilities continued until April 2002 when Savimbi was murdered, prompting the MPLA and UNITA to sign a new cease-fire.

There is no shortage of possible explanations for the failure of UNAVEM II. Many commentators criticize the mission for failing to ensure that the factions were fully demobilized before elections took place.[36] Others submit that the "winner-take-all" electoral system used in the Angolan elections, which offered few incentives for the losing party to accept the results, was a principal cause of the mission's failure.[37] Another interpretation blames the design of the Bicesse accords themselves, suggesting that they were vague and lacked "procedures for dealing with violations."[38] A variant of this argument is that the peace agreement was flawed in assigning the primary responsibility for the implementation of the accords to the Angolan parties, rather than to the UN itself.[39] Yet others contend that the United Nations and the international community devoted insufficient personnel and material resources for overseeing the implementation of the accords.[40]

Perhaps the simplest and most obvious explanation for the failure of the mission is that the Angolan parties themselves lacked sufficient political will to achieve a lasting peace.[41] Savimbi, in particular, was widely portrayed as the "spoiler" of the peace process: a man who, despite his stated commitment to peace, had no intention of demobilizing his forces or respecting the results of the elections, unless they advanced his goal of becoming president of Angola.[42]

Whatever the actual causes of renewed violence may have been, at least one conclusion seems clear in the aftermath of UNAVEM II: The 1992 election in Angola did not facilitate a reconciliation of the formerly warring parties. On the contrary, the election forced the latent conflict between Savimbi and dos Santos into the open, generating a climate of competition and hostility between their two parties, who approached the election as "war by other means."[43] During the campaign period, both Savimbi and (to a lesser degree) dos Santos used rhetoric that played upon Angola's existing social and political divisions, including urban–rural and ethnic–tribal

[35] Security Council Resolution 1299 (February 26, 1999). The UN mission had been reorganized and renamed the UN Observer Mission in Angola in 1997. On the rationale for ending the mission, see "Report of the Secretary-General on the United Nations Observer Mission in Angola (MONUA)," S/1999/49 (January 17, 1999).
[36] Meldrum 1993b, p. 24; Marcum 1993, p. 223; Bertram 1995, pp. 398–399; Fortna 1995, p. 294; Vines 1995, p. 8; Malaquias 1996, p. 95; and Krška 1997, pp. 92–93.
[37] Cohen 1993; Pereira 1994, pp. 15–16; Knudsen with Zartman 1995, p. 136; Ciment 1997, p. 20; and Rothchild 1997, p. 135.
[38] Fortna 1993b, p. 402; and Walter 1994, p. 152.
[39] Walter 1994, p. 120; Malaquias 1996, pp. 94–95; and Krška 1997, p. 92.
[40] Hampson 1996, p. 122; Rothchild 1997, p. 134; and Ciment 1997, p. 20.
[41] Fortna 1995, p. 292.   [42] Brittain 1998. On "spoilers," see Stedman 1997.
[43] Wesley 1997, pp. 98–109.

differences, in order to generate popular fear of the other party's intentions.[44] These verbal battles reduced the prospects of peaceful cooperation by making it even more difficult for the parties to accept any type of postelection democratic coexistence with their adversaries. Although it was ultimately Savimbi who rejected the vote (and who, therefore, bore primary responsibility for the collapse of the peace process), neither of the Angolan leaders seemed willing to accept the possibility of electoral defeat in the weeks leading up to the election or during the vote-counting period.[45]

The ordinary citizens of Angola may have had a clearer understanding of the election's likely effects than the international peacebuilders. "The people are full of fear," reported one Roman Catholic bishop in the days before the vote, "and a lot of them are leaving their villages because they don't know what will happen during the elections."[46] International agencies, by contrast, made unrealistic best-case assumptions about the elections. Indeed, the entire plan for the democratization of Angola was based on the flimsy hypothesis that encouraging democratic competition among recently warring rivals would reduce the likelihood of renewed violence in Angola. In practice, however, the elections brought the long-running contest between the MPLA and UNITA to a head, with devastating results. Not only did the elections fail to reconcile the formerly warring parties; they also apparently served as a catalyst for renewed fighting and helped to destroy the fragile peace that had prevailed since the signing of the Bicesse accords. As one observer wrote in the aftermath of these events, "No longer can it be assumed that a ceasefire and internationally monitored elections are sufficient to establish a lasting peace in a country torn by years of bitter civil strife."[47]

This fighting might have been avoided if the international peacebuilding agencies had ensured that the parties were completely disarmed before the elections took place – certainly, UNITA's military capacity gave Savimbi some flexibility in deciding whether or not to renew fighting. Be that as it may, the attempts to transform Angola into a democratic state in 1992 seemed to have a detrimental impact on the country's peace process.[48]

Rwanda

Rwanda is a small Central African country whose population is divided into two main ethnic groups: According to the 1991 census, just over 90 percent

[44] Wesley 1997, p. 102; Heywood 2000, pp. 216–218.
[45] Wesley 1997, pp. 102–105.   [46] Quoted in Noble 1992.   [47] Meldrum 1993a, p. 24.
[48] The economic dimension of peacebuilding was virtually nonexistent in Angola during the 1990s, and therefore is not addressed in this chapter. The World Bank conducted a few small projects in the country, and the IMF did not commit any financial resources or negotiate an adjustment program with Angola, due to the country's failure to meet the most basic macroeconomic and policy "benchmarks" that the IMF required as a precondition for beginning discussions of an adjustment program. See Hodges 2001.

of the country's inhabitants were ethnic Hutu, while roughly 8 percent were ethnic Tutsi.[49] During the period of Belgian colonial rule prior to 1959, virtually all the chiefs and subchiefs who dominated Rwandan political and economic life had been Tutsi. In 1959, however, Belgian officials found themselves under pressure, both internationally and from Hutus within Rwanda, to "democratize" the country's indigenous ruling structures, which in practice meant replacing the Tutsi elite with Hutus.[50] This goal was largely accomplished by the time Rwanda formally became independent in July 1962.

Tutsi resistance to Hutu rule continued in the following years, which in turn provoked waves of repression by the Hutu government against the Tutsi population, spurring the emigration of tens of thousands of Tutsis from Rwanda. Many of these Tutsi refugees settled in neighboring Uganda, some achieving positions of influence under the regime of Uganda's president, Yoweri Museveni. In 1990, approximately four thousand Tutsis who had served in the Ugandan army established an armed wing of the expatriate Tutsi organization, the Rwandan Patriotic Front (RPF). Together with about three thousand other exiles, this force invaded Rwanda in October 1990 with the goal of overthrowing the Hutu regime.[51] After the invasion was repulsed by Rwandan government forces, the RPF reverted to guerrilla tactics. Sporadic fighting continued until July 1992, when a cease-fire agreement was reached with the assistance of mediation from the Organization of African Unity. After a year of further negotiations, the RPF and the Hutu-dominated Rwandan government signed a comprehensive peace accord in Arusha, Tanzania, in August 1993.

The Arusha Accords provided for the creation of a transitional government in which Tutsis would share power with Hutus, the integration of the two armies, the return of refugees to Rwanda, and the organization of parliamentary elections for 1995, all of which was to be supervised by a neutral international force.[52] "The principal purpose of the Arusha accord," writes Samuel Makinda, "was to create a participatory, multi-party democracy in which a government could be voted out of power and opposition parties could function freely."[53] Indeed, the Hutu president of Rwanda, Juvénal Habyarimana, had been under considerable pressure to liberalize the country's political system and to hold democratic elections – pressure that came not only from the RPF, which demanded a share of governmental power in Rwanda, but also from opposition groups within Rwanda, as well as from international donors, many of whom argued that democratization and a multiparty system were necessary to end the war.[54]

[49] Sellström and Wohlgemuth 1996.   [50] Prunier 1995, pp. 41–54.
[51] Vaccaro 1996, p. 370.   [52] United Nations 1994, p. 2.   [53] Makinda 1996, p. 562.
[54] De Waal and Omaar 1995, p. 156; Adelman, Suhrke, with Jones 1996; Uvin 1998, p. 62; Clapham 1998, p. 202; and Human Rights Watch 1999, p. 47.

Habyarimana and his supporters had long resisted calls for power sharing with Hutu and Tutsi opposition groups. Habyarimana's political party, the Mouvement Révolutionnaire National pour le Développement (MRND), was the only legal party in existence from 1975 until 1990, when the regime was compelled by foreign donors and rising internal opposition to recognize the existence of new parties. The clique that controlled the ruling MRND party included Habyarimana's relatives and closest political allies – known as the *akazu* or "little house" – who were mostly Hutu and predominantly from northwestern Rwanda, the president's home region. As elsewhere in Africa, control of the state itself was the main avenue of rapid wealth creation, and members of the *akazu* enriched themselves by diverting state revenues, doling out patronage, and administering international development aid.[55] Many ordinary Rwandans also depended on the central administration for employment and perquisites: Local administrators, village chiefs, security agents, policemen, and local party cadres were all appointed by the central government.

The desire to hold onto these advantages likely contributed to the growing opposition within the MRND to the Arusha Accords and to the notion of sharing power and democratizing Rwanda's political system. By July 1993, however, international donors had lost patience with Habyarimana's recalcitrance and, working in combination with the World Bank, informed the Rwandan president that international funds for his government would be halted if he did not sign the Accords, including the provisions for temporary power sharing with opposition groups during a transitional period leading up to free and fair elections.[56] Given that Rwanda was relying on foreign donors to subsidize at least 70 percent of its public investment, the threat to cut off aid was effective: Habyarimana signed the agreement.

The Arusha Accords devoted little attention to the country's economic policies, but the Rwandan government had also been under pressure from the international financial institutions to implement structural adjustment programs. During the late 1980s, Rwanda's fiscal condition had deteriorated following a sharp decline in world coffee prices (coffee exports provided more than two-thirds of the country's foreign revenues) and a severe drought.[57] After resisting structural adjustment for several years, Habyarimana finally agreed in September 1990 to implement a package of economic reforms in exchange for financial assistance from the IMF and World Bank. The main elements of this package included measures to reduce the government budget deficit through a combination of improved revenue collection and spending cuts; the liberalization of imports; the elimination of controls on domestic prices and other regulations impeding private

---

[55] Uvin 1998, p. 21.   [56] Human Rights Watch 1999, p. 124.
[57] Sellström and Wohlgemuth 1996.

enterprise; the elimination of subsidies for coffee producers; and the privatization of state-owned enterprises.[58] Although the immediate goal of these reforms was to restore macroeconomic stability and competitiveness to the Rwandan economy, a number of international donors argued that these measures would also help to reduce political tensions within the country by bringing the Rwandan economic crisis to an end.

In sum, the government of Rwanda committed itself to a dual process of political and economic liberalization in the early 1990s, largely at the behest of international agencies and Western states.[59] The process was intended, at least from the perspective of these external actors, to promote political and economic stability in the country. Yet the faith of the international community in the pacifying effects of democratization and marketization turned out to be tragically misplaced.

In October 1993, two months after the signing of the Arusha Accords, the United Nations approved the UN Assistance Mission for Rwanda (UNAMIR) to oversee the implementation of the peace agreement.[60] The principal functions of UNAMIR were to ensure the security of the capital city of Kigali, to monitor Rwanda's border with Uganda, to verify compliance with the cease-fire agreement, and to oversee implementation of military reforms, including the demobilization of both armies, as well as a number of humanitarian tasks.[61] In 1995, the operation was to shift its principal focus to preparing for municipal, parliamentary, and presidential elections.[62] The entire complement of more than 2,500 UNAMIR military and civilian personnel was fully deployed by the end of February 1994.[63]

During this period, however, tensions were mounting between Habyarimana and other members of his regime who opposed the peace settlement. Senior ministers in Habyarimana's own party, along with high-ranking military officers in the armed forces and Presidential Guard, issued veiled warnings that attempts to implement the Arusha Accords would have dire results.[64] Many of these individuals apparently had direct links to the Coalition pour la Défense de la République (CDR), a new Hutu-based party that was formed in 1992 with an openly anti-Tutsi platform.[65] In the months that followed the signing of the Arusha Accords, Hutu hard-liners in the CDR and elsewhere pushed ahead with plans to organize ordinary Rwandans into "self-defense" units, nominally directed against the threat of invasion from abroad, but also apparently in preparation for possible attacks upon Tutsi civilians inside the country.[66] The CDR's principal vehicle for spreading its concepts of Hutu ethnic supremacy to the population of Rwanda was a private radio

---

[58] Ibid.   [59] Jones 2001, pp. 62–63.
[60] UN Security Council Resolution 872 (October 5, 1993).
[61] United Natioms 1996b, p. 343.   [62] Sellström and Wohlgemuth 1996.
[63] Vaccaro 1996, p. 382.   [64] Adelman, Suhrke, with Jones 1996.
[65] Prunier 1995, pp. 128–129.   [66] Human Rights Watch 1999, pp. 101–103, 126.

station – Radio-Télévision Libres des Milles Collines (RTLM) – whose broadcasts were, according to one Western observer, "the most virulent and effective incitement to hatred and violence" against Rwanda's Tutsi population.[67] During and immediately after the negotiation of the Arusha Accords, the killing of Tutsi civilians became more frequent. Evidence mounted that Hutu militia groups associated with the CDR and the ruling party were responsible for some of these killings.[68]

On April 6, 1994, President Habyarimana died when his plane crashed after being struck by a missile near the Kigali airport; within minutes, members of the Presidential Guard and CDR militias established roadblocks throughout the capital.[69] Beginning that evening and extending over the following thirty-six hours, members of the Guard conducted a series of political assassinations that targeted Hutu and Tutsi politicians, activists, journalists, and clerics who had voiced support for the planned democratic transition or criticized the government for its delay in implementing the Arusha Accords.[70] Members of local militias and ordinary Hutu peasants soon began killing Tutsi civilians throughout the country. Over the next three months, somewhere between five hundred thousand and one million Rwandan Tutsis were murdered by their Hutu compatriots, and an estimated four million (roughly half of Rwanda's prewar population) were displaced from their homes in "one of history's most intensely violent acts."[71]

Efforts to reinforce UNAMIR failed due to lack of interest from the international community in deploying a larger force to Rwanda.[72] Given the inability of the existing UNAMIR force to carry out its responsibilities in the midst of intense violence, the UN ordered the bulk of the force to leave Kigali, leaving behind a token contingent of 450 soldiers.[73] It was therefore

---

[67] Chege 1996/97, p. 34.

[68] Sellström and Wohlgemuth 1996; and Adelman, Suhrke, with Jones 1996.

[69] Vaccaro 1996, p. 373. The identity of those who launched the missile against Habyarimana's plane remains unknown (Human Rights Watch 1999, pp. 181–185). However, the speed with which the Presidential Guard and militias set up roadblocks following Habyarimana's assassination suggests that they may have had advanced warning.

[70] Prunier 1995, pp. 230–231 and 242–243. See also the report of the UN Commission on Human Rights (UN document E/CN.4/1995/7, June 28, 1994).

[71] Jones 2001, pp. 1–2 and 43–44.

[72] The deciding factor appears to have been the lack of support from the United States for expanding the size and mandate of UNAMIR. See Burkhalter 1994/95.

[73] Jones 1995, p. 230. The UN commander in Rwanda at the time, Major General Roméo Dallaire of Canada, explained in an interview why his force of 2,600 blue-helmeted troops were unable to perform their mandate under these circumstances: "[T]hey [UNAMIR personnel] couldn't move all around. They couldn't do their job. They did not have the self-protection. They did not have the ammunition. They did not have the weapons" (CBC 1995). Dallaire has argued that the genocide could have been stopped if the UN contingent had been reinforced with well-equipped and well-trained troops in the early days of the killing (Buckley 1998; and Straus 1998).

left to the RPF, which had resumed military operations on April 8, to stop the massacres through force of arms. By the time the RPF gained control of most of the country's territory, however, an estimated 80 percent of Rwanda's resident Tutsi population had been killed.[74]

The mass murder of Rwanda's Tutsis between April and July 1994 has been labeled a genocide because of the magnitude of the killings and because a specific ethnic group was targeted for extermination. Most observers of Rwandan politics have concluded that the genocide was carefully planned and orchestrated by a relatively small group of Hutus belonging to the regime's political, military, and economic elite, including members of Habyarimana's own party, who had created and were in control of the network of local militias that conducted the initial wave of killings (although the genocide became less organized as ordinary Hutu villagers, spurred on by government-controlled radio stations, joined in the frenzy).[75] The genocide effectively ended the UN peacebuilding mission in Rwanda, as the international community's attention shifted to the new refugee crisis caused by hundreds of thousands of Hutus fleeing into neighboring countries. Since that time, the RPF has remained in control of Rwanda's government and territory, and the fighting has largely subsided, although there is still disagreement about exactly what happened, who was responsible, and why the international community failed to foresee and avert the massacres.

Why did Hutu extremists plan and conduct the genocide? The evidence suggests that the mass killing of Tutsis was a last-ditch effort to block implementation of the Arusha Accords.[76] Plans for political liberalization, including the transitional coalition government and democratic elections, would have challenged the dominance of the Hutu clique that surrounded Habyarimana and controlled the military. As Howard Adelman and Astrid Suhrke put it, the accords "represented a frontal attack on the power base erected by the Habyarimana regime during 20 years of rule – a denial of authoritarian rule, of 'Hutu power,' and especially Northwestern-based Hutu power which was the regional constituency and political backbone of the regime."[77] Hard-line members of Habyarimana's party and the CDR had openly displayed their opposition to the Arusha Accords by boycotting

---

[74] Prunier 1995, p. 265.

[75] Prunier 1995, pp. 239–248; Sellström and Wohlgemuth 1996; and Longman 1997, p. 300. For firsthand reports of the premeditated character of the genocide, see the testimonies cited in Prunier 1995, p. 242, n. 51. See also the report of the UN Commission on Human Rights (UN document E/CN.4/1995/70, November 11, 1994), which refers to "reliable testimony" that orders to carry out the massacres were issued by the central government via local political and administrative authorities.

[76] Burkhalter 1994/95, p. 44; Jones 1995, p. 227; Prunier 1995, pp. 241–242; Makinda 1996, p. 266; Sellström and Wohlgemuth 1996; Longman 1997, pp. 287–300; and Jones 2001.

[77] Adelman, Suhrke, with Jones 1996.

cabinet meetings and organizing violent demonstrations, and early plans for a "final solution to the ethnic problem" had circulated in extremist circles in late 1992, while negotiations at Arusha were still ongoing.[78] Faced with the prospect of sharing power with their Tutsi adversaries, this group apparently decided to assassinate its political enemies, including Hutu moderates within the government, and then physically eliminate the Tutsi population of Rwanda. The enactment of these plans "marked the culmination of a program of government-sponsored violence and intimidation intended to frustrate efforts to change the structures of power and democratize the political system."[79] Political liberalization, in other words, not only failed to reconcile the warring parties in Rwanda but also apparently served as a catalyst for the genocide by threatening Hutu elements with the prospect of losing power.

The tragedy cannot be explained *entirely* as a response to the internationally sponsored democratization plan; the genocide clearly had multiple and complex causes. The growing power of the RPF relative to Rwandan government forces, for example, may have convinced some members of the Hutu-dominated regime of the urgency of solving the "Tutsi problem" once and for all.[80] The regime also faced mounting internal political pressure from disgruntled Hutus, particularly those who were not from the privileged northwestern region of the country. Less obviously, the causes of the genocide could be traced back to the colonial history of Rwanda, which helped to create the very ethnic divisions and resentments that played themselves out in April 1994; and to the perverse tradition of tit-for-tat civilian massacres by Hutus and Tutsis throughout the postindependence period, which effectively established the "strategy" of genocide as a conceivable option for members of the embattled Habyarimana clique. Any of these factors may have contributed to the conditions that produced the genocide, and should figure in a comprehensive explanation of the genocide.

However, our more limited task in these case studies is to evaluate the effects of liberalization on the prospects for stable and lasting peace in peacebuilding host states. Although the internationally sponsored plans for democratization and power sharing do not provide a complete explanation for the events of April 1994, they do appear to have provoked extremist members of the regime to act quickly – both in preparing for the massacres and in initiating the genocide immediately after Habyarimana's death – in order to prevent the Arusha Accords from being implemented. At the very least, then, the effort to move Rwanda in the direction of democracy did not have

---

[78] Prunier 1995, pp. 160–161, 166, 173, and 200.

[79] Longman 1997, p. 287. Makinda (1996, p. 556) reaches a similar conclusion, arguing that the Hutu leadership was "so strongly opposed to the competitive political system that they tried to sabotage every effort to make it work." See also Clapham 1998.

[80] Destexhe 1995, p. 46.

the pacifying influence that international peacebuilders had hoped for and apparently expected. The international community had presented the plan for power sharing followed by democratic elections as a means of resolving Rwanda's civil war, but attempts to foster peace and stability in Rwanda by promoting political liberalization ultimately backfired, and in the worst possible way. As one student of Rwandan politics notes: "The push for democratization had unforeseen and ultimately negative effects, and it was a key tactical error."[81]

Other dimensions of the Rwandan case also cast doubt on the Wilsonian assumptions of peacebuilding. First, although some commentators have argued that *greater* political liberalization – such as more freedom of association and expanded press freedom – might have helped to avert the genocide, there is little reason to believe this is true. Many international development agencies that were involved in Rwanda before the genocide worked to increase the number of nongovernmental, voluntary organizations in the country on the assumption that the latter would enhance the "social trust" and "civic engagement" that are the pillars of a democratic, pluralistic society.[82] Yet this assumption depended on these local organizations' choosing to embrace democracy and human rights. As it turned out, however, many local NGOs in Rwanda either were apolitical and thus disconnected from the events of April 1994, or were virulently anti-Tutsi and antidemocratic.[83] Efforts to promote a more active "associational life" in Rwanda, in other words, did not appear to further the goals of either democracy or peace because many indigenous NGOs subscribed to the dominant bigotry of the larger society.

Similarly, the partial liberalization of Rwanda's popular media in the early 1990s may have made the genocide more, not less, likely to occur: Although the Hutu regime monopolized the radio, a vibrant but irresponsible press came into existence after 1990. This press was highly polarized between supporters and opponents of the Habyarimana regime, with some of the new publications advocating the destruction of Rwanda's Tutsi population and others openly expressing sympathy for the RPF's war effort.[84] Jack Snyder and Karen Ballentine have argued that inflammatory publications on both sides of the conflict worked against the cause of peace: Some pro-government newspapers worked in tandem with RTLM to incite the Hutu population to violence against Tutsis, while virulent attacks on the Habyarimana regime in some antigovernment publications may have reinforced the Hutu extremists' determination not to accept the power-sharing provisions of the Arusha Accords.[85] Thus, the liberalization of the media did not appear to have the moderating effects that some international agencies predicted.

[81] Jones 2001, p. 164.   [82] Uvin 1998, chap. 8.   [83] Ibid.
[84] Prunier 1995, pp. 131–132.   [85] Snyder and Ballentine 1996, pp. 30–34.

A further aspect of the Rwandan case that raises doubts about Wilsonianism is the seemingly deleterious impact of *economic* liberalization on the Rwandan peace process in the years preceding the genocide. As noted, the government of Rwanda had committed itself to a structural adjustment plan in September 1990 at the insistence of the international financial institutions, a plan that included government spending cuts, reductions in price subsidies, and deregulation of the domestic economy. These policies may have contributed to the worsening of economic conditions in the early 1990s, and thereby made the Rwandan population more susceptible to the government's hate propaganda. Some commentators put this case in very strong terms. Michel Chossudovsky, for example, argues that "the imposition of sweeping macro-economic reforms by the Bretton Woods institutions exacerbated simmering ethnic tensions and accelerated the process of political collapse."[86] However, the precise impact of structural adjustment policies on economic and political conditions in Rwanda is difficult to discern, given that the introduction of these policies coincided with the collapse in international coffee prices, a prolonged drought, and the RPF invasion in October 1990 – the combined effects of which resulted in an absolute decline in the country's GDP in every year from 1990 to 1994.[87] Nevertheless, specific elements of the structural adjustment program did apparently contribute to the impoverishment of many Rwandans in the early 1990s: Higher fees for health and education, for example, added to the already heavy burdens of Rwanda's poor, while a freeze on public wages, combined with successive currency devaluations, decreased the real income of many middle-class Rwandans.[88]

Whether these conditions increased the willingness of ordinary Rwandans to participate in mass murder remains a matter of debate, but it does appear that the economic crisis placed additional stress on the social and political fabric of the country in the lead-up to the genocide.[89] Indeed, whatever connection may exist between the economic liberalization policies and the genocide, these policies clearly did not enhance Rwanda's political stability during the Arusha peace process, and they seem to have contributed to the impoverishment of many Rwandans at a time of acute political and social tension. Nor did the international community, including the World Bank and IMF, consider the potentially explosive political consequences of these policies when they designed the structural adjustment program.[90]

---

[86] Chossudovsky 1997, p. 111.

[87] Per capital GDP fell by almost 40% from 1989 ($330) to 1993 ($200), according to figures cited in Sellström and Wohlgemuth 1996.

[88] Ibid.

[89] Prunier (1995, pp. 284 and 243) points out, moreover, that there was an element of material interest in the killings: Most of the members of the militias were poor, and looting of victims' possessions was widespread.

[90] Uvin 1998.

All told, the peacebuilding experience in Rwanda challenges the liberal peace thesis in a number of ways. Efforts to democratize Rwanda facilitated the rise of political parties that were "masks for ethnic groups that organized murderous militias"[91] and provoked Hutu extremists to plan and launch a genocidal attack on the country's Tutsi population; the liberalization of the media and civil society organizations did not produce political moderation and may have simply offered extremist groups a means of organizing and conveying their inflammatory messages; and market-oriented economic reforms seem to have worsened, not ameliorated, the climate of insecurity in Rwanda that the perpetrators of the genocide were able to exploit. The precise degree to which the liberalization process may have ultimately contributed to the resurgence of violence in Rwanda has yet to be determined, and responsibility for the horrors of April 1994 must rest with those who perpetrated the genocide. But it seems safe to conclude, at the very least, that international efforts to transform Rwanda into a market democracy did not advance the goal of establishing a stable and lasting peace.

Conclusion

The two missions investigated in this chapter indicate that the liberalization process in Angola and Rwanda did not have the pacifying effects that peacebuilders had anticipated. Indeed, the cases also offer circumstantial evidence that the liberalization process may have worked against the goal of creating a stable and lasting peace in these two states. Nevertheless, Angola and Rwanda represent only two of eleven operations that we will examine in depth, and in many respects these two missions offer the worst outcomes of internationally sponsored liberalization efforts in war-shattered states during the 1990s. As we investigate more cases in the following chapters, our conclusions about the Wilsonian assumptions of peacebuilding will therefore need to be revised and elaborated.

[91] Kaplan 1997.

5

Cambodia and Liberia

Democracy Diverted

In contrast to Angola and Rwanda, where the democratization process might well have served as a catalyst for renewed conflict and the collapse of peacebuilding efforts, the results of postconflict democratization efforts in Cambodia and Liberia were widely viewed as positive. Both countries held largely free and fair elections under international supervision, and in both cases peacebuilding agencies declared their efforts a "success" and terminated their operations shortly after the elections. At first glance, then, Cambodia and Liberia seem to corroborate the Wilsonian hypothesis that liberalization fosters peace in war-shattered states. Closer examination, however, raises serious doubts about the pacifying effects of democratization in these two cases. Even though both countries experienced a period of relative political stability following the departure of international peacebuilders, the adoption of democracy itself cannot be credited because the newly elected governments of both countries immediately backed away from their commitments to democracy and reverted to more autocratic forms of rule; and one country, Liberia, ultimately slipped back into war.

The Wilsonian hypothesis holds that violent conflict can be transformed into peaceful political competition when groups are allowed to pursue their interests freely through democratic political institutions. While this may help to explain the initial success of elections in Cambodia and Liberia, it does not explain the ensuing period, during which there was little real freedom to challenge the policies of governing cliques, and the behavior of both countries' elected leaders – Hun Sen in Cambodia and Charles Taylor in Liberia – was more despotic than democratic. Their regimes do not lend support to the proposition that free political competition fosters peace.

Cambodia

Cambodia enjoyed little peace in the years after it gained its independence from France in 1953. During the 1960s, Vietnamese communist guerrillas used Cambodian territory to move supplies and establish bases in their fight against the forces of South Vietnam and the United States, and in response, American forces began a secret bombing campaign of Cambodia in 1969.[1] Soon after, American and South Vietnamese troops crossed the border into Cambodia to destroy communist bases and supply lines, a campaign that pushed the guerrillas and the fighting deeper into Cambodian territory. As the Vietnam war drew to a close in April 1975, Cambodian communist guerrillas known as the Khmer Rouge captured the country's capital of Phnom Penh. The leader of the Khmer Rouge, Pol Pot, immediately ordered the city emptied of all of its inhabitants, many of whom were sent to labor camps in the countryside for "reeducation." Over the following three years and eight months, the Pol Pot government orchestrated a perverse reengineering of the society during which an estimated 1.7 million Cambodians – or approximately 20 percent of the population – died as a result of forced labor, torture, execution, malnutrition, or disease.

In December 1978, Vietnamese troops invaded Cambodia and overthrew the Khmer Rouge regime, driving Pol Pot and his supporters into jungle areas close to the border with Thailand. Tens of thousands of Cambodian civilians also fled over the Thai border and found their way to sprawling refugee camps. Meanwhile, the Vietnamese established a new Cambodian government, which continued the military campaign against the Khmer Rouge with the assistance of Vietnamese combat troops. With Chinese equipment and funding, however, the Khmer Rouge was able to defend its jungle redoubts and wage a guerrilla war against the Phnom Penh government and its Vietnamese backers for most of the 1980s. Two smaller Cambodian opposition groups also fought alongside the Khmer Rouge. The Front Uni Pour Un Cambodge Indépendant, Neutre, Pacifique et Coopératif (FUNCINPEC) was led by Prince Norodom Sihanouk, who had been Cambodia's head of state from its independence until he was deposed in 1970; the second group, the Khmer People's National Liberation Front (KPNLF), was led by former prime minister Son Sann. Both of these noncommunist factions received support from Thailand and Western countries, including the United States and Britain.

The rise of Mikhail Gorbachev to power in the Soviet Union in 1985 initiated a series of events that led eventually to the negotiated settlement of the Cambodian conflict. Vietnam had relied on the Soviet Union for material support since the relationship between Vietnam and China had cooled in the late 1970s. When Gorbachev indicated that his government intended to reduce its international spending and seek peaceful solutions to the regional conflicts in which it was involved, Vietnam's policy toward Cambodia began to shift. In late 1985, the Hanoi government informed its Southeast Asian neighbors that Vietnam might be willing to withdraw its troops from

[1] Shawcross 1994, p. 7.

Cambodia. In 1986, the member states of the Association of Southeast Asian Nations (ASEAN) and Vietnam began to discuss possible compromise solutions to the Cambodian conflict. One year later, Prince Sihanouk met for the first time with the leader of the Phnom Penh regime, Hun Sen. After several rounds of negotiations, the four Cambodian parties (the government, FUNCINPEC, the KPNLF, and the Khmer Rouge) finally agreed on a framework for the comprehensive settlement of the Cambodian conflict in September 1990.[2] The framework had been devised by the five permanent members of the Security Council – China, France, Britain, the Soviet Union, and the United States – who met again in November to draft a comprehensive peace agreement, building upon the framework agreement.[3] The document ultimately produced by these states was, after several months of further negotiation, formally accepted by the Cambodian parties at a peace conference in Paris on October 23, 1991.[4]

The agreement set out a detailed plan for transforming Cambodia into a peaceful liberal democracy. Factional armies would be disarmed and demobilized, refugees returned to their homes, political prisoners released. A Supreme National Council consisting of representatives from all four Cambodian parties would act as the country's sovereign authority until multiparty elections could be held for a constituent assembly. This assembly, once elected, would draft a new constitution and then transform itself into the country's first postwar government. The peace agreement set out the main principles for a new constitution: Cambodia would follow "a system of liberal democracy, on the basis of pluralism," including "periodic and genuine elections" by secret ballot and universal suffrage, civil liberties enshrined in a declaration of fundamental rights, and an independent judiciary empowered to enforce these rights.[5] In short, the formula that the "permanent five" members of the UN Security Council presented to the Cambodian parties, and which these parties accepted with slight modifications, reflected the Wilsonian assumption that transforming the Cambodian state into a liberal democracy would facilitate the transition from civil war to lasting peace. Indeed, the Security Council explicitly justified its support for the Cambodian peace accords on the grounds that "free and fair elections

---

[2] For a description of the negotiations that led up to the 1990 framework agreement, see Heininger 1994, pp. 12–22.

[3] Indonesia was also present at the meeting, in virtue of its position as the co-chair (along with France) of the most recent peace conference on Cambodia.

[4] The text of the agreement is reproduced in UN document A/46/608-S/23177 (October 30, 1991), annex.

[5] Ibid., section II, "Agreement on a Comprehensive Political Settlement of the Cambodia Conflict," annex 5, "Principles for a New Constitution for Cambodia." As Michael Doyle (1996b, p. 500) notes, the peace agreement "specified all the elements necessary for a constitutional democracy" in Cambodia, with free and fair elections as the "hallmark and linchpin" of the settlement.

are essential to produce a just and durable settlement to the Cambodia conflict."[6]

A new United Nations field operation – the UN Transitional Authority in Cambodia (UNTAC) – was created to oversee implementation of the accord. UNTAC's extensive duties included supervising Cambodia's civilian police, monitoring the cease-fire and the demobilization of factional armies, investigating human rights complaints, repatriating refugees, and coordinating an international campaign to reconstruct Cambodia's war-damaged infrastructure, as well as organizing and conducting national elections.[7] The operation was also given a wide-ranging mandate to supervise the conduct of Cambodia's existing governmental administration in order to "ensure a neutral political environment conducive to free and fair general elections." This meant, in practice, that UN officials were to be involved in the day-to-day operations of individual government ministries.

"Not since the colonial era and the post–World War II Allied occupations of Germany and Japan," writes Michael Doyle, "had a foreign presence held so much formal administrative jurisdiction over the civilian functions of an independent country."[8] James Schear elaborates this point:

By the latter stages of the operation, UNTAC personnel could be found doing such things as probing into the country's penal code, investigating its defense procurement decisions, vetting editorials in state-run media, reviewing regulations on national heritage preservation, scrutinizing admissions policies at public educational institutions, monitoring passport and visa procedures, managing monetary and fiscal decisions, and delving into a host of other civil administrative activities.[9]

Not only did the peace accords explicitly prescribe the remolding of the Cambodian state into a liberal democracy, but they also empowered international civil servants, working under the auspices of the United Nations, to oversee and expedite these reforms by occupying positions within the Cambodian government ministries themselves.

In the realm of economic policy, the accords carefully avoided endorsing any particular economic model for postwar Cambodia, and explicitly warned international donors against interfering in the country's economic policymaking process: "No attempt shall be made to impose a development strategy on Cambodia from any outside source."[10] In practice, however, the international financial institutions encouraged Cambodia to adopt

---

[6] UN Security Council Resolution 745 (February 28, 1992).
[7] The operation's mandate is set out in detail in UN document S/23613 (February 19, 1992) and its addendum, UN document S/23613/Add.1 (February 26, 1992).
[8] Doyle 1995b, p. 13.   [9] Schear 1996, p. 158.
[10] UN document A/46/608-S/23177 (October 30, 1991), annex, part IV, "Declaration on the Rehabilitation and Reconstruction of Cambodia," para 2.

market-oriented economic reforms.[11] In mid-1992, the government of Cambodia reached an agreement with the IMF to implement an economic stabilization program that involved deep cuts in capital and social spending, along with wage and salary limits for public employees, in order to restore balance to the government's finances.[12] This was followed, in October 1993, by the negotiation of an IMF structural adjustment loan to Cambodia that committed the government to further market-oriented reforms, some of which were implemented "under the tutelage of UNTAC officials" working within the Cambodian bureaucracy.[13]

Although external peacebuilding agencies played a central role in promoting and effecting Cambodia's transition to a market economy, this transition does not appear to have been "imposed" on the Cambodian parties. After all, these parties opted to pursue market-oriented economic reforms rather than an alternative development strategy. But there is little doubt that the principal peacebuilding agencies in Cambodia were predisposed in favor of liberal economic policies, and that they communicated this predisposition to the Cambodian government through the offer of concessional loans and technical advice.

These observations lead to the following conclusion: The peacebuilding operation in Cambodia, like the others examined in this volume, sought to transform Cambodia into a particular kind of society – a liberal market democracy – on the assumption that doing so would create the most propitious conditions for a stable and lasting peace. As Joakim Öjendal argues, "one of the intrinsic aspects of the operation certainly was the establishment of a liberal order," which in practice meant the promotion of democratic elections, civil liberties, and market-oriented economic reforms in Cambodia.[14]

The mission got off to a rocky start. Although UNTAC officially became operational on March 15, 1992, many of its offices were not fully staffed until December, just six months before the scheduled elections in May 1993.[15] The mission's military component was not fielded in time to begin the process of disarmament and demobilization scheduled for June 1992.[16] Necessary vehicles, prefabricated housing, office and communications equipment, and other items were also slow to arrive in Cambodia.[17]

---

[11] At a meeting of international donors on June 22, 1992, for example, the international financial institutions "stressed the importance of market-based reforms in Cambodia to increase the output in major sectors of the economy" (UN doc A/47/285-S/24183 of June 24, 1992, annex).

[12] Irvin 1993, pp. 128–132.

[13] Ibid., p. 132. Indeed, UNTAC took over responsibility for financial and macroeconomic operations of the Cambodian government in March 1992 (United Nations 1996b, p. 191).

[14] Öjendal 1996, p. 194.   [15] Prasso 1995, p. 39.   [16] USGAO 1993, p. 41.

[17] United Nations 1995, p. 16. Many reasons have been cited for UNTAC's delayed deployments, including inadequate planning by UN headquarters (Heininger 1994, p. 85; and Jennar 1994, p. 153), the organization's cumbersome recruitment and procurement system

While the UN scrambled to assemble teams of military and civilian personnel and transport them to Cambodia, the operation suffered another serious setback: The Khmer Rouge simply refused to prepare its forces for demobilization as required by the peace agreement.[18] The cantonment of the factional armies was to have been completed by the end of July, but the three other Cambodian parties were reluctant to disarm their forces in the face of Khmer Rouge recalcitrance. As a result, by mid-November, only some 55,000 troops had reported to the cantonment sites, most of whom appeared to be untrained teenagers with antiquated weapons, while superior forces and caches of weapons remained in the field.[19] After several unsuccessful attempts at convincing the Khmer Rouge to comply with the accords, UNTAC abandoned its demobilization effort and allowed the soldiers who had already been cantoned to return to their respective armies on "agricultural leave."[20]

On November 30, the Security Council imposed a selective trade embargo on the Khmer Rouge and ordered UNTAC to proceed with the planned elections with or without the cooperation of the Khmer Rouge.[21] The operation's military component was subsequently redeployed "to protect voter registration and, subsequently, the electoral and polling processes, particularly in remote or insecure areas."[22] Thus, after the failed demobilization effort, UNTAC shifted its attention to the goal of ensuring a peaceful environment for free and fair elections. But as the May 1993 elections drew closer, the security situation in Cambodia deteriorated.

The opening of the campaign period in March unleashed a wave of political violence, which intensified as election day neared.[23] Opposition political offices were "attacked, ransacked, and burned, and party members were beaten, kidnapped and killed."[24] In the ten weeks leading up to the

---

(USGAO 1993, pp. 35–41), the sheer size and complexity of the Cambodia operation (United Nations 1995, p. 16), and the fact that UNTAC found itself in competition for scarce resources with the UN operation in the former Yugoslavia (Schear 1996, p. 152).

[18] To justify their noncompliance with the accords, Khmer Rouge officials asserted that "a great number" of Vietnamese military personnel remained in Cambodia in contravention of the accords (United Nations 1995, p. 17; and Schear 1996, p. 157). In response, UNTAC conducted an extensive investigation, which revealed no evidence of any organized Vietnamese military presence in Cambodia.

[19] Berdal and Leifer 1996, p. 43.   [20] Doyle 1995b, p. 35.

[21] The trade embargo included stopping the supply of petroleum products "to areas occupied by any Cambodian party not complying with the military provisions" of the peace accords, and a moratorium on the export of logs from Cambodia. Regarding the elections, the Council determined that UNTAC should proceed with preparations for free and fair elections "in all areas of Cambodia to which it has full and free access as at 31 January 1993." Security Council Resolution 792 (November 30, 1992), paras. 5, 10, and 13.

[22] Boutros-Ghali's third progress report on UNTAC, UN document S/25154 (January 25, 1993), para. 41.

[23] Chopra 1994, p. 27.   [24] Doyle 1995b, p. 56.

vote, political violence resulted in a reported 176 deaths, 316 injuries, and 67 abductions.[25] Two groups were thought to be primarily responsible for these attacks: Agents of Hun Sen's incumbent regime apparently perpetrated much of the violence against supporters of the two noncommunist opposition parties, FUNCINPEC and the KPNLF; while the Khmer Rouge was held responsible for killing dozens of ethnic Vietnamese civilians and for several attacks against UNTAC officials in the Cambodian countryside, which was apparently intended to disrupt the polling.[26] Hostile intimidation also interfered with the registration of eligible voters at refugee camps along the Cambodian border.[27] To many observers, the election-related violence represented a "looming disaster" for UNTAC.[28]

Nevertheless, preparations for the elections continued, and for reasons that are still unknown, the Khmer Rouge did not ultimately carry out its threat to launch a large-scale military offensive when polls opened on May 29.[29] The relative peacefulness of Cambodia during the two days of voting came as an "astonishing, welcome surprise" after weeks of mounting violence,[30] with nearly 90 percent of registered voters casting ballots.[31] FUNCINPEC, under the leadership of Prince Sihanouk's son, Norodom Ranariddh, took more than 45 percent of the votes; Hun Sen's Cambodian People's Party (CPP) won roughly 38 percent; and the KPNLF came in a distant third with 3.8 percent.[32]

However, Hun Sen's reluctance to accept his loss to Ranariddh led to further confrontations in the days after the vote.[33] In an effort to create a stable postelection government, Prince Sihanouk announced on June 16 the formation of an Interim Joint Administration, with himself as head of state and both Ranariddh and Hun Sen as co–prime ministers. Ministerial posts were to be split evenly between the two leading parties.

From the vantage point of late 1993, the effects of political liberalization on the prospects for lasting peace in Cambodia appeared to be mixed. On the one hand, democratic elections seemed to provide a formula for three of the four formerly warring parties to shift their political disputes from the battlefield to the ballot box. In late 1992, when it became apparent that

---

[25] Plunkett 1994, p. 71.
[26] Boutros-Ghali's fourth progress report on UNTAC, UN document S/25719 (May 3, 1993), paras. 4–5, and United Nations 1995, pp. 41–44.
[27] Hampson 1996, p. 198.   [28] Doyle 1995b, p. 51.
[29] At a public lecture at Yale University in 1996, I asked the former UN administrator for Cambodia, Yasushi Akashi, why the Khmer Rouge did not seek to disrupt the elections, and Akashi said that he did not know.
[30] Shawcross 1994, p. 21.   [31] United Nations 1995, p. 46.
[32] Ibid. The remaining vote was shared among seventeen other political parties. The KPNLF contested the election under the banner of its political wing, the Buddhist Liberal Democratic Party.
[33] Will 1993, pp. 399–400.

important elements of the peace accords, including the planned demobilization, would not be fulfilled, the UN had redirected its efforts toward organizing free and fair elections. This gamble had apparently paid off when the new coalition government was formed, and Cambodia seemed to enter a new period of political stability.[34] On the other hand, the process of political liberalization had also served to exacerbate tensions among the Cambodian parties in the period leading up to the elections – tensions which, according to many observers at the time, had threatened to destroy the fragile truce between FUNCINPEC and the CPP. James Schear underscores this point: "The injection of political pluralism into the country, though welcome in many respects, opened the door to an upsurge in violence that UNTAC was ill prepared to handle."[35] Although UNTAC helped to stabilize the situation – for instance, by posting guards at party offices and campaign rallies to deter attacks – the fact remains that election-related violence could have easily escalated into renewed civil war.

By the end of 1993, after the Cambodian parties had formally approved the constitution and the new coalition government had been formed, the UN Security Council declared UNTAC a "success" and ordered the withdrawal of the operation.[36] Relations between the coalition partners – Ranariddh's FUNCINPEC and Hun Sen's CPP – were tense but peaceful. The Khmer Rouge, though still an active insurgency, was beset by internal divisions and weakened by a steady stream of defections. Most analysts agreed that Cambodia was more at peace than it had been at any time since the early 1960s.[37]

But, in fact, the situation was fundamentally unstable. The quick departure of the UN mission and the precarious power-sharing arrangement "set the course for the inevitable overthrow of the democratic process four years later," as UNTAC's military commander later publicly acknowledged.[38] In theory, Ranariddh was "first prime minister" because his party had won more votes in the election, and Hun Sen was "second prime minister." In practice, however, Hun Sen continued to control the apparatus of the state and the largest armed force in the country, and was unwilling to cooperate with Ranariddh.

Anticipation of new elections scheduled for 1998 soon led to a deterioration in relations between Cambodia's two co–prime ministers. Ranariddh was determined to bolster the military forces loyal to FUNCINPEC before

[34] This was certainly the opinion of the UN's point man in Cambodia, Yasushi Akashi, who declared that the elections had provided "an important basis for eventually consolidating peace and preparing for national reconciliation" in Cambodia (Akashi 1994, p. 258).

[35] Schear 1996, p. 174.

[36] "Statement of the President of the Security Council Concerning the Successful Completion of the Mandate of UNTAC," UN document S/26531 (October 5, 1993).

[37] Mabbett and Chandler 1995, p. 257.

[38] Sanderson 2001, p. 165. See also Sanderson and Maley 1998.

the 1998 elections in order to deter CPP-sponsored violence and intimidation, which he and his supporters had faced during the 1993 campaign. Hun Sen was similarly determined to weaken FUNCINPEC before the 1998 elections in order to avoid another embarrassing loss at the polls.[39] By early 1996, political violence was once again on the rise.[40] Later that year, Ranariddh began to pursue contacts with the remaining leaders of the Khmer Rouge in the hopes of enlisting their support against the CPP.[41] Hun Sen saw these moves as a threat and responded by launching a military campaign against Ranariddh's supporters in July 1997, which led to renewed fighting between forces loyal to the two governing parties.[42] Although the bulk of Ranariddh's forces were defeated in two days, fighting between the CPP and individual FUNCINPEC units continued for several months.[43]

Ranariddh was outside Cambodia at the time and escaped arrest and possible assassination, but approximately forty of his supporters in Phnom Penh were executed and hundreds arrested.[44] According to the United Nations, moreover, at least fifty opponents of Hun Sen were killed in the subsequent eight months from August 1997 to March 1998.[45] The underlying cause of this renewed violence was the ongoing rivalry and distrust between FUNCINPEC and the CPP, but the approaching elections appear to have been the major precipitating factor that brought this rivalry to a head.[46] As one Western journalist, who was in Cambodia throughout this period, commented: "The only reason that there was a coup [in 1997] was that Hun Sen saw himself as being politically outflanked and realized that he would have lost the election [if he had not taken action]."[47]

This is not to say that the democratization process was solely responsible for the resurgence of political violence in Cambodia. Nevertheless, political competition and violence among the Cambodian parties did intensify in the period leading up to both the 1993 and the 1998 national elections, sparking new fighting between the CPP and FUNCINPEC in the latter period. While it is true that the 1993 vote permitted FUNCINPEC and the CPP to establish a new relationship as partners in a governing coalition, this partnership was untenable, and the political violence of the 1993 campaign period foreshadowed the more serious fighting that erupted in the lead-up to the 1998 elections, when both parties attempted to outmaneuver the other in advance of the vote. UNTAC, it seems, took advantage of the moment of relative

---

[39] Karniol 1997; and Jeldres 1997.   [40] Ott 1997, p. 434.
[41] Ott 1997, p. 435; Karniol 1997; and Roberts 2001, p. 140.   [42] Mydans 1997b.
[43] Mydans 1997a; Associated Press 1998.   [44] Ott 1997, p. 435.   [45] Reuters 1998.
[46] Doyle 2001, p. 92.
[47] Nate Thayer, in a personal communication to the author on May 15, 1998. Others have reached a similar conclusion, including Richard Solomon, former U.S. assistant secretary of state for East Asia (*Newshour* 1997 [July 14]).

calm immediately after the 1993 election to declare victory and withdraw from the country before the chaos returned.[48]

Although Cambodia has experienced greater political stability since the signing of the Paris Peace Accords, the traditional sources of violent conflict in the country – including the recurring pattern of authoritarianism and rebellion – seem not to have been fundamentally altered by the peacebuilding mission. The country's internal politics have historically been marked by distrust and lack of cooperation among charismatic leaders, who have generally sought absolute power and engendered similarly intolerant and extreme forms of opposition. As David Roberts writes: "No Khmer leader since independence, whether regal, communist, republican or former peasant, has accepted without resistance a challenge to the absolutism of their authority."[49] Longtime Cambodia observer Sorpong Peou concurs: "From Sihanouk to Hun Sen, the state leadership always seemed interested in preserving or enhancing its hegemonic status quo, even if it later grew vulnerable to challenges from within and/or from without the state. As these leaders tightened their grips on power, they succeeded in turning foes into friends, but later risked turning friends into foes."[50]

Both Roberts and Peou express doubt that the post-1993 "democratization" substantially changed this pathological characteristic of Cambodian politics. While the country was *more* democratic after 1993 than in the past, and the elections of 1993 and 1998 were freer and fairer than many observers had predicted, Hun Sen also used a strategy of violence and intimidation to undermine the ability of his political opponents to challenge his authority.[51] Starting immediately after the 1993 elections, he maneuvered himself and the CPP into the dominant position in the coalition with FUNCINPEC, even though they had received fewer votes. The 1997 coup d'état seriously weakened FUNCINPEC – the CPP's only major rival – and represented "a glaring example of violence against the democratic spirit."[52] Those who harmed or threatened opposition elements escaped prosecution by a police and court system that remained dominated by Hun Sen supporters, and the CPP leadership "used every occasion to make sure that anyone accused of harming its political interests or its party leaders was punished – severely."[53] By the end of the decade, Cambodia had only the "veneer" of democracy, and Hun Sen ruled "by virtue of a monopoly of muscle, the readiness of thuggish subordinates to use it and a tight grip on the machinery and resources of the state."[54]

Indeed, one could argue that Cambodia's relative stability after 1997 was due primarily to Hun Sen's largely successful but patently illiberal maneuverings to reestablish his de facto hegemonic control of Cambodian

---

[48] Fleitz 2002, p. 129.   [49] Roberts 2001, p. 171.   [50] Peou 2000, p. 427.
[51] Sanderson and Maley 1998.   [52] Ibid., p. 298.   [53] Ibid., p. 304.
[54] Roberts 2001, p. 202; *Economist* 2002 (February 9).

politics.[55] In other words, it is unclear to what degree Cambodia's relative stability can be attributed to the internationally sponsored democratization process, or instead to Hun Sen's efforts to suppress political opposition in the country. From this perspective, the 1997 coup d'état and its aftermath represented a return to traditional yet fundamentally undemocratic methods for establishing political order in Cambodia: Through violence and intimidation, the CPP undercut the ability of opposition parties to participate effectively in the democratic process.[56]

It is doubtful that this form of authoritarian quasi-democracy will offer a lasting solution to the cycle of violence that the country has experienced since its independence, since the ascendancy of Hun Sen seems to have followed the long-standing tendency toward zero-sum competition for absolute control in Cambodian politics – a tendency that has provided the country with brief periods of stability, but ultimately has always elicited violent counterreactions from opposition groups. Put differently, the partial democratization of Cambodian society that took place during the early 1990s under the supervision of international peacebuilders did not appear to alter the "underlying tenor" of the conflict.[57]

This is not to suggest that the peacebuilders' efforts in promoting political liberalization left Cambodia in a worse condition than before. On the contrary, whatever the weaknesses of the peacebuilding mission, it helped to implement a peace settlement that brought an end to a prolonged period of pervasive violence and brutality. The fact that Cambodia is no longer a "killing field" is something to be celebrated, and the UN and other international peacebuilders deserve partial credit for this accomplishment. But the question we are investigating is more specific: Does Cambodia corroborate the assumptions of Wilsonianism? To be more precise, did internationally sponsored liberalization efforts in Cambodia help to create the conditions for a stable and lasting peace? On the basis of record to date, the answer must be both yes and no. On the one hand, multiparty elections provided a formula that the warring parties were willing to adopt as the basis for determining who would rule Cambodia in the postconflict period. Further, elections have been generally free and fair, and in 1998 the populace expressed its support for Hun Sen and the CPP. But on the other hand, the transition to liberal democracy was very limited, and to some extent the modest achievements of 1993 were reversed in the ensuing years as Hun Sen undermined his political opponents and consolidated his near-absolute powers using decidedly illiberal means.

---

[55] Freedom House, a U.S.-based organization that analyzes the political and civil liberties of every country in the world, downgraded Cambodia from "partly free" to "not free" in the mid-1990s: http://www.freedomhouse.org/research/freeworld/FHSCORES.xls, accessed in August 2002.

[56] Fleitz 2002, p. 128.   [57] Roberts 2001, p. xv.

At this writing, the government continues to control the police and judiciary, and there is effectively no opposition in the country. As noted in Chapter 1, the liberal peace thesis – of which Wilsonianism is one variant – is based on the premise that peace derives not only from elections but also from real political contestation within the rule of law, respect for political and civil liberties, constitutional limitations on the exercise of governmental power, and the maximization of individual freedom. Cambodia has had elections but lacks many other characteristics of liberal democracy.[58] We must therefore treat with skepticism any suggestion that the Cambodian experience corroborates the Wilsonian hypothesis. Indeed, the country became *more* stable in the late 1990s as Hun Sen increasingly backed away from his earlier democratic commitments.

Liberia

In the early nineteenth century, the American Colonization Society purchased land that would later became part of Liberia, a small country on the west coast of Africa that shares a border with Guinea, Ivory Coast, and Sierra Leone, and began resettling freed American slaves to the territory.[59] When Liberia gained independence in 1847, it was governed by a small group of Americo-Liberians, who subjugated the indigenous population in a series of wars. Ironically, given the new arrivals' origins as former slaves themselves, the Americo-Liberian elite created a system of forced labor that continued well into the twentieth century. (The League of Nations condemned it as virtual slavery in 1930.)[60] Approximately three hundred closely knit families formed the ruling elite, which preserved its "feudal oligarchy" intact for over a century.[61]

In 1980, a small group of indigenous army officers overthrew the Americo-Liberian regime in a violent coup and installed Master Sergeant Samuel Doe as Liberia's new head of state. At first, the native population welcomed the coup and the new regime, believing that their "needs and interests, which had long been overlooked, would now claim the full attention of their government."[62] But their hopes soon met the reality of Doe's increasingly authoritarian, self-serving, and nepotistic rule. Like the Americo-Liberians before him, Doe created a governmental system that benefited a small minority within the country – in this case, his own ethnic group, the Krahns, who constituted about only 4 percent of the population.[63] Many of the president's non-Krahn supporters were gradually eliminated and all forms of opposition were suppressed.[64] To the surprise of many, Doe agreed to

[58] Sanderson 2001.   [59] Conteh et al. 1999.   [60] Dalton 1965.
[61] Alao et al. 1999, pp. 12, 14.
[62] W. Nah Dixon, *Great Lessons of the Liberian Civil War,* quoted in Alao et al. 1999, p. 18.
[63] Alao 1998, p. 11; Ero 2000, p. 197.   [64] Sesay 1996; Alao et al. 1999, p. 18.

hold general elections in 1985, but after early returns indicated that he was losing the vote, he brazenly manipulated the vote count and announced his victory.[65] Critics of these results faced "brutal reprisals."[66]

Animosity against the Krahn hegemony – and against the person of Doe – was widespread in Liberia by the late 1980s, and it created propitious conditions for a former Doe ally, Charles Taylor, to launch an insurrection against the government in December 1989. Taylor's rebel force, the National Patriotic Front for Liberia (NPFL), gained the support of peasants in the hinterland as Doe's army terrorized non-Krahn ethnic groups that he suspected of treason.[67] The insurgents advanced quickly, reaching the outskirts of the Liberian capital, Monrovia, in July 1990. In response, the Economic Community of West African States (ECOWAS), led by Nigeria, sponsored peace negotiations and deployed a ceasc-fire monitoring group (ECOMOG) comprised of approximately four thousand troops from Gambia, Ghana, Guinea, Nigeria, and Sierra Leone. However, fighting in Liberia did not stop. President Doe was captured and killed in 1990, and opposition forces fragmented into several tribally based militia factions, each led by a warlord. Interfactional violence was particularly brutal, characterized by widespread atrocities against civilian populations and an "abandonment of all rules and conventions of war."[68]

From 1990 to 1997, one-tenth of the country's prewar population of 2.5 million died, one-third became refugees, and nearly all the rest were displaced at one time or another.[69] ECOWAS, and increasingly the United Nations, were involved in numerous unsuccessful efforts to establish peace in Liberia during this period. Twelve separate peace settlements among the warring parties were successfully negotiated, but each of them quickly collapsed – until the signing of the second Abuja Accord in 1996. The Abuja agreement laid out a timetable for the disarmament and demobilization of factional forces, the deployment of an expanded international monitoring mission, and the creation of an interim power-sharing government that would rule Liberia in the transitional period leading up to democratic elections, originally scheduled for May 1997.

Given that previous attempts to hold elections in the country had "failed hopelessly," many commentators were pessimistic about the possibilities of conducting a free and fair vote.[70] Nevertheless, preparations for the elections proceeded only slightly behind schedule, and the warring factions transformed themselves into political parties, including the dominant faction – Taylor's NPFL – which converted itself into the National Patriotic Party (NPP). Under the supervision of ECOMOG and the United Nations

---

[65] Harris 1999, p. 433; and Lyons 1999, p. 21.
[66] Alao et al. 1999, p. 19; and Ero 2000, p. 197.   [67] Lyons 1999, p. 22.
[68] Alao et al. 1999, p. 20.   [69] Lyons 1999, p. 20.
[70] Tanner 1998; and Alao et al. 1999, p. 102.

Observer Mission in Liberia (UNOMIL), more than 21,000 combatants were disarmed and demobilized between November 1996 and February 1997.[71] Meanwhile, the UN Development Program, the European Union, and a private organization, the International Foundation for Electoral Systems, provided technical assistance in preparation for legislative and presidential elections, which were ultimately held in July 1997. Electoral rules provided for run-off ballots in the event that no single presidential candidate received a majority of votes on the initial ballot, but as it turned out, Taylor won 75.3 percent of the vote in the first round, while his NPP party took 49 of 64 seats in the House of Representatives and 21 of 26 seats in the Senate.[72] Taylor's nearest rival for the presidency won 9.6 percent of the vote, and the remaining 11 contenders received a combined total of less than 10 percent.[73] It was a landslide victory.

By all accounts, the election results broadly reflected the will of the Liberian people. Turnout was estimated at over 80 percent of registered voters. Balloting was scrutinized by approximately five hundred international observers from a panoply of intergovernmental and nongovernmental agencies, including the UN, the Organization of African Unity, the European Union, the Carter Center, and the Friends of Liberia, and judged to be generally free and fair.[74] According to the UN, polling was conducted "in an organized and efficient manner and without reports of violence or intimidation."[75] However, whether the campaign itself offered candidates an equal opportunity to convey their messages to voters is a different question. In fact, Taylor's organizational network and resources were far superior to those of any other candidate. Taylor alone had a fleet of Land Rovers, buses, motorcycles, loudspeaker trucks – even a helicopter – at his disposal during the campaign.[76] Because he was also the only candidate with a national political network already in place, he also benefited from the quick election timetable and short campaign period.

Yet despite this uneven playing field, the sheer margin of Taylor's victory quieted skeptics and convinced most observers that the Liberian population did, in fact, want Taylor as their president.[77] The consensus interpretation was that Liberians had voted out of the fear that Taylor would resume fighting if he lost the election. As one commentator put it, Liberians were anxious that Taylor would "do a Savimbi" – referring to the violent outcome of the 1992 elections in Angola.[78] "In the eyes of these voters," wrote another observer, "a victory for anyone else would have meant almost certain

[71] Lyons 1999, p. 42.   [72] Harris 1999, p. 436.   [73] Alao et al. 1999, p. 103.
[74] Harris 1999, p. 437.
[75] "Letter from the Secretary-General to the President of the Security Council," UN document S/1997/581, July 24, 1997.
[76] Tanner 1998, p. 138; and Lyons 1999, p. 58.   [77] Harris 1999, p. 442 and passim.
[78] Ero 1999, p. 195. See also Tanner 1998, p. 140; Alao et al. 1999, p. 105; Lyons 1999, p. 59; and Harris 1999, p. 452.

resumption of the bush warfare that [had] cost the lives of so many of their family members and friends."[79]

With the completion of elections and Taylor's inauguration as president in August 1997, the United Nations and ECOWAS declared their missions a "success" and withdrew most of their personnel from the country.[80] The period immediately following the elections was one of relative calm, with some commentators proclaiming the arrival of a "new era" of tranquility and hope in Liberian politics.[81] But to what degree did this outcome lend support to the Wilsonian hypothesis of peace-through-liberalization? While the election was a central mechanism in the implementation of the Abuja peace accord, which ended a seven-year-long war,[82] the holding of one reasonably successful election does not demonstrate that liberalization has fostered the conditions for a stable and lasting peace in Liberia. In fact, on closer examination, the Liberian case does not appear to lend support to the Wilsonian approach to conflict management and peacebuilding, for several reasons.

First, as in Cambodia, the process of political liberalization in Liberia was superficial and temporary. President Taylor immediately began to suppress the activities of his political opponents, effectively reversing the fragile and preliminary movement toward democracy that was accomplished during the peacebuilding mission. Initially, Taylor seemed interested in continuing the democratization process: In his inaugural address, he promised to pursue the goals of reconciliation and political inclusion and to give high priority to human rights and the rule of law, and he matched these words with actions, inducting four opposition members into his initial cabinet of nineteen ministers.[83] But soon after, Taylor's style of rule revealed the "increasingly paranoid and bellicose attitude of a leader who continues to rely on security forces to stifle opposition movements or remove those considered to be likely coup plotters."[84]

Instead of neutralizing the country's security forces, Taylor absorbed the most reliable fighters of his former guerrilla organization into a so-called Anti-Terrorist Unit, which was soon linked to a series of attacks upon his political rivals, including his erstwhile ally, Samuel Dokie, who was abducted and brutally murdered in late 1997.[85] Many other political leaders subsequently left the country. By 2001, Taylor had "all but put an end to organized opposition" to his government, routinely threatening and jailing journalists.[86] When university students demonstrated peacefully against the arrests

---

[79] Fitzpatrick 1997.
[80] The UN's self-congratulatory final report on UNOMIL uses the words "success" and "successful" no fewer than ten times in thirty-four paragraphs (UN doc. S/1997/712, September 12, 1997; see also S/1997/581, July 24, 1997). After the termination of UNOMIL, the UN established a small peacebuilding office in Monrovia.
[81] Alao et al. 1999, p. 102.   [82] Lyons 1999.   [83] Ero 2000, pp. 200–201.
[84] Ibid., p. 201.   [85] Ero 2000, p. 202; United States Department of State 2002.
[86] Farah 2001b.

of four prominent journalists in the spring of 2001, the Anti-Terrorist Unit physically beat and dispersed the demonstrators.[87] In addition, according to both the U.S. State Department and the nongovernmental organization Human Rights Watch, "President Taylor's government functioned without accountability, independent of an ineffective judiciary and legislature that operated in fear of the executive."[88] In short, the president and his party used their positions to "entrench their power, limit political freedom, and make it less likely that future elections will be competitive."[89] Given all this, crediting Liberia's relative postelection stability to the supposed liberalization of political life in the country would do violence to the liberal peace thesis.

Second, the peacebuilding mission did not address the underlying patterns of conflict in Liberian society, including the historical tendency of Liberian leaders to achieve power by hijacking the institutions of the state for the personal enrichment of their kinsmen, loyalists, and themselves, while ruthlessly suppressing rival leaders and groups.[90] This is the pattern that was first established by Americo-Liberian rule, which dominated and exploited the indigenous majority and elicited the violent coup in 1980 that brought Samuel Doe to power. Perversely, Doe reproduced the same style of kleptocratic and fiercely repressive rule – to the detriment of almost everyone in Liberia except members of his own Krahn ethnic group – which in turn created conditions of general resentment that Charles Taylor and his allies were able to exploit as they organized their own violent uprising against the state.

The 1997 elections did little to alter this pattern, and may have served only to strengthen an authoritarian leader who offered rhetorical support for multiparty democracy but began immediately consolidating a "monolithic political party system and presidential autocracy" based on violence, suppression, and nepotism.[91] By attacking his rivals, by abolishing what few political liberties were established during the peacebuilding mission, and by establishing a network of semiofficial business ventures – including some that the UN Security Council claims are involved in the smuggling of contraband diamonds – to finance his personal security forces,[92] Taylor appeared to be "repeating the mistakes of the Americo-Liberians and the Doe regime."[93] The peacebuilding mission – which oversaw a partial demobilization of the factions and hastily organized elections, and then quit the country – did little to curb the cycle of oppressive kleptocracy and violent rebellion that has marked Liberia's history as an independent state.[94]

---

[87] Ibid.

[88] The quotation is from Human Rights Watch 2002; see also United States Department of State 2002.

[89] Lyons 1999, p. 63.   [90] Dolo 1996; Bøås 2001.

[91] Barclay 1999, p. 303. See also Adebajo 2002.   [92] Farah 2001a.

[93] Ero 2000, pp. 210–211.   [94] Tanner 1998, pp. 145–146.

Indeed, fighting soon resumed. A new armed opposition group – Liberians United for Reconciliation and Democracy (LURD) – launched attacks on Taylor's government forces in July 2000 and quickly advanced to positions near the capital.[95] In response, Taylor mobilized fifteen hundred of his former fighters to combat the insurgency.[96] As rebels continued to close in on the capital, Taylor declared a national state of emergency in February 2002, under which the government began widespread arrests of suspected "dissidents" in Monrovia, including street youths and members of ethnic groups that Taylor viewed as untrustworthy.[97] Amnesty International subsequently accused Taylor's security forces of using the state of emergency as a justification to increase human rights violations against the civilian population, including widespread torture and rape.[98] As the *Washington Post* editorialized in February 2002, "Liberia is now on the verge of a civil liberties meltdown and a return to unrestrained bloodshed."[99]

Indeed, conditions continued to deteriorate over the coming months, until Taylor, who faced imminent military defeat and intense international pressure to leave the country, resigned his office and fled Liberia in August 2003 (reportedly with several million dollars of public funds in his baggage). One month later, the United Nations deployed yet another peacebuilding operation to the country – the UN Mission in Liberia (UNMIL), with up to fifteen thousand international troops – to support the implementation of a new peace agreement, which was negotiated among the warring parties when Taylor departed. Among other things, the Security Council instructed UNMIL to monitor the cease-fire and to prepare the country for a new set of national elections, scheduled for 2005.

Given all this, the assessment offered by the Africa scholar Terrence Lyons in 1999 seems to have been prescient. Lyons suggested that the critical weakness of the Abuja Accord and the ensuing international peacebuilding mission was that they paid too little attention to "the longer and more difficult problems of reconciliation and the rebuilding of social relationships necessary to promote long-term conflict management."[100] Although the 1997 elections themselves were largely free and fair, and helped to create a measure of stability in the short run, they did not yield the conditions for a stable and lasting peace in Liberia.

The Liberian case may be interpreted in one of two ways. Either the partial democratization overseen by international peacebuilders was so insubstantial that it offers little or no insight into the effects of political liberalization on war-shattered states, or alternatively, the pacifying effects of Liberia's partial democratization were themselves transitory and largely illusory. Whichever

---

[95] Human Rights Watch 2002.　　[96] Farah 2001b.
[97] Reuters 2002; and Amnesty International 2002.　　[98] Amnesty International 2002.
[99] *Washington Post* 2002 (February 14).　　[100] Lyons 1999, p. 63.

interpretation one chooses, the Liberian case does not appear to lend support to the Wilsonian hypothesis.

Conclusion

Internationally sponsored liberalization efforts did not have the immediately destabilizing effects in Cambodia and Liberia that they apparently had in Angola and Rwanda, but neither of these cases demonstrates that liberalization promotes the conditions for a stable and lasting peace in war-shattered states. Although Cambodia has enjoyed relative tranquility since the termination of the peacebuilding mission, this does not corroborate the Wilsonian hypothesis, since early efforts to democratize political life in Cambodia have been progressively reversed by the country's authoritarian prime minister. In Liberia, the partial movement toward democratization that culminated in the 1997 elections did little to address the historical pattern and sources of conflict in the country, which slipped back into violence in 2000. Both countries emerged from their peacebuilding missions as quasi-democracies based on the power of strongmen who brook little dissent and use intimidation and threats to suppress political opposition. In Cambodia, this form of rule may offer the basis for continued stability; in Liberia, it quickly gave way to renewed conflict. But in neither case can peace be attributed to democratic freedoms, open political contestation, effective constitutional limitations on the exercise of power, or any other conditions that might corroborate the liberal peace thesis. Indeed, the cases of Cambodia and Liberia seem to reinforce the preliminary findings of the previous chapter: that hasty liberalization efforts might actually work against the goal of establishing a stable and lasting peace in countries that are just emerging from civil wars.

6

Bosnia and Croatia

Reinforcing Ethnic Divisions

The territory of the former Yugoslavia has hosted several peacebuilding missions. The first major postconflict operation was deployed to Bosnia in 1995. Other missions were created for Croatia (1995) and Kosovo (1999). This chapter focuses on the Bosnia operation and concludes with an analysis of the much smaller Croatia operation. The subsequent mission to Kosovo will be examined in Chapter 11.

Bosnia

War in the former Yugoslavia broke out in June 1991, after two of the country's then-constituent republics – Slovenia and Croatia – declared their independence from the Yugoslav federation. Fighting between Slovenian nationalists and the Yugoslav National Army (JNA) lasted only ten days before the JNA withdrew from Slovenia. In Croatia, however, ethnic Serb residents formed paramilitary units (which were supplied and supported by the JNA) and waged a war against Croatian nationalist forces throughout the second half of 1991. A cease-fire came into effect at the end of the year, but only after Serb militias and the JNA had gained control of roughly one-quarter of the republic's territory. In February 1992, the UN Security Council created the United Nations Protection Force (UNPROFOR) to monitor the cease-fire in Croatia.[1]

One month later, in March 1992, a referendum on independence was held in neighboring Bosnia, which at the time was still part of Yugoslavia. The vote divided Bosnia along ethnic lines. Muslims (who represented 44 percent of the republic's population in 1991) and Croats (17 percent of the population) strongly favored independence, while Serbs (31 percent of the population) vigorously opposed the secession of Bosnia and abstained from the

---

[1] Security Council Resolution 743 (February 21, 1992).

vote.[2] Like their compatriots in Croatia, most Serbs in Bosnia preferred to remain part of the Yugoslav federation – in which Serbs were the dominant group – rather than become a permanent minority in a newly independent state. With Serbs boycotting the referendum, Bosnia's independence resolution was approved by an overwhelming margin.[3] Sporadic fighting between paramilitary groups from each of the three major ethnic groups soon developed into a full-scale civil war, which continued, despite several short-lived cease-fires, until the end of 1995. From the beginning of the war, Bosnian Serb militias – with direct support from the government of Serbia – instituted the practice that came to be known as "ethnic cleansing," forcibly ousting and, in some cases, executing Muslims and Croats who lived in Serb-controlled territory.[4] Although Muslims and Croats had earlier cooperated to achieve Bosnian independence, their military coalition quickly disintegrated and they began fighting each other. Until the final months of the conflict, Serbian forces enjoyed a considerable military advantage over both Muslims and Croats. They used this to gain control of more than 70 percent of Bosnian territory.

In 1992, the United Nations responded to the Bosnian war by deploying peacekeeping troops to ensure the delivery of humanitarian relief supplies, and later to protect civilian "safe areas." The mission (an extension of the existing UNPROFOR operation in Croatia) was unable to prevent Bosnian Serb forces from blockading and eventually storming two of the designated safe areas, the Muslim towns of Srebrenica and Zepa. International efforts to mediate a negotiated settlement of the conflict took place concurrently with the UN mission, but repeatedly failed to gain the agreement of all the warring parties. The Bosnian Muslims, in particular, refused to accept any peace proposal that granted ethnic Serbs political control over areas that had been ethnically "cleansed"; the Bosnian Serbs, for their part, had little incentive to negotiate a settlement of the war as long as they continued to dominate the battlefield. In the summer of 1995, Croats and Muslims joined forces to reconquer territories held by the Bosnian Serbs since 1992. With the tide of battle turning against them, Serb leaders finally indicated that they were willing to engage in serious peace negotiations.

[2] Population figures are from Steinberg 1993, p. 41. The remaining 8% was made up of "others," including self-described "Yugoslavs."

[3] More than 99% of valid votes favored independence (Cohen 1993, p. 237).

[4] According to Cigar (1995, p. 4), ethnic cleansing was "the direct and planned consequence of conscious policy decisions taken by the Serbian establishment in Serbia and Bosnia-Herzegovina. This policy was implemented in a deliberate and systematic manner as part of a broader strategy intended to achieve a well-defined, concrete, political objective, namely, the creation of an expanded, ethnically pure Greater Serbia." On JNA support for Bosnian Serb paramilitary forces, see Silber and Little 1996, p. 243. The connections between the Serbian government and the Bosnian war are a central issue in the ongoing trial of former Yugoslav president Slobodan Milosevic at the International Criminal Tribunal for the Former Yugoslavia in the Hague.

American-mediated talks convened in November 1995 at a military base near Dayton, Ohio.[5] After three weeks of intensive negotiation, the parties initialed the General Framework Agreement for Peace in Bosnia and Herzegovina (the Dayton Accord) on November 21 and formally signed the agreement in Paris on December 14. The Dayton Accord contained eleven annexes detailing the responsibilities of the Bosnian parties and the international agencies that would oversee its implementation.[6] National elections would be held for new pan-Bosnian political institutions, including a three-member presidency (one from each of the three major ethnic groups) and a bicameral parliament. At the same time, however, the country was to be divided into ethnic subunits, according to a detailed map. Areas controlled by Muslims and Croats would together form the "Federation of Bosnia and Herzegovina," whereas areas controlled by Serbs would form "Republika Srpska." Each of these "entities" would possess its own democratically elected political institutions. A draft constitution, also annexed to the Dayton agreement, set out the federal division of powers between the national and entity-level governments.[7] In addition, the parties agreed to maintain the existing cease-fire, to withdraw their military forces from a four-kilometer-wide "zone of separation" dividing the two entities, to negotiate numerical limits on military forces, to ensure the free movement of civilians throughout Bosnia, including the return of refugees to their homes, and to cooperate in the investigation and prosecution of war crimes.

The Dayton Accord explicitly sought to transform Bosnia into a liberal democracy on the assumption that doing so would reduce the likelihood of renewed fighting. The preamble of the new constitution made this assumption clear, asserting that "democratic governmental institutions and fair procedures best produce peaceful relations within a pluralist society." In the body of the constitution, the parties agreed that Bosnia "shall be a democratic state, which shall operate under the rule of law and with free and democratic elections." They also promised to uphold the civil liberties of all persons within the territory of Bosnia, including freedom of expression, assembly, movement, thought, conscience, and religion.[8] In the economic realm, the Accord affirmed the parties' desire "to promote the general welfare and economic growth through the protection of private property

---

[5] At the talks, the Bosnian Serbs were represented by the president of Serbia, Slobodan Milosevic; the Bosnian Croats by the president of Croatia, Franjo Tudjman; and the Bosnian Muslims by the president of Bosnia, Alija Izetbegovic.

[6] The agreement is reproduced in UN document S/1995/999, annex.

[7] The federal government would be responsible for foreign policy; international trade and customs; monetary policy; national-level finances; immigration, refugee, and asylum policy and regulation; inter-entity and international criminal law enforcement, communications and transportation; and air traffic control. All other governmental powers would be exercised at the entity level.

[8] A list of these rights are enumerated in article 2(3) of the constitution.

and the promotion of a market economy."[9] Support for market-oriented economic policies was further reinforced by provisions in the Accord authorizing the IMF to appoint the first governor of Bosnia's new central bank.[10]

The agreement also called for the creation of a new International Force (IFOR) under NATO command to oversee the military elements of the settlement and assist in the implementation of nonmilitary aspects, such as providing security for elections and helping to ensure the relocation of refugees and displaced persons. The United Nations was to terminate the existing UNPROFOR operation, and replace it with a contingent of unarmed police monitors to help train civilian law-enforcement personnel throughout Bosnia. The OSCE was assigned the task of supervising the election process, monitoring human rights, and assisting with the negotiation and implementation of arms control and confidence-building measures. The agreement also called upon the United Nations High Commissioner for Refugees to develop a repatriation plan that would allow an early, peaceful, and phased return of refugees and displaced persons.

The formal transfer of authority from UNPROFOR to IFOR took place on December 20, 1995.[11] By mid-January 1996, IFOR troops had cleared the four-kilometer buffer zone separating the opposing armies. Between early February and mid-March, IFOR supervised the redeployment of Bosnian forces on either side of the "inter-entity boundary line." Under its supervision, the formerly warring parties placed heavy weapons in cantonment sites and demobilized approximately three hundred thousand fighters.[12] Despite the failure of the Bosnian Serbs to reduce their armed forces to the extent required by the accords, the military component of the peacebuilding operation met most of its initial goals. Not only did the Bosnian parties complete their planned redeployment but they also continued to observe the October 1995 cease-fire.

In the meantime, preparations for national elections in September 1996 continued. These elections were intended to begin the process of knitting back together the country's physically and ethnically separated communities – specifically, by reconstituting Bosnia's national political institutions with representation from all three communities. Under considerable pressure from the United States,[13] the OSCE certified that conditions for effective elections existed in Bosnia, despite the warnings of many observers that elections held so soon after the cessation of hostilities would merely consolidate the power of extremist nationalists who had a vested interest in

---

[9] Preamble of the constitution.   [10] Article 7(2) of the constitution.

[11] IFOR consisted of approximately 54,000 troops from thirty-four countries. This total included approximately 17,000 troops who had been serving in UNPROFOR and came under the control of the IFOR commander when the official transfer of authority took place.

[12] USGAO 1997a.   [13] Glitman 1996/97, p. 78.

resisting the reconciliation of Bosnia's ethnic communities.[14] In fact, this is precisely what happened. The most belligerent and narrowly nationalistic political parties within each of the three communities – the Muslim Party of Democratic Action (SDA), the Croatian Democratic Union (HDZ), and the Serbian Democratic Party (SDS) – swept the legislative elections at both the national and the "entity" level.[15] Similarly, in elections to the tripartite Bosnian presidency, voters in each ethnic group elected the respective leaders of these parties by overwhelming margins.[16] Although numerous technical objections were raised to specific decisions that OSCE had made in administering the elections,[17] few observers doubted that the outcome of the vote generally reflected the preferences of the Bosnian electorate. Yet as American negotiator Richard Holbrooke later pointed out, "The election strengthened the very separatists who had started the war."[18]

With the power of hard-liners in each community reaffirmed by the elections, the prospects of establishing a viable pan-Bosnian government were greatly diminished. Many of the newly elected Bosnian Croat and Serb leaders, in particular, were reluctant to participate in the very national institutions to which they had been elected. The pan-Bosnian parliament was scheduled to hold its first meeting in October, but it did not actually convene until January 1997 because Serbian representatives refused to swear allegiance to a united Bosnia. Members of the new central bank were selected, but they disagreed on the bank's role and were unable to conduct business. Bosnian Serb and Croat leaders refused to appoint members to the new constitutional court. Similar stonewalling delayed efforts to endow the new council of ministers with effective authority. Within the Muslim-Croat Federation as well, Bosnian Croats attempted to retain their separate institutions, rather than merge them into the new "entity-level" government. The Bosnian Croat HDZ apparently had "no intention of abandoning what it consider[ed] to be its national rights to territorial sovereignty and economic assets" within the areas of the Federation that they controlled.[19]

---

[14] See, for example, Anthony Borden's prediction in Borden, Drakulic, and Kenny 1996, p. 14; and Human Rights Watch/Helsinki 1996, p. 2.

[15] In elections to the national-level House of Representatives, these three parties took 36 of 42 seats (or 86%). In the Bosnian-Croat Federation, voters elected members to two bodies: the Federation House of Representatives and the Federation Cantonal Assemblies. The SDA and HDZ together captured 114 of 140 seats (or 81%) in the House of Representatives, and 345 of 406 seats (or 85%) in the Cantonal Assemblies. In Republika Srpska, voters cast ballots for the Republika Srpska National Assembly, and for the presidency of Republika Srpska. The SDS won 45 of 83 seats (or 54%) in the National Assembly, and 59% of votes cast for the presidency.

[16] The leader of the SDA took 80% of Bosnian Muslim votes, the leader of the SDS took 67% of Bosnian Serb votes, and the leader of the HDZ took 89% of Bosnian Croat votes.

[17] See Cousens 1997, pp. 811–812, for a brief description of these objections.

[18] Holbrooke 1998, p. 344.   [19] Woodward 1997, p. 102.

Political leaders of all three ethnic groups also obstructed the return of minority refugees and displaced persons to their homes,[20] and the returns that did take place consisted mainly of people going back to areas controlled by their own ethnic group "because returns across ethnic lines proved nearly impossible."[21] Many factors hindered the repatriation process, including fear of violent attacks, poor economic prospects, and lack of suitable housing; but political leaders were also responsible for hampering returns by failing to provide adequate security, by maintaining discriminatory property laws, and by transferring minority-owned housing to members of their own ethnic group.[22] Furthermore, all three parties resisted international efforts to track down and arrest persons indicted as war criminals by the International Criminal Tribunal for the Former Yugoslavia, despite their earlier pledges to cooperate in these efforts. As one group of observers wrote in late 1997, "real cooperation between the still dominant nationalist parties has been slight and grudging, while progress on the ground, in terms of the return of refugees, freedom of movement, and the arrest of indicted war criminals, has been minimal."[23]

The September 1996 elections did not facilitate greater cooperation among the formerly warring parties; on the contrary, they served to consolidate and legitimize the political power of those nationalist leaders who were least willing to implement the provisions of the Dayton Accord that called for cooperation among the formerly warring parties – an outcome that appeared to diminish the prospects of achieving a stable and lasting peace in Bosnia. Although the Dayton agreement recognized the de facto division of Bosnia into ethnic entities, it also sought to establish a "common roof" of national political, judicial, and economic institutions that would permit the country's three ethnic communities to coexist peacefully within a single state. Dayton's international sponsors had assumed that peace was unlikely to endure in Bosnia beyond the departure of foreign troops unless a network of functioning national institutions was established with representation from all three groups. Indeed, it is difficult to imagine how the Bosnian parties could peacefully manage their intercommunal disputes in the absence of a functioning set of pan-national political institutions.[24]

Dayton's international sponsors insisted that these institutions be constituted through democratic elections – on the assumption that democratic governmental institutions would "best produce peaceful relations" among Bosnia's ethnic communities.[25] This Wilsonian assumption proved to be

---

[20] Boyd 1998, pp. 47–48.   [21] USGAO 1997b, p. 4.

[22] Ibid., p. 5. Displaced Serbs from Sarajevo, for example, have been encouraged by Bosnian Serb authorities to repopulate the formerly Muslim towns of Brcko and Srebrenica (International Commission on the Balkans 1996, p. 99).

[23] EIU 1997a, p. 5.   [24] I explore this point in greater detail in Chapter 10.

[25] Dayton Accord, Annex 4.

wrongheaded: As we have seen, the elections paradoxically filled the new institutions with individuals who were openly opposed to cooperating with their ethnic adversaries. As one Sarajevo commentator noted, although elections were intended to create mechanisms that would facilitate cooperation among Bosnia's ethnic groups, they served instead to reaffirm "the ethnic fault lines that tore the country apart."[26] Municipal elections held in September 1997 further reinforced the power of the most nationalist parties: Only 6 percent of local council seats were won by candidates who did not exclusively represent the rights of one ethnic group.[27] In recognition that little progress had been made toward the political and economic reintegration of Bosnia, IFOR's mandate was extended for a further eighteen months beyond its originally scheduled termination date in December 1996.[28] In the spring of 1998, the force's mandate was again renewed, without any specific time limit.

Following the 1996 national elections, several international agencies – most notably, the OSCE and NATO – sought to diminish the influence of the most extreme nationalists and simultaneously to increase the power of more moderate politicians, particularly in the Bosnian Serb entity. Because the Bosnian Serb's wartime leader, Radovan Karadzic, had been prohibited from contesting the 1996 elections on the grounds that he had been indicted for war crimes by the Hague tribunal, his supporters promoted the candidacy of another hard-core Serb nationalist, Biljana Plavsic, for the presidency of the Bosnian Serb entity. Plavsic was elected president, but tensions soon emerged with Karadzic over the issue of who actually controlled the Bosnian Serb government. International peacebuilding agencies and Western governments encouraged Plavsic to defy Karadzic and his supporters by providing millions of dollars in financial assistance to Plavsic loyalists and by funding aid projects in parts of Republika Srpska where Plavsic had the strongest support, while denying similar funding to areas controlled by Karadzic.[29]

In July 1997, a majority of legislators in the Bosnian Serb parliament called for Plavsic's dismissal. She responded by dissolving the parliament and calling new elections. During the subsequent election campaign, peacebuilding agencies took actions clearly aimed at helping Plavsic supporters win seats in the Bosnian Serb parliament: NATO troops, for example, seized television transmitters and police stations under the control of Karadzic supporters and turned them over to Plavsic loyalists.[30] In spite of this assistance, when

[26] Soloway 1996.
[27] International Crisis Group 1997, p. 8. In many Bosnian cities, municipal legislators representing nationalist parties refused to share power with their ethnic adversaries and boycotted local assembly meetings, thereby paralyzing several municipal governments (Smith 1998).
[28] The mission was given a new name at this time: Stabilization Force (SFOR).
[29] Wilkinson 1998.   [30] Hedges 1997.

the election was held in November, candidates belonging to Plavsic's new political party, the Serb People's Alliance – which had been formed "with Western advice and money" – won only fifteen of eighty-three seats in the Bosnian Serb parliament.[31] Although their rival, Karadzic's SDS party, lost its majority in the parliament, it still remained the most powerful faction and joined with another hard-line nationalist party to control a near majority of the seats.[32]

Because Karadzic controlled the largest group in the assembly, Plavsic was unable to gain parliamentary approval for her relatively moderate nominee for prime minister of Republika Srpska, Milorad Dodik. In order to overcome this opposition, her supporters maneuvered to hold a vote for prime minister within the parliament in January 1998, but only after the chamber had been formally adjourned and Karadzic's loyalists had left the building.[33] In these circumstances of questionable legality, Dodik was elected prime minister by the legislators who remained in the parliament building, all of whom were Plavsic supporters. International peacebuilding officials not only provided financial and rhetorical backing for Dodik in this nomination fight, but also openly supported the maneuvering that led to his election.[34] After the vote was held, international officials publicly declared their intention to provide ongoing political and financial assistance to the Dodik government.[35] Dodik reciprocated by pledging to implement all the provisions of the Dayton Accord, including those governing the repatriation of refugees and the prosecution of alleged war criminals.[36]

The behavior of international peacebuilders during and after the 1997 Bosnian Serb elections contrasted sharply with their behavior at the time of the 1996 national elections. In 1996, representatives of peacebuilding agencies and Western governments in Bosnia had focused their efforts on creating conditions for a free and fair election and had made no effort to promote particular parties or candidates over any others. The result was a landslide victory for candidates and parties that openly opposed reconciliation among Bosnia's ethnic communities – an outcome which appeared to diminish rather than enhance the prospects for a durable peace in the country. In 1997, international peacebuilders pursued a different strategy, encouraging a split within the ruling Bosnian Serb party, precipitating new entity-level elections, and providing overt financial and political assistance to the more moderate

[31] Ibid.   [32] Hedges 1998b.   [33] O'Connor 1998.
[34] According to Michael Kelly (1998), international officials dispatched NATO troops to track down a pro-Plavsic legislator and return him to the Bosnian Serb parliament for the vote, deployed NATO guards around government buildings, and persuaded the World Bank to release $65 million in reconstruction aid to the Bosnian Serb entity to bolster local support for Dodik.
[35] See, for example, the comments of Carlos Westendorp, the international community's High Representative in Bosnia, in Hedges 1998a.
[36] Smith 1998.

candidates in the ensuing electoral campaign. Despite this effort, moderate candidates still fared poorly in the vote compared to the performance of extremist nationalists loyal to Karadzic, who remained the most powerful faction in the legislature. Several Bosnian Serb leaders responded by accusing peacebuilding officials of imposing the new Dodik government on their people in what amounted to an internationally orchestrated coup.[37] Their complaints were not entirely unfounded: In seeking to bolster the power of moderate politicians, international peacebuilding agencies effectively defied the popular will of the Bosnian Serb electorate by openly working to undermine the authority of extremist nationalists who had twice been elected as the dominant faction in the Bosnian Serb legislature.

The actions of international officials in Republika Srpska in the aftermath of the 1996 national elections underscore the broader point about the potentially destabilizing effects of political liberalization in postconflict peacebuilding operations. On the basis of their experience with the 1996 national elections, peacebuilders apparently recognized that "free and fair" elections could impede, rather than facilitate, the consolidation of a lasting peace in Bosnia, and therefore undertook to intervene in the 1997 entity-level elections on the side of candidates who preached moderation but who lacked sufficient popular support to gain power through the democratic process alone. International officials, in short, seemed to retreat from their earlier faith in the putatively pacifying effects of political liberalization in postwar Bosnia. Only by "rigging" the democratic process in favor of moderate politicians did peacebuilders succeed in installing a government in Republika Srpska that supported the full implementation of the Dayton Accord.

A new round of national elections in 1998, also organized under international auspices, ended up further reinforcing the power of the wartime nationalist political parties. In the Muslim-Croat federation, the Muslim-dominated SDA under its president Alija Izetbegovic, and the Croatian-dominated HDZ under its president Ante Jelavic, increased their respective share of the vote, with Izetbegovic's vote climbing from 80 percent in 1996 to 86 percent in 1998.[38] In Republika Srpska, Nikola Poplasen – described as a "hard-line nationalist" by several observers[39] – defeated the Plavsic-Dodik government that the international community had heavily supported.[40] Once again, peacebuilders intervened to change the result of the election: Carlos Westendorp, the senior peacebuilding official in Bosnia, removed Poplasen from office for, in Westendorp's words, "consistently acting to trigger instability."[41] Even with these major intrusions in the electoral process, the most extreme parties in Bosnia retained their firm grip on political power and

---

[37] O'Connor 1998; and Wilkinson 1998.   [38] Woodward 1999, p. 6.
[39] Sullivan 1999; Smith 1999; Dinmore 1999; and Watson 1999.   [40] Woodward 1999, p. 6.
[41] Quoted in Dinmore 1999. Westendorp's successor, Wolfgang Petritsch, similarly fired the Croat member of the tripartite Bosnian presidency, Ante Jelavic, in March 2001 because

"continued to propagate ethnic insecurity and separatism in order to maintain control over the country's political, military, and economic resources."[42]

Although peacebuilders have succeeded in preventing a resurgence of fighting, the goal of the mission was to create the foundations for a stable and lasting peace by supplanting "militant ethnic nationalism with pluralism."[43] However, democratization in Bosnia has had "the opposite effect," reinforcing the societal schisms that fueled fighting in the first place.[44] One commentator put it this way in 2000:

The unified, democratic, multi-ethnic nation the international community delivered at the Dayton peace talks was stillborn. The great powers quickly rushed the corpse into the operating room, surrounded it with highly trained specialists and expensive equipment, then stood around watching it decompose. After four years as an international protectorate, Bosnia is more divided than ever.[45]

"In these circumstances," writes another pair of observers, "prospects of reconciliation and long-term stability are virtually non-existent."[46]

If political liberalization has, in various ways, worked against the goal of reconciling Bosnia's formerly warring groups, what about the process of *economic* liberalization? As we noted earlier, the Dayton Accord specified that the Bosnian and entity-level governments would promote a market economy. After the Accord was signed, the World Bank and European Union assumed joint responsibility for overseeing reconstruction efforts in Bosnia and coordinating the activities of international donors. From December 1995 until May 1998, the economic dimensions of the peacebuilding mission focused primarily on two areas: 1) repairing war-damaged physical infrastructure, including bridges, roads, water and sewage facilities, and housing; and 2) establishing the institutional structures necessary for the management of a market economy, including regulatory bodies to govern the banking and private commercial sector, a central bank, and a common currency. Some economic liberalization measures were also introduced during this period, including a plan for the privatization of state-owned enterprises and policies to reduce fiscal deficits, which were approved by both the World Bank and the International Monetary Fund.[47]

More comprehensive reforms in economic policy, however, were not pursued during this initial period. The IMF, in particular, preferred to wait before implementing a full-scale structural adjustment program in Bosnia until the institutional structures for managing the economy were in place. After significant delays in this process caused, in part, by disagreements over

Jelavic was attempting to form an illegal "Croat National Assembly" as a new center of power for Bosnian Croats.
[42] USIP 2000, p. 2.   [43] Singer 2000.
[44] Woodward 1999, p. 7. See also Belloni 2001, pp. 165–166.   [45] Woodard 2000.
[46] Dahrendorf and Balian 1999, p. 20.   [47] World Bank 1996a.

the design of Bosnia's common currency,[48] the IMF and Bosnian authorities agreed on the provisions of a comprehensive structural adjustment loan in May 1998.[49] At this writing, it is too early to evaluate even the preliminary impact of structural adjustment policies on the Bosnian peace process.

Nevertheless, the experience of the former Yugoslavia in the 1980s and early 1990s should serve as a cautionary tale for postwar Bosnia. During this earlier period, the IMF and other international donors required the government of Yugoslavia to implement far-reaching austerity measures, to undertake trade and price liberalization, to remove food subsidies, to devalue the currency, and to freeze new investment in social services, infrastructure, and government projects, among other things.[50] These policies led to a sharp rise in unemployment and increased the level of economic polarization between rich and poor regions of the country, exacerbating social tensions and straining relations between Yugoslavia's central government and its constituent republics in the period immediately preceding the country's violent disintegration.[51]

In many respects, the circumstances of prewar Yugoslavia and postwar Bosnia are dissimilar: For one thing, national and entity-level governments in Bosnia have already achieved a degree of macroeconomic stability that the former Yugoslav government lacked. But Yugoslavia's experience in the 1980s and early 1990s does provide an object lesson regarding the potentially conflict-inducing effects of economic liberalization and structural-adjustment policies in deeply divided societies such as Bosnia. Whether these policies ultimately help or hinder efforts to consolidate peace in Bosnia remains to be seen.

Croatia

The peacebuilding mission in Croatia following the negotiation of the Dayton agreement was a much smaller and shorter operation, lasting from 1995 to 1998 and involving approximately 2,800 uniformed personnel. Fighting between Croat and Serb forces in the territory of Croatia had occurred in two major phases. During the latter half of 1991, ethnic Serbs backed by the Yugoslav National Army captured approximately one-quarter of Croatia's territory, including the lands of Eastern and Western Slavonia and the Krajina where ethnic Serbs had lived for centuries. From early 1992 until mid-1995, while fighting in Bosnia raged, the front lines in the Croatian conflict remained largely unchanged, and a UN-brokered cease-fire remained in force under the supervision of UNPROFOR. In May 1995, however, the

[48] International Crisis Group 1997, p. 14.   [49] IMF 1998.
[50] Woodward 1995, pp. 49–51.
[51] Woodward 1995, pp. 15–17, 51, 73, 127 and 383; Daalder 1996, p. 38; and Orford 1997, pp. 454–456.

Croatian army began a series of attacks on Serb positions in Croatia, culminating in "Operation Storm," a large-scale assault in Western Slavonia and the Krajina that routed Serb forces and sparked a massive flight of ethnic Serb civilians into neighboring Bosnia and Serbia proper.

At the Dayton peace conference in November 1995, Slobodan Milosevic effectively abandoned Serbia's claims to those parts of Croatia that had long-standing ethnic Serb populations and indicated that he was willing to support the transfer of territories that were still in ethnic Serb hands to Croatia – notably, the region of Eastern Slavonia. Deprived of military and political support from Belgrade, local Serb leaders in Eastern Slavonia agreed to give up control of the territory to the Croatian government, and to do so under the auspices of a new UN mission, the United Nations Transitional Administration for Eastern Slavonia, Baranja, and Western Sirmium (UNTAES).[52]

UNTAES began its operations in January 1996 (at the same time that the NATO-led mission arrived in Bosnia to begin implementing the Dayton peace accords). The operation had both a military and civilian component. The military component was to supervise the demilitarization of the region; monitor the voluntary and safe return of refugees and displaced persons to their homes of origin; and help to maintain peace and security. The civilian component set out to establish a temporary police force; develop a training program and oversee its implementation; administer the government of the territory on a temporary basis; facilitate the return of refugees; and organize elections, assist in their conduct, and certify the results.[53] Despite isolated shootings, the process of transferring control of Eastern Slavonia to the Croatian government went forward with few major setbacks.[54] Demilitarization was completed on June 20, 1996, and a transitional police force was established a few days later.[55] UNTAES conducted local and regional elections in April 1997, leading to the formation of a temporary power-sharing arrangement among the victorious parties.[56]

The mission terminated on January 15, 1998, having achieved most of the elements of its mandate, including the return of the territory to Croatian jurisdiction.[57] UNTAES was replaced by a smaller UN civilian mission whose job was to monitor the performance of the Croatian police.[58] In

---

[52] Another UN mission – UNMOP – was authorized to oversee the demilitarization of the Prevlaka Peninsula.

[53] United Nations Security Council resolution 1037 (January 15, 1996).

[54] "Report of the Secretary-General on the United Nations Transitional Administration for Eastern Slavonia, Baranja, and Western Sirmium," S/1997/953 (December 4, 1997).

[55] Ibid.

[56] "Report of the Secretary-General on the Situation in Croatia," S/1997/487 (June 23, 1997).

[57] Šimunović 1999, pp. 126–142.

[58] The UN Civilian Peace Support Group (UNPSG), comprised of 180 international police officers plus administrative staff.

October 1998, this UN mission handed over its responsibilities to the OSCE, which subsequently monitored Croatia-wide elections in January and February 2000, including areas of the country, such as Eastern Slavonia, that had been affected by the war.

In contrast to those in Bosnia, postconflict elections in Croatia have not reinforced the political power of the most nationalist elements of the society; on the contrary, voters in the 2000 elections rejected the ruling Croatian Democratic Union (HDZ), the party of the late president Franjo Tudjman.[59] Tudjman and the HDZ had unapologetically promoted the interests of Croat nationalists, and came under sharp international criticism in the post-Dayton period for failing to meet international commitments on the protection of human rights and democratic standards – in particular, for failing to provide the remaining ethnic Serb residents of Croatia with the full rights and protections of Croatian citizenship. Popular rejection of the HDZ was, therefore, "little short of a quiet revolution" because the newly elected regime explicitly eschewed Tudjman's parochial nationalism and has, among other things, worked to eliminate legislative provisions that discriminate against non-Croat residents of the country.[60] The new government, in effect, espoused a multiethnic conception of Croatian citizenship and sought to encourage the return of Serb refugees who fled the country during the war.[61]

While ethnic Serbs continue to be subject to sporadic attacks and intimidation, the process of political liberalization in Croatia since the Dayton peace settlement has, at this writing, yielded a government that appears to be committed to creating conditions for the peaceful reconciliation of Serbs and Croats in the country. Simply put, the people of Croatia used the electoral mechanism to put the past behind them by voting for the most prominent opponents of narrow nationalism.[62]

At first glance, this outcome lends support to the Wilsonian approach to postconflict peacebuilding, but closer analysis suggests that conditions in Croatia were atypical of most war-shattered states: One of the two parties that fought the war in Croatia – namely, the Serbian side – was for practical purposes no longer present in the country when the war ended. Of course, tens of thousands of ethnic Serb civilians were still living in Croatia when the Dayton Accord was signed in November 1995, and one pocket of territory – Eastern Slavonia – was effectively under the control of ethnic Serbs. But the prewar population of Croatia had included approximately six hundred thousand Serb residents, who were backed during the war by the power of the Yugoslav National Army. By the end of the conflict, however, well over half of Serb residents had fled Croatia,[63] and the Yugoslav army (and

---

[59] Tudjman died in office in 1999. [60] Judah 2000. [61] Denitch 2000.
[62] Strobel 2000, p. 39.
[63] The UN High Commissioner for Refugees reports more than 340,000 refugees from Croatia living in Bosnia and Yugoslavia at the end of 2000, most of whom were ethnic Serbs. This

its leaders in Serbia proper) was no longer willing to provide support to the Serbs still remaining in Croatia. With a greatly diminished (and elderly) Serb population remaining in Croatia, and the government of Yugoslavia no longer offering military or political aid, the Serbian "side" in the Croatian civil war had, in effect, quit the country.

These conditions appeared to reduce the danger that political liberalization would promote, rather than moderate, ethnic tensions. The residual Serbian community in Croatia did not pose a threat to the majority population within the country (unlike the situation in Bosnia, where Croats, Muslims, and Serbs continued to exist as vital communities and political actors). Under these conditions, voting for moderate candidates may have been more likely to occur. Although there was no shortage of politicians making ethnic nationalist and xenophobic appeals to the Croatian electorate during the 2000 balloting, including some who accused moderates of betraying the "heroes of the Homeland War,"[64] the de facto departure of one of the formerly warring parties in Croatia – the Serbs – seems to have reduced the political traction of ethnic nationalism. As Milton Esman writes, "the most likely cause of ethnic mobilization is a serious threat to the vital interests or established expectations of an ethnic community, to its political position, cultural rights, livelihood, or neighborhood."[65] In Croatia, the virtual elimination of the Serbian community as a serious political force removed the immediate threat to Croatian cultural security and may help to explain why political liberalization did not seem to exacerbate divisions and tensions among formerly warring parties, as happened in Bosnia.

As we will see, however, the propitious conditions in Croatia for peace-through-democratization were relatively uncommon among the countries that hosted postconflict peacebuilding operations in the 1990s – most of which remained home to warring parties that only recently laid down their weapons. In this sense, the task of peacebuilding in Croatia was relatively easy compared to elsewhere, and the perils of democratization less pronounced.

Conclusion

Both the Bosnia and Croatia missions were "successful" in the sense that fighting has not resumed in either country. Given the brutality of the conflict that preceded these missions – which led to the deaths of an estimated 250,000 people in Bosnia alone – the persistence of relative peace must be

number does not include internally displaced Serbs who remained within the borders of Croatia. See UNHCR 2001.

[64] Judah 2000.   [65] Esman 1990.

considered a major accomplishment. Nevertheless, the question at hand is whether the liberalization process promoted a stable and lasting peace in these states. In the case of Croatia, the prospect of lasting peace seems favorable; the internationally sponsored democratization yielded a government that seems committed to implementing the Dayton Accord in full. Yet the circumstances of the Croatia mission may have been exceptional: One of the parties to the preceding conflict was largely eliminated as its external sponsor, Belgrade, abandoned support for the ethnic Serb community in Croatia – a community whose numbers were decimated when hundreds of thousands were "cleansed" from the territory in the latter stages of the war. By contrast, the warring parties and communities in Bosnia remained in place at the end of the war – each perceiving the other as a threat – and democratization in Bosnia reinforced the power of the most extremist, nationalist parties, who continued to obstruct the implementation of measures in the Dayton Accord that were intended to promote political moderation and a more lasting reconciliation of the formerly warring groups.

7

Nicaragua, El Salvador, and Guatemala

Reproducing the Sources of Conflict

Central America has historically suffered from chronic civil violence, insurgencies, coups, and military dictatorships.[1] During the latter stages of the Cold War, armed revolutionary movements sought to overthrow the governments of Nicaragua, El Salvador, and Guatemala. In Nicaragua, a group of dissidents backed by the United States and known as Contras fought an insurgency campaign against the left-leaning Sandinista government in Managua throughout the 1980s. In El Salvador, the Farabundo Martí Liberation Front (FLMN) launched a guerrilla war against the government in 1981 that cost an estimated seventy-five thousand lives and displaced roughly one-quarter of the country's population.[2] In Guatemala, when revolutionary movements challenged the military government in the late 1970s and early 1980s, the Guatemalan regime responded with a brutal counterinsurgency effort that lasted into the early 1990s, mainly targeting indigenous Mayan communities in which many revolutionaries, including the major rebel group, the Guatemalan National Revolutionary Unity (URNG), were based.

Central American leaders met on several occasions during the 1980s to discuss possible solutions to these conflicts.[3] At one such meeting – on August 7, 1987 in Esquipulas, Guatemala – the presidents of Guatemala, El Salvador, Honduras, Nicaragua, and Costa Rica formally endorsed a peace plan presented by the Costa Rican president, Oscar Arias, which called for a cease-fire, national reconciliation, amnesty, democratization, termination of external aid to insurgent movements, and free elections.[4] This pact, widely known as the Esquipulas Accord, ultimately provided the basis for the peaceful settlement of conflicts in Nicaragua, El Salvador, and Guatemala,

---

[1] An earlier version of this chapter appeared as Paris 2002b.
[2] Karl 1992, p. 150; and United Nations 1996c, p. 195.
[3] For a description of these efforts, see Child 1992; and Chernick 1996.
[4] This agreement, which is reproduced in Child 1992, appendix 4, pp. 178–184, was a slightly modified version of the plan that Arias had presented to the meeting.

which were negotiated with the help of international mediators, including the United Nations. Nicaragua was the first to reach a settlement in 1989, followed by El Salvador in 1992 and Guatemala in 1996. All three countries subsequently hosted international peacebuilding operations that assisted in implementing these agreements.

By the early twenty-first century, many commentators were concluding that these missions had been largely successful. Indeed, the armed conflicts that had plagued Central America during the 1980s were now over, and the formerly warring parties were pursuing their interests through electoral politics, rather than by force of arms, in all three countries. These are significant accomplishments both for the local parties and for the international peacebuilders who helped them. As UN Secretary-General Kofi Annan wrote regarding El Salvador in 1997:

El Salvador has largely been demilitarized: the armed structure of [the] FMLN has disappeared and its combatants have been reintegrated into civilian life; and the armed forces have been reduced and have respected the profound changes in their nature and role called for by the peace accords. But the most notable development has been that the peace process has also allowed for the opening up of space for democratic participation. A climate of tolerance prevails today, unlike any the country has known before. Since the signing of the peace agreements, no national sector has taken refuge in or supported violence as a form of political action.[5]

In Nicaragua and Guatemala, too, guerrilla wars have ended and the formerly warring parties appear to be committed to peaceful democratic politics.

This largely favorable outcome, and the fact that all three peacebuilding missions promoted the formula of peace through political and economic liberalization, suggest that the Wilsonian approach to postconflict peacebuilding scored important successes in Central America. Once again, however, this assessment depends a great deal on the operative definition of "success" in peacebuilding. If the goal of peacebuilding is to address the underlying causes of conflict and establish the conditions for a stable and lasting peace, or a peace that is likely to endure beyond the departure of the peacebuilders themselves and into the foreseeable future, then there is in fact reason to doubt the success of peacebuilding efforts in Central America. The liberal economic policies pursued by the governments of Nicaragua, El Salvador, and Guatemala in the postconflict period have enriched a very small portion of their populations and left the most vulnerable sectors relatively untouched or even worse off. This inequality between the impoverished majority and the affluent minority has been the most important cause of the region's recurring bouts of revolutionary violence in the past, and peacebuilding agencies have done little to remedy the problem. On the contrary, economic liberalization

---

[5] Quoted in Canas and Dada 1999, p. 69.

was a central prescription of international peacebuilding in these countries. Thus, while the peacebuilding operations in Nicaragua, El Salvador, and Guatemala have succeeded in some respects, they have also helped to reproduce the very conditions that contributed to the outbreak of fighting in the first place, which is not a formula for stable and lasting peace.

On balance, then, the Central American cases offer a mixed verdict for Wilsonianism. On the one hand, the holding of internationally monitored elections appears to have encouraged former combatants to think that peaceful politics was a viable alternative to armed struggle. Unlike in Angola and Rwanda, political liberalization in Central America has not sparked a resurgence of the war that the elections were intended to help terminate. Nor, as in Bosnia, has political liberalization reinforced the power of extremists who have little interest in peaceful compromise. On the other hand, however, the Central American cases challenge a different dimension of Wilsonianism: the notion that economic liberalization helps to promote the consolidation of peace in war-shattered states. Although it is still too early to reach definitive conclusions, the process of economic liberalization in Nicaragua, El Salvador, and Guatemala appears to have weakened the prospects for a stable and lasting peace in these countries. In this sense, these cases seem to reveal further problems in the Wilsonian assumptions of post–Cold War peacebuilding.

Nicaragua

In the late nineteenth century, local elites in Nicaragua and other Central American states responded to the rising international demand for certain primary products, including coffee, by carrying out a series of reforms in the countryside, which was (and remains) populated primarily by mestizo peasants. The reforms legally transformed communally held indigenous properties into "unoccupied" territory that could be purchased by wealthy agricultural elites who wished to produce lucrative export commodities. Not only were peasant farmers displaced from the land they cultivated, but new laws also prohibited the growing of plantain, the staple food of the peasantry, and made "vagrancy" punishable by forced labor in productive enterprises (including the giant coffee plantations that often replaced indigenous farms).[6] Indian communities rebelled against this treatment, most notably in the 1881 War of the Comuneros, and waged a guerrilla war against the Nicaraguan government (and U.S. troops) in the 1920s and 1930s, as policies supporting the agro-export economy continued to favor the existing elite and disadvantage the rural peasantry.

Anastasio Somoza García became the country's autocratic president after rigged elections in 1936 and ruled until his assassination in 1956, and his sons continued the Somoza family dictatorship until 1979. Throughout this

---

[6] Walker 1997, p. 2.

period, new lands were expropriated from Indian farmers for mass production of export commodities, including cotton in the 1950s. The Somoza family, its supporters, and the agricultural elite prospered, but living conditions in
the countryside remained dismal: While the size of the rural population increased, the amount of food produced for domestic consumption declined
in absolute terms as more and more land was dedicated to the cultivation
of export goods. Widespread perceptions of the regime as both exploita-
tive and corrupt fueled the country's insurgency, whose members called
themselves Sandinistas (after Augusto César Sandino, a guerrilla leader who
was assassinated in 1934). Following a series of attacks in the late 1970s,
Sandinista guerrilla forces defeated the Nicaraguan army in 1979, marched
into Managua, and installed a new regime, which immediately undertook
agrarian reforms by creating state-owned and communally owned farms,
in part using assets that had been abandoned by supporters of the former
regime who fled the country.

The Sandinista government adopted other policies aimed at alleviating
the hardships of the majority of poor Nicaraguans, including wage increases,
food price subsidies, and expanded public services in health, welfare, and education.[7] In addition to new spending on social services, the government also
conducted an expensive military campaign against a new armed opposition
group known as the Contras, who were backed by the United States, and who
sought to topple the Sandinista regime by launching raids from their bases
in neighboring Honduras. By 1985, over half of the national budget was devoted to military spending alone.[8] While government expenditures mounted
throughout the 1980s, tax revenues fell precipitously, not only because domestic and foreign investors were suspicious of the Sandinista regime's Marxist leanings, but also because the U.S. government largely succeeded in cutting
off foreign economic aid to Nicaragua by blocking loans from international
lending agencies, such as the World Bank and Inter-American Development
Bank.[9] The combination of rising government expenditures and falling tax
revenues generated an economic crisis that the Nicaraguan regime initially
attempted to manage by printing more money – a policy that further com-
pounded the country's economic crisis by triggering high rates of inflation,
which peaked at over 33,000 percent in 1988.[10]

Under the Esquipulas process, the Nicaraguan government and the Contra
rebels agreed on a peace settlement in 1989 that included the demobilization
of the Contras and the holding of free and fair democratic elections.[11] Central
American presidents quickly endorsed the agreement and called on both the
UN and the Organization of American States to oversee its implementation.[12]

---

[7] Booth and Walker 1999, p. 88.   [8] Walker 1991, p. 84.   [9] Ibid., p. 81.
[10] Ibid., p. 52.
[11] For a description of the negotiations that ended Nicaragua's civil war, see Child 1992.
[12] Child 1992, pp. 63–69; Chernick 1996, p. 284.

A joint UN-OAS commission subsequently reviewed Nicaragua's plans for elections (including provisions to guarantee freedom of association and expression) and concluded that the plans conformed with basic liberal democratic norms.[13] Two new peacebuilding operations were then launched: first, the UN Observer Group in Central America (ONUCA), which monitored international frontiers and verified the cessation of cross-border aid to irregular forces and insurrection movements in the region;[14] and second, the UN Observer Group for the Verification of Elections in Nicaragua, which was sent to oversee the country's first postconflict election and to ensure that the vote was conducted in a free and fair manner.[15]

The election took place in February 1990 under international supervision. Two Nicaraguan political parties were leading contenders: the incumbent Sandinista party led by President Daniel Ortega and a coalition of opposition groups led by Violeta Barrios de Chamorro. Despite minor violence, the elections were "universally regarded as free and fair."[16] To the surprise and dismay of the Sandinista government, the Chamorro opposition grouping emerged with over 50 percent of the popular vote and a majority of seats in the National Assembly.[17] For the first time in Nicaragua's history, a governing party peacefully handed over power to its democratically elected opponents.

The new government quickly implemented a sweeping program of economic liberalization and reform, including extensive layoffs of government employees, privatization of most state-owned enterprises, the lowering of import barriers, reductions in social spending, elimination of price controls and subsidies, and liberalization of the financial and banking sector, among other things.[18] The Sandinistas had begun to liberalize the Nicaraguan economy during their final years in power as a response to the country's economic crisis, but their reform efforts lacked the full support of the international financial institutions and foundered thanks, in part, to lack of external funding.[19] The Chamorro administration, which was more committed to economic liberalization than the Sandinistas, intensified and accelerated the deregulation of Nicaragua's economy at the behest of the International Monetary

---

[13] Child 1992, p. 75.

[14] ONUCA was later also called upon to police five "security zones" within Nicaragua where Contras were disarmed and demobilized. On the expansion of ONUCA's mandate, see UN 1996b, pp. 416–417. For an analysis of the ONUCA mission, see Smith and Durch 1993. In addition to ONUCA, the UN and OAS also created an International Support and Verification Commission (ICVN), which facilitated and oversaw demobilization, repatriation, and relocation of Contras from their camps in Honduras.

[15] "Report of the Secretary-General," UN document A/46/609 (November 19, 1991).

[16] Moreno 1994, p. 140. See also Williams 1990; and Walker 1997.

[17] Chamorro's coalition won 51 of 92 seats, the Sandinistas won 39 seats, and two independent opposition parties won 1 seat each.

[18] Gibson 1993, p. 445; DGAP 1995; Spalding 1996, p. 20; and World Bank 1996b, p. 367.

[19] Aravena 1996.

Fund, World Bank, and the U.S. Agency for International Development, which designed a detailed stabilization and structural adjustment program for the country and made their financial support contingent on Managua's compliance with the program.[20] While the new government generally supported these policies, in fact the Chamorro regime had little choice but to accept the conditions established by major international donors in order to gain access to foreign resources.[21]

The economic reforms succeeded in reducing inflation to 12 percent in 1994 – a "remarkable success," in the estimation of the World Bank.[22] This success, however, came at a cost. The austerity measures that the government implemented to control inflation, and related reforms aimed at deregulating the country's economy, deepened the distributional inequalities in Nicaraguan society and contributed to an absolute decline in living conditions for many – if not most – Nicaraguans. In early 1995, for example, the unemployment rate was double that of 1990 and ten times that of 1984, due partly to the elimination of some thirty thousand public sector nonmilitary jobs from 1990 to 1994, and partly to the general economic contraction that was a side effect of efforts to control inflation in the early 1990s.[23] Although economic growth resumed in the mid-1990s, the problem of unemployment and underemployment in Nicaragua improved little between 1994 to 1998, with roughly half of the country's workers still unemployed or underemployed.[24] The situation was particularly grave in the countryside, where some observers estimated that as much as 80 percent of the economically active population was out of work.[25]

Reductions in redistributive social spending and massive public-sector layoffs – all part of the internationally mandated economic restructuring program – also contributed more generally to a widening of the gap in living conditions between rich and poor, even after the return of economic growth in the mid-1990s. One commonly used measure of income inequality is the so-called Gini index, which is scaled from a minimum of zero to a maximum of one, with zero representing no inequality and one representing a maximum possible degree of inequality. The Gini index for Nicaragua increased from 0.5669 in 1993 to 0.6024 in 1998, indicating that the income gap between the richest and poorest Nicaraguans widened during this period.[26] Indeed, between 1992 and 1997, while Nicaraguans involved in the newly deregulated export and financial sectors generally prospered, overall per capita income in the country fell from $920 to $340, meaning that most of the

---

[20] Robinson 1997, p. 34.   [21] Arana 1997, p. 83; and Neira 1999.
[22] World Bank 1996b, p. 367.
[23] In early 1995, the rate of unemployment was 20.2% of the economically active population, while the combined rate of unemployment and underemployment was 53.9% (Arana 1997, p. 84). See also EIU 1997c, pp. 31, 62.
[24] MacDonald 1998; EIU 1999b, p. 21.   [25] Jonakin 1997, p. 106.
[26] Székely and Hilgert 1999, p. 34.

country's inhabitants became poorer.[27] Another telling statistic is that the daily caloric intake of the average Nicaraguan also decreased between 1990 and 1998 – in a country where more than one-third of the urban population (which is generally better off than the rural population) already lacked the personal income to cover the cost of a basic "food basket."[28] While there were some signs of improvement in the area of health care,[29] it seems that the living conditions of most Nicaraguans either remained stagnant or worsened during the 1990s, and that the income gap between the rich minority and poor majority became even more pronounced than before.

In sum, economic adjustment and liberalization measures designed by the international financial institutions did help to restore fiscal balance and economic stability to Nicaragua, but the social costs of these adjustments appeared to be significant. As the resident representative of the UN Development Program in Nicaragua, Carmelo Angulo, communicated to his colleagues in the International Monetary Fund in 1997, the internationally sponsored economic reform program "has not succeeded in correcting the social imbalances," but instead has served "to aggravate the living conditions of a majority of the population."[30]

The deterioration of living conditions in postwar Nicaragua appeared to fuel an increase in criminal and gang-related violence. Armed bands roaming the countryside were responsible for an estimated one thousand deaths and six hundred kidnappings between 1990 and 1996,[31] while the number of reported homicides in the country continued to increase in the latter part of the decade.[32] Even the army chief, charged with controlling this violence, linked the problem to the pervasiveness of poverty and unemployment.[33] Another factor contributing to the violence was the presence of large numbers of ex-combatants who had few legitimate economic opportunities but ready access to automatic weapons. Former fighters from both sides in the civil war had been promised access to land, credit, and other resources, but few received these benefits, in part because of continuing conflicts over land titles, and because the Nicaraguan government was under pressure from international financial agencies to reduce spending.[34] Put another way, government austerity measures not only contributed to conditions of economic distress in the

---

[27] Everingham 1998, p. 251.   [28] EIU 1999b, p. 21; IADB 2001a.
[29] Despite real decreases in spending on health care, life expectancy increased over the decade, infant mortality decreased, more people had access to potable water, and the number of cholera cases fell from more than 3,000 in 1992 to just over 500 in 1999. On the other hand, the incidence of dengue fever, tuberculosis, and intestinal infections has increased, as has the rate of maternal mortality and the percentage of babies born with low birth weight. See UNDP 2000b.
[30] Quoted in *Envío* 1997a, p. 6.
[31] Nicaraguan government statistics, cited in Reuters 1997b.
[32] World Health Organization 2003; Interpol 2003.   [33] Quoted in Reuters 1997b.
[34] Dunkerly 1994, p. 58.

countryside but also imposed limits on the ability of Nicaraguan authorities to fund peacebuilding programs, such as efforts to reintegrate ex-combatants into productive civilian life. Many of these ex-fighters subsequently joined criminal bands, primarily in the more remote, northwestern part of the country.[35] By mid-1993, an estimated 1,200 former combatants from both sides were operating in Nicaragua, along with an unknown number of ordinary criminals who had no previous connection to military or guerrilla groups.[36] These so-called rearmados or "rearmed ones" conducted sporadic attacks on government security forces and terrorized civilians in the countryside throughout the 1990s.[37] Urban areas also experienced a rapid increase in criminal violence, due largely to the spread of youth gangs – a phenomenon unknown even during the country's most violent periods of civil war, and apparently related to increases in youth unemployment and urban poverty.[38] Police statistics indicate that the number of crimes reported in the capital city, Managua, increased by 100 percent between 1989 and 1996,[39] while anecdotal accounts suggest that the city's crime problem grew even worse between 1996 and 2002.[40]

All of these developments cast doubt on the durability of peace in Nicaragua, for several reasons. First, while the Sandinistas have behaved as a loyal opposition since they lost power in 1990 (in the sense that they remain committed to operating within the constitutional framework, rather than seeking to achieve power by other means), the upsurge of criminal violence in postwar Nicaragua, including "assassinations of former Contras and Sandinistas, politically inspired kidnappings, takeovers of towns, public buildings and roads, armed attacks against security forces, and land invasions," have made it difficult to conclude that the country is now "at peace," even if the period of organized insurrection is over.[41]

Second, the socioeconomic conditions that fueled previous periods of organized revolutionary violence in Nicaragua – namely, the existence of large and growing distributional inequalities between the largely rural peasantry and the wealthy elite – have not been remedied in the postwar period. Indeed, as we have seen, by some measures living conditions for most Nicaraguans have worsened and the gap between rich and poor has widened.

---

[35] Child 1992, pp. 120–127. As Spalding (1996, p. 19) notes, this phenomenon was not limited to former Contras but included ex-soldiers of the Sandinista military: "Economic frustration, combined with political discontent, pulled some ex-soldiers back into armed groups as well."

[36] Dye et al. 1995, p. 40.   [37] Rogers 2001.

[38] McMohan 1996. An estimated 55% of Nicaragua's youth between the ages of fourteen and twenty-four do not work or attend school (EIU 1996b). The independent research institute Nitlapán-UCA published a report concluding that 36.6% of the urban population was "severely impoverished," meaning that their minimum caloric needs could not be met, even if all their income were to go for food (EIU 1997c, p. 31).

[39] Reuters 1996 (October 8).   [40] Rodgers 2002.   [41] Armony 1997, p. 205.

Further, reductions in subsidies to small-scale farmers and the privatization of state-owned farms have also led to a restratification of land ownership patterns in the countryside, with large estate owners once again acquiring farmland at the expense of peasant farmers.[42] Given that these are issues that drove large numbers of ordinary Nicaraguans to support the violent overthrow of the Somoza regime in the first place, the reconcentration of wealth in postwar Nicaragua seems to be a recipe for renewed conflict, not lasting peace.

Third, unless socioeconomic conditions improve for the majority of Nicaraguans, popular anger over the perceived inaction of the government in the face of economic distress – anger that has been visible and widespread – may undermine support for the country's new liberal democratic constitution, along with the institutions of electoral democracy.[43] In the words of then–UN Secretary-General Boutros-Ghali, "The major threat to the democratic system [in Nicaragua] is not political conflict, but the deterioration of living conditions and the consequent loss of faith in democracy and its institutions."[44]

More generally, the economic aspects of postconflict peacebuilding in Nicaragua appear to challenge the notion that economic liberalization fosters peace in states that are just emerging from civil wars. Proponents of economic liberalization and orthodox structural adjustment in war-shattered states argue that these reforms are necessary in order to create the conditions for economic growth, which can help to reinforce a fragile peace by increasing incomes and living standards in formerly warring states. What these proponents often overlook or underemphasize, however, is that the strategy of promoting growth through economic liberalization tends to exacerbate distributional inequalities, which in the case of Nicaragua is a prescription for social unrest, given the historic causes of conflict in the country. As Argentine political scientist Carlos Vilas writes, the postconflict economic liberalization policies pursued in Nicaragua, including deregulation and reductions in social spending, have offered "the same old mode of development against whose effects peasants, workers, and middle sectors rebelled more than twenty years ago, sparking a revolutionary cycle that is coming to a close only now."[45] In other words, a strategy of rapid marketization is most likely to promote a type of economic growth whose benefits are concentrated in a very small segment of the population.

It is precisely this type of inequitable growth that has historically fueled revolutionary violence in the country. During the Somoza years of the 1960s and early 1970s, for example, overall economic growth statistics in Nicaragua were impressive: Per capita gross domestic product (GDP) rose

---

[42] Jonakin 1997.
[43] Vilas 1995b, p. 186; Vickers 1995, p. 57; Isbester 1996; and Spalding 1996, pp. 20–22.
[44] Quoted in DGAP 1995.   [45] Vilas 1995b, p. 186.

an average of almost 3.9 percent for the decade 1962–1971, and an average of 2.3 percent between 1972 and 1976, while real GDP per capita rose by no less than 54 percent between 1960 and 1970.[46] Yet it was partly because so few benefits of this new economic activity found their way into the pockets of poorer Nicaraguans that popular support for the Sandinista insurrection gathered strength. Economic growth alone is not enough to promote a stable and lasting peace in Nicaragua; what is needed is balanced, or equitable, growth to address the underlying sources of conflict.[47]

Thus, the experience of peacebuilding to date in Nicaragua yields mixed results. On the one hand, democratization efforts have proceeded relatively smoothly. New national elections were held in 1996 and 2001, and once again opposition parties accepted their electoral loss in stride.[48] Further, the process of political liberalization has not sparked renewed fighting in Nicaragua, as it did in Rwanda and Angola; nor has this process reinforced the power of the most recalcitrant and least peace-oriented local parties, as it has done in Bosnia. But the prevailing doctrine of peacebuilding presupposes that political *and* economic liberalization together help to foster peace in war-shattered states – a presumption that the Nicaraguan case does not seem to support, given the apparently destabilizing effects of rapid economic liberalization on the society. In addition to the fact that marketization appears to be recreating precisely the socioeconomic conditions that ignited the Nicaraguan conflict in the first place, it also seems to be eroding popular support for the country's new liberal democratic institutions, all of which suggests that the effects of economic liberalization may be undermining the accomplishments of democratization efforts in Nicaragua. More generally, the Nicaraguan case offers further evidence that liberalization sometimes works against the goal of promoting a stable and lasting peace in countries that are just emerging from civil wars, not only because the political or economic dimensions of liberalization can be destabilizing in and of themselves, but also because the processes of marketization and democratization are capable of working at cross-purposes.

Nor are there any signs that the government of Nicaragua will pursue more balanced growth strategies in the foreseeable future. In 1998, the government signed a new agreement with the IMF that made international loans and debt relief contingent on Managua's implementing new austerity policies, including a further round of cuts to government spending and public-sector layoffs – policies that the president of Nicaragua, Arnoldo Alemán, has described as necessary, but "painful and bitter" for the poor.[49] Other commentators, however, do not view such rapid and radical adjustment as necessary; they advocate instead a more equitable approach to reforms that recognizes the importance of spreading the benefits of economic growth and,

---

[46] Booth and Walker 1999, p. 69.   [47] Kay 2001.   [48] Anderson and Dodd 2002.
[49] Quoted in EURODAD 1998; see also MacDonald 1998.

if necessary, delaying liberalization in order to enhance the prospects for a lasting and stable peace in Nicaragua.[50]

El Salvador

El Salvador's civil war began in the wake of a failed attempt to introduce agrarian and social reforms in late 1970s. The reforms were intended in part to change a "very unequal system of land tenure" and to reduce the political, social, and economic control of the country's small but powerful "coffee oligarchy."[51] All previous efforts to challenge the dominance of this elite had been squelched by the Salvadoran army, acting in concert with members of the oligarchy. In 1980, when it was clear that the latest reform effort had also failed, five communist revolutionary groups formed a new coalition – the FLMN – which in early 1981 launched an armed rebellion against the Salvadoran regime. Thus began a twelve-year-long civil war that cost an estimated seventy-five thousand lives and displaced roughly one-quarter of El Salvador's population.[52]

After the 1987 meeting of Central American leaders in Esquipulas, progress toward a peace settlement in El Salvador was slow. Periodic discussions between the government and the FMLN in 1988 and 1989 brought no significant results,[53] but in April 1990 the parties jointly declared their desire to end the war and appealed to then–UN Secretary-General Javier Pérez de Cuéllar for help in mediating the ensuing negotiations.[54] The secretary-general agreed, and a process of staged negotiations began, leading eventually to the signing of a preliminary cease-fire agreement on December 31, 1991, and a comprehensive peace settlement two weeks later.[55] This settlement became known as the Chapúltepec Accord for the Mexican location at which it was signed, bringing together several agreements that the parties had reached over the preceding months.

The Chapúltepec agreement comprised a detailed plan (filling nine chapters and several annexes) for the demobilization and reintegration of former combatants into civilian life, legalization of opposition parties, free and fair elections, limited land reform, investigation of alleged human rights abuses, retraining and professionalization of the judiciary and national police, establishment of civilian control over the armed forces, and reconstruction of physical infrastructure, including roads, bridges, schools, and clinics. In addition to setting out a vision for political and economic life in El Salvador,

---

[50] See Chapter 10, where alternative approaches to economic adjustment in war-shattered states are explored in the section "Adopt Conflict-Reducing Economic Policies."
[51] Baloyra 1982, pp. 2 and 22–32; and Moreno 1994, p. 31.
[52] Karl 1992, p. 150; and United Nations 1996c, p. 195.   [53] Fagan 1996, p. 217.
[54] Dunkerly 1994, p. 72.   [55] The cease-fire took effect on February 1, 1992.

Chapúltepec also provided the blueprint for the subsequent peacebuilding mission. The United Nations was the primary international agency called upon to monitor the implementation of the Accord. A new UN peacebuilding operation – known by its Spanish acronym, ONUSAL – was deployed to verify all aspects of the cease-fire, along with the demobilization and reintegration of former combatants into civilian life, and to monitor the maintenance of public order while the new civilian police force was set up. ONUSAL also established offices in El Salvador to receive and investigate complaints of human rights violations, and to verify compliance with the human rights provisions of the peace agreement.[56]

In May 1993, the operation's mandate was further expanded to include oversight of El Salvador's first postconflict elections, including voter registration, the campaign, voting, and every stage of vote counting. Although the election, which was held in March and April 1994, was marred by sporadic violence and polling irregularities, the outcome was regarded as reasonably fair by most observers.[57] The ruling party, the Alianza Republicana Nacionalista (ARENA), retained the presidency in a runoff ballot with 68 percent of the popular vote, and took thirty-nine of eighty-four National Assembly seats; while the FMLN (which, in the words of one observer, had "succeeded remarkably in transforming itself from a clandestine operation into an open, well-organized party")[58] won twenty-one seats in the Assembly.[59]

Peacebuilders also promoted economic liberalization in El Salvador. At the behest of the international financial institutions, former Salvadoran President Alfredo Cristiani had implemented economic stabilization and structural adjustment policies shortly after taking office in mid-1989, eliminating price controls, restructuring the tax system,[60] and increasing water, electricity, and transportation fees. These measures were reinforced and deepened in 1991 in conjunction with the peace process, under the guidance of the International Monetary Fund, the World Bank, and the Inter-American Development Bank, which offered additional financial assistance to the Salvadoran government in exchange for extensive market-oriented reforms.[61] The FMLN, which had previously endorsed Marxist goals for the reorganization of Salvadoran society, apparently made a strategic decision to accept the liberal economic model that the ARENA government insisted on continuing in the postconflict period.[62]

---

[56] See Johnstone 1995.
[57] Boyce 1995, p. 2074; Vilas 1995a, p. 8; and United Nations 1996b, p. 440.
[58] Montgomery 1995, p. 253.
[59] The Christian Democratic Party (PDC) took 18 seats, with the remaining 6 seats divided among three smaller parties. Hampson 1996, p. 95.
[60] DGAP 1995; and del Castillo 2001.   [61] Ibid.   [62] Wood 1996, p. 77.

Despite delays in implementing various aspects of the peace agreement,[63] El Salvador, like Nicaragua, is widely regarded as a peacebuilding success.[64] At the time of this writing, the FMLN and other opposition groups remain committed to pursuing their political goals through peaceful means. New legislative and local elections were held in 1997, in conditions that the U.S. State Department described as "free and peaceful," and presidential elections in 1999 were also accepted as legitimate by local parties.[65] Moreover, the government's liberal economic policies appear to have yielded relatively high levels of growth and low levels of inflation. El Salvador's real GDP, for example, expanded at a yearly average of 6.0 percent from 1992 to 1996[66] – a record that the World Bank deemed "a remarkable success story."[67] At first glance, then, the experience of El Salvador to date suggests that peacebuilding promoted both political stability and economic prosperity, and set the country on the path to a stable and lasting peace.

As in Nicaragua, however, closer examination reveals a more complex story. Democratic elections helped to transfer the conflict from the battlefield to the political arena, but economic liberalization policies promoted by the IMF and World Bank appear to have exacerbated the very socioeconomic conditions that precipitated war in the first place. Since the arrival of Spanish settlers in the mid-sixteenth century, the inhabitants of what is now El Salvador have always been sharply divided between a wealthy landowning elite and an impoverished peasantry, and the country's history is punctuated by a series of popular uprisings that have sought to overturn the political and economic domination of the elite and to achieve a more equitable distribution of land, wealth, and political power across Salvadoran society. All of these uprisings were eventually suppressed by the armed forces, but the perpetuation of high levels of poverty and income inequality laid the foundation for future uprisings, followed in turn by further authoritarian repression – a pattern which, over time, produced recurring cycles of revolutionary violence in the country.

El Salvador's internationally mandated economic reforms have included cutbacks in government expenditures and public-sector employment, aimed at restoring balance to national finances and reducing the state's role in the economy. These cutbacks have had a disproportionately detrimental effect on the less affluent members of society, particularly the rural poor and urban working class, and living conditions for the bulk of the population have not improved significantly since the implementation of these reforms. El Salvador's human development index – a measure of general social

[63] There were delays in demobilization (see CIIR 1993, pp. 12–13; and Dunkerly 1994, pp. 4–75), land reform (see Fagan 1996, p. 232), and establishing the new civilian police force (see Wood and Segovia 1995, p. 2093).

[64] Hampson 1996, p. 69; and Montgomery 1997, p. 61.

[65] Associated Press 1997 (March 18).   [66] EIU 1997b, p. 76.   [67] World Bank 1996b, p. 1.

well-being that includes per capita income, literacy, and life expectancy – fell by over 10 percent in the first six years of the economic adjustment program, although it had recovered by the late 1990s.[68]

While there have been improvements in the areas of health and education,[69] postwar economic growth has primarily enriched a very narrow segment of the population, including urban elites that originally made their money from coffee and sugar and are now involved in a wider range of export and financial enterprises.[70] Parts of the countryside, by contrast, such as the province of Morazán, remain stuck at human development levels similar to those of sub-Saharan Africa.[71] As a result of this unequal growth, wealth became even more concentrated in El Salvador during the period of economic liberalization and restructuring: The country's Gini index, for example, was 0.5050 in 1995; and despite relatively high levels of annual GDP growth, the index rose to 0.5589 by 1998, meaning that the benefits of economic liberalization were concentrated in the hands of a small minority and that the distributional inequalities had widened.[72]

If the principal purpose of peacebuilding is to remediate the underlying sources of conflict in states that have recently experienced internal wars, then one might expect, given El Salvador's history, that peacebuilding efforts would attempt to ameliorate the problems of pervasive poverty and distributional inequality that have precipitated civil violence in the past, including the most recent war. As Carlos Acevedo writes: "If El Salvador's history during the first three-quarters of the twentieth century offers any lesson for the current postwar period, it is that the success of the peace process in the long run will hinge on the country's ability to redress the great inequalities of wealth and power that imperil both economic and political stability."[73] In practice, however, economic policies promoted by international peacebuilding agencies seem to have had precisely the opposite effect, worsening rather than ameliorating these problems. At best, the underlying conditions that drove people to openly challenge the regime in the 1980s have remained largely unchanged.[74] Kimbra Fishel puts it this way: "Widespread structural adjustment policy has resulted in micro-economic difficulties which exacerbate the initial social and economic causes of conflict."[75] Economic liberalization policies, in short, appear to have worked against the consolidation of a stable and lasting peace in El Salvador.

---

[68] El Salvador's human development index fell from 0.651 in 1987 (the first year of structural adjustment) to 0.576 in 1993 (a decline of 11.5% over six years) despite the fact that the Salvadoran GDP grew by an average of over 3% per annum over this period.
[69] UNDP 1999a. This report was published before a major earthquake struck the region in January 2001.
[70] DGAP 1995.   [71] Rivera Cámpos 2000, pp. 220–221.
[72] Székely and Hilgert 1999, p. 34.   [73] Acevedo 1996, p. 19. See also Kay 2001.
[74] Walker and Armony 2000, p. 40.   [75] Fishel 1998, p. 33.

Indeed, as living standards for the bulk of the population have stagnated, the incidence of violent and nonviolent crime in El Salvador has increased dramatically, particularly in impoverished rural areas where the rate of unemployment in 1994 was estimated to be near 80 percent of the economically active population.[76] The Economist Intelligence Unit summarized the situation in 1996: "Kidnappings, assaults, gangland-style assassinations and organized, often drug-related, crime appear to be occurring more frequently, as the influence of drug-traffickers and car thieves spreads."[77] A study published by the Inter-American Development Bank showed that El Salvador had the highest per capita homicide rate in the world in the mid-1990s.[78] The total number of violent deaths far exceeded the estimated annual figure during the final years of the civil war, including both civilian and military deaths,[79] and reported homicides continued to climb through 2001.[80] Many of these murders were being committed by armed gangs that roamed the cities and countryside, and which reportedly included ex-fighters from both sides of the civil war.[81] A large proportion of Salvadorans blame the difficult economic conditions, including high unemployment, for this crime wave.[82] As in Nicaragua, the upsurge in crime was also linked to the presence of thousands of former guerrilla fighters, many of whom, unemployed, unsupported by the state, and with no means of making a living, joined roving criminal bands.[83]

Pervasive criminal violence has not only made living conditions for most Salvadoran citizens more dangerous in the postwar period than in the preceding period of civil war,[84] but has also led to the creation of private vigilante "crime control" groups.[85] The Salvadoran government has implemented measures to combat the violence, including emergency anticrime legislation that increased penalties and simplified the process for convicting alleged criminals, and it has deployed army units to assist police in high-crime areas

[76] Vilas 1995a, p. 11.
[77] EIU 1996a, p. 40. For additional descriptions of the crime problem in El Salvador, see Dalton 1996; *Envío* 1997b; Evans 1998; and Fishel 1998.
[78] Cited in EIU 1999a, p. 42.
[79] In 1996, there were 8,047 reported homicides (EIU 1997b, p. 71). The annual number of violent deaths in El Salvador in the latter years of the war was approximately 5,000 (Farah 1996).
[80] Interpol 2003.
[81] CIIR 1993, p. 16; Montgomery 1997, pp. 61–62; Boyce and Pastor 1997, p. 90; and Kovaleski 1997.
[82] See Montgomery (1997, p. 61) for the results of public opinion polls conducted in El Salvador in 1996.
[83] Muoz 2000.
[84] As Spence et al. (1997, p. 6) write: "For a majority of [Salvadoran] citizens life is less safe now than during most of the war." Farah (1996) makes the same argument.
[85] Human Rights Watch 1994, p. 1; de Soto and del Castillo 1995, p. 190; Tracey 1995; Vilas 1995a, p. 6; and Stanley 1996, p. 11.

of the country, but these measures have not succeeded in reducing the rate of violent crime.[86] Some observers argue that the government's solution to the crime problem is just as dangerous as the problem itself, because expanding the role of the army for domestic crime fighting violates the spirit if not the letter of El Salvador's postwar constitution, which prohibits the army from playing a domestic policing role.[87] There is evidence of government security officials using illegal methods against suspected criminals, including excessive violence and human rights abuses – techniques which have historically been employed by Salvadoran governments to silence political opposition groups.[88] In short, the problem of rampant crime is not only a symptom of persistent poverty, unequal economic growth, and social decay, which are conditions that threaten the long-term political stability of the country; the crime problem has also induced the government to respond in a manner that raises concerns about the future of El Salvador's new liberal democratic constitution.

Kimbra Fishel concludes that for all of these reasons, peace in El Salvador is an "illusion." This judgment, however, is too severe: Although violent crime is endemic and the dangers of renewed political unrest still exist, the war between the government and the FMLN is over, there is greater freedom and tolerance of political activity, human rights violations have declined and are openly monitored, and most former combatants have returned to civilian life.[89] The country's economy has also revived since the end of the war, with overall growth rates ranging from 1.7 percent to 7.5 percent annually in the 1990s.[90] As in the case of Nicaragua, however, the benefits of this growth have gone mainly to the country's small and already wealthy elite. Economic growth in the aggregate is not sufficient to address the underlying sources of recurring conflict in El Salvador. During the 1960s and 1970s, for example, the Salvadoran economy grew rapidly, with GDP per capita rising at an annual average of over 2 percent from 1962 to 1978,[91] yet economic gains were unevenly divided. In practice, Salvadoran workers actually lost one-fifth of their real purchasing power between 1973 and 1980.[92] A similar pattern recurred in the 1990s: Despite relatively high levels of aggregate economic growth, real wages for working-class laborers in El Salvador *declined* by 7 percent between 1991 and 1999, which helps to explain why, as noted earlier, distributional inequalities have also widened.[93]

Responsibility for the widening gulf between rich and poor in postwar El Salvador lies partly with the international financial institutions that guided the Salvadoran government through various adjustment programs in the 1990s. These policies emphasized rapid liberalization and the achievement

---

[86] Stanley and Loosle 1998; Interpol 2003.
[87] Stanley 1996, p. 12; and Montgomery 1997, p. 62.
[88] Stanley 1996, p. 2; EIU 1996a, p. 46.   [89] Studemeister 2001   [90] IADB 2001b.
[91] Booth and Walker 1999, p. 101.   [92] Ibid., p. 102.   [93] ILO 2002.

of macroeconomic stability above other goals, such as poverty reduction, in order to create the conditions for sustainable economic growth. But relying so heavily on market forces as a strategy for economic development does little, particularly in the short run, to address the long-standing grievances of the poor majority of Salvadorans – in fact, as we have seen, by some measures the adjustment programs promoted by the IMF and World Bank have left the poorest worse off than before. This is not the prescription for stable and lasting peace in El Salvador, where disparities in wealth and living conditions are factors that produced the conflict that only recently ended. In the words of James Boyce and Manuel Pastor, "A failure to achieve broad improvements in living standards would fuel social tensions and heighten the risk of renewed war – and a return to war would shatter hopes for economic revival."[94] Rapid and far-reaching economic liberalization policies have stimulated economic growth, but a type of growth that has done little to remedy the underlying sources of conflict in the society, or what one author describes as "impoverishing growth."[95] Indeed, the current combination of endemic poverty, widening income inequalities, and pervasive criminal violence suggests that liberal economic policies have, in several important ways, impeded rather than facilitated the consolidation of peace in El Salvador.

Guatemala

International peacebuilding in Guatemala began in early 1997, after the signing of a comprehensive peace accord in December 1996. Given that little time has passed between then and the time of this writing, conclusions about the outcome of the Guatemala mission must be even more provisional than in the case of Nicaragua and El Salvador. Nevertheless, the Guatemala case is worth exploring for several reasons: First, the international financial institutions apparently recognized the adverse effects of rapid liberalization in Nicaragua and El Salvador; second, these institutions have attempted to correct such problems in their dealings with Guatemala; and third, despite their efforts to learn from previous experiences in Nicaragua and El Salvador, the World Bank and IMF have still not gone far enough in tempering and targeting their economic adjustment policies to the particular circumstances of deeply divided states that are just emerging from civil conflicts.

Although Guatemala differs from its neighbors in that it possesses a very large and relatively unintegrated Indian community (which makes up approximately 65 percent of the total population and is concentrated mainly in rural areas), the country has much in common with El Salvador and Nicaragua, including persistent and extreme socioeconomic inequalities that have fueled recurring rounds of revolutionary violence. In fact, of all the

---

[94] Boyce and Pastor 1997, p. 287.   [95] Perez-Brignoli 1989.

countries in the world, Guatemala has the third most unequal distribution of resources between rich and poor, according to the Gini index.[96] This inequality reflects the historical domination of large-scale landowners over the Guatemalan economy, which became especially pronounced in the late nineteenth century, when huge estates in the countryside were dedicated to growing coffee beans for export. By 1900, coffee accounted for 85 percent of Guatemala's exports, and land ownership was concentrated in the hands of the so-called agro-elite, who also controlled the country's politics through a series of authoritarian regimes backed by the armed forces.[97] As in neighboring countries, Guatemalan peasants were often forced from their lands, labeled "vagrants," and coerced into providing cheap labor for the plantations.

Elections in 1944 brought to power populist governments, led by Juan José Arévalo and Jacobo Arbenz, who implemented social and agrarian reforms, including the formation of farming cooperatives, social security, rural education, a labor code, and ultimately the confiscation and redistribution of farmland to a hundred thousand peasants. These reforms faced strong opposition from large landowners, including the U.S. banana company United Fruit. In 1954, the Arbenz government was overthrown in a U.S.-backed invasion and replaced with a succession of right-wing military and civilian governments. These governments responded forcefully to the rural-based insurgency – an insurgency that gained varying degrees of support from urban dissidents, including student activists, labor unionists, and opposition parties. Between 1981 and 1984 alone, an estimated 440 villages were totally destroyed by security forces and private vigilantes; 50,000 people were killed; 150,000 fled to Mexico as refugees; and roughly 500,000 were internally displaced.[98]

In 1990, three years after the Esquipulas meeting, the Guatemalan government entered into peace negotiations with what remained of the main rebel group, the Guatemalan National Revolutionary Unity (URNG). Over the next several years, the parties reached several agreements: on human rights (March 1994), the resettlement of displaced populations (June 1994), the creation of a "historical clarification commission" to investigate past violence and human rights abuses (June 1994), the protection of indigenous rights (March 1995), a cease-fire (November 1995), socioeconomic and land issues (May 1996), and civilian control of the armed forces (September 1996). They also reached a final agreement that set out liberal democratic constitutional reforms and rules for elections, legalized the URNG, and declared a "definitive" cease-fire (December 1996).[99] From 1994 onward, representatives from the United Nations served as the facilitators of these talks, thus

---

[96] Reding 2000, p. 1. Sierra Leone and Brazil have the world's most unequal distribution.
[97] Booth and Walker 1999, p. 45.   [98] Louise 1997, p. 53.   [99] Jonas 2000, chap. 3.

"paving the way for significantly increased involvement by the international community" in the Guatemalan peace process.[100]

The United Nations deployed a monitoring mission in 1994 (called the UN Human Rights Verification Mission in Guatemala, or MINUGUA), whose mandate was gradually expanded to include supervision of all aspects of the peace accords, including the demobilization of approximately three thousand URNG guerrillas and their weapons and the creation of a new civilian police force. Paralleling earlier peacebuilding achievements in Nicaragua and El Salvador, the demobilization of the URNG proceeded successfully, and national elections were held under relatively calm conditions in December 1999. In the area of human rights, however, international observers continued to express concerns about the treatment of journalists and activists, and some feared that para-statal death squads continue to operate in the country. In April 1998, the Roman Catholic Church released its "Recovery of Historical Memory" report that detailed the impact of the war's violence; two days later, the bishop who oversaw the project was murdered, and the Church sees military complicity in the homicide.[101] The next two years witnessed an increase in the number of reported threats and attacks on political activists, human rights workers, members of the judiciary, and opposition politicians.[102] MINUGUA, whose mandate was extended through 2001, reported assaults, death threats, and other acts of intimidation directed against journalists, prosecutors, and judges who were directly or indirectly involved in the investigation of government security forces.[103] Whether these isolated reports augur a return to systematic human rights abuses in Guatemala remains to be seen.

In the area of economic reform, the provisions of the Guatemala peace settlement differed from the economic measures undertaken in Nicaragua and El Salvador. Three major international donors – the IMF, the World Bank, and the Inter-American Development Bank – were in close communication with UN mediators during the negotiation of the Guatemalan accords, and apparently resolved to correct some of the problems that had arisen from the economic adjustment process in El Salvador and Nicaragua.[104] Specifically, they pressed for agreement on a so-called socioeconomic accord that endorsed liberalization and macroeconomic stabilization but also committed the Guatemalan government to increased levels of social welfare spending. The rationale for this policy was drawn from the lessons learned by the donor agencies in El Salvador and Nicaragua, where traditional structural adjustment policies emphasized rapid movement toward fiscal balance, low inflation, and economic liberalization, but at the expense of distributional equity. The financial institutions now argued that lasting peace would not be possible without a reduction in Guatemala's sharp social and economic

---

[100] Jonas 1998.   [101] Holiday 2000, p. 80.   [102] MacDonald 2001; Rosenberg 2001.
[103] A/55/174, July 26, 2000, para. 13.   [104] Jonas 2000, p. 167.

inequities,[105] and regarded the country as a test case for a new approach to "postconflict sustainable development" in the fragile circumstances of war-shattered states.[106]

Among other things, the socioeconomic accord set detailed targets for increased state expenditure on education, health, social security, and housing; committed the government to raising literacy and to providing at least three years of schooling to all children between the ages of seven and twelve; and set the goal of providing access to jobs in which real wages increased over time. Regarding taxation, the accord mandated an increase in the ratio of taxes to GDP from under 8 percent to 12 percent by 2000 – in order to pay for the increased social spending. Furthermore, the accord called for the creation of a more progressive system of taxation in the country, that is, one that would make individual tax burdens more proportionate to income. So while Guatemala's postconflict economic reform package retained the traditional elements of structural adjustment, including liberalization and deregulation of the economy, it also placed greater emphasis than the Nicaraguan and Salvadoran economic reforms did on measures aimed at immediately reducing social and economic inequalities.

That, at least, was how the reforms were designed. In practice, however, certain business interests in Guatemala (spearheaded by the Coordination Committee of Agricultural, Commercial, Industrial, and Financial Associations) put pressure on the government not to increase taxation levels or reform the tax system to the detriment of wealthier citizens of Guatemala.[107] In the face of this resistance, the government delayed full implementation of these elements of the socioeconomic accord. In 2001, a year after the ratio of taxes to GDP was supposed to have been raised to 12 percent in order to pay for new social spending, the tax rate was still only 9.75 percent of GDP, one of the lowest in Latin America.[108] The government, in other words, was fulfilling its commitments to privatization and fuller liberalization of the economy, apparently because these policies served the interests of the Guatemalan business elite, but the government was dragging its feet in executing elements of the socioeconomic accord that were intended to even out the asymmetrical benefits of marketization and to redistribute resources from the wealthy to the poor.[109]

The international financial institutions called on the Guatemalan authorities to fulfill their commitments under the socioeconomic accord, but their actions were not as strong as their words: They compromised with the government, allowing it to implement these commitments more slowly and over

---

[105] Ruthrauff 1998.   [106] Jonas 2000, pp. 168, 171, 174.   [107] EIU 1999a, p. 18
[108] IMF 2001.
[109] As William Stanley and David Holiday (2002, p. 453) point out, "Without progress on the tax front, all other measures the government takes to [address the problem of socioeconoic inequality] are unsustainable."

a longer period. Further, the donor organizations backed away from their insistence on more progressive taxation in Guatemala, accepting the government's proposal to increase indirect, value-added taxes, which are borne by all consumers regardless of their income level, rather than increasing personal income taxes.[110]

According to some observers, the IMF, World Bank, and Inter-American Development Bank did not press the issue as vigorously and consistently as they could have. "One rather imagines," writes Susanne Jonas, for example, "that the international financial institutions would have sent an extremely clear, consistent, and unified message if the Guatemalan government were refusing to privatize or repay the foreign debt, rather than refusing to tax the rich."[111] Be that as it may, international pressure and threats to terminate their aid did finally induce the Guatemalan regime to negotiate a "Fiscal Pact" with business and civil society groups in May 2000. The pact recommitted the government to raising the level of tax revenues to 12 percent by 2002, and to increasing the minimum tax rate and eliminating tax loopholes, while meeting specific targets for social spending.[112] But soon after signing the pact, the government backed out of it.[113]

Although the effects of these economic policies will become clearer in the coming years, the benefits of several years of aggregate economic growth in Guatemala have not trickled down to the poor majority.[114] As the UN secretary-general reported in mid-2000, "Guatemalans do not see the peace process as having brought about any major, tangible improvements in their lives."[115] This situation is problematic for those who hope that peace will be lasting and stable in Guatemala. As in Nicaragua and El Salvador, failure to address the underlying sources of recurrent revolutionary violence in Guatemala – including profound social and economic inequalities – poses a serious threat to the durability of the peace settlement. Indeed, there is widespread agreement among observers of Guatemalan politics that "the question of development remains central to the overall equation of building peace" in the country.[116] Unemployment rates remain very high (estimated at over 40 percent), half the population earns less than a dollar a day, more than a quarter of children under five years old are moderately to severely underweight, and almost 90 percent of the indigenous population lives below the poverty line.[117]

The historical record in Guatemala – as well as Nicaragua and El Salvador – indicates that high levels of economic growth alone are not a sufficient remedy for the problem of recurring social unrest: In the 1960s and 1970s, the Guatemalan economy grew at an average of almost 3 percent

[110] Ruthrauff 1998; Jonas 2000, pp. 177–180.   [111] Jonas 2000, p. 178.
[112] IADB 2001c.   [113] *Economist* 2001 (February 24).
[114] *Business Week* 2000 (November 6); Holiday 2000, p. 81.
[115] A/55/175 (July 26, 2000), para. 48.   [116] Louise 1997, p. 55. See also Preti 2002.
[117] Reding 2000.

annually, yet revolutionary movements gathered force as real wages fell and income distribution worsened.[118] Since the peace settlement was signed in 1996, the country has also experienced a period of economic growth, but addressing the underlying causes of conflict will require further efforts to convert this growth into improvements in living conditions for the majority of Guatemalans – that is, more equitable growth than the country has experienced in the past. This, in turn, requires the international financial institutions to act more forcefully in emphasizing income redistribution as a condition of assistance, and to move even further away from the traditional model of structural adjustment that emphasizes economic efficiency over equity.

Moreover, there may be limited time to address these problems. Persistent poverty, unemployment, and easy access to weapons have contributed to an upsurge in violent crime in Guatemala since 1996, including soaring rates of kidnapping, theft, and homicide.[119] As two World Bank observers wrote in 2000, "Guatemala has become a substantially more violent country since the end of the internal armed conflict."[120] In the countryside, a major source of violence and insecurity is disputes over landownership, which reflect the government's failure to carry out its commitment in the peace settlement to address the country's long-standing land tenure problem – over 70 percent of arable land is still owned by less than 3 percent of the population.[121] Some commentators express concern that the crime problem may encourage the government to expand the domestic policing role of the Guatemalan military, opening the door to a return of political repression under the cover of crime fighting.[122] Indeed, MINUGUA's July 2000 report on the situation in Guatemala contained this warning: "Faced with the high crime rate, and especially the impact of kidnappings, which serve to heighten the perception of a climate of insecurity, the State has allowed persons or groups outside the competent institutions to become involved in police investigations, on the pretense of supporting prosecutors, judges and victims."[123] MINUGUA also stated – with remarkable bluntness for a United Nations document – that serious human rights violations have been committed by government security forces, including extrajudicial executions.[124] These developments pose a danger not only to the integrity of the 1996 peace settlement, which called for a demilitarization of the society, but also to the survival of Guatemala's fledgling democracy.

Conclusion

The process of political liberalization in Nicaragua, El Salvador, and Guatemala has provided opportunities for former belligerents to pursue their

[118] Booth and Walker 1999, pp. 118–120.
[119] Jonas 1997, p. 9; UNDP 1999b, pp. 5–6; Child 2000, p. 181.
[120] Moser and McIlwaine 2000.   [121] Holiday 1997, p. 68; Black 1998; Reding 2000, p. 21.
[122] Jonas 1998.   [123] A/55/174 (July 26, 2000), para. 83.   [124] Ibid., paras. 8, 19.

respective political objectives through peaceful means, but the effects of internationally sponsored economic-adjustment policies appear to be eroding the relative success of democratic reforms and undermining the prospects of a stable and lasting peace in all three countries. The principal weakness in the Wilsonian prescription for postconflict peacebuilding in Central America is that it has failed to address the underlying sources of violent conflict in the region. "Central America's warring nations," wrote the *New York Times* in a March 1999 editorial,

have essentially returned to the conditions of misery and inequality that caused the wars to begin with. While El Salvador has experienced steady economic growth, poverty in rural areas remains unchanged. In Nicaragua, the poor are worse off than at its war's end. . . . Even the local governments admit that free-market changes have so far mainly served the urban wealthy and middle class.[125]

These observations correspond to the view that now prevails among many commentators: Peace will not last in these countries if it means a return to the living conditions that sparked the wars.[126] Economic growth is important, but it is not enough, since unbalanced growth will not reduce the enormous disparities in wealth and well-being that have traditionally fueled unrest in these countries. Unless these disparities are reduced, democratic consolidation will remain uncertain, and the threat of renewed violence will likely persist.

All of this suggests that the Wilsonian emphasis on simultaneous political and economic liberalization as a remedy for civil conflicts is problematic. Economic liberalization and adjustment programs have promoted free markets, helped to restore macroeconomic balance and led to several years of economic growth in Nicaragua, El Salvador, and Guatemala, but they have also "reinforced historical tendencies toward profound social inequality" in these countries.[127] As we shall see in Chapter 10, the international financial institutions have established "social investment funds" to counterbalance the deleterious effects of liberal economic adjustment on vulnerable communities, but in Central America, these funds have been too small and temporary to have significant effects on poverty and distributional inequalities.[128] The Guatemalan case, however, suggests that international lenders may be starting to recognize that market-based development strategies can have dangerous effects in countries that are just emerging from civil wars.

---

[125] *New York Times* 1999 (March 11).
[126] Vilas 1995b; Vickers 1995; Arias 1997; Boyce and Pastor 1997; Robinson 2000.
[127] Vilas 2000, p. 227.   [128] McCleary 1999, p. 426.

8

Namibia and Mozambique

Success Stories in Southern Africa?

In the wake of peacebuilding missions in Namibia and Mozambique, the danger of resurgent conflict in both countries appears remote. Namibia has enjoyed more than a decade of domestic peace with little internal unrest, and at the time of this writing, there are no signs of renewed insurgency or intergroup violence. Although the durability of peace in Mozambique seems less secure than in Namibia, Mozambique has enjoyed the longest period of peace and stability in its history since its conflict came to an end in 1994. Yet the apparent success of Wilsonian peacebuilding policies in these two countries is not without qualification: Like Croatia, both countries offered unusually propitious conditions for postconflict liberalization, not least because major parties to their conflicts were external parties who effectively withdrew from the countries when the wars ended, thereby reducing the risks of rapid liberalization exacerbating tensions among formerly warring parties within these states. Indeed, neither the conflict in Mozambique nor that in Namibia was primarily indigenous or "homegrown" because both wars were instigated and sustained by external actors, and when outsiders abandoned the conflicts, there was little "demand" for continued fighting.

Namibia

South West Africa, as Namibia was previously known, was colonized by Germany in 1884, and it remained a German possession until World War I, when South African troops seized control of the territory and imposed military rule for the duration of the war.[1] Following the war, the League of Nations authorized South Africa to administer Namibia as a League mandate and to prepare Namibians for their eventual independence. However,

---

[1] For a comprehensive history of Namibia, see Kaela 1996. This section also draws upon Fortna 1993c and 1995; Forrest 1994; and United Nations 1996b, chap. 11.

during the negotiations in San Francisco at the end of World War II that led eventually to the creation of the United Nations, the South African government declared that Namibia should be formally incorporated into the Union of South Africa on the grounds that there was "no prospect of the territory ever existing as a separate state."[2] The UN subsequently refused to give its consent for Namibia's annexation, insisting that South Africa place the territory under the control of the United Nations Trusteeship Council – the successor to the League's mandate system. South Africa responded by rejecting the United Nations' authority over the disposition of Namibia. Thus began a dispute between the world body and the South African government over the status of Namibia, which eventually led the UN to declare that South Africa's occupation of Namibia was illegal and to press for the country's independence.

Meanwhile, several black nationalist organizations inside Namibia joined forces in 1960 to form the South West African People's Organization (SWAPO), which soon initiated a military and political campaign to oust South African authorities from Namibia and secure the territory's independence. SWAPO's guerrilla army was based in neighboring Angola and Zambia, from which it launched attacks on South African military units inside Namibia. In response, South Africa established permanent bases for thousands of South African counterinsurgency troops, who waged a small-scale but persistent bush war against the guerrillas in the northern part of the country. International negotiations were conducted sporadically during the 1970s and 1980s, eventually linking Namibia's independence with the withdrawal of Cuban troops from Angola, a formula that finally led to the signing of a comprehensive peace agreement in December 1988.

The agreement envisaged a "free and fair" election of an indigenous Constituent Assembly, which would then write a constitution for an independent Namibia. These elections would be supervised by the United Nations Transitional Assistance Group (UNTAG), an international mission of military and civilian personnel, which, in addition to its electoral duties, would be responsible for monitoring the demobilization of SWAPO guerrillas and the phased withdrawal of South African troops from Namibia, the conduct of local police, and the return of refugees, among other things.[3] The implementation of this agreement was delayed by a resurgence of fighting in early April 1989, but peace was quickly restored and demobilization proceeded with relatively few problems. Ninety-six percent of Namibians cast ballots in the November elections, which were relatively free of intimidation and violence, according to international observers.[4] SWAPO won forty-one of the Constituent Assembly's seventy-two seats, while its main opponent, the

[2] Cited in Kaela 1996, p. 12.   [3] United Nations 1996b, pp. 209–214.
[4] Fortna 1995, p. 287.

Democratic Turnhalle Alliance, secured twenty-one seats.[5] Later in the month, the newly elected Constituent Assembly convened and began negotiating the contents of a draft constitution, which the Assembly unanimously approved on February 9, 1990. Six weeks later, the leader of SWAPO, Sam Nujoma, was formally sworn in as the first president of independent Namibia.

International actors were instrumental not only in securing a peace settlement in Namibia but also in promoting a particular model of domestic governance for the country that Namibian leaders quickly embraced: liberal market democracy. Indeed, the main elements of the peace settlement were not set out by Namibians at all but by the "Contact Group" of Western countries – Canada, France, Germany, Great Britain, and the United States – in 1978, more than ten years before the conflict ended. The Western settlement plan, endorsed by the UN Security Council later that year,[6] provided for "free and fair elections" to a Constituent Assembly, which would adopt a constitution for an independent Namibia, as well as guarantees of free speech, assembly, movement, and the press, and the repeal of "discriminatory or restrictive laws, regulations, or administrative measures" that might interfere with free elections. The plan also provided for the release of political prisoners and the "demobilization of the citizen forces, commandos, and ethnic forces."[7] In 1982 the Contact Group went one step further and promulgated a detailed set of guidelines for Namibia's future constitution, which read like a checklist of liberal democratic principles: The government of Namibia would be constituted through periodic and genuine elections by secret ballot and universal suffrage, and fundamental rights would be guaranteed, including "the rights to life, personal liberty and freedom of movement; to freedom of conscience; to freedom of expression, including freedom of speech and a free press; to freedom of assembly and association, including political parties and trade unions; to due process and equality before the law; to protection from arbitrary deprivation of private property without just compensation; and to freedom from racial, ethnic, religious or sexual discrimination." Moreover, there would be an independent judicial branch of government, which would be "responsible for the interpretation of the Constitution and for ensuring its supremacy and the authority of the law."[8]

When the Constituent Assembly first met in November 1989 following the internationally supervised elections, the special representative of the UN

---

[5] United Nations 1996b, p. 227. The remaining ten seats were shared among five parties.

[6] See UN Security Council Resolution 435 of September 19, 1978.

[7] "Proposal for a Settlement of the Namibian Situation," UN Security Council document S/12636 (April 10, 1978).

[8] "Principles Concerning the Constituent Assembly and the Constitution for an Independent Namibia," UN Security Council document S/15287 (July 12, 1978).

secretary-general formally communicated the 1982 constitutional principles
to the Assembly, which adopted these principles, in accordance with the provisions of the 1988 peace settlement, as the basis for Namibia's new Constitution. Thus, the most difficult and important work of Namibia's founding
constitutional congress – that of defining the fundamental organizational
principles of the country's governing institutions – was effectively completed
by international actors long before the congress ever met.[9]

In the economic realm, the new Namibian government quickly adopted
an internationally endorsed plan for market-oriented reform. This was a remarkable development given SWAPO's long-standing advocacy of socialist
economics. SWAPO's 1976 political program, for example, had committed
the organization to the goal of uniting "all Namibian people, particularly
the working class, the peasantry and progressive intellectuals into a vanguard party capable of safe-guarding national independence and building a
classless, nonexploitative society based on the ideals and principles of scientific socialism," which included public ownership of "all the major means of
production and exchange of the country."[10] The months immediately following independence, however, witnessed a sea change in SWAPO's economic
policies that "astonished many observers, at home and abroad."[11] The new
Namibian government emphasized the crucial role of the private sector in
promoting economic growth and the importance of creating an "enabling
environment" for foreign investment.[12] At an international donors' conference in New York in June 1990, Namibia presented a economic plan that
explicitly endorsed both liberal democracy and "a free-market path to development," along with a draft code to protect foreign investments.[13] The
meeting resulted in pledges of almost $700 million in development aid to
Namibia, along with the country's membership in the International Monetary Fund, the World Bank, and the Lomé Convention of the European
Union. SWAPO's commitment to capitalist economics was reaffirmed in the
government's July 1990 budget and in the Foreign Investment Act, passed
by the National Assembly five months later, which guaranteed security of investments, nondiscriminatory treatment between foreign and local investors,
and freedom to repatriate profits and dividends.[14]

SWAPO's abrupt conversion to free-market economics appeared to underscore the influence of international actors over the domestic policies of
the new Namibian government. The incoming government was virtually
bankrupt and in pressing need of foreign financial assistance, and it was
offered such assistance by international lending agencies and donors on the

---

[9] This fact was not lost on the Namibian leaders themselves, some of whom complained
    bitterly that the new constitution was drawn up as much for international approval as for
    the approval of the Namibian people. See Cliffe et al. 1994, p. 213.
[10] Cited in Strand 1991, pp. 27–28.   [11] Dobell 1995, p. 171.   [12] Ibid.
[13] Cliffe et al. 1994, p. 230; and Dobell 1995, pp. 177–178.   [14] Murray 1992, p. 34.

condition that the government agree to adopt liberal economic (and, to a lesser extent, political) domestic policies.

Namibia has emerged from a quarter century of conflict as one of the most peaceful societies in Africa. Elections were held on schedule and without major disturbances in 1992, 1994, 1998, and 1999. Relations between SWAPO and the white minority population remain amicable, and the political climate is, by some accounts, "the most tolerant and free in the Third World."[15] A wide range of constitutionally protected freedoms are respected, including personal liberties, nondiscrimination in employment, property rights, and women's rights.[16] Moreover, the economy has grown strongly since independence.[17] The country faces its share of economic and political challenges, including allegations of corruption among government officials,[18] high levels of poverty in the black community,[19] and demands for prosecution of those alleged to have committed atrocities during the war.[20] Despite these problems, the prospect of renewed armed conflict in the foreseeable future remains vanishingly small. The process of political and economic liberalization appears not to have destabilized the peace in Namibia, but rather to have created the conditions for political stability and economic growth, just as defenders of the liberal peace thesis might expect.

Much of the credit for this outcome must go to the leaders of SWAPO, who eschewed vengeance against Namibia's white minority in favor of an official policy of "national reconciliation," which has included a "hands off" policy with regard to the white community.[21] There was, for example, no wholesale purge of white Namibians from the country's civil service, or expropriation of white businesses or property (including the huge swatches of white-owned commercial farmland in areas formerly under the control of South African police). In return, white settlers have responded to the political changes in Namibia with considerable restraint. Furthermore, the SWAPO leadership has insisted on "full inclusion of the country's racial and ethnic groups in the national political system" and has made special efforts to ensure "ethnic and racial representation across a broad spectrum of political posts, from the cabinet level through the lower ranks of the civil service."[22]

While the accomplishments of peacebuilding in Namibia have been noteworthy, the Namibian case should not be viewed as an unmitigated endorsement of the Wilsonian notion that liberalization will generally foster stable and lasting peace in war-shattered states. First, one of the principal belligerents in the war – the South African military – withdrew its forces entirely from the country as part of the peace process, thereby greatly reducing the

[15] Forrest 1994, p. 96. See also Constantine 1996.   [16] Forrest 2000, p. 98.
[17] Namibia's real GDP growth rate averaged 3.5% annually between 1995 and 2001 (OECD 2002, p. 231).
[18] See McNeil 1997.   [19] Kaela 1996, pp. 126–127.   [20] Africa Watch 1992.
[21] Forrest 1994, p. 97.   [22] Forrest 2000, p. 100.

danger that liberalization would exacerbate tensions among formerly war-ring parties in the postconflict state. The departure of the South African military effectively made a continuation or renewal of hostilities impossible: White settlers who remained in Namibia simply lacked the capacity to wage a war against the new government. Under these conditions, the willingness of white Namibians to accommodate themselves to a black-led regime is less remarkable than it might appear at first glance; indeed, it was their only possible course of action.

Unlike most other countries that have hosted postconflict peacebuilding missions, then, Namibia benefited from the fact that one of the parties to the conflict largely abandoned the territory at the end of hostilities. Indeed, one could argue that Namibia's war was to a considerable degree not a "civil" war at all but a liberation struggle against South Africa's quasi-colonial rule of the territory. When South Africa abandoned its efforts to maintain con-trol of Namibia, the principal impetus for violence effectively ceased to ex-ist. These conditions appear to have facilitated the peaceful liberalization of postconflict Namibia. Because these conditions are uncommon among coun-tries that are just emerging from civil wars, the Namibian case lends only qualified support to the peace-through-liberalization hypothesis.

Second, there are doubts about the degree to which Namibia can be char-acterized as a multiparty democracy. Although the administration of free and fair elections has been exemplary, there is virtually no opposition to SWAPO or to President Nujoma, and some commentators argue that Namibia has been developing into a one-party state.[23] Not only have the number and strength of viable political parties (apart from SWAPO) declined since inde-pendence, but the distinction between the ruling party and the government has also been steadily blurred.[24] Further, in the lead-up to the 1999 national election, Nujoma used his two-thirds majority in parliament to amend the country's constitution in order to allow him to serve for a third term (al-though he later announced that he would not run for a fourth term in the 2004 elections).[25] This is not to suggest that the government is acting ille-gally or extraconstitutionally to subvert the opposition – as has been the case in Liberia and Cambodia – but rather that the overwhelming dominance of SWAPO and Nujoma in Namibian politics raises questions about the degree to which the Namibian case corroborates the liberal peace thesis, given the absence of real political competition. Indeed, one could argue that it is pre-cisely the *non*competitive nature of Namibian politics that has made the country's peaceful democratic transition so relatively smooth.

None of these observations diminishes the fact that Namibia is now at peace after decades of war. Yet despite these very positive outcomes of Namibia's peacebuilding operation, it would be a mistake to interpret the Namibian case as strongly supporting the general proposition that liberalization fosters peace in war-shattered states: not only because postwar

[23] Mallet 1998; Bauer 1999.   [24] Bauer 1999, pp. 432–433.   [25] Swarns 2001.

conditions in Namibia were unusually propitious for liberalization due to the departure of South African forces, but also because the country's democratic system has been only nominally competitive.

Mozambique

Mozambique gained its independence from Portugal in 1975, when the Frente de Libertação de Moçambique (Frelimo), which had led the struggle against Portuguese rule, formed the first postindependence government. The ensuing period of peace lasted less than two years. The new Frelimo government provided support to black nationalist groups fighting the white minority regime in neighboring Rhodesia, and the government of Rhodesia responded by covertly recruiting a group of Mozambican expatriates to wage a campaign of terror and destruction in Mozambique.[26] The guerrilla organization, which eventually called itself the Resistência Nacional Moçambicana (Renamo), included Mozambican-born soldiers who had fought alongside the Portuguese against the independence movement, and was financed and sustained by the Rhodesian intelligence service.[27] For most of the Cold War, the Frelimo government received support from the Soviet Union and Soviet allies in Eastern Europe. Fighting between Frelimo and Renamo lasted for sixteen years and resulted in the deaths of approximately one million people.[28]

Throughout the 1980s, numerous attempts to end the war were made by third parties, but with little success.[29] It was not until July 1990, after both sides had lost most of their foreign support, that the first direct talks between the government and Renamo took place, mediated by the Italian government and a Catholic lay organization in Rome, the Community of Sant'Egidio. The negotiation process was slow and fitful, as both parties maneuvered for strategic advantage on the battlefield and at the bargaining table.[30] Over time, additional outside parties were brought into the negotiations as observers and advisors, including France, Portugal, Britain, the United States, and the United Nations. Two years of talks yielded a formal peace agreement in October 1992, which finally brought fighting in Mozambique to a halt. The main provisions of this agreement included plans for multiparty elections, the liberalization of the popular media, freedom of association and movement, the creation of nonpartisan commissions to monitor respect for civil rights and the activities of police and intelligence services, the demobilization of armed forces and the creation of a new national army, and the reintegration of ex-combatants into civilian life.[31]

---

[26] Newitt 1995, pp. 559 and 563–564; Reed 1996, p. 278; and Ciment 1997, p. 14.
[27] Rupiya 1998.   [28] Lloyd 1995, p. 155; and United Nations 1996b, p. 321.
[29] Jett 1995, p. 23.   [30] For a detailed account of the negotiations, see Hume 1994.
[31] "The General Peace Agreement for Mozambique," UN document S/24635 (October 8, 1992), annex.

Once again, the United Nations took on the principal task of monitoring and verifying implementation of the peace agreement. The UN Operation in Mozambique (ONUMOZ) included almost seven thousand international military personnel and was fully deployed by May 1993. The military functions of the UN mission included monitoring the local parties' compliance with the cease-fire agreement, preparing the assembly sites where combatants from both sides would assemble for demobilization, overseeing the demobilization itself, and maintaining a secure environment, particularly along transportation corridors, for other peacebuilding activities.[32] Civilian employees of several international agencies – including the European Union, the World Health Organization, the United Nations Children's Fund, and the Swiss Development Cooperation Agency – also worked alongside ONUMOZ personnel as observers of the cease-fire and demobilization process.[33] The humanitarian program involved the resettlement of nearly two million Mozambicans displaced by the war, overseen by the UN High Commissioner for Refugees. The special representative of the UN secretary-general, Aldo Ajello, was assigned the responsibility of establishing a political environment in which national elections, scheduled to be held in October 1993, would be judged as "free and fair." This meant, among other things, overseeing the design and implementation of electoral laws and monitoring respect for civil liberties, including freedom of the press and freedom of association, as well as mediating disagreements among the formerly warring parties in the postconflict period.

Due to delays in the demobilization process, national elections were not held until October 1994, one year after they were originally planned. Approximately twenty-three hundred international observers monitored the polling, including personnel from the UN, the European Union, the Organization of African Unity, and several nongovernmental organizations.[34] Despite last-minute complaints from Renamo about the fairness of the electoral process, the vote was judged generally free and fair by most international observers, with nearly 90 percent of registered voters casting ballots.[35] The incumbent president, Joaquin Chissano of the Frelimo party, won a narrow majority in the presidential election with 53 percent of the popular vote, while the Renamo candidate finished second with 34 percent. Frelimo also won a majority of seats in the country's National Assembly.[36]

The elections represented a milestone in Mozambique's transition away from a one-party socialist state and toward a market-oriented democracy – a process which had been ongoing for several years, and which was driven primarily by Mozambique's need for financial aid and other types of assistance from international agencies and Western governments. In the period

[32] United Nations 1996b, p. 324.   [33] Reed 1996, p. 286.
[34] United Nations 1996b, p. 333; and Reed 1996, p. 301.   [35] Jett 1995, p. 24.
[36] United Nations 1996b, p. 334.

immediately following independence in 1975, Frelimo had explicitly rejected Western models of political and economic organization, opting instead to pursue a program of "pragmatic Marxism." In practice, this meant authoritarian rule combined with anti–free market economic policies that emphasized large-scale, centrally planned, capital-intensive development projects both in industry and agriculture, including the establishment of state farms and collectives on the Soviet model.[37] In the early 1980s, however, the government of Mozambique found itself unable to meet its obligations to international creditors, due in part to the poor economic performance of the state farms, along with the increasing costs of the war against Renamo and the crippling effects of floods, drought, and famine on the rural economy.[38] The collapse of the economy and decline in state revenues led Frelimo reluctantly to solicit financial assistance from Western governments and the International Monetary Fund.[39] The conditions for such aid were clear: Mozambique would have to liberalize its socialist economy and replace it with a market-oriented one, which would entail privatizing state farms and other state-run enterprises, lowering government subsidies, removing wage and price controls, and lifting barriers to foreign investment and trade, among other things.[40] Mozambique became a member of the IMF and World Bank in 1984. Three years later, in 1987, the Frelimo government implemented an extensive structural adjustment program and economic liberalization, which had been developed in large part by the Bretton Woods institutions,[41] and which amounted to a "complete change of direction in economic strategy."[42]

Political liberalization followed economic liberalization in Mozambique. The Frelimo government, in order to shore up its support in the West, renounced Marxism-Leninism as its official ideology and dropped the words "People's Republic" from the country's name in 1989.[43] In November 1990, the government introduced a new constitution for Mozambique, which for the first time authorized multiparty elections, freedom of the press, and a legal right to strike – reforms that were designed, in part, to elicit further support from Western governments and donor agencies, while signaling a

---

[37] Alden and Simpson 1993, p. 123; Alden 1996, p. 42; and Ciment 1997, pp. 17 and 176. Whether or not Frelimo was a truly "socialist" government in its first few years in power, or whether Frelimo's commitment to "socialist" principles was primarily rhetorical, is a subject of ongoing debate among scholars. See, for example, Cahen 1993; and Saul 1993.

[38] Abrahamsson and Nilsson 1995, pp. 48–55 and 97–100; Newitt 1995, p. 566; Alden 1996, p. 42; and Ciment 1997, p. 17.

[39] Willett 1995, pp. 38–39. Frelimo turned to the West instead of the Soviet bloc for financial help in the early 1980s partly because the Soviet Union had, in 1981, rejected Mozambique's request for closer commercial relations with socialist countries, including membership in Comecon, the Soviet trading bloc. See Alden and Simpson 1993, p. 111.

[40] Abrahamsson and Nilsson 1995, p. 100; and Newitt 1995, pp. 566–567.

[41] Hume 1994, p. 20; and Abrahamsson and Nilsson 1995, p. 111.   [42] Plank 1993, p. 411.

[43] Ciment 1997, p. 142.

willingness to pursue more serious peace negotiations with Renamo, which had long called for democratic elections in the country.[44] Frelimo's endorsement of liberal democratic principles represented an abrupt reversal of the party's long-standing refusal to hold multiparty elections in Mozambique.[45] The shift in Frelimo's position came in response to "immense pressure from outside interests," including the Western governments and international mediators who were urging Frelimo in the direction of market democracy.[46] The peacebuilding mission, which oversaw the preparation and conduct of the 1994 elections in Mozambique, served to reinforce and to expedite a process of economic and political liberalization that had been ongoing since the early 1980s.

As in the case of Namibia, the outcome of peacebuilding in Mozambique has been generally positive. At the time of this writing, more than a decade has passed since the signing of the peace accord, and the country's two formerly warring parties remain at peace. Renamo has successfully transformed itself from a guerrilla army into a legal opposition party in the country's legislature, showing no signs of contemplating a return to violence, in spite of the fact that Frelimo flatly refused to appoint any Renamo officials to positions of authority in the government following the 1994 election. The two parties appear to have settled into a stable, albeit quarrelsome, relationship as parliamentary adversaries.[47] A new round of national elections in 1999 resulted in the reelection of President Chissano and a small increase in Frelimo's majority of seats in the Mozambican parliament.

On the economic front, structural adjustment reforms, which were initiated in the 1980s and extended into the postconflict period at the behest of the IMF and World Bank, have yielded relatively high levels of economic growth with low levels of inflation: Mozambique's real GDP grew by an annual average of 9.3 percent between 1996 and 1999, a figure that the OECD described as "remarkable" because it was so high in comparison to most other African countries.[48] Indeed, Mozambique is widely touted as an economic success story with the potential for continued high rates of growth.[49] Positive economic reports have contributed to the perception, shared by many if not most international observers of Mozambique, that the peacebuilding mission was a resounding success that effectively helped the

[44] Alden and Simpson 1993, p. 118; and Newitt 1995, pp. 572–573.

[45] President Chissano and the Frelimo Central Committee had reiterated their strong opposition to multiparty elections as recently as November and December 1989. See Hume 1994, pp. 29–30.

[46] Harrison 1996, p. 20. As Ciment (1997, p. 143) writes, Frelimo reluctantly agreed to elections "as the price to be paid for peace."

[47] *Economist* 1997b, p. 44.

[48] OECD 2002, p. 217. Growth slowed after a series of major floods struck the country in 2000 and 2001 but was expected to rebound quickly.

[49] For example, Rosenblum 1997; Matloff 1997; and Alden 2001, p. 101.

country emerge from a long history of chronic war and economic stagnation and begin a new period of peaceful democratic politics and economic growth.

But like Namibia, Mozambique offers only qualified support for the Wilsonian hypothesis of peace-through-liberalization in countries that have just experienced civil wars, for a number of reasons. First, the conflict in Mozambique was not primarily an indigenous or "homegrown" war – it was instigated and sustained chiefly by outside parties. As noted, Renamo began its existence as an instrument of the white minority government of Rhodesia. Renamo raids into Mozambique were organized by the Rhodesian intelligence service and supported by the Rhodesian army. As one scholar writes, Renamo was "simply a mercenary group of a white colonial army" and not a genuine "political movement" when it was founded.[50] After the fall of the Rhodesian government in 1979, Renamo was adopted by South Africa, which was committed to a "total strategy" of destabilizing nearby black African regimes through a campaign of sabotage and subversion.[51] At that time, most of Renamo's membership and equipment were transferred to South African territory. The rebel organization aimed to undermine the Frelimo government of Mozambique, but beyond that goal, it lacked a political program and received little encouragement from the population within Mozambique.

When Renamo did eventually acquire territorial bases inside Mozambique, it still "could not gain a critical mass of support" and consequently maintained its bases by terrorizing the local population into compliance.[52] Techniques for building popular "support" included mutilating civilians by cutting off ears, noses, lips, and sexual organs.[53] Only in the latter stages of the war did the group gain some measure of popular backing from rural groups disaffected with the government, which ultimately translated into electoral support in the postconflict period.

Although scholars disagree about the depth of support for Renamo within Mozambique by the end of the war, there is widespread agreement that the war itself was a foreign imposition on the country.[54] Renamo would not have posed a serious military, or even political, threat to the government without the sponsorship and prodding of Rhodesia and South Africa. Furthermore, the available evidence suggests that there was little popular support for Renamo's guerrilla campaign itself; rather, the vast majority of ordinary Mozambicans wanted to have nothing to do with the conflict.[55] Thus, when the rebel group lost its foreign backing in the early 1990s, there was virtually no popular support within Mozambique for a continuation of the armed struggle, which in turn reduced the danger of renewed fighting in the postconflict period.

[50] Newitt 1995, p. 564.   [51] Pitcher 2000, p. 192.   [52] Ibid., p. 194.   [53] Rupiya 1998.
[54] For an overview of this debate, see Young 1994.
[55] For further discussion of these points, see Finnegan 1992; and Ciment 1997.

On the one hand, then, conditions were particularly conducive for reconciliation in Mozambique after the war, due in part to the fact that the
war itself had only shallow domestic roots. But on the other hand, to the
extent that Renamo did obtain a measure of popular support, it apparently
stemmed from the disaffection of some rural dwellers with Frelimo's policies
of "modernization," which focused on spurring industrial growth and large-
scale agriculture while offering few benefits to individual peasant farmers.[56]
These tensions – between the wealthier urban industrial class and the poorer
rural peasantry – were not resolved by the end of Mozambique's war. On the
contrary, rapid economic liberalization has widened these socioeconomic inequalities dramatically since the termination of the conflict.[57] Foreign investment and economic growth have been concentrated in cities such as Maputo
and Beira – urban areas which were already the most highly developed in the
country, and therefore better able to attract new investment.[58] At the same
time, cutbacks in government social spending mandated by the international
financial institutions made it more difficult for many Mozambicans (80 percent of whom live in the countryside) to obtain basic necessities, including
food, shelter, and medical treatment.[59]

This is the second reason that the Mozambican case offers a less-than-
complete corroboration of Wilsonianism: As in Central America, the marketization policies that were part of postconflict peacebuilding in Mozambique
have exacerbated long-standing socioeconomic divisions that today remain
"the greatest threat to peace."[60] Although the immediate danger of violent
conflict seems remote, the widening of distributional inequalities is probably
not conducive to a stable and lasting peace in a country in which the principal lines of conflict are between a wealthy elite and a marginalized rural
peasantry.[61] As Mozambique's prime minister, Pascoal Mocumbi, observed
in 1997: "[S]ocial inequalities and regional asymmetry could endanger the
climate of peace, calm and social harmony that is a basic prerequisite for
balanced and self-sustaining socio-economic development."[62]

Furthermore, economic hardship has given rise to increased levels of criminal violence and banditry, including robberies, hijackings, and armed attacks,
particularly in rural areas of Mozambique.[63] As a result of this new violence, many parts of the country previously considered safe are now subject

---

[56] Hanlon 2000.
[57] Ohlson and Stedman 1994, p. 198; Hanlon 1996, p. 20; Pitcher 2000, p. 202; and Hanlon
2000. Moreover, de Sousa (2003) and Wuyts (2003) note that income inequality *within* rural
areas has also increased in the postwar period.
[58] Abrahamsson and Nilsson 1995, pp. 161 and 189; EPSA 1997; Hanlon 2000; and OECD
2002.
[59] Willett 1995, p. 35.   [60] Hanlon 2000. See also Thusi 2001.   [61] Wuyts 2001.
[62] Cited in *Economist* 1997b.
[63] Lloyd 1995, p. 155; Alden 1996; Daley 1996, p. 54; Dique 1996; Ciment 1997, p. 226; and
Alden 2001, p. 113.

to armed attacks.[64] While the precise causal relationship between increased deprivation and rising violence in postwar Mozambique is difficult to pinpoint, students of Mozambican history point out that sudden shocks to the rural economy in the past have been accompanied by increased levels of violent crime and banditry in the countryside.[65] This pattern appears to be playing itself out again, as ex-combatants and ordinary peasants have responded to declining living standards by joining the ranks of criminal gangs. In the words of one former government soldier: "We want to eat, or if not, we will have to rob."[66] The upsurge in violent crime has, in effect, denied the benefits of the Frelimo-Renamo armistice to the many Mozambicans who continue to be menaced by armed groups that roam the countryside with relative impunity. Commentators who contend that peace has been consolidated in Mozambique tend to focus too narrowly on the relatively peaceful relationship between Frelimo and Renamo, while underemphasizing the proliferation of postwar criminal violence. Nor is it possible to rule out the possibility that this unrest could eventually take on a more explicitly antigovernment character. As Chris Alden writes: "[I]t is not far-fetched to suggest that the criminal violence of today – mediated through growing social disaffection – could well end up as the political violence of tomorrow."[67] Others have similarly warned that declining living conditions in the countryside have made Mozambique a "potential powder keg."[68]

Whether Mozambique continues to live up to its reputation as a peacebuilding success story remains to be seen. As of this writing, the record of Mozambique's postwar democratization has been relatively favorable, with the former adversaries apparently shifting their disagreements from the battlefield to the ballot box. Economic liberalization policies have also been beneficial in many ways – most notably, by contributing to high levels of GNP growth and encouraging new flows of foreign investment. But these same economic reforms have also deepened existing schisms and traditional sources of political tension in the country, and have apparently contributed to the spread of criminal violence, which at least casts doubt on the Wilsonian claim that liberalization promotes stable and lasting peace, even in what is generally viewed as one of the most successful cases of peacebuilding in the 1990s.[69]

Conclusion

The accomplishments of the international peacebuilding missions in Namibia and Mozambique are impressive: The wars in both countries show no sign of

[64] EIU 1997d, p. 9; Amnesty International 1998.   [65] See Newitt 1995, pp. 575–576.
[66] Cited in Dolan and Schafer 1997, p. 166.   [67] Alden 1996, p. 55.
[68] Willett 1995, p. 48. See also Ohlson and Stedman 1994, p. 199.
[69] Weinstein 2002 characterizes Mozambique as a "fading success story," or one that is less successful than it may have first appeared, for many of the reasons mentioned here.

rekindling in the foreseeable future. Both countries, moreover, have adopted liberal political and economic institutions and policies less problematically than other peacebuilding host states that we have examined. Nevertheless, Namibia and Mozambique are also unlike most other countries that have recently emerged from civil wars: In both cases, conflicts that preceded the deployment of peacebuilders were instigated and sustained primarily by outside actors, a condition that facilitated postwar reconciliation and quite likely diminished the destabilizing effects of rapid liberalization. Put another way, the conflicts in Namibia and Mozambique were, in important respects, not "civil" wars at all. This is particularly true of Namibia, where SWAPO fought what amounted to an anticolonial war against the South African army. To a lesser extent, it is also true of Mozambique, where one faction in the war was created and maintained by foreign governments and only started to build a domestic political base after several years of trying to do so. Furthermore, in Mozambique, economic liberalization policies have led to a worsening of poverty and inequality – circumstances that have historically been a source of political unrest in the country.

PART III

PROBLEMS AND SOLUTIONS

9

The Limits of Wilsonianism

Understanding the Dangers

Despite the many differences among the eleven peacebuilding operations launched between 1989 and 1998, these missions have pursued a broadly common strategy, seeking to transform war-shattered states into liberal market democracies on the assumption that doing so would help to consolidate a stable and lasting peace. As noted in Part I, this strategy rested on a proposition that liberal thinkers have propounded in one form or another since the eighteenth century, and which gained widespread acceptance among scholars and policymakers at the end of the Cold War: that liberal democracy and market-oriented economics offer the surest formula for peace, both in relations between states and within their borders. I labeled this the Wilsonian approach to conflict management and noted that this method of conflict management is still largely unproven, because questions such as whether the process of liberalization fosters peace, and whether democratization and marketization are reliable remedies for intrastate violence, remain largely unanswered. The case studies examined in the preceding chapters were conducted in the hope of gaining new insights into these questions.

Some missions were clear successes (Namibia and Croatia); others were obvious failures (Angola and Rwanda). The remaining operations fell in between these two extremes. In most of these eleven cases, the process of political liberalization, or economic liberalization, or both, produced destabilizing side effects that worked against the consolidation of peace. In some countries, liberalization exacerbated societal tensions, and in others it reproduced traditional sources of violence. The approach to peacebuilding that prevailed in the 1990s was, it seems, based on overly optimistic assumptions about the effects of democratization and marketization in the immediate aftermath of civil war. (Operations launched after 1998 will be discussed in Chapter 11.)

This conclusion points not only to weaknesses in the prevailing peacebuilding strategy as a conflict management method but also to the limitations of the liberal peace thesis itself. Although well-established market democracies do tend to be more peaceful and prosperous than other types of states, the actual process of transforming a country into a market democracy is tumultuous and conflictual, particularly in the fragile circumstances of war-shattered states that typically lack governmental institutions capable of managing the disruptive effects of liberalization. Contemporary students of the liberal peace thesis and practitioners of peacebuilding have paid too little attention to this problem. They have, it seems, largely forgotten classical liberalism's pragmatic emphasis on authoritative and effective – in addition to limited – government as a precondition for domestic peace.

This is not to suggest that peacebuilders should abandon their efforts to promote the principles and practices of market democracy. In the next chapter, I shall argue that peacebuilders should *continue* to pursue the goal of transforming war-shattered states into liberal market democracies, but using a different strategy – one that starts from the assumption that the liberalization process is capable of undermining the very peace that it is intended to uphold.

The remainder of this chapter proceeds as follows: After reviewing and summarizing the findings of the case studies, I shall attempt to explain *why* rapid liberalization has been a problematic peacebuilding strategy, an explanation that is divided into two parts. The first part describes five "pathologies" that can arise during a process of democratization and marketization in any state undergoing these transitions. The second part explains why countries that are just emerging from civil wars are especially susceptible to these pathologies.

Learning from the Case Studies

The Wilsonian approach to conflict management yielded problematic results in many of the countries that hosted peacebuilding missions in the 1990s. The main question I posed at the outset of these case studies was whether efforts to transform war-shattered states into liberal market democracies had fostered conditions for a stable and lasting peace, or a peace that is likely to survive for the foreseeable future. I suggested that if we discovered that the liberalization process had 1) contributed to a resurgence of fighting, 2) recreated or exacerbated conditions that had historically been the cause of civil violence in the host states, or 3) created new conditions within the host states that seemed likely to spark a renewal of fighting, these findings would cast doubt on the Wilsonian assumptions of peacebuilding, since they would indicate that the liberalization process had been, in some respects, inimical to the establishment of a stable and lasting peace.

The case studies offer a mixed verdict on the effects of liberalization in war-shattered states. In the worst examples – Angola and Rwanda – democratization efforts precipitated renewed violence. In the best – Croatia and

Namibia – the process of political and economic liberalization was relatively unproblematic and appeared to facilitate the peaceful settlement of disputes that show no sign of rekindling at present. The remaining seven cases fall somewhere between these two extremes. Nicaragua, El Salvador, and Guatemala underwent relatively smooth transitions to multiparty democracy, but rapid marketization appears to have reproduced some of the socioeconomic conditions that sparked unrest in these countries in the first place; and in Mozambique, economic liberalization also appears to have exacerbated conditions that have traditionally fueled violence in the country. In Bosnia, political liberalization has reinforced the power of the parties who are least committed to peaceful reconciliation. In Cambodia, elections spurred deadly competition between the formerly warring groups – competition that was ultimately squelched by the repressive tactics of the country's prime minister, Hun Sen, who effectively reversed the country's initial movement toward multiparty democracy. Similarly, in Liberia, Charles Taylor immediately began to suppress the political freedom of his opponents after being elected president in 1997, and was forced out of power in 2003 in the face of renewed fighting in the country.

A closer look at the results suggests that these eleven peacebuilding cases might be divided into three broad categories. The first category includes Namibia and Croatia, where major belligerents effectively abandoned the territory at the end of the conflict: In Namibia, the South African army gave up all claims to the territory at the end of the conflict. In Croatia, a large portion of the ethnic Serbian population fled during the latter stages of the war, and the government of Yugoslavia abandoned its support for the remaining Serbian community. The disengagement of these belligerents almost certainly facilitated the task of reconciling the parties who remained in the state after the war, and tempered the dangers of destabilization arising from the effects of postconflict liberalization. These conditions are relatively unusual among countries that seek international peacebuilding assistance to help implement negotiated settlements. More commonly, the existence of a negotiated settlement in a civil conflict indicates that the formerly warring parties will continue to share the same territory and play an active role in postwar politics. So while international liberalization efforts had a largely positive outcome in Croatia and Namibia, we must also recognize that these countries offered unusually propitious conditions for postconflict stabilization.[1]

---

[1] To a lesser extent, Mozambique could also fall into this category, since one of the parties to the country's conflict – Renamo – was created and sustained by foreign actors and had relatively little domestic support. However, because the process of economic liberalization in Mozambique has apparently reproduced conditions that have traditionally fueled unrest in the country, as I argued in Chapter 8, I have included it in the third category of cases in this chapter.

The second category is comprised of those cases in which initial democratization efforts were diverted by newly elected leaders, resulting in what might be called "demagogue democracies," characterized by the de facto suppression of political opposition through violence and intimidation.[2] Cambodia and Liberia fall into this category. Both countries experienced a period of relative stability in the aftermath of peacebuilding – stability which continues in Cambodia as of this writing but which quickly gave way to renewed conflict in Liberia. Yet it is difficult to reach firm conclusions about the effects of liberalization in Cambodia and Liberia because both countries quickly reverted to a system of de facto one-party – indeed, one-person – rule. Furthermore, during the brief period of genuine political competition in Cambodia, which lasted from approximately 1992 to 1997, democratic elections became a catalyst for new bouts of violent conflict among the leading political parties, which ended only when Hun Sen forcefully subdued his rivals in the July 1997 coup. More generally, the Cambodian and Liberian cases suggest that the "quick and dirty" style of democratization promoted by international peacebuilders can be readily diverted by opportunistic local actors who have little interest in sustaining liberal reforms. This outcome poses a particular danger for countries such as Cambodia and Liberia, whose history is marked by cycles of governmental repression followed by violent counterreactions from equally ruthless opposition groups.

The third category of peacebuilding encompasses the remaining seven operations: Angola, Rwanda, Bosnia, El Salvador, Nicaragua, Guatemala, and Mozambique. This group is diverse, and the effects of democratization and marketization have varied widely. In some cases – including Angola, Rwanda, and Bosnia – the process of *political* liberalization sparked renewed violence or reinforced the power of the most belligerent groups in the society. In other cases – including El Salvador, Nicaragua, Guatemala, and Mozambique – some of the effects of *economic* liberalization seemed to work against the establishment of a stable and lasting peace. The outcome of each mission was in many respects unique, but in various ways and to different degrees, the liberalization process produced unanticipated problems that threatened to destabilize – or did destabilize – the fragile peace.

This is not to suggest that peacebuilding missions left all eleven host states in a worse condition than they would have otherwise been. On the contrary, many are at peace for the first time in decades, thanks in part to the assistance offered by international agencies. After decades of revolutionary violence and repression in Central America, for example, the relative tranquility of the region today is an accomplishment worthy of celebration. Yet the question I posed at the outset was not whether peacebuilding does more harm than good, or vice versa, but whether the assumptions of the Wilsonian

---

[2] I define a "demagogue democracy" as a type or subclass of "illiberal democracy" (Zakaria 1997 and 2003) that is ruled by a charismatic strongman.

approach to conflict management are borne out by the record of peacebuilding. Specifically, have internationally sponsored democratization and marketization efforts helped to create the conditions for stable and lasting peace,
which is the stated goal of peacebuilding? Given the limited number of cases
to evaluate, and the varied circumstances of each mission, I cannot offer a
final and definitive answer to this question. Nevertheless, the case studies
do suggest that the liberalization process either contributed to a rekindling
of violence or helped to recreate the historic sources of violence in many of
the countries that have hosted these missions – a conclusion that casts doubt
on the reliability of the peace-through-liberalization strategy as it has been
practiced to date.

Some observers might respond to this conclusion with skepticism. George
Downs and Stephen Stedman, for example, argue that it is based on an unrea-
sonably high standard of peacebuilding "success" and that it consequently
yields "very little information that can be used to improve future missions."[3]
As noted in Chapter 3, Downs and Stedman prefer to judge the effectiveness
of peacebuilding primarily on whether or not peace exists at the moment
peacebuilders go home. I have already explained why their standard for
evaluating peacebuilding is inappropriate: It pays too little attention to the
declared purpose of peacebuilding – the creation of self-sustaining peace –
and therefore sets the bar too low. One of the unfortunate results of using
this reduced standard is that it deflects attention away from conditions that
have previously precipitated violence in peacebuilding host states, as well
as the impact of peacebuilding policies on these conditions. Thus, Stedman
ends up dismissing distributional inequalities and related violence in the
Central America cases as "the mundane reality of life in crime- and poverty-
ridden insecurity," but he does not consider the relationship between these
conditions, the actions of peacebuilders, and the prospects for establishing a
durable peace in these countries.[4] More fundamentally, Downs and Stedman
misunderstand the nature of my investigation. Rather than simply applying
a standard of "success" and evaluating individual missions against this standard, I have evaluated one specific aspect of peacebuilding – the promotion of
market democracy as a remedy for civil strife – which, it turns out, seems to
have worked against the consolidation of self-sustaining peace in a number
of ways, contrary to the Wilsonian assumptions of peacebuilding.

These observations lead, in turn, to another question that will be addressed in the remainder of this chapter: *Why* exactly does the Wilsonian
approach to peacebuilding generate such destabilizing side effects? I shall
argue that many of the problems identified in the peacebuilding case studies can be traced back to tensions in the logic of market democracy itself –
tensions that make the liberalization process potentially dangerous in the

[3] Stedman and Downs 2002, p. 49, responding to my earlier work on the subject.
[4] Stedman 2002, p. 19.

fragile circumstances of countries just emerging from civil wars. As we shall see in Chapter 10, this analysis offers useful and concrete recommendations for improving the design and conduct of future peacebuilding operations.

The Paradoxical Logic of Market Democracy: Peace Through Conflict

If it is true that democracies rarely go to war against one another and that they are less likely than nondemocracies to experience internal unrest, then democratization would seem, at first glance, to be a sensible solution for states suffering from civil strife. Similarly, if capitalism has generated the highest levels of wealth and economic growth in human history, and if capitalism and democracy are mutually reinforcing systems of organizing political and economic life, as many Western commentators contend, then market democracy should be a promising formula for managing domestic conflict and creating prosperity in war-shattered states.

The problem with this reasoning is that it overlooks another important feature of democracy and capitalism: Both systems *encourage* conflict and competition – indeed, they thrive on it.[5] Democracy, for example, requires competitive multiparty elections as well as a politically active and involved citizenry, or a vibrant "civil society," meaning the space or arena between the household and the state in which citizens engage in organized activities that are not governmental in nature but are nevertheless "public."[6] Sites of such activity include trade unions, churches, political parties and movements, cooperatives, neighborhood groups, and even bowling leagues. From the mid-nineteenth-century writings of Alexis de Tocqueville to the present day, political observers have argued that civil society serves at least two important functions in liberal democracies: First, private associations help to scrutinize and counterbalance the power of the state, thus serving as an informal check against "tyranny" and complementing formal constitutional arrangements.[7] Second, these associations serve as "great free schools" that train citizens in the habits of compromise and negotiation that underpin the success of a democracy.[8]

More recently, scholars have added a third, related argument: Simultaneous membership in many different associations produces a network of "cross-cutting cleavages," or overlapping commitments to different social groupings, which is said to minimize the salience of any single line of conflict

---

[5] In this chapter I use the term "conflict" in its broadest sense as a synonym for competition, or a struggle in which the aim is to "gain objectives" against the wishes of rivals (Coser 1956). Conflict, in this sense, can be violent or nonviolent.

[6] Walzer 1991; Putnam 1995; and Hall 1995. For a genealogy of the term "civil society," see Gellner 1991; and Kumar 1993.

[7] De Tocqueville 1988, pp. 189–195.   [8] Ibid., p. 522.

and "temper the severity of social antagonisms."[9] R. J. Rummel explains the rationale behind this argument: "Because of the multitude of diverse groups and separate interests, [and] because of the lack of coincidence of interests across groups and issues, if political conflict escalates to violence it is usually limited to an issue or so, a neighborhood or urban area, or particular individuals."[10] Walter Morris-Hale similarly notes that

ethnic disharmonies are less likely to be . . . violent in a political community that has a significant number of voluntary associations, because citizens who belong to numerous and diverse associations will be exposed to a variety of divergent points of view. . . . The resulting compromises mean the clash of interests is less vehement; social and political tensions are less strident; and ethnic groups are more willing to trust their ethnic opposites and less likely to respond violently to their success.[11]

For these and other reasons, a vibrant civil society is commonly viewed as a factor that strengthens and enhances liberal democracy and domestic peace.[12]

The existence of an active civil society, however, requires sustained mobilization on the part of a large number of citizens and a willingness to engage in continuous competition in the pursuit of often conflicting interests. Thus, as Robert Dahl writes, "in democratic countries political conflict is not merely normal, it is generally thought to be rather healthy."[13] Conflict is salubrious, according to this perspective, because it facilitates the reconciliation of competing interests through peaceful debate and compromise, which can serve to co-opt potential revolutionaries who might otherwise turn to violence in order to achieve their goals.[14]

Herein lies a fundamental paradox within the workings of democracy, which relies on political competition as a means of limiting the intensity of this competition. Lewis Coser, one of the first scholars to describe the "stabilizing" effects of societal conflict, put it this way: "By permitting the immediate and direct expression of rival claims," open societies "are able to readjust their structures by eliminating the sources of dissatisfaction."[15] E. E. Schattschneider describes the paradox in even blunter terms: "The most powerful instrument for the control of conflict is conflict itself."[16]

Nothing illustrates the reliance of democracy upon political contestation better than multiparty elections, the "indispensable marker" of democratic government.[17] While a central function of elections is to channel political conflict through peaceful institutions, elections also presuppose energetic

[9] Schattschneider 1973, p. 65. The classic work on cross-cutting cleavages is Simmel 1955.
[10] Rummel 1997, p. 147.   [11] Morris-Hale 1996, p. 1.
[12] In Robert Putnam's words: "Tocqueville was right: Democratic government is strengthened, not weakened, when it faces a vigorous civil society" (Putnam 1993, p. 82).
[13] Dahl 1986, p. 14.   [14] Rummel 1997, p. 146.   [15] Coser 1956, p. 154.
[16] Schattschneider 1973, p. 65.   [17] Clark 2000, p. 27.

competition among candidates and parties seeking office. Leaders must offer contending programs and visions of public policy if voters are genuinely
to participate in the decision-making process. In the absence of incentives
for politicians to compete for votes, the mechanism of representative accountability to the electorate would founder, since leaders would have little
motivation to adjust their policies in response to public preferences.[18] Similarly, the possibility of democratically replacing governments – which allows
disaffected citizens to effect policy changes without resorting to violence –
presupposes voting systems in which there is not only widespread public participation in the electoral process but at least two leaders or parties actively
competing for power. In short, political contestation is no less a requirement
of democracy than is popular participation.[19] Like the idea of a vibrant
civil society, competitive elections reveal the paradoxical logic upon which
democracy is based: that political contestation itself provides a means of
containing and reconciling social conflicts.

The notion that self-interested competition engenders stability and other
social benefits is, of course, a core tenet of liberal economic theory as well.
Competition for profit among individuals and firms allows markets to allocate resources efficiently and productively. In the absence of competition,
inefficient firms are not driven out of the marketplace; instead, they continue
to tie up resources that could be used for more productive purposes. Although
most contemporary economists have abandoned the sweeping laissez-faire
philosophy of classical liberalism, the notion that free markets generally allocate resources efficiently remains a central principle of modern capitalism,
along with the attendant belief that encouraging competition among individual profit seekers is the key to greater prosperity, not just for those who
"win" in the market but for society as a whole.

The benefits of capitalist competition, however, are more than just
monetary: Competition in the market also provides a peaceful outlet for
aggressive impulses and a mechanism through which "our activities can be
adjusted to each other without coercive or arbitrary intervention of authority."[20] In the words of John Maynard Keynes, "dangerous human proclivities
can be canalized into comparatively harmless channels by the existence of
opportunities for money-making and private wealth, which, if they cannot
be satisfied in this way, may find their outlet in cruelty, the reckless pursuit of
personal power and authority, and other forms of self-aggrandizement."[21]
The market is said to temper social conflicts by giving individuals the freedom
to pursue their respective interests, and by providing a mechanism through
which self-interested behavior can be translated into mutual gains, thus tap-
ping into what Adam Smith called the "natural harmony of interests." Thus,
the putatively pacifying qualities of capitalism, like those of democracy, rest

---

[18] Holler 1987, p. 21.   [19] Dahl 1971.   [20] Hayek 1944, p. 41.
[21] Quoted in Hall 1987, pp. 47–48.

on a paradox: that self-interested competition contributes to the maintenance of a well-ordered society.

However, competition in the political and economic marketplace is not entirely self-regulating, even in the most permissive market democracies: Competition takes place within a *framework of institutions* that resolve disputes, translate public debate into governmental policy, and enforce a system of rules and regulations that govern the operation of the polity and economy. When such institutions exist and function well, political and economic competition generally works in the manner suggested by liberal peace theorists, who argued that competition would promote efficiency in the economic realm and democratic accountability in the political realm. But problems can arise if societal contestation becomes so intense that it cannot be channeled through existing institutions. Under these circumstances, encouraging further competition could lead to violence.

Problems of this type are relatively rare in the well-established democracies of the West, but they are not uncommon in countries that are undergoing the transition to liberal market democracy, particularly those that lack either a tradition of peaceful competition or governmental institutions that are capable of "processing" societal demands, for reasons I will discuss in the next section. Market democracy's emphasis on public contestation can give rise to a number of different pathologies – including violent conflict – which can themselves impede further progress toward market democracy in countries undergoing political and economic liberalization. Exploring these "pathologies of liberalization" is essential to understanding the shortcomings of Wilsonianism as a peacebuilding strategy. In what follows, I identify these pathologies, describe the circumstances under which they are most likely to arise, and examine their implications for the theory and practice of postconflict peacebuilding.

The Pathologies of Liberalization

In any country undergoing a transition to market democracy, democratization and marketization may produce unanticipated consequences that can undermine the liberalization process itself or endanger internal peace. These pathologies include: 1) the problem of "bad" civil society; 2) the behavior of opportunistic "ethnic entrepreneurs"; 3) the risk that elections can serve as focal points for destructive societal competition; 4) the danger posed by local "saboteurs" who cloak themselves in the mantle of democracy but seek to undermine democracy; and 5) the disruptive and conflict-inducing effects of economic liberalization (see Figure 9.1).

A common theme unites these problems: They arise, in part, from the fact that democratization and marketization foster societal competition, as we shall see. Although these pathologies are not inevitable consequences of

1. Bad Civil Society

2. Ethnic Entrepreneurs

3. Elections as Focal Points for Harmful Competition

4. Saboteurs and Failed Transitions

5. The Dangers of Economic Liberalization

FIGURE 9.1. Five Pathologies of Liberalization

liberalization, they do periodically occur and therefore should be directly addressed by students and practitioners of peacebuilding.

Bad Civil Society

Democracy, I have argued, presupposes an active civil society to counterbalance and scrutinize the state, to educate the populace in the practices of peaceful compromise, and to create a network of cross-cutting social groups, thereby diminishing the intensity of any particular social cleavage. Accordingly, the various governmental and nongovernmental organizations that have sought to promote democracy abroad – sometimes labeled the "democracy industry"[22] – have almost universally subscribed to the view that democratization must involve, among other things, measures aimed at stimulating the growth of civil-society activity within these states, including liberalization of the press, the promotion of free assembly and association rights, and financial and technical assistance to local NGOs.[23]

Yet encouraging the growth of civil society does not necessarily promote pluralism, moderation, accommodation – or democracy. Much of the discourse in the 1990s focused on increasing the *quantity* of civil society organizations, rather than considering their specific *qualities*. Organizations that preach hatred and intolerance, for example, may not perform the kind of educative functions that de Tocqueville and others viewed as supportive of democracy. Rather than inculcating pluralist compromise, they might instead spread prejudice, insularity, and extremism, resulting in what Simone Chambers and Jeffrey Kopstein call "bad civil society," or private political activity that rejects the liberal principle of toleration.[24] There are many historical and contemporary examples of this phenomenon. Sheri Berman argues, for instance, that high levels of associational involvement in Weimar Germany contributed directly to the rise of the Nazi movement and the collapse of Germany's nascent interwar democracy.[25] "Germans

---

[22] Bjornlund 2001.   [23] For example, Human Rights Watch 1995.
[24] Chambers and Kopstein 2001.   [25] Berman 1997.

threw themselves into their clubs, voluntary associations, and professional organizations out of frustration with the failures of the national government and political parties," Berman writes,

thereby helping to undermine the Weimar Republic and facilitate Hitler's rise to power. In addition, Weimar's rich associational life provided a critical training ground for eventual Nazi cadres and a base from which the National Socialist German Workers' Party (NSDAP) could launch its *Machtergreifung* (seizure of power). Had German civil society been weaker, the Nazis would never have been able to capture so many citizens for their cause or eviscerate their opponents so swiftly.[26]

Rwanda offers a more recent example of the potentially perverse effects of civil society mobilization. Rwanda had "an extremely high civil society density" in the 1980s and early 1990s.[27] By some estimates, there was approximately one farmers' organization per 35 households, one commercial cooperative per 350 households, and one local NGO per 3,500 households, along with very active and widespread membership in Christian churches throughout the country.[28] But this network of organizations did not prevent the mass killings of April 1994. Indeed, many civil society groups subscribed to the dominant racism in the society and eventually took part in the genocide.[29] Some members of Rwanda's human rights NGOs reportedly played roles as instigators, leaders, and participants.[30] Furthermore, as noted in Chapter 4, efforts to liberalize the country's popular media seemed to cause more, not less, polarization in society through the publication and broadcast of incendiary and ethnically intolerant opinion.

The broader problem illustrated by these examples is that while active civil-society associations may be an essential ingredient for a functioning liberal democracy, some kinds of associations can, in the words of Robert Dahl, "foster the narrow egoism of their members at the expense of concerns for the broader public good, and even . . . weaken or destroy democracy itself."[31] The promotion of civil society can have positive *or* deleterious effects both on the prospects for democratic consolidation and on domestic peace. When efforts to encourage political participation do not result in greater support for democratic compromise, but instead serve to increase polarization, intolerance, and antagonism in a transitional society, they do not further the cause of either democracy or peace.

Ethnic Entrepreneurs
In addition to fostering "bad civil society," liberalization can also be manipulated by opportunistic leaders who exploit intercommunal distrust as a means of building political support in ethnically divided societies. For such ethnic entrepreneurs, playing upon the "fear of domination by ethnic strangers" can help to consolidate a political following among members of

[26] Ibid., p. 402.   [27] Uvin 1998, p. 166.   [28] Ibid., pp. 166–167.   [29] Ibid., p. 172.
[30] Ibid.   [31] Dahl 1982, p. 1.

their own ethnic group, encouraging other ethnic groups and leaders to respond in kind and resulting in the polarization of the emerging democracy's
party system along mutually exclusive ethnic lines.[32] Jack Snyder has explored this dynamic in depth, showing how "political entrepreneurs who
want to gain mass support to seize or strengthen state power find that traditional cultural networks based on a common religion or language provide
convenient channels to mobilize backers."[33] The strategy is most likely to
succeed, according to Snyder, "when the democratizing country is poor, when
its citizens lack the skills needed for successful democratic participation, and
when its representative institutions, political parties, and journalistic profes-
sionalism are weakly established during the early phase of the democratic
transition."[34] It is a particularly dangerous strategy because "exclusionary
forms of nationalism often make enemies of the excluded groups."[35] At the
very least, the emergence of ethnically based party systems in a transitional
democracy can make the mediation of intergroup differences and interests
more difficult.[36] At worst, elites' efforts to persuade ordinary people to accept divisive nationalist ideas can increase the danger of ethnic violence and
failed democratization.[37]

Recent studies of the polarizing effects of ethnic entrepreneurs in democratizing states have focused on Africa, Eastern Europe, and the former Soviet
Union.[38] Yugoslavia's abortive attempt to democratize at the end of the Cold
War offers a particularly striking illustration of this pathology. The power
of the central government in the Yugoslav federation had been weak relative to the other communist states of Eastern Europe, even before the death
of Marshal Tito in 1980. But the centrifugal tendencies of regionalism and
ethnic nationalism remained largely under control until the end of the Cold
War, when the Yugoslav communist party – and the communist ideology
of the ruling elite – disintegrated and plans for democratic elections were
drawn up. The easiest strategy for establishing political support in the post-
communist Yugoslavia was through appeals to ethnic unity and communal
fears. As Bogdan Denitch writes, "the new politicians did not build their
programs out of wholly new materials. Rather, they used whatever political materials were available in the conscience of the electorate, and what
was available was, by and large, pretty terrible, or at the very least inappropriate for democratic politics and pluralist give-and-take in what was a
complicated, modern, multinational federation."[39]

In all six of the country's constituent republics – Slovenia, Croatia, Serbia,
Bosnia, Macedonia, and Montenegro – nationalist leaders employed rhetoric
of intolerance and hatred in the lead-up to the 1990 elections, stirring up

[32] Horowitz 1985, pp. 188, 306, and 323 (quotation from p. 188); and Sisk 1995, p. 23.
[33] Snyder 2000, p. 271.   [34] Ibid., p. 37.   [35] Ibid., p. 66.   [36] Horowitz 1985, p. 298.
[37] Snyder 2000, p. 32.   [38] For example, Ottaway 1994; Roeder 1998; and Snyder 2000.
[39] Denitch 1996, p. 157.

long-suppressed ethnic fears and "prepar[ing] the way for war by emphasizing group danger."[40] The strategy was stunningly successful: The electorate became polarized along ethnic lines, and politicians who campaigned on a nationalist platform won easily in all of the republics. In gaining victory at the polls, these politicians unleashed forces that led ultimately to the violent disintegration of Yugoslavia and a prolonged civil war in Bosnia. The American ambassador to Yugoslavia, Warren Zimmermann, summed up the impact of the 1990 elections bluntly: "In bringing nationalism to power, the elections helped to snuff out the very flame of democracy that had been kindled."[41]

In this way, Yugoslavia's ethnic entrepreneurs exploited the country's new civil and political freedoms to mobilize support by rousing xenophobic nationalism, illustrating a danger that one commentator calls the "dark side of democracy" in ethnically divided societies.[42] It is the elite-level counterpart of "bad civil society" pathology – instead of grassroots mobilization of intolerant and antidemocratic private associations from the "bottom up," this pathology involves political leaders encouraging hatred from the "top down." Societies in the earliest phases of liberalization, where ethnic identities are stronger than democratic traditions, seem to be particularly vulnerable to such mobilization strategies. As Susan Woodward explains:

In a world of competing symbols and personalities at a point of political transition, nationalism has a particular advantage. The message is simple and can be largely emotional. It relies on the familiar, using little time or money to develop a new political language appropriate to the new times of democratic governance and to communicate or explain the complexities of policy for an entire social and economic transformation. Nationalist appeals thus provide the easiest route to political visibility for politicians without established constituencies.[43]

Elections as Focal Points for Harmful Competition

In similar ways, democratic elections can serve as catalysts and focal points for destructive competition among factions and groups in a transitional country. In the best cases, elections help to channel societal conflicts through peaceful political institutions, and in so doing they replace the breaking of heads with the counting of heads. We saw in the case studies of peacebuilding, however, that democratic elections can also polarize the electorate, exacerbate existing societal conflicts, weaken the prospects for further democratization, and even precipitate large-scale violence. This problem is not limited to Angola, Rwanda, and Bosnia: In the Sudan, elections provided an opportunity for fundamentalist groups, such as the Islamic National Front, to "use the rhetoric of Islamic revival" in order to gain political power, thereby

---

[40] Woodward 1995, pp. 132–134 and 233.   [41] Zimmermann 1996, p. 68.
[42] Mann 2001, p. 83.   [43] Woodward 1995, p. 124.

reinforcing the ethnic, regional, and religious tensions that continue to fuel the country's civil war.[44] In Ethiopia, an attempt by the Tigrean People's Liberation Front to exclude other ethnic parties from participating in the June 1992 elections elicited renewed violence from the excluded parties.[45] In Sri Lanka, voters helped precipitate civil war by turning out in large numbers for radical Sinhala-based parties and Tamil-supported movements.[46] In Papua New Guinea, democratic elections have invariably exacerbated communal tensions and fueled political violence in the country by reinforcing the "tribalization" of electorates.[47] Elections have also served as an "indispensable prelude to civil war" in Nigeria, Uganda, Chad, and Pakistan.[48]

Violence and damaging polarization are by no means the inevitable result of holding elections, even in the most ethnically divided societies. "Ties of blood do not lead ineluctably to rivers of blood," as Donald Horowitz puts it.[49] But elections – including elections conducted in a "free and fair" manner – do have the potential to cause violence and impede democratization. This observation challenges the tendency of many people in government, international organizations, academia, and NGOs to portray elections as inherently helpful in promoting democracy and peace.[50] While it is true that periodic and genuine elections are a necessary precondition for liberal democracy, to place one's faith in the universally beneficial effects of elections is to oversimplify and mischaracterize the complex and sometimes negative relationship between voting and peace. Terry Lynn Karl labels this faith "electoralism," or the belief that "merely holding elections will channel political action into peaceful contests among elites and accord public legitimacy to the winners in these contests."[51] A more realistic view would recognize that elections can be either beneficial or detrimental, and that vote-driven violence is one of the pathologies of liberalization.

Saboteurs and Failed Transitions
Elections can also serve to legitimize the power of politicians who use their new status as freely elected leaders to sabotage their own country's transition to democracy so that they will never again face a democratic challenge.[52] Not only did this predicament mar the outcome of the Cambodian and Liberian peacebuilding operations; it has also occurred in other parts of sub-Saharan Africa and in the former Soviet bloc. In the late 1990s, students of democratization began to note the emergence of a new form of regime

[44] Chiriyankandath 1991, p. 84. The 1986 elections, in particular, strengthened the position of Islamist parties who insist on retaining *sharia,* or Islamic law, which non-Muslims in southern Sudan have been fighting against. See Salih 1991; and Deng 1995.
[45] NDIIA and AAI 1992, p. 4; Ottaway 1994, p. 22; and Ottaway 1995, pp. 238–239.
[46] Snyder 2000, pp. 275–280; and DeVotta 2002.
[47] Strathearn 1993, p. 49; Dinnen 1996; and Standish 1996.
[48] Horowitz 1991, p. 97.   [49] Horowitz 1985, p. 684.   [50] Carothers 2002.
[51] Karl 2000, p. 95.   [52] Walzer 1996.

occupying a "gray zone" between liberal democracy and dictatorship, in which elected leaders maintain a veneer of democracy but in practice use violence and threats of violence to suppress political dissent and opposition, thereby preserving the uncontested power of one-party, or in some cases one-man, regimes.[53]

Mauritania provides an example. In 1991, the military ruler of the West African country, Colonel Ould Taya, announced his plans to hold multiparty elections the following year. In order to reduce his chances of losing, Ould Taya personally drafted a new constitution (arresting and temporarily exiling to remote villages the opposition's major leaders) and manipulated the field of presidential candidates by "flooding the market" with pro-government candidates.[54] After winning the election with 63 percent of the vote, the president reverted to "open repression and judicial machinations" to undermine his opponents.[55] In late 2000, dozens of students and intellectuals accused of a graffiti campaign against the regime were reportedly arrested and tortured, and a major opposition party was banned.[56] Nevertheless, Mauritania continues to exhibit many of the "trappings" of democracy, including a National Assembly and Senate.[57]

Like many countries whose transitions to democracy have been sabotaged, Mauritania illustrates the rise of what one commentator calls "pseudodemocracy"[58] and another "the new authoritarianism,"[59] characterized by authoritarian leaders manipulating the language and symbols of democracy and human rights to conceal the repressive and noncompetitive reality of their regimes. Other countries in this category include Cameroon, Burkina Faso, Equatorial Guinea, Tanzania, Gabon, Kenya, Armenia, Azerbaijan, Georgia, Kyrgystan, and Kazakhstan.[60] In addition, there are numerous, less ambiguous examples of elected leaders subverting their own democracies and reestablishing outright dictatorial rule, including Uzbekistan, Turkmenistan, Belarus, and Togo.

One of the hazards of pseudodemocracy is that populations subject to the doublespeak of democratic rhetoric and repressive rule may become disillusioned with the idea of democracy itself. Where democracy is still "young and fragile," chronic dissatisfaction and alienation can be an obstacle to consolidation.[61] Another danger is the possibility that reversions to authoritarian rule may reinforce historical patterns of conflict in some war-shattered states, as seen in Cambodia and Liberia. More generally, the ability of newly elected leaders to purposely subvert democratic openings highlights the inadequacy of the rushed democratization formula that peacebuilders applied in the 1990s.

---

[53] For example, Diamond 1996; Ihonvbere 1996b; Kaplan 1997; Zakaria 1997 and 2003; Schedler 2002; and Carothers 2002.

[54] N'Diaye 2001, p. 92.   [55] Ibid., p. 94.   [56] Ibid., pp. 88–89.   [57] Ibid.

[58] Diamond 1996.   [59] Kaplan 1997.   [60] Carothers 2002, p. 13.   [61] Diamond 2001.

The Dangers of Economic Liberalization

Economic liberalization is also full of pitfalls. Most developing countries that initiate major marketization programs do so under the auspices of one or both of the Bretton Woods institutions, which offer structural-adjustment loans aimed at creating the conditions for market-driven growth.[62] As noted in Chapter 1, these adjustment programs typically require recipient states to undertake a number of institutional and economic reforms, including the privatization of state-owned enterprises; the reduction or elimination of subsidies and other market-distorting government interventions in the domestic economy; the liberalization of regulatory structures, including barriers to international trade and investment and constraints on the domestic labor market; and reductions in overall government spending, which often involve cuts in public-sector employment.

Since the early 1980s, when the idea of linking international financial assistance to neoliberal adjustment formulas first took hold, scholars have debated the effects of structural-adjustment programs on the recipient states. This debate has focused on two main issues: the influence of these programs on economic growth rates; and the so-called social effects of adjustment, or the impact on poverty levels, distributional inequalities, and vulnerable sectors of recipient country populations. Twenty years after the advent of structural adjustment, the quarrel over both of these issues remains largely unresolved: Neither the IMF nor the World Bank has been able to demonstrate convincingly that structural-adjustment programs promote economic growth,[63] and the precise relationship between these programs and levels of poverty and distributional inequality is still hotly contested.[64]

While structural adjustment may or may not create the conditions for sustainable economic growth in the long term, there is widespread agreement that it usually imposes significant social costs in the short term. Most studies have shown that in addition to adversely affecting some groups within recipient states – including those most dependent on government subsidies and social spending – market-oriented adjustment policies have tended to worsen the overall distribution of wealth, widening the gap between rich and poor.[65] Manuel Pastor and Michael Conroy explain:

Wages tend to fall, both because of rising employment caused by demand contraction and because of real devaluation that raises the costs of imports. Fiscal retrenchment, in the form of increased taxes and reduced government subsidies, tends to have a

---

[62] Milward 2000b.   [63] Milward 2000a; and Easterly 2001.

[64] On the difficulties of measuring the distributional impacts of structural adjustment, see Roemer and Radelet 1991; Thomas 1993; and Faruqee and Husain 1994.

[65] See Cornia, Jolly, and Stewart 1987; Richards and Waterbury 1990, p. 47; Nelson 1994; Walton and Seddon 1994; Benería and Mendoza 1995; Gayi 1995, pp. 79–80; Karl 1995; Morley 1995a and 1995b; Engberg-Pedersen et al. 1996; Nonneman 1996, pp. 3–30; Bird and Helwege 1997; Díaz 1997; Heredia 1997; Peeler 1998, p. 151; and Milanovic 1999.

regressive effect, because the easiest taxes to raise and collect are often sales and value-added taxes, which fall more heavily on lower-income consumers.[66]

In some cases, increased income inequality results directly from large-scale public-sector layoffs, which serve to "hollow out" the middle-income sectors of a transitional society.[67] For these and other reasons, the "neoliberal cure" prescribed by international financial institutions is almost always a painful one.[68]

There is also extensive evidence that the economic dislocations and asymmetrical effects of marketization programs on different groups in transitional societies can spawn political unrest and violence.[69] Examples of countries in which structural-adjustment policies were greeted by violent protests and riots include Brazil, Egypt, Jordan, Madagascar, Mali, Nigeria, Peru, Sudan, Tunisia, Venezuela, and Zambia.[70] Such policies also appear to have exacerbated intercommunal divisions in a number of places, including Tanzania, where the worsening of religious and racial tensions has been linked to these policies.[71] Rapid economic liberalization seemed to have similar effects in some of the peacebuilding host states I have profiled in this book, including Rwanda and Yugoslavia, where internationally mandated austerity measures fostered an atmosphere of economic insecurity that strained intergroup relations in the vital period leading up to a genocide in the former and the violent disintegration of the latter; and which appear to be reproducing conditions that have traditionally spurred conflict in Nicaragua, El Salvador, and Guatemala.

It is worth emphasizing that marketization policies do not inevitably undermine social cohesion, nor do they prove that violence is "an essential and permanent feature of the capitalist economy."[72] But the record of these policies in peacebuilding host states and in other states does suggest that economic liberalization can exacerbate societal tensions and endanger domestic peace in countries undergoing these reforms. Underlying these destabilizing effects is a simple fact: Capitalism, as we have already noted, is inherently competitive. It inevitably creates winners and losers, which can fuel social unrest. As Seymour Martin Lipset puts it, the market system "at best . . . holds out the promise of an unrigged lottery, but as in all such contests, the jackpots go to a minority of players."[73]

Social tensions arising from the marketization process can also imperil concurrent democratization efforts. Many studies find strong associations

---

[66] Pastor and Conroy 1996, p. 159.   [67] Milanovic 1999.   [68] Przeworski 1993, p. 50.
[69] Walton and Seddon 1994.
[70] Haggard and Kaufman 1992, p. 337; Skogly 1993, pp. 751–778; Walton and Seddon 1994; Adekanye 1995, p. 368; Ake 1996, p. 118; Ihonvbere 1996a, pp. 196–197; Jeong 1996, pp. 155–167; Wright 1997, p. 27; and van de Walle 1997, pp. 26–29.
[71] Kaiser 1996; and Ake 1996, p. 118.   [72] This claim is made by Salmi 1993, p. 119.
[73] Lipset 1993, p. 129.

between high levels of income inequality and the disintegration of democratic governments.[74] Market-oriented reforms often exact a particularly
high price from precisely those organized groups – university students, professionals, civil servants, and urban workers – who usually form the core of
pro-democracy movements.[75]

To varying degrees, the problems described in this section can afflict any
country undergoing a transition to market democracy, but before spelling
out the implications of these pathologies for postconflict peacebuilding, two
questions must be addressed: Is there any reason to believe that war-shattered
states are particularly prone to these pathologies? And if so, what can be
done?

The Vulnerability of War-Shattered States

There are three reasons why the process of democratization and marketization may be especially disruptive in countries just emerging from
civil wars. First, war-shattered states begin the liberalization process with
particularly intense societal conflicts already in place. Domestic peace
consequently tends to be more fragile in these states than in other developing countries, and the stimulation of further political and economic contestation correspondingly more dangerous. Second, war-shattered
states typically lack natural "conflict dampeners" that exist elsewhere, including a tradition of nonviolent dispute resolution. Third, countries just
emerging from civil wars often lack effective governmental institutions that
might otherwise help to contain and manage the pathologies of liberalization. (See Figure 9.2.)

Intense Societal Conflicts

States with intense societal conflicts appear to be less well-equipped than
others to withstand the competition-inducing effects of democratization and
marketization. The intensity of societal conflicts can be arrayed along a
spectrum, "depending on how strongly committed the partisans are about
the goals they wish to reach, how hostile they feel toward each other, and how
much they want to harm and injure each other."[76] At one end of the spectrum are low-intensity conflicts[77] involving friendly competition in which
the partisans are not strongly committed to a particular outcome and not
hostile toward their rivals. Access to desirable picnic sites in public parks, for

---

[74] Muller 1988 and 1995; Muller and Seligson 1994; Lakoff 1996, p. 292; and Robinson 1996,
   p. 344.
[75] Sandbrook 1996, p. 69.   [76] Kriegsberg 1973, p. 6.
[77] Not to be confused with low-intensity *armed* conflicts, which necessarily involve the use of
   force.

1. Intense Societal Conflicts

2. Weak Conflict Dampeners

3. Ineffective Political Institutions

FIGURE 9.2. Three Common Problems in War-Torn States

example, may pit one group's interests against another's and even prompt the creation of a regulatory system of permits and fees to govern the allotment of this shared resource. At the other end of the spectrum are higher-intensity conflicts in which partisans are so committed to achieving the desired outcome that they seek the physical destruction of their rivals. As expected, states with intense social conflicts are more prone to internal unrest and violence than are other states.[78]

Few states suffer from more intense societal conflicts than those in which groups have recently been killing each other, and not surprisingly, these states are particularly prone to experiencing further civil violence. "It is an empirical regularity," note Paul Collier and Nicholas Sambanis, "that the risk of war recurrence in postwar societies is higher than the risk of onset of a new war in countries with no prior war history."[79] Accordingly, peacebuilders have tried to inoculate such societies against further violence by promoting political and economic liberalization. But stimulating political and economic contestation in places that *already* suffer from intense societal conflicts can be dangerous, particularly if democratization spurs destructive forms of political mobilization, including "bad civil society," ethnic entrepreneurship, polarization, and violence. States that begin the transition to market democracy with lower levels of intergroup tensions are generally better equipped to withstand the competition-inducing effects of the liberalization process without slipping into violence. Simply put, there seems to be less "room" for political and economic contestation in deeply conflicted societies.

Weak Conflict Dampeners
War-shattered states also tend to lack two key domestic attributes that often serve as countervailing and moderating influences on societal conflict. The first of these is the existence of a tradition, or culture, of peaceful dispute resolution. Societies typically hold different beliefs about the uses of political violence in specific situations, beliefs they acquire through experience.[80] Where violence is viewed as an illegitimate and intolerable form of political

[78] Leatherman, DeMars, Gaffney, and Väyrynen 1999, chap. 4.
[79] Collier and Sambanis 2002, p. 5.
[80] Gurr 1970, p. 155. See also Ross 1993, p. 2; and Kriegsberg 1998, p. 29.

expression, societal conflicts are less likely to escalate into open violence. Karl Deustch calls this a "security community" – one in which people have a "dependable expectation" that social problems will be addressed "without resort to large-scale physical force."[81] Others have talked about the tradition of "civility" – or the willingness to view political opponents as fellow citizens worthy of respect – as an impediment to communal violence.[82] These arguments have a clear basis in social psychology: Viewing one's adversaries as members of a morally inferior "outgroup" has been shown to be a "precondition for harmdoing."[83]

It follows that countries characterized by high levels of "civility" and by taboos against the use of violence in the resolution of political disputes should be partially insulated from the disruptive effects of liberalization – because, all other things being equal, social conflicts are less likely to escalate into open violence. As Larry Diamond, Juan Linz, and Seymour Martin Lipset write:

> If political freedom and competition are not to descend into extremism, polarization, and violence, there must be mechanisms to contain conflict within certain behavioral boundaries. One of the most important factors in this regard is a country's political culture; that is, the beliefs and values concerning politics that prevail within both the elite and the mass.[84]

War-shattered states tend to be particularly lacking in cultural constraints on violent behavior that might otherwise help to contain democratic and capitalist competition within peaceful bounds. While nothing precludes the construction or reconstruction of "civility," this process takes time, and during the *immediate* postconflict period, formerly warring parties typically still regard each other with distrust, detestation, and fear.[85] Further, the experience of intercommunal killing tends to destroy any existing taboos on the use of violence in politics.[86] For these reasons, war-shattered states tend to have particularly weak cultural conflict dampeners, which might otherwise help to insulate them from the disruptive effects of liberalization.

In addition to cultural attitudes, the "cleavage structure" of a society (or the number and depth of divisions among the various communities that comprise the state) might also serve to dampen or intensify societal conflicts. A country with "cross-cutting" cleavages is one in which political, ideological, ethnic, racial, religious, or linguistic divisions overlap one another, such

---

[81] Deutsch et al. 1957, p. 5. As Deutsch notes, the creation of a security community requires that its members learn "habits" of peaceful conflict resolution (p. 37). Nonviolence, in other words, can be a learned or cultural attribute of a society. Deutsch applied these concepts to relations across borders, but they are relevant to conditions within warring states as well.

[82] For example, Shils 1991, pp. 12–13; and Bryant 1993, p. 399.

[83] See, for example, Staub 1989, pp. 48–49 and 60–62.

[84] Diamond, Linz, and Lipset 1990, p. 16. See also Lipset 1994, p. 3.   [85] Maynard 1997.

[86] Lumsden 1997.

that individuals on opposite sides of one divisive issue are often allies on another issue. By contrast, when the principal subgroup divisions reinforce one another very closely, the society can be described as having a "cumulative" cleavage structure. Individuals in such a society tend to be divided into clearly separated communities, in contrast to the overlapping group memberships that characterize countries with cross-cutting cleavages.

An increase in the level of competition and contestation tends to follow existing lines of social division, thus reinforcing the existing structure of cross-cutting or cumulative cleavages.[87] Consider the example of India and Sri Lanka. Although the cleavages in Indian society are often described solely in terms of the schism between Hindus and Muslims, this depiction is in fact inaccurate: Many other divisions including class and regional affiliations actually transcend the Hindu–Muslim rift, and these cross-cutting cleavages appear to have discouraged most Indian politicians from seeking to build electoral support by mobilizing the population along religious lines. Even the Hindu-nationalist Bharatiya Janata Party (BJP), which became the leading partner in a coalition government in 1998, was able to attract national support only by putting "its ideology on the shelf"[88] and by promoting conciliatory policies aimed at securing votes in the country's South and East, "where the Hindu-Muslim rivalry is of limited appeal."[89] Thus, while religious violence continues to be a problem in India, the cross-cutting character of the country's social conflicts appears to diminish the political payoffs to ethnic entrepreneurs.

In Sri Lanka, on the other hand, prevailing linguistic, regional, religious, ethnic, and class cleavages are mutually reinforcing and have "cumulatively" divided the country's Sinhalese and Tamil communities. As a result, the process of political liberalization in Sri Lanka has fostered *further* competition along the Sinhalese–Tamil lines as voters democratically cast their votes for ethnic parties "intent on conflict."[90] Thus, while India's cross-cutting cleavages seem to have limited the prospects for political mobilization along exclusionist ethnic lines, democratization efforts in Sri Lanka, where cleavages are more cumulative, appear to have deepened and perpetuated that country's seemingly intractable ethnic violence.

Some writers have gone so far as to argue that democracy "is simply not viable in an environment of intense ethnic preferences."[91] Yet it is worth noting that democratic political institutions have survived, albeit tenuously, in conditions of intense ethnic loyalties (Malaysia, Belgium) and even in the midst of ethnic violence (India, Philippines).[92] Liberalization does not

---

[87] Leatherman, DeMars, Gaffney, and Väyrynen 1999, pp. 59–60.
[88] Raman 2000.   [89] Schaffer and Saigal-Arora 1999, p. 146.
[90] Austin 1994, p. 3   [91] Rabushka and Shepsle 1972, p. 86.
[92] As Charles Beitz (1981) points out, the academic literature on the "preconditions for democracy" has identified a wide range of contextual factors that increase or diminish the prospects

inevitably spawn violence, nor is democratization doomed to failure even in the most deeply divided societies.

A more plausible argument is offered by Harvey Glickman, who contends that ethnic conflict can readily coexist with "institutions of democratic government if [the ethnic conflict] finds expression as a group interest *among other interests.*"[93] His point is that the existence of cross-cutting cleavages can help to offset even deeply rooted intercommunal divisions and thereby facilitate peaceful democratization. Although Glickman is more optimistic than some others about the possibility of successful liberalization in deeply divided societies, he acknowledges that this process tends to be more difficult and dangerous in countries with cumulative social cleavages. All else being equal, we should expect countries with cumulative cleavage structures to be more susceptible to the pathologies of liberalization than are countries with cross-cutting cleavage structures.

The problem is that war-shattered states normally suffer from deep and cumulative social cleavages.[94] As Chaim Kaufmann and others have shown, large-scale violence almost always serves to "harden" narrow and exclusive social identities.[95] When intercommunal killing starts, social groupings and identities that transcend the boundaries of the warring communities tend to become delegitimized; the possibility of multiple-group memberships diminishes, as individuals are compelled by social pressures or overt threats to identify themselves exclusively with one camp. I shall argue in Chapter 10 that Kaufmann exaggerates the rigidity and permanence of the resulting social cleavages, and that wartime communal divisions may, over the long term, be transcended and eroded through the growth of new overlapping associations. But in the period immediately following the termination of hostilities, when peacebuilding operations are launched, war-shattered states tend to

---

for the survival of democracy, but none that makes democracy *impossible.* Lipset (1994, p. 17) makes a similar observation.

[93] Glickman 1995, p. 3 (emphasis added).

[94] Although not all civil wars take place along *ethnic* lines, the experience of fighting a civil conflict inevitably sharpens the boundary between warring communities within a state. These communities may be defined primarily by ascriptive characteristics, such as ethnicity (as in Rwanda), religion (as in the former Yugoslavia), race (as in Namibia), or tribe (as in Liberia and Angola), or they may be based mainly in regional rivalries, socioeconomic class, or ideology (as in Central America, Cambodia, and Mozambique). Many observers argue that "identity conflicts," or those rooted in ascriptive differences, are generally more difficult to resolve than "nonidentity conflicts," because ethnicity, race, religion, and tribe are more resilient filaments of group attachment than are ideology, class, or residence. Indeed, among the eleven peacebuilding case studies we examined in the previous chapters, those countries in which warring groups defined themselves primarily by ascriptive characteristics tended to also be the *least* successful in making the transition from war to stable and lasting peace. But more generally, whether a particular civil war is identity based or not, countries just emerging from internal conflicts tend to be deeply polarized.

[95] Kaufmann 1996b, p. 153.

be deeply polarized. Put differently, countries just emerging from civil strife typically lack the network of cross-cutting cleavages that might otherwise help to moderate the disruptive effects of postconflict liberalization.

Ineffective Political Institutions

Finally, war-shattered states tend to lack effective political institutions – that is, the formal apparatus of the state: constitutions, executives, legislatures, bureaucracies, courts, and the like. States with "ineffective" or "weak" political institutions are commonly defined as those that lack the capability to implement policies, or to process societal demands into authoritative decisions, or to maintain the rule of law.[96] Ineffective institutions can lead to a "security dilemma" in which societal groups cannot rely on the state to defend them against their enemies and consequently have an incentive to mobilize for war in self-defense. One group's preparation for war generates a corresponding fear among its rivals, who respond by enhancing their own military capacities. The result can be a spiral to ethnic war.[97]

Functioning political institutions are required not only to overcome the "security dilemma" but also to reconcile competing societal demands. If institutions are incapable of processing societal "inputs" into authoritative "outputs," individuals and groups will likely seek to pursue their interests through more direct means – that is, extrainstitutionally.[98] The ability of such institutions to respond to conflicting demands is especially important in times of rapid change, such as during periods of rapid liberalization. Students of international development have found that the marketization process is more likely to be completed in countries whose governmental institutions have the capacity to "identify problems, formulate policies to respond to them, implement activities in pursuit of policy goals, and sustain these activities over time."[99] Failed efforts at economic reform, according to this line of argument, have stemmed in part from an absence of technical expertise and administrative efficiency. Thus, an effective bureaucracy may be necessary to implement the policy changes associated with economic reform and to uphold the system of rules that market economies require in order to function smoothly – including the enforcement of contracts and the mechanisms for resolving disputes and regulating monopolies.[100]

Another group of scholars have pointed out that successful *democratization* also depends upon the existence of "a functioning state" with a "useable bureaucracy," and that nascent democracies would be less likely to survive if

---

[96] On strong versus weak states, see Jackson and Rosberg 1982; and Evans, Rueschemeyer, and Skocpol 1985.

[97] Byman and Van Evera 1998, pp. 37–38; and Snyder and Jervis 1999.   [98] Easton 1965.

[99] Hilderbrand and Grindle 1997, p. 31. See also World Bank 1994 and 1997; Brautigam 1996.

[100] Kochanowicz 1994.

newly elected leaders lacked the institutional apparatus necessary to exercise a "monopoly on the legitimate use of force," to "command, to regulate, and to extract tax revenues," and to "coordinate the relations among contending social and economic interests."[101] Although these writers acknowledge that excessive governmental power can itself endanger democracy, they nevertheless contend that successful transitions to democracy demand some minimal level of institutional effectiveness in order to implement and sustain the reforms themselves.

War-shattered states undergoing simultaneous democratization and marketization tend to lack effective political institutions; indeed, some emerge from civil conflicts with no functioning political institutions at all. Intercommunal violence is the antithesis of "normal" institutionalized politics, as the warring parties pursue their interests not through rule-governed procedures involving negotiation and compromise but by seeking to physically destroy their opponents. As a result, prewar political institutions rarely survive these conflicts intact, and where institutions do survive – as in the case of the dos Santos regime in Angola – they tend to be little more than an appendage of a combatant group, staffed with factional loyalists who are dedicated to prosecuting the war rather than mediating societal differences through institutionalized politics, and are consequently viewed as illegitimate by their rivals.[102]

In either case – where there are effectively no functioning political institutions in a war-shattered state or where remnant institutions have been co-opted by one of the parties to the former conflict – international peacebuilders have attempted to rebuild institutional capacity by promoting multiparty democracy. In doing so, however, they have encountered a dilemma: Some of the techniques to promote democracy have, as we have seen, stimulated increased societal competition *at the same time* that new institutions are being established. In other words, without the presence of effective political institutions, war-shattered states may be faced with the destabilizing effects of liberalization before they have developed the institutional capacity to manage these instabilities.

Samuel Huntington made a similar observation in *Political Order in Changing Societies,* first published in 1968: Violence and instability frequently occurred in developing countries due to the effects of "rapid social change and rapid mobilization of new groups coupled with the slow development of

---

[101] Diamond, Linz, and Lipset 1990, p. 23; Haggard and Kaufman 1995, p. 335; and Linz and Stepan 1996, pp. 19–20.

[102] Legitimacy, according to Juan Linz (1978, p. 16), is "the belief that in spite of shortcomings and failures, the existing political institutions are better than any others that might be established, and that they therefore can command obedience." The perceived legitimacy of a political institution tends to increase compliance with the institution's outputs, and thereby enhances the institution's effectiveness. See Lipset 1981, p. 64; and Linz 1988, p. 65.

political institutions."[103] Huntington was referring to urbanization, industrialization, and increased levels of literacy and education, but his argument could be applied more generally to the competition-inducing effects of democratization and marketization in war-shattered states, which also tend to lack effective political institutions.[104] I shall revisit Huntington's thesis in the next chapter, but for now, suffice it to say that countries just emerging from civil wars typically lack the institutional capacity to manage social conflicts and maintain domestic order during the process of democratization and marketization.

To summarize, there are good reasons to believe that war-shattered states are particularly prone to destabilizing pathologies that sometimes arise during transitions to liberal market democracy. In addition to suffering from very intense societal conflicts, these states tend to possess neither a culture of peaceful dispute resolution nor cross-cutting social cleavages, and they typically emerge from civil wars with weak or nonexistent political institutions. Given these conditions, why should we expect the process of political and economic liberalization, which encourages societal competition, to have a pacifying effect on war-shattered states? If anything, we should expect the opposite.

The Faulty Assumptions of Wilsonianism

Peacebuilders in the 1990s apparently failed to anticipate the destabilizing potential of democratization and marketization in countries that had just emerged from civil wars, and consequently failed to take preemptive action specifically designed to avert the pathologies of liberalization. The standard peacebuilding formula involved holding postconflict elections and launching a full range of market-oriented economic reforms, followed by a declaration of peacebuilding "success" and the termination of the operation usually within two or three years of its creation.[105] As we have seen, not only did this formula fail to produce stable and lasting peace in most of the countries that hosted missions, but it was also based on an overly optimistic view of the

---

[103] Huntington 1968, p. 4.

[104] In recent years, a number of scholars have pursued this line of reasoning: In addition to Sheri Berman's work on Weimar Germany (see Berman 1997), Richard Rose and Don Chull Shin (2001) have attributed the cause of stalled democratization efforts in Russia, the Czech Republic, and Korea to the fact that these countries held elections before the "institutions of the modern state" were fully secured. This argument also reappears under a slightly different guise in writings claiming that countries with higher levels of "state capacity" are better equipped to manage the transition to democracy and capitalism than are countries with ineffective institutions (see n. 96).

[105] The principal exception is the Bosnia mission, which continued to operate at the time of this writing, six years after its deployment. For further discussion of this mission, see the next chapter.

pacifying effects of liberalization in war-shattered states and on insufficient attention to the pathologies of this process.

It is interesting to note that international peacebuilders seemed to reproduce the flawed logic of "modernization theory," which dominated the thinking of American policymakers and scholars about international aid policies during the 1950s and 1960s, and which optimistically but incorrectly predicted that economic growth in developing countries would naturally culminate in liberal capitalist economies and stable polities resembling Western democracies.[106] Writing in 1973, Robert Packenham critiqued modernization theory's erroneous premise that "all good things go together," referring to the widespread but false expectation that the transition to market democracy, once initiated, would be largely self-reinforcing and unproblematic.[107] The same critique can be applied to the practice of peacebuilding in the 1990s: The liberalization process can, it seems, exacerbate rather than moderate conflicts in countries just emerging from civil wars.

However, it would be unfair to hold the peacebuilding agencies solely responsible for the failure to anticipate, and forestall, these destabilizing effects. The ideas that informed peacebuilding in the 1990s were widely shared within academic and policymaking circles at the end of the Cold War: namely, the notion that liberal market democracy offered a general recipe for peace, both within, and between, states. The weaknesses of peacebuilding described here reflected problems in the underlying *theory* of peacebuilding: the liberal peace thesis itself.

In Chapter 1, I traced the development of this thesis from the eighteenth century to the present, noting the resurgent interest in the ideas of these philosophers and other thinkers during the latter part of the twentieth century. I also argued that recent scholarship on the liberal peace differed from the work of the classical liberals in at least one important respect: Rather than theorizing about the conditions necessary to lift societies out of a "state of nature" (a subject typical of classical liberalism), contemporary students of the liberal peace have tended to take the existence of functioning states as a given, allowing them to focus on the question of whether certain governmental regime types (democratic, authoritarian, etc.) or economic systems (market-oriented, state-directed, mixed, etc.) tend to be more peaceful than others. Because the recent scholarship has largely ignored the problem of *constituting* governments, little guidance has been provided to those concerned with building stable market democracies virtually from scratch.

By contrast, earlier versions of the liberal peace thesis tackled this problem directly. Classical liberals from John Locke to James Madison argued that limitations on governmental power, and respect for individual liberties,

---

[106] For an overview of modernization theory, see So 1990, pp. 17–87.
[107] Packenham 1973.

were necessary but not sufficient conditions for the establishment of durably peaceful and just societies. The other necessary condition was *effective* government, or state institutions capable of upholding the rule of law and of protecting society against external and internal threats. The alternative, argued Locke, was the "state of nature" – a world "full of fears and continual dangers" due to the lack of central authority.[108] In this respect, most classical liberals shared Thomas Hobbes's conviction that domestic peace could not be achieved, or maintained, in the absence of effective government. They sought to tame Hobbes's absolutist sovereign – to impose constitutional constraints on the exercise of power by a central authority – but they never dispensed with the Leviathan. On the contrary, reconciling the dual (and often conflicting) imperatives of limited and effective government became a leitmotiv in liberal political thought.

The early liberals' dual emphasis on justice and domestic order also reflected the times in which they wrote. In the eighteenth century, European nations were still consolidating their power, and the defining problem of the early modern state – how to establish effective national authority over a bounded territory – was a recurring theme in political philosophy, as was the fear of civil violence. As the coercive powers of the state increased, attention shifted to the dangers posed by arbitrary and tyrannical rule. But even the most libertarian of the classical liberals (such as Adam Smith) continued to acknowledge that the attainment of domestic peace and justice presupposed the existence of a functioning (and constitutionally limited) central authority, or what Hobbes called "a Common Power, as may be able to defend them from the invasion of Forraigners, and the injuries of one another."[109] The modern state was still new in the eighteenth century. Commentators could not take it, or its security-providing function, for granted.

The late-twentieth-century revival of the liberal peace thesis – and the related enthusiasm in scholarly and policymaking circles for market democracy as a remedy for civil violence and other social ills – also reflects the historical circumstances in which we live. The preoccupations of political thinkers in well-established Western democracies have moved beyond the problems of constituting effective states out of an anarchical "state of nature," perhaps because they inhabit states in which the Hobbesian dilemma of establishing domestic peace through a common authority has been largely resolved. Some contemporary theorists of American politics in particular have discounted the relevance of the state itself, overlooking the fact that democratic politics take place within "a framework of controls and institutions" that enforces rules, structures political and economic competition, and translates societal demands into public policy.[110] Given this context, it is not surprising that modern liberal peace scholars have tended to ignore – or set

---

[108] Locke 1963 [1698], book II, para. 123, p. 395.
[109] Hobbes 1968 [1651], part II, chap. 17, p. 406.   [110] Lowi 1969.

aside as "unproblematic" – the question of how market democracies are to be constituted from scratch, including the effects of political and economic liberalization in countries that lack a functioning central authority. These scholars have focused on the empirical relationship between *limited* government and peace, ignoring the antecedent requirement for limited government: namely, *effective* government. The relatively few studies that have explored the relationship between regime change and peace have typically assumed that countries undergoing transitions to market democracy already possess functioning states.

For peacebuilders, the relevant question is not whether well-established market democracies are more peaceful than other states, but rather, what can be done to help consolidate peace in countries that effectively lack governments and are prone to civil violence.

An appropriate starting point for theorizing about peacebuilding might be closer to the "state of nature" of classical liberalism. The early liberals recognized that peace and freedom presupposed a working system of controls and rules to structure societal competition and contain it within peaceful bounds, and they acknowledged that these rules needed to be upheld, in extremis, by the coercive powers of the state. Their understanding of the need for effective authority makes the earlier versions of the liberal peace thesis particularly relevant to the contemporary problem of postconflict peacebuilding. The recognition that the Hobbesian "state of nature" is often typical of countries just emerging from civil wars, that the Wilsonian solution to internal violence pays inadequate attention to this dilemma, and that in spite of its successes and good intentions, liberalization can generate destabilizing side effects that work against the consolidation of peace would offer a stronger intellectual basis for effective peacebuilding practice.

IO

Toward More Effective Peacebuilding

Institutionalization Before Liberalization

Might another approach to peacebuilding be better suited to creating stable and lasting peace in war-shattered states? I shall begin by considering two sweeping alternatives to Wilsonianism. The first is to abandon liberalization as a core element of peacebuilding in favor of establishing authoritarian regimes with international military and financial backing. The other is the strategy of partition, or the physical separation of warring communities and perhaps the creation of new states. I conclude that neither of these strategies offers a sound basis for peacebuilding, although there are limited circumstances in which they might be warranted.

Second, I shall propose a more feasible and prudent approach to peacebuilding: a modified form of Wilsonianism. Peacebuilders should continue to seek to transform war-shattered states into liberal market democracies, but with a different technique – by constructing the foundations of effective political and economic institutions *before* the introduction of electoral democracy and market-oriented adjustment policies, a strategy that I call Institutionalization Before Liberalization (IBL). This approach rests, I believe, on a more realistic understanding than that which has guided the practice of peacebuilding to date. Rather than assuming that liberalization will foster peace in countries just emerging from civil wars, we should start from the assumption that liberalization is an inherently tumultuous and conflict-inducing process that is capable of undermining a fragile peace. The chapter concludes by considering three possible criticisms of the IBL strategy.

Alternatives to Wilsonianism

Authoritarian solutions for war-shattered states should not be rejected out of hand. Even the most stalwart defenders of liberalization might support the establishment of an authoritarian regime if the alternative were more abhorrent – a genocide, for example. Over the years, many students of development have argued that democracy is an unaffordable luxury for developing countries in which the need for effective government outweighs the need for accountable government.[1] Within the context of peacebuilding, the international community could effectively choose a local "champion" – an individual or a party – to rule over the war-shattered state with international financial, or even military, support. Indeed, this was the strategy that both the Soviet Union and the United States often pursued during the Cold War in order to maintain friendly regimes in power.

But promoting authoritarianism would be a problematic peacebuilding strategy. It offers little hope of establishing a "self-sustaining" peace in war-torn countries because it would rely on the permanent, forcible suppression of political contestation, rather than on the development of mechanisms that might ultimately be capable of resolving conflicts of interest through conciliation and negotiation. The end of the Cold War demonstrated that many authoritarian regimes that were previously supported by the superpowers were more fragile than they had appeared. Without massive and continuing military and financial aid from the international community, local "strongmen" would generally have difficulty maintaining domestic order in deeply divided societies. A more sensible solution – and one that is more faithful to the goal of establishing a self-sustaining peace in the long run – would involve the creation of mechanisms that can resolve competing societal demands in a manner that is perceived by the local parties themselves as fair and consistent.

A related problem with the authoritarian option is that it would likely inhibit the growth of cross-factional social and political groupings in the postconflict period. If, as I have suggested, the cleavage structure of a society affects its capacity to survive periods of increased conflict without descending into large-scale violence, then peacebuilding strategies should be consciously designed to nurture the growth of cross-cutting social cleavages within war-shattered states. The establishment of authoritarian government, however, would virtually ensure that cross-factional social groups that do emerge in the aftermath of civil war would be unable to play a role in the government of the war-shattered states, since those in power would likely have a vested interest in preventing the formation of rival political groupings who might challenge their authority.

Finally, local parties are unlikely to embrace peace settlements that involve what amounts to the creation of a permanent dictatorship to rule over them. Although the issues and grievances that drive civil conflicts vary widely, belligerents rarely agree to lay down their arms unless they face imminent defeat or believe that they will be able to successfully pursue their political interests in the postconflict period. Parties to the negotiation of peace settlements need to have a realistic hope that their concerns will be heard and addressed

[1] For example, see Ake 1967, chap. 7; Huntington 1968, chap. 4; Packenham 1973, p. 338; and Ayoob 1995, p. 195.

by any newly created government – that they will be able to participate in the shaping of government policy. The authoritarian option restricts such opportunities.[2]

A second possible approach to peacebuilding is the strategy of partition, or the division of a war-shattered state into territorially discrete, politically independent units, with the resulting entities designated as sovereign countries or autonomous regions within an existing state. Strictly speaking, partition is not an alternative to Wilsonianism, since Wilson himself advocated the redrawing of international borders after World War I along the lines of nationalities. Nor does it preclude promoting political and economic liberalization within the resulting states or autonomous regions. Nevertheless, embracing partition as a key strategy of postconflict peacebuilding would represent a significant departure from the standard operating procedures that have guided the conduct of peacebuilding to date. With the partial exception of the Bosnia operation, which recognized two distinct, ethnically based political units within Bosnia, all of the peacebuilding missions conducted since 1989 have eschewed the redrawing of political boundaries or the physical separation of populations, and have sought instead to promote the peaceful coexistence of formerly warring parties within existing states.

Those who promote partition as a peacebuilding strategy contend that "separation breeds peace," particularly in the aftermath of ethnically based civil wars.[3] According to a leading proponent of partition, Chaim Kaufmann, intercommunal fighting tends to "harden ethnic identities to the point that cross-ethnic political appeals are unlikely to be made and even less likely to be heard."[4] Consequently, the reconciliation of these groups under a single government is very difficult, if not impossible. As Kaufmann writes, "intermingled population settlement patterns create real security dilemmas that intensify violence, motivate ethnic 'cleansing,' and prevent de-escalation unless the groups are separated."[5] Stable settlements are possible "only

---

[2] Alternatively, former belligerents could agree to share dictatorial powers themselves, thereby ensuring a central place in government, but such an arrangement would, in most cases, be a recipe for deadlock or further civil conflict – unless there were mechanisms to resolve disputes among the ruling parties themselves.

[3] Mearsheimer and Van Evera 1999. See also Kaufmann 1996a, 1996b, and 1998; Mearsheimer and Van Evera 1996; and Mearsheimer 1997.

[4] Kaufmann 1996b, p. 137.

[5] Ibid. This argument builds on Barry Posen's (1993) argument that situations of state collapse in domestic politics represent the anarchical international order, and that the concept of the "security dilemma" in international politics can also be applied to the relationship among ethnic groups in states that lack effective central governments. The security dilemma emphasizes that one party's efforts to increase its own security by improving its military forces may be perceived as threatening to other states, and thus spark a competitive spiral of mobilization (Herz 1950). Other scholars who have applied the security-dilemma concept to ethnic civil conflict include Walter 1994; Lake and Rothchild 1996; Ganguly 1996; and S. J. Kaufman 1996.

when the opposing groups are demographically separated into defensible enclaves."[6] For these reasons, Kaufmann and others have advocated a more definitive partition strategy for Bosnia, where rival communities are already largely (but not entirely) separated as a result of the war.[7] "Partition is in Bosnia's future and no Western policy can avoid it," argues Robert Pape. "Rather than allow ethnic boundaries to be written in blood after SFOR leaves, the West should help to manage a peaceful partition while it still has troops on the ground."[8]

The partition strategy has intuitive appeal: Why should warring groups be compelled to live together if they would prefer to live apart? Furthermore, political separation might make postconflict democratization and marketization easier, since the resulting polities would generally be less internally divided and societal cleavages less intense, thereby reducing the threat that the liberalization process will rekindle violence.[9] Indeed, we have noted that in Namibia and Croatia, the task of postconflict liberalization seemed to be simplified by the effective departure of a major combatant group from the territory of each state. Perhaps, then, the international community should routinely seek to separate rival communities into discrete political units as a means of promoting stable and lasting peace in war-shattered states.

Closer examination of this option, however, reveals major flaws. There is little firm evidence that violence is less likely to recur in states that are partitioned after civil wars than in states that are not partitioned. Scholars continue to debate this question, but the most comprehensive analysis to date has found little support for the proposition that partition reduces the risk of war recurrence.[10] Although there are circumstances in which promoting partition may be the most sensible course of action for peacebuilders – circumstances that I shall describe in a moment – partition raises serious and ultimately insurmountable problems as a peacebuilding strategy in most postconflict situations.

One difficulty is the role that peacebuilders would be called upon to play in its implementation, particularly when rival communities are not *already* completely separated. In such circumstances, Kaufmann advocates "separation campaigns" in which international intervenors would forcibly transfer civilian populations to create ethnically homogeneous regions. This procedure would involve several steps.[11] First, international forces would

[6] Kaufmann 1996b, p. 137.
[7] In addition to the references in n. 3, see also Pape 1997; and the comments of U.S. Senator Kay Bailey Hutchinson (1997) and *Washington Post* columnist Robert Novak (1997).
[8] Pape 1997, p. 27.
[9] This may explain Kaufmann's (1998, pp. 152–155) finding that the successor states of partitions tend to be no less democratic than their predecessors, and in some cases are considerably more democratic.
[10] Sambanis 2000. For an overview of the debate, see Kumar 2000.
[11] Kaufmann 1996a, pp. 91–92; and Kaufmann 1996b, pp. 164–166.

have to intervene militarily in support of "the weaker side" in the local conflict. Second, they would need to decide upon the geographic boundary line for the partition. Third, the international forces would need to take physical control, through a conventional military operation, of the territory on the side of the boundary line and in the process drive "enemy" forces out of the target region. Fourth, once the territory was occupied, civilians of the enemy ethnic groups who remain behind would be interned, to be exchanged after the war. Finally, intervention forces would withdraw after guaranteeing the separation lines, by international agreement if possible, or by ongoing military assistance if necessary.

Kaufmann should be lauded for carrying through his prescriptions to their logical conclusions, but in doing so he exposes a deep flaw within the partition strategy: namely, the requirement that international intervenors adopt the role of "ethnic cleansers." Kaufmann himself notes that the strategy is "not pretty,"[12] but he fails to spell out its full implications. He assumes, in particular, that "enemy" civilians will be cowed into giving up their homes without a fight.[13] This assumption is dubious: International forces would almost certainly find themselves in situations in which they would be required to use deadly force (or threats of deadly force) in order to remove civilians who adamantly refused to abandon their homes. If civilian resistance to mandatory resettlement is widespread, or if it sparks violent riots, peacebuilders may be called upon to kill large numbers of noncombatants in the name of effecting a partition.[14] So long as international actors remain unwilling to perform such odious tasks, partition strategies will be impractical for warring states in which rival communities are not already separated into homogeneous, or nearly homogeneous, enclaves.[15]

---

[12] Kaufmann 1996a, p. 92.

[13] "At first glance internment of enemy forces may seem to risk inflicting a heavy loss of life, but it need not. While forcible relocation is distasteful for the intervenors and very unpleasant for the internees, given adequate planning, discipline, and resource it need not be very dangerous" (Kaufmann 1996a, p. 95).

[14] Indeed, partitions have historically tended to be quite messy, particularly when the rival groups are geographically intermixed and must therefore be separated. In the violence that accompanied the partition of India, for example, hundreds of thousands of people were killed, with some estimates citing more than a million deaths (Hardgrave 1994, p. 71; and MacFarquhar 1997, p. 26, n. 3). For a recounting of the "sordid history" of partitions, see Kumar 1997. In the particular case of Bosnia, American mediator Richard Holbrooke (1998, p. 363) offered this analysis of the partition option: "Dividing the country along ethnic lines would create massive new refugee flows. Serbs, Croats and Muslims who still lived as minorities in many parts of the country would be forced to flee their homes, and fighting would be certain to break out as the scramble for land and houses erupted again. Thus, contrary to the arguments of the partitionists, the chances of fighting would be increased, not decreased, by partition and the relocation that would follow."

[15] As Sisk (1995, p. 32) writes, "Secession and partition can work only in societies where communal groups are homogeneously concentrated in territories."

The third problem with the partition strategy flows directly from the second: If the international community were to adopt partition as a standard peacebuilding formula, it would almost certainly create incentives for violent nationalists in other states to launch ethnic cleansing campaigns in the hopes of gaining international support for the creation of new, ethnically based political units. Kaufmann assumes that this would not happen, arguing that local actors would be dissuaded from launching such campaigns on the grounds that "secession attempts are very costly,"[16] but he appears to miss the point that international peacebuilding strategies in support of partition would *reduce* the expected costs of a secession attempt and might therefore make it a more attractive option to local actors. This is not to argue that the international community should never support the partition of war-shattered states: In countries where warring communities are already physically separated, such a strategy may be appropriate, particularly if it does not require international agencies to perpetrate or endorse ethnic cleansing. The point, rather, is that even in these rare circumstances, the partition strategy should be used as a last resort because of the "moral hazard" that disaffected groups in other countries will launch their own ethnic cleansing campaigns in order to secure international assistance in carving out their own, ethnically pure states.

More generally, Kaufmann espouses partition because he believes that the alternative is continued fighting and "intercommunal slaughter."[17] This proposition is rooted in yet another dubious assumption: that ethnic identities cannot "soften" in the period following the termination of hostilities. I argued in Chapter 9 that we should expect social cleavages in war-shattered states to be deep and cumulative because of the polarizing effects of civil conflict. On this point, I agree with Kaufmann. However, I disagree with his assessment of how durable these cumulative cleavages will be in the postconflict period. According to Kaufmann, once the genie of ethnic mobilization is out of the bottle, there is no way to put it back in; ethnic identities that are hardened by civil war will remain hard indefinitely.[18] Only a physical partition, or an overpowering and permanent military occupation by an outside power, can prevent such a state from experiencing renewed violence. Yet, if one accepts that ethnic identities are in some measure "socially constructed" rather than innate, fixed, and timeless phenomena, there is at least a possibility that hardened communal identities will soften over time.[19] Kaufmann responds to this argument by claiming that conditions of continuing distrust in states that have experienced intense ethnic violence will tend to reinforce the hardness of these communal identities ad infinitum.

---

[16] Kaufmann 1996b, p. 170.   [17] Kaufmann 1996a, p. 99.   [18] Kaufmann 1996b, p. 153.
[19] On the social construction of ethnic identities, see Brass 1974; Eller and Coughlan 1993; Eriksen 1993; Little 1994; and Nagel 1994.

This seems to be an overly deterministic argument.[20] As I will argue in the next section, peacebuilding policies can be designed in ways that promote the gradual reintegration of rival groups in a war-shattered state, together with a concomitant softening of communal identities.

Rethinking the Wilsonian Approach to Peacebuilding

Neither outright authoritarianism nor routine partition offers a viable alternative to the Wilsonian peacebuilding formula of the 1990s. A more sensible option is to modify only those aspects of Wilsonianism that are problematic, rather than rejecting Wilsonianism in its entirety. To this end, we need to distinguish once again between the ends and means of the Wilsonian approach. The end goal is to consolidate peace in war-shattered states by transforming these states into liberal market democracies. This aim is not, in itself, unsound, for well-established market democracies tend to be peaceful both in their internal affairs and in their relations with other democracies. Furthermore, there are other reasons (aside from peace) to promote the principles and practices of market democracy, since the political and economic freedoms that underpin market democracy have their own intrinsic value as human rights.

The problem with Wilsonianism, rather, lies in the methods that it employs to achieve this goal, and the assumptions upon which these methods are based. It is the process of liberalization, rather than the end point of market democracy, that has generated the destabilizing side effects described in the previous chapters. The challenge for peacebuilders, then, is to devise methods of placing war-shattered states on a long-term path toward market democracy, while avoiding the pathologies of liberalization itself.

How can this be done? Revisiting Samuel Huntington's work on political development offers a useful starting point. Huntington argued in the 1960s that the very process of political and economic development could have dislocating effects on developing states, due primarily to social changes that accompany the modernization process, such as increased levels of urbanization, industrialization, and literacy, all of which serve to disrupt traditional mechanisms of social control.[21] By creating new demands within a society while simultaneously undermining existing sources of political authority, the modernization process produces "political instability and disorder" in

---

[20] For an excellent critique of Kaufmann's "essentialist" view of identity in relation to Bosnia, see Campbell 1998.

[21] Huntington 1968. For a similar argument emphasizing the potentially destabilizing effects of the modernization process, see Deutsch 1961; Pye 1963; Apter 1970; Connor 1972; Packenham 1973; Ake 1974; and Smock and Smock 1975. As Horowitz (1985, p. 99) points out, Deutsch (1953 and 1961) appears to have been the first scholar to suggest that the modernization process itself could engender social conflict.

many developing states and thus derails efforts to transform these states into market democracies.[22] Huntington's solution to this problem was to argue in favor of restricting political participation and political mobilization in the early phases of modernization, if necessary through the establishment of authoritarian military governments in developing societies. Military rule, he claimed, often represents the only viable method of managing the most destabilizing effects of the modernization process, while creating effective political institutions that could, at a later date, be placed under civilian and democratic control.[23]

Huntington's analysis is relevant to peacebuilding in many respects, but his conclusions and recommendations are problematic. Particularly troublesome is his suggestion that military officers should be relied upon to serve as midwives for democracy – a suggestion that he makes on the grounds that military organizations are "cohesive, bureaucratized, and disciplined" and therefore uniquely equipped to govern states undergoing political and economic change.[24] Experience in many parts of the developing world suggests that military rulers are often reluctant to give up their power voluntarily to civilian authorities.[25] In addition, his analysis presupposes the existence of a coherent national military, which rarely exists in countries that are just emerging from civil conflicts. War-shattered states tend to lack even this minimal degree of central authority.

On the other hand, several features of Huntington's analysis (in contrast to his specific recommendations) do relate directly to the problems of post-conflict peacebuilding. His main argument is that "political order depends in part on the relation between the development of political institutions and the mobilization of new social forces."[26] In the absence of political institutions capable of processing societal demands and ensuring compliance with the rule of law, the stimulating of political mobilization can lead to civil strife and unrest. Modern liberals, particularly in the United States, tend to view the task of government building as a process of limiting and dividing power, but Huntington points out that political stability is a precondition for political liberty, and that political stability requires the existence of effective and authoritative political institutions. "Authority has to exist before it can be limited," he writes.[27]

---

[22] Huntington 1968, p. 5. Other commentators placed greater emphasis than Huntington on the psychological sources of social unrest during the modernization process. For example, Apter (1970, p. 159) wrote: "As societies modernize, the normative integration of the previous system begins to weaken," which leads to "less predictability in social action" and "greater uncertainty by individuals both of themselves and of the anticipated responses of others." For a similar view, see Pye 1963, pp. 54–55.

[23] Huntington 1968, chap. 4.   [24] Ibid., p. 239.

[25] Huntington (1968) notes this danger (on pp. 233 and 237) but remains unaccountably optimistic about the prospects for military officers to give way to democratic rule.

[26] Ibid., p. viii.   [27] Ibid., p. 8.

Despite surface appearances to the contrary, this argument is not an illiberal one. Huntington does not reject the importance of constitutional constraints on the exercise of governmental power. Rather, he argues that a functioning liberal democracy must have both limited *and* effective government. His argument thus recapitulates the classical liberal formula for a peaceful (and just) polity: that there be respect for individual freedoms, protected by limitations on the arbitrary exercise of governmental power, and that a central authority exist in order to maintain a basic regulatory framework for political and economic life.

Peacebuilders, in other words, have been insufficiently attuned to the "Hobbesian problem" that the classical liberals addressed and that modern scholars of the liberal peace have largely assumed away. Peacebuilders have sought to transform war shattered states into liberal market democracies by drafting rights-based constitutions, holding multiparty elections, liberalizing the popular media and political activity, and implementing market-oriented economic reforms. But these measures have, in several cases, spurred societal competition before effective governmental structures could be established to regulate this competition.

Yet it is not only the absence of effective governmental institutions that makes war-shattered states vulnerable to the pathologies of liberalization. As noted earlier, these states also tend to lack other domestic characteristics that might otherwise help to moderate the intensity of societal conflicts, including a tradition of peaceful dispute resolution and a cross-cutting cleavage structure. Putting more emphasis on the construction of effective institutions is only one part of the solution; other measures that aim more directly at limiting the intensity of societal conflicts should also be part of the revised peacebuilding strategy. Among other things, this means rejecting the "shock therapy" approach to economic liberalization, which is ill suited to the task of minimizing societal conflict in the immediate postwar period. It also means that the guiding doctrine of peacebuilding should emphasize the gradual and controlled liberalization of political and economic life.

Institutionalization Before Liberalization

The peacebuilding strategy I propose would preserve the Wilsonian goal of transforming war-shattered states into liberal market democracies in the long run, while minimizing the destabilizing effects of the liberalization process in the short run. I call the strategy Institutionalization Before Liberalization (IBL) because the central recommendation is that peacebuilders should concentrate on constructing a framework of effective institutions prior to promoting political and economic competition. What is needed in the immediate postconflict period is not democratic ferment and economic upheaval, but political stability and the establishment of effective administration over the territory. Only when a working governmental authority has

---

1. Wait Until Conditions Are Ripe for Elections

2. Design Electoral Systems That Reward Moderation

3. Promote Good Civil Society

4. Control Hate Speech

5. Adopt Conflict-Reducing Economic Policies

6. The Common Denominator: Rebuild Effective State Institutions

---

FIGURE 10.1. Key Elements of the IBL Peacebuilding Strategy

been reestablished should peacebuilders initiate a series of gradual democratic and market-oriented reforms. Put another way, peacebuilders should delay liberalization and limit political and economic freedoms in the short run, in order to create conditions for a smoother and less hazardous transition to market democracy – and durable peace – in the long run.

The main elements of this strategy include the following: 1) postponing elections until moderate political parties have been created, and mechanisms to ensure compliance with the results of the election have been established; 2) designing electoral rules that reward moderation instead of extremism; 3) encouraging the development of civil-society organizations that cut across lines of societal conflict, and proscribing those that advocate violence; 4) regulating incendiary "hate speech"; 5) promoting economic reforms that moderate rather than exacerbate societal tensions; and 6) developing effective security institutions and a professional, neutral bureaucracy. (See Figure 10.1.) Some of these elements have been implemented in missions launched after 1998, but, as we shall see later, these newer operations have continued to emphasize rapid liberalization at the expense of institutionalization and have consequently suffered from many of the weaknesses that characterized earlier missions.

Wait Until Conditions Are Ripe for Elections

Peacebuilders have sponsored elections in war-shattered states as a means of facilitating the peaceful management of societal conflicts through competition at the ballot box, rather than through combat on the battlefield. But elections do not always foster peaceful forms of competition, nor do they necessarily produce governments committed to resolving disputes through negotiation and compromise – or, for that matter, governments committed to preserving democracy. If the parties that win elections are dedicated to the violent destruction of their rivals, or if they seek to undermine the very democratic institutions that brought them to power, elections may actually work against the goal of establishing a stable liberal democracy. Moreover, if the parties that contest elections attempt to build popular support by appealing to intercommunal fears and hatreds, the election campaign can itself rekindle the very conflicts that peacebuilders seek to mitigate.

Rather than recognizing that elections can sometimes serve as focal points for destructive forms of competition, peacebuilders in operations conducted between 1989 and 1998 tended to portray elections as simply serving the cause of peace. In all eleven cases, preparations for elections began immediately, and they were held (or were about to be held, in the case of Rwanda) within three years of the deployment of the operation. Peacebuilders also typically presented the holding of an election as a signal of "success" and a rationale for the termination of the operation. In some instances, postconflict elections facilitated a peaceful transition of government and an important development in the transition to stable democracy. But in other cases, elections spurred new violence or installed leaders who immediately began to reverse the movement toward democracy. Peacebuilding agencies' seemingly doctrinaire belief in the pacifying effects of elections allowed little room for serious consideration of the potentially damaging consequences of rushed elections.

So the first element of the IBL strategy is to delay the holding of elections until conditions are propitious for a successful vote – a vote that not only is conducted in a free and fair manner but also furthers the development of stable democracy and diminishes the risk of renewed violence. Judging whether such conditions exist requires an assessment of 1) the political parties that are likely to contest the election, and 2) the institutional setting in which the election will take place.

With regard to the parties, the most dangerous circumstances are those in which the principal contenders for election are the very individuals or organizations that recently fought the civil war, particularly if these individuals and groups exploit intercommunal fears and hatreds in order to build electoral support. Although involvement of former belligerents in postconflict elections may be unavoidable because they often remain the most prominent leaders in war-shattered states, peacebuilders can nevertheless use a variety of means to promote greater moderation in the parties contesting elections. By resisting calls for early elections, peacebuilders can allow passions to cool with the passage of time. International agencies can also use inducements and punishments – carrots and sticks – to encourage the rise of new moderate parties and leaders in the period leading up to elections. These inducements may include significant financial support to parties that publicly eschew violence and violent rhetoric and make concerted efforts to gain popular support from voters across communal lines. Punishments may include the banning of parties that preach violence or hatred from participating in elections. Peacebuilders should proceed with elections only when there is evidence that "moderate" parties – or those that seem genuinely committed to resolving disputes through peaceful negotiation and to intercommunal reconciliation – have sufficient popular support (as demonstrated by internationally sponsored opinion surveys) to prevail over "immoderate" parties at the polls.

Although international peacebuilding agencies have assisted in the drafting and oversight of electoral laws in war-shattered states, they have generally been reluctant to become directly involved in regulating the activities of political parties. In only one mission – Bosnia – did international officials prohibit certain individuals from contesting public office: namely, individuals indicted for war crimes. As we shall see, the willingness of peacebuilders (in Bosnia and elsewhere) to regulate participation in postconflict elections has increased since 1998, but only marginally. Holding elections soon after the termination of hostilities is still treated as a top priority that trumps virtually all others, including the question of whether peace can survive the pressures of electoral mobilization, given the character of the political parties that are likely to contest the election. If local parties preach intolerance and hatred toward their rivals, or display little commitment to sustaining democracy once in power, there is little to be gained by proceeding with elections. Instead, peacebuilders should use the period leading up to elections to promote moderation within existing parties, to foster the growth of new democratic and moderate parties, and if necessary, prevent the most intolerant individuals and parties from running for public office.

The second consideration when judging the ripeness of conditions for successful postconflict elections is whether the country's governmental institutions are capable of resolving disputes arising from the election and of enforcing compliance with the election's outcome. Before holding elections, peacebuilders should ensure that a functioning, professional, and neutral judicial mechanism to rule on election-related disputes is already in place. Achieving this objective would typically require training or retraining judges and legal advocates, and creating a working high court or constitutional court to render authoritative judgments. (The existence of an effective constitutional court would also diminish the threat of an unconstitutional usurpation of power by the newly elected government.) The court would also require reliable enforcement mechanisms for upholding the court's decisions – at the very least, a police force that is not beholden to any of the formerly warring groups or to any individuals or parties running for election.

Although peacebuilders have worked toward the reconstruction of a functioning judiciary and police force in many missions, in practice elections have generally taken place prior to the establishment of effective judicial and police institutions. The danger of conducting elections without such institutions was most graphically illustrated in Angola, but problems of resolving election-related disputes also arose, and threatened to escalate into violence, in Cambodia and Mozambique. Moreover, in the absence of effective mechanisms to enforce constitutional norms, the undemocratic maneuverings of newly elected leaders in Liberia and Cambodia went largely unchecked.

To date, peacebuilders have been reluctant to delay elections or to slow the pace of democratization, even in the most adverse circumstances and in spite of mounting evidence that hasty elections can have pathological effects in war-shattered states. Minor scheduling adjustments have occurred in a few cases: Mozambique's first national elections were delayed from October 1993 to October 1994; and Bosnia's first municipal elections were deferred from September 1996 to September 1997 because of "massive registration irregularities."[28] The IBL strategy, by contrast, would permit the postponement of elections for as long as it takes to establish the right institutional and political conditions for a constructive vote that advances, rather than hinders, efforts to consolidate a stable and lasting peace.

Design Electoral Systems That Reward Moderation

If and when the decision is made to proceed with elections, the design of the electoral system itself could help to promote reconciliation among formerly warring parties. "For most leaders, most of the time," writes Donald Horowitz, "there are greater rewards in pursuing ethnic conflict than in pursuing measures to abate it. One of the great challenges of political engineers is to make moderation rewarding and to penalize extremism."[29] Recent studies have shown that certain electoral systems can indeed "encourage moderate, centrist forms of political competition, rather than the polarizing extremes and centrifugal patterns that characterize so many divided societies."[30]

Presidential elections in Nigeria, for example, have previously required presidential aspirants to win not only an absolute majority of national votes but at least 25 percent of votes cast in no fewer than two-thirds of the nineteen states – a requirement that, in practice, encouraged serious candidates to "reach out and conciliate and propitiate the interests of groups other than the ones [that they were] accustomed to appealing to."[31] The Nigerian experiment lasted only from 1979 to 1983. It ultimately failed not because of the presidential election formula, which successfully reduced the ethnic partisanship of presidential candidates, but because the country's national legislature continued to be dominated by ethnic parties, and because vote rigging and other forms of corruption undermined popular support for the regime as a whole.[32]

---

[28] Pomfret 1996.   [29] Horowitz 1990b, p. 452.
[30] Sisk and Reynolds 1998; and Reilly 2001, p. 7 and passim.
[31] Horowitz 1990a, p. 127. See also Esman 1994, pp. 43–44. The Nigerian arrangements bore a close resemblance to a scheme that was proposed, but not implemented, by the Muslim leader Mohamed Ali in India in 1935. According to Ali's plan, Muslim and Hindu electorates in India were to be kept separate, but no candidate would be declared elected unless he had secured at least 40% of the votes cast by his own community and 5% of the votes cast by the other community (Laponce 1957, p. 324).
[32] Nmona 1985, pp. 324–327; and Horowitz 1985, pp. 636–638.

Contrast the Nigerian presidential election formula with the arrangements governing Bosnia's presidency. Both systems were designed to produce politically moderate chief executives, but they sought to achieve this goal in very different ways. In Nigeria, candidates were constitutionally required to gain support from rival communities in order to win election. This requirement created a strong political incentive for aspiring candidates to promote policies that would appeal to moderate voters across lines of social cleavage. The Bosnian constitution adopted at Dayton in 1995, on the other hand, provided for a tripartite presidency, with one representative from each of the three major ethnic communities. The constitution called upon the co-presidents to "adopt all Presidency Decisions ... by consensus," although the legal requirement for measures to pass was only two affirmative votes, not three.[33] In order to prevent two members of the presidency from ganging up on the third, the constitution also permitted each co-president to exercise a veto over specific decisions that were deemed to be "destructive of a vital interest."[34] These arrangements, it was hoped, would encourage the Bosnian presidency to devise policies that balanced the interests of the country's constituent communities.

However, the Bosnian constitution provided few incentives for aspiring presidential candidates to solicit political support in different ethnic groups. Indeed, quite the opposite: The population was divided into separate ethnic electorates, with voters permitted to cast ballots only for the presidential seat that corresponded to their individual ethnic affiliation. This electoral system reinforced the propensity for political mobilization in war-shattered states to follow the existing lines of communal cleavage. With the electorate thus divided, and with no electoral advantages to be gained by campaigning for votes in more than one ethnic community, it is little wonder that the candidates who won the 1996 presidential election gained power precisely because they appealed to ethnic nationalist sentiments within their respective constituencies. The duly elected co-presidents thus came into office with little interest in compromising with the other members of the presidency, since it was on the basis of their credentials, not as conciliators but as defenders of their own group's interests over and above the interests of their ethnic adversaries, that they had each gained power. The result was the virtual paralysis of the presidency as a decision-making institution, and the perpetuation in power of groups that are determined "to prevent their

---

[33] Constitution of Bosnia-Herzegovina, Article V, Section 2(c).

[34] Ibid., Section 2(d). The veto procedure is actually quite involved: Briefly, vetoes must be reconfirmed by a two-thirds vote of those members of the *entity-level* legislature who belong to the same ethnic group as the presidency member who initially employed the veto. If such a vote does not pass within ten days of the matter's being referred to the relevant entity-level legislature, then the veto would not take effect, and the original measure would pass.

separate power structures from being subject to constitutional and demo-cratic control."[35]

The shortcomings of Bosnia's presidential power-sharing formula appear to be shared more generally by "consociational" models of governance. Consociationalism, according to Arend Lijphart, who first coined the term, describes a form of democratic government that has been employed in sev-eral countries with well-defined cumulative cleavages, most notably Austria, Belgium, the Netherlands, and Switzerland.[36] Consociational democracies have four distinguishing characteristics: 1) Government consists of "a grand coalition of the political leaders of all significant segments of the society," meaning that all the major social groupings share power in all the institu-tions of government; 2) representation in these institutions is proportionate to each segment's share of the population as a whole; 3) policymaking is subject to a "concurrent majority rule," requiring joint decisions on matters of common interest to be approved by all major segments in the society; and 4) each segment retains exclusive decision-making authority over mat-ters that are of concern only to that segment.[37] Although Bosnian political institutions do not display all the characteristics of consociationalism, the institution of the presidency rests on many of the same principles, including the notion that government should consist of a "grand coalition" of the ma-jor social groupings in a country, and that each of these groupings should have the power to veto joint decisions (which is the logical corollary of the "concurrent majority rule").

Lijphart promotes consociationalism as "the best type of democracy that can realistically be expected" in deeply divided societies,[38] but the record of Bosnia's multiheaded presidency suggests that consociationalism is ill suited to the domestic conditions of war-shattered states. Both the Bosnian pres-idency and the consociational model presume that government institutions will be comprised of individuals who, in Lijphart's words, "have the ability to transcend cleavages and join in a common effort with the elites of a rival subculture."[39] Yet for reasons I have already described, such individuals are unlikely to achieve electoral victory in the highly polarized environment of a war-shattered state – unless, of course, the electoral rules themselves re-quire candidates to secure a minimum level of support in communities other than their own. Lijphart's consociationalism and the Bosnian presidential formula call for the division of the electorate into separate voting constituen-cies according to communal affiliation, which makes cross-factional voting impracticable. Nor should we expect nationalist political parties in war-shattered states to be willing to form alliances with parties in rival ethnic camps (which, in theory, might be another way of moderating the policies of

---

[35] Cox 2001, p. 8.
[36] The classic work on consociationalism is Lijphart 1977. See also the essays in McRae 1974.
[37] Lijphart 1977, pp. 25–52.   [38] Ibid., p. 48.   [39] Lijphart 1969, p. 216.

these parties in the absence of cross-factional voting). If individual politicians in these circumstances have little to gain and much to lose by appearing to be "soft" on their ethnic adversaries, political parties would presumably also face strong political incentives to maintain a hard line toward rival groups.

The challenge for peacebuilders, therefore, is to devise electoral and constitutional rules that compel serious candidates to secure significant political support across different communal groups. There is no magic formula to achieve this goal – electoral arrangements must be adapted to the circumstances of each state. In Bosnia, for example, an alternative to the Dayton plan might have been a *one*-person presidency with a dual requirement for victory: a plurality of votes cast in the entire country and a given percentage of votes cast in each of the ethnic communities or geographical regions of Bosnia.[40] Like the Nigerian election rules, these requirements would have likely created stronger incentives for candidates to appeal to moderate voters in each ethnic camp, which might have ultimately encouraged the growth of cross-factional political movements. Whatever specific formula is chosen, the broader point is that peacebuilders should deliberately design electoral institutions to elicit moderation and cross-factional compromise from the parties vying for election and from governments seeking reelection.

Promote Good Civil Society

Not all civil-society associations are conducive to peaceful democratic politics, particularly those that espouse violence against members of other groups or that reject the idea of democracy itself.[41] Promoting the development of civil-society associations can therefore have quite different results depending on the nature of the associations created. At one extreme, pluralistic organizations can help to break down social barriers between formerly warring communities and provide grassroots support for political parties that support intergroup accommodation. At the other extreme, chauvinistic organizations can reinforce existing social cleavages, exacerbate tensions, and discourage cross-communal compromise. The challenge for peacebuilders, therefore, is to promote "good" civil society while simultaneously restraining its "bad" variant, particularly during the early phases of a peacebuilding mission when governmental institutions are still being constructed.

---

[40] In addition, using an "alternative vote" system could have helped preclude the possibility of no candidate meeting the minimum requirements for electoral victory. This system – the current method of electing Australia's House of Representatives – requires voters to rank candidates on the ballot in order of preference. If no candidate meets the conditions for election after all the first preferences have been counted, then the last-place candidate is eliminated and all of his or her votes are transferred to the remaining candidates according to second preferences indicated on the ballots, and so on, until a winner emerges with the required levels of support. See Rae 1967, p. 24; and Palley 1978, pp. 16–17.

[41] See the section on Bad Civil Society in Chapter 9.

Peacebuilding agencies have begun to experiment with programs aimed at promoting the development of cross-factional social groups in countries that recently experienced civil conflicts. The Organization for Economic Cooperation and Development, for example, has conducted "culture of peace" programs in El Salvador and Rwanda that are designed to increase grassroots dialogue and cooperation among members of formerly warring communities.[42] Similar initiatives have also been undertaken in Tajikistan and the Philippines.[43] Yet these programs remain largely experimental and peripheral to the activities of the principal peacebuilding agencies.

A stronger commitment to nurturing the development of cross-factional social groupings in war-shattered states should become a central element of a broader strategy aimed at preventing the process of political liberalization from intensifying intercommunal conflict. In particular, peacebuilding agencies should offer greater financial and logistical support to cross-factional associations in different areas of social, economic, and political life, from political lobbying groups to trade unions to private social clubs.[44] Clear criteria should be established for groups seeking international support: For example, groups might be required to have a cross-factional membership, to hold regular meetings, to adopt a set of guiding principles for their organization that includes the goal of enhancing intercommunal cooperation and tolerance, and to revoke the membership of any individual who openly espouses violence against another group.

Peacebuilders must also be prepared to shut down organizations that openly and repeatedly advocate violence against other groups in the society when such behavior poses a threat to the consolidation of peace and democracy. The precedent for such action is postwar Germany, in which the occupying Allied powers sponsored the reconstruction of political parties and civil-society groups on the condition that these groups repudiate nationalism and embrace democracy and tolerance. Organizations that failed to comply with these guidelines were banned. This "denazification" process initially targeted not only organizations but individuals as well: The Allies agreed to remove former Nazi Party members from "public and semi-public office, and from such positions of responsibility in important private undertakings," and to replace them with persons "deemed capable of assisting in developing genuine democratic institutions in Germany."[45] This form of social regulation may seem heavy-handed, but it was also crucial in restoring civility to Germany and in creating conditions for a stable, free, and peaceful democracy in the long term.

---

[42] See UN General Assembly document A/51/395, September 23, 1996, annex, for an overview of OECD activities in this area.

[43] See Slim and Saunders 1996, and Saunders 1999, chap. 7, for descriptions of the program in Tajikistan. On the Philippines, see Garcia 1989.

[44] Prendergast and Plumb 2002.   [45] From the Potsdam Agreement of 1945.

The regulation of extremist groups and individuals – that is, those who preach hatred and violence – is one means of placing limits on the conflict-exacerbating effects of political liberalization, while at the same time fostering the development of civil-society associations that support democracy and cross-factional compromise. In practice, however, peacebuilders have been hesitant to exercise such powers, even when they have explicitly reserved for themselves the right to dismiss officials or to prevent certain individuals from serving in government. In Cambodia, for example, UNTAC had formal powers to "require the reassignment or removal of any personnel" in the Cambodian government[46] but UN officials never actually used this power, despite "numerous cases" of bureaucrats acting illegally in support of one of the Cambodian political parties while undermining the others.[47] The Bosnia operation was the only other mission deployed between 1989 and 1998 in which international personnel had the formal authority to remove local officials who obstructed the peace process – a power that international officials began to use, with great effect, in 1999. In general, peacebuilders could be much more assertive in regulating the conduct of groups and individuals in war-shattered states, focusing on those that promulgate ethnic hatred – just as nationalist and antidemocratic groups and members of the former Nazi regime were proscribed from public life in postwar Germany.

Control Hate Speech

A free press, which provides a forum for debating public issues and criticizing government policies, is vital to a functioning democracy.[48] Encouraging the development of free media should therefore be one of the central goals of peacebuilding, as it has been in many operations. But the liberalization of the media in war-shattered states can also lead to the proliferation of "news" outlets that deliberately seek to incite hatred and violence against particular groups within the society. When these messages find receptive audiences – as they did in Rwanda, for example – new rounds of civil violence, including attacks on innocent civilians, may result. As one observer writes: "A biased or hatemongering media can sabotage almost any other peacebuilding effort."[49]

Peacebuilders should pursue a two-track media policy. The first track involves the development of responsible news outlets and the provision of reliably accurate sources of information to the inhabitants of war-shattered states; the second track involves regulating the activities of news media that incite hatred and violence against particular groups. The UN and other international agencies have actively pursued the first track since the earliest post–Cold War peacebuilding missions were launched.[50] In Cambodia, for example, Radio UNTAC transmitted a mixed format of news and entertainment

---

[46] United Nations 1995, p. 100.   [47] McLean 1994, pp. 55–56.   [48] Lichtberg 1990.
[49] Howard 2001, p. 12.   [50] For an overview of these efforts, see Lehmann 1999.

programming, which became very popular in the country and provided a neutral forum in which the political factions contesting election could communicate their policy positions. At the same time, a panoply of governmental and nongovernmental agencies – from the United Nations Educational, Scientific and Cultural Organization (UNESCO) to the U.S.-based Asia Foundation – have offered technical and financial assistance to local newspapers and radio stations with the goal of promoting "independent, open, and accountable" sources of information to the public, while also seeking to protect responsible journalists from government intimidation.[51] Similarly in Bosnia, funding from the European Union and the Open Society Foundation (among other donors) supported the creation of the Open Broadcasting Network, a group of local television stations that receive international financial and training support in exchange for their compliance with an editorial charter that mandates factual accuracy in reporting and prohibits the use of any "language or representation which incites discrimination, prejudice or hatred."[52]

While peacebuilders have offered extensive assistance to independent local media in war-shattered states, they have been reluctant to pursue the second track, which involves suppressing publications or broadcasting outlets that disseminate maliciously distorted and inflammatory "news" directed against a particular group. This reluctance is understandable: Censorship, even for the purposes of promoting a free and responsible press, sets a troubling precedent that could make it easier for subsequent governments to suppress legitimate political dissent. But when "hate media"[53] incite genocidal violence or rekindles civil conflicts, peacebuilders should not adhere so blindly to the principle of press freedom that they allow greater harm to occur through their inaction.

The argument that jamming incendiary broadcasts is never permissible[54] ignores the role that Radio-Télévision Libres des Milles Collines and other radio stations played in orchestrating the Rwandan genocide of 1994. The UN commander in Rwanda, General Roméo Dallaire, called for the jamming of these broadcasts, but UN headquarters refused,[55] a decision that was applauded by Western anticensorship groups, including the London-based Article 19 organization.[56] The rigid anticensorship position is rooted in the notion that promoting unconditional freedom of expression is the key to countering inflammatory propaganda,[57] but as Jack Snyder and Karen Ballentine point out, "from the French Revolution to Rwanda, sudden liberalizations

[51] For example, see Sharpe 2001.
[52] Open Broadcasting Network's website: http://openbn.hypermart.net, accessed in July 2002.
[53] Reporters Sans Frontières 1995.
[54] Jeffery Heyman, the head of the UNPROFOR Radio Unit, is quoted making this argument in Lehmann 1999, p. 100.
[55] Metzl 1997, p. 15.   [56] Article Nineteen 1995.   [57] Human Rights Watch 1995.

of press freedom have been associated with bloody outbursts of popular nationalism."[58] Given the costs of inaction, peacebuilders would be well advised to shut down newspapers and jam broadcasts that openly incite violence in the fragile circumstances of a war-shattered state.[59] Only once have peacebuilders done so: In 1997, NATO soldiers in Bosnia took over a key transmitter belonging to a Bosnian Serb radio station that had been broadcasting inflammatory propaganda. NATO acted under a provision of the Dayton Accord, which authorized peacebuilders to "suspend or curtail programming that is hostile to the spirit" of the Accord. But all peacebuilding missions should be given both the means and the mandate to block the dissemination of hate propaganda.

One method of regulating hate speech is by establishing enforceable "codes of conduct" for print and broadcast media, along with a licensing system. As we shall see, peacebuilders in Kosovo have adopted this approach with considerable success. Codes of conduct should include a positive commitment to accuracy in reporting the news and prohibitions on the publication of material that incites hatred or violence. International officials should interpret these codes, rule on alleged violations, and impose sanctions, if necessary, within a framework that allows for appeals. In Western democracies, broadcast media are normally regulated and licensed by government agencies, given the need to allocate broadcast frequencies across a limited spectrum. Print media, by contrast, tend to regulate themselves through "press councils" and the like, and both print and broadcast journalists are typically also subject to libel laws. Some Western democracies, such as Germany and Canada, have also criminalized the willful incitement of hatred against particular groups. Thus, neither the licensing of broadcast media nor the existence of rules governing the content of media are unknown in Western democracies. What makes such regulation controversial in the context of peacebuilding is the degree to which foreign officials ought to impose rules on the indigenous media. However, given the absence of domestic institutional structures to manage hate speech in most of these countries, and the potential dangers of allowing hate media to flourish, there is little alternative to doing so.

As in other areas of social, political, and economic life, the rapid and unfettered liberalization of the media in war-shattered states does not necessarily aid in the consolidation of peace or the transition to stable market democracy. Creating institutional structures to manage the potentially pathological effects of media liberalization is a sensible strategy for promoting a free and responsible press. Over time, mechanisms for the self-regulation of the media should largely replace those operated by peacebuilders. Independent press councils, for example, might be created to interpret the codes of conduct and impose sanctions on violators, if necessary. Initially, perhaps,

[58] Snyder and Ballentine 1996, pp. 5–6.   [59] See Metzl 1997 for a similar argument.

peacebuilding agencies should retain a final veto over the operation of these press councils, and ultimately this final veto power should be phased out or transferred to the civilian court system once such a system is established and functioning. At that point, media regulation in peacebuilding host states would more closely resemble the regulatory arrangements that exist in many Western democracies. But the key to this strategy is that it emphasizes institutionalization before liberalization and a managed transition to a free press.

Adopt Conflict-Reducing Economic Policies

In Chapter 9 we examined some of the dangers and pathologies of rapid economic adjustment in war-shattered states. Although "orthodox" structural adjustment programs may create the conditions for sustainable economic growth in the long term, they usually impose significant short-term social costs. The economic reforms typically required by the IMF and World Bank tend not only to lower the living standards of certain groups within states undergoing adjustment but also to worsen the overall distribution of wealth in these states.

Proponents of orthodox structural-adjustment models do not deny the short-term social pains of economic reform, but they argue that temporary dislocation is justified in order to create the conditions for sustainable economic growth in the long term. There are, in fact, excellent reasons to encourage war-shattered states to pursue a market-oriented growth strategy, rather than protecting uncompetitive local industries from domestic or international competition. The second half of the twentieth century demonstrated that centrally planned and state-dominated development strategies – including not only Soviet-style communism but also import substitution strategies pursued in many parts of Latin America and Africa – generally produced lower levels of economic growth than market-oriented development strategies. Although debates continue over the appropriate balance between the market and the state in economic development, there is near-universal agreement today that non-market-oriented economic policies (that is, those that do not give the market the primary role in allocating scarce resources) are too inefficient to generate sustained economic growth. This is not to say that market-oriented economic policies are a sufficient condition for sustained economic growth, but that these policies appear to be a necessary condition.

Nevertheless, there are different methods of promoting market-oriented reform, some of which may be more suited to the needs of postconflict peacebuilding than others. The prevailing model of structural adjustment is a problematic approach to economic reform in war-shattered states, for several reasons. First, as we noted earlier, the economic hardships that rapid adjustment tends to impose on specific population sectors, along with the regressive widening of distributional inequalities, have been generally associated with higher levels of political unrest and violence in states undergoing these reforms. Given the fragile political conditions that exist in most war-shattered states, particularly in the period immediately following the termination of hostilities, it is unwise to pursue a strategy of rapid and immediate adjustment in these states. A better approach would be to delay reforms until political conditions are less fragile, or to stretch the reforms over a longer period in order to temper the disruptive effects of adjustment.[60] Some commentators argue that rapid reform is essential because slow reform "allows the [domestic] opposition to coalesce, often in defense of the disproportionate benefits that it receives from public expenditure."[61] While this may be true, the requirements of successful adjustment must be balanced against the need for political stability in states just emerging from civil wars. As Thomas Callaghy puts it, "economic liberalization without attention to domestic political stability . . . is likely to prevent successful economic and political adjustment."[62] This is particularly important for war-shattered states in which economic deprivation or distributional inequalities have fueled violent conflict in the past.

Second, orthodox structural-adjustment policies make it difficult to provide the inhabitants of war-shattered states with a "peace dividend," or tangible improvements in economic conditions, which could help to reinforce popular support for peace. If peace comes along with material rewards, ordinary citizens may be less willing to heed extremist members of their own community who seek to scuttle the peace. But orthodox adjustment models are based on a different set of priorities: namely, establishing conditions for economic growth in the long term, even at the expense of an initial economic downturn. The IMF and World Bank typically require states undergoing adjustment to implement fiscal austerity policies aimed at establishing budgetary balance, along with reductions in the money supply designed to keep inflation in check. But fiscal retrenchment and monetary contraction tend to suppress economic growth in the short run, in part because they increase the cost of credit and reduce the amount of disposable income in the hands of consumers. As a result, the use of fiscal or monetary policy to stimulate immediate economic growth in the aftermath of a civil conflict becomes difficult under prevailing models of adjustment. Rather than enjoying a peace dividend, the inhabitants of war-shattered states that embrace orthodox adjustment are assessed what amounts to a "peace penalty" in the form of policies that artificially suppress growth in the short term, in

---

[60] Paul Collier and Anke Hoeffler (2002) argue, for example, that special postwar recovery funds should be channeled to war-shattered states for at least a decade, and that placing emphasis on "social policies," including funding for education and health care, as opposed to focusing primarily on macroeconomic reforms, is especially important for preserving peace in countries that have emerged from civil conflict. These arguments are elaborated in Collier et al. 2003.

[61] Graham 1995, p. 144. See also Bhattacharya 1997, p. 1047.

[62] Callaghy 1993, p. 165. See also Boyce 2002, pp. 48–50.

exchange for assurances about the possibility of economic improvement in the long term. By delaying the implementation of these reforms or spreading them out over a longer period, peacebuilders would have greater flexibility to pursue policies that stimulate economic growth in the crucial period immediately following the war's end.[63]

Third, war-shattered states typically lack the institutional capacity to successfully manage market-oriented reforms. One of the most important functions that governments can perform in market systems is to maintain a sound legal framework that is capable of upholding property rights, resolving business disputes impartially, enforcing contracts, protecting consumers from fraud, collecting taxes, and regulating the banking system. At the most fundamental level (as Adam Smith and other classical liberal economists recognized long ago), a successful market economy presupposes the rule of law – that is, an environment in which the "rules of the game" are for the most part predictable, clear, and enforced in a consistent and disinterested manner. Promoting economic liberalization in the absence of a sound legal framework is a recipe for a malfunctioning and inefficient market economy in which the boundaries between business and crime are blurred: for example, the Russian economy in the 1990s.[64]

Partly in response to the problematic marketization of Russia and other former Soviet bloc states, the IMF and World Bank have since the mid-1990s acknowledged the importance of effective governmental and legal institutions to the success of market-oriented adjustment programs.[65] Under the rubric of "good governance," the Bretton Woods institutions (along with major national aid donors) have increasingly made their financial assistance conditional on recipient states implementing institutional reforms, including not only measures to ensure a sound legal framework for the market economy but also improvements in the management of public resources. The IMF in particular has emphasized the importance of reforming public-sector institutions in recipient states in order to increase the efficiency and transparency of their operations and reduce the problems of wastage, corruption, and misallocation of resources. The World Bank has also pointed out that administrative competency facilitates the provision of public services upon which the market economy depends, including education, health care, and physical infrastructure.

War-shattered states, however, represent a special category of underinstitutionalized states. Within the larger class of countries undergoing transitions to capitalism under the guidance of international donor agencies, war-torn territories tend to be particularly lacking in functioning legal systems and governmental institutions. Despite the World Bank and IMF attention to "good governance," these organizations remain overly confident in the

---

[63] Jeffrey Sachs (1994) and Jenny Pearce (1998) have made similar arguments.
[64] Nellis 1999.   [65] IMF 1997; World Bank 1997; James 1998.

ability of markets to organize themselves spontaneously, and have tended to push for economic liberalization in war-shattered states prior to the construction of necessary governmental and legal institutions.[66]

Nowhere is this problem more apparent than in Bosnia, where liberalization programs undertaken in the absence of effective institutions have served, as Michael Pugh puts it, to "reinforc[e] the dominance of clientelistic and mafia political economies."[67] Following the signing of the Dayton Accord in 1995, international donors immediately launched economic reforms that included a far-reaching privatization program aimed at selling off inefficient government-owned enterprises. But in Bosnia's "especially acute institutional vacuum," there was little to prevent the dominant nationalist parties from manipulating the selling of these public enterprises "to themselves or to their allies through shady and non-transparent privatization deals."[68] This process had adverse effects both for the economic and political reconstruction of the country. Economically, it reinforced the underlying corruption and cronyism of the Bosnian economy, which "remains controlled by a political elite at odds with the very reform policies that would lead to greater openness."[69] This elite reportedly misappropriated as much as $1 billion of international assistance during the first four years of peace.[70] Politically, it strengthened the power of the very nationalist groups who are least interested in achieving interethnic reconciliation in Bosnia. While peacebuilding agencies have made some strides in building public-sector institutions to govern the market economy – including the capacity of the central and regional governments in Bosnia to collect revenues, perform audits, and conduct economic forecasts – the fact that these agencies launched a comprehensive economic liberalization program in the underinstitutionalized setting of post-Dayton Bosnia did little to spur economic growth or promote cross-factional reconciliation.[71]

Attempts by the Bretton Woods institutions to moderate the social costs of structural adjustment in war-shattered states have also been inadequate. In response to criticisms that orthodox adjustment models impose disproportionate costs on the poorest and most vulnerable sectors of transitional states, both the IMF and World Bank have made much-vaunted but essentially minor changes in their lending policies. These initiatives included not only the introduction of "poverty assessments" for each recipient state to evaluate the effects of economic reforms on the poor, but also support for "social investment funds" in a number of countries undergoing economic adjustment. Many of these funds mirrored Bolivia's Emergency Social Fund, which was established in 1986 in response to the economic and social turmoil

[66] This critique draws generally on Kolodko 2000.   [67] Pugh 2000a, p. 2.
[68] Donais 2002, pp. 11, 7.   [69] O'Driscoll, Holmes, and O'Grady 2001, p. 121.
[70] Hedges 1999.   [71] Donais 2002, p. 2.

that accompanied structural adjustment reforms in that country, and which disbursed money to local projects that sought to "create temporary employment, build social and economic infrastructure, and provide basic social services to low-income populations."[72] Among the countries that subsequently introduced similar social funds are Brazil, Chad, Chile, Ghana, Honduras, Mexico, Peru, Poland, Senegal, Uganda, Uruguay, and Zambia, as well as El Salvador and Nicaragua.[73]

Some commentators argue that these funds have helped to "dull the pain" of economic adjustment by providing temporary assistance to vulnerable populations,[74] but there is also widespread agreement that they have had little or no discernible impact on overall rates of poverty or distributional inequality.[75] In fact, one of the World Bank's vice presidents, Shavid Burki, acknowledged in 1996 that the Bank's efforts to minimize the ill effects of adjustment, including the social investment funds, had largely failed.[76] With the possible exception of the Chilean program, which was "big enough to reverse the regressive impact of recession and adjustment on the income of the poor,"[77] most social investment funds have lacked the financial backing necessary to make substantial headway against the poverty problem in states undergoing economic adjustment.[78] In the period 1988–1993, for example, the World Bank committed $4 billion for adjustment programs, while programs aimed at moderating the ill effects of adjustment received only $141 million.[79] The government of Denmark concluded in 1995 that social investment funds have been "of little financial significance compared to the overall magnitude of adjustment lending."[80]

It should be noted, however, that this state of affairs reflects the broader priorities of the international financial institutions: Social investment funds do not impel developing country governments to "get the fundamentals right" or to open their economies to market forces, and are therefore viewed as peripheral to the adjustment process. The only long-term solution to poverty and distributional inequality, both the IMF and World Bank argue, is sustained economic growth; and efforts to alleviate poverty in the short run, no matter how well intended, risk diverting resources from the adjustment process and perpetuating inefficiencies.

The Bretton Woods institutions have also been criticized, more specifically, for treating war-shattered states as any other transitional countries, rather than as special cases that require policies specifically designed to

---

[72] Jayarajah, Branson, and Sen 1996, p. 105.
[73] For a description of the various social funds that have been instituted in these states, see Glaessner et al. 1994; Graham 1994 and 1995; Vivian 1995; and IMF 1995.
[74] Morley 1995a, p. 69. See also Glaessner et al. 1994.   [75] See Vivian 1995.
[76] Cited in Caufield 1996, p. 163.   [77] Morley 1995a, pp. 68–69.
[78] Sandbrook 1997, p. 504.   [79] Denmark 1995, p. 56.   [80] Ibid.

moderate, not exacerbate, societal tensions.[81] Both agencies responded in
the late 1990s and early 2000s by devising a new set of lending principles
for postconflict countries and by pledging to disburse emergency funds to
such countries in an expedited manner.[82] The Bank's new goals were to
"jump-start" the economy through investment in key productive sectors;
to support the reconstruction of governmental institutions, the rule of law,
physical infrastructure, and basic social welfare programs; and to facilitate
the demobilization of combatants and the removal of land mines.[83] The
IMF's revised goals were more limited: to help war-shattered states cope with
urgent macroeconomic imbalances and to assist in rebuilding "the administrative and institutional capacity required to put a comprehensive economic
program in place."[84] How these policy statements will ultimately be implemented, and whether they will lead to substantive changes in lending practices for war-shattered states, remain to be seen. But the apparent willingness
of the Bretton Woods institutions to place a high priority on institutional
reconstruction in countries just emerging from civil conflicts is a welcome
development.

Ideally, comprehensive economic liberalization should be delayed while
the governmental and legal frameworks needed to regulate a market economy are being established. Moreover, economic reforms should generally be
implemented in a gradual and phased manner, rather than all at once in the
orthodox "shock therapy" style, which tends to be politically destabilizing.
Schedules for achieving fiscal balance and low rates of inflation should also
be extended in order to reduce pressures on social spending and the funding
of rehabilitation projects during the fragile period immediately following the
termination of hostilities.

Finally, international donors should be more responsive to the fact that
economic reforms that worsen income inequalities can work against the
consolidation of peace in countries with a history of civil violence arising
from distributional grievances. Contrary to the assertions of IMF and World
Bank officials, doing more to promote income equity in such countries need
not involve a trade-off with economic growth: Several recent econometric
studies have concluded that societies with more equitable distributions of
income tend to experience higher levels of economic growth over the long
term.[85] Even if greater emphasis on distributional issues *did* ultimately reduce the rate of economic growth, this trade-off would still be sensible if it
diminished the risk of renewed civil war. Furthermore, as we noted earlier, a
strong relationship exists between the distribution of wealth and the stability
of democratic regimes: Democracies with higher levels of income equality

[81] For example, Boyce 2002.   [82] IMF and World Bank 2001.   [83] World Bank 1998.
[84] IMF and World Bank 2001, pp. 8–9.
[85] For a review of this literature, see Birdsall and Jaspersen 1997.

tend to be more stable than democracies with lower levels of income equality, independent of their level of economic development.[86]

At bottom, managing this problem in the context of peacebuilding requires reordering funding priorities and redirecting some donor resources away from traditional adjustment projects in order to provide much-expanded support to such redistributive programs as the aforementioned safety net funds, along with public education and health-care services, start-up money for "microenterprises" and other job-creation programs in poorer communities, and perhaps even temporary price controls for food staples. Whatever specific devices are selected, they should be part of a more serious effort to moderate the polarizing effects of market-oriented adjustment on the income distribution of war-shattered states, particularly those in which distributional inequities have fueled violent conflict in the past. Attempts to effect such changes in the Guatemala operation represented a step in the right direction but were incomplete, as we have already noted.

The Common Denominator: Rebuild Effective State Institutions

All of the recommendations outlined in this chapter are based on the observation that promoting democratization and marketization in institutionally weak, conflict-prone environments is an unreliable and potentially counterproductive approach to peacebuilding. Democratic politics and capitalist economics are not self-organizing; they depend on public institutions to uphold basic rules, to maintain order, to resolve disputes impartially, and to regulate behavior incompatible with the preservation of market democracy itself. At the most basic level, democracy and capitalism presuppose a functioning state apparatus. I have described several institutional elements that peacebuilders should seek to construct before they launch comprehensive political and economic liberalization programs in countries that are just emerging from civil wars. These elements include a constitutional court to resolve disputes surrounding elections and to uphold the articles of the constitution against challenges; a reliable police force to maintain domestic order and enforce the rulings of the constitutional court and any other court legally constituted under the constitution; a procedure for regulating hate speech in the media; a system for overseeing the conduct of political parties and civil-society organizations; electoral rules specifically designed to reward moderation; a legal framework capable of regulating the market economy; and a redistributive mechanism to protect the welfare of the most vulnerable sectors of the population. The common denominator across all of these recommendations is that institutionalization should precede liberalization to a considerable degree in order to limit the destabilizing effects of the liberalization process itself.

[86] Muller 1988 and 1995. See also Diamond, Linz, and Lipset 1990, p. 19.

The ultimate success of the IBL strategy, however, will depend not only on the willingness of peacebuilders to delay liberalization. The proper sequencing of reforms is only part of the prescription for more effective peacebuilding. Just as importantly, peacebuilding organizations (and the states that support these organizations) need to commit the time and the political and financial resources necessary to restore functioning central governments in war-shattered states, sometimes from scratch. If the peacebuilding record of the 1990s demonstrated anything, it was this: There is no easy, quick, and cheap method of establishing stable and lasting peace in war-shattered states. Rebuilding effective governmental institutions, managing a phased and gradual transition to market democracy, and ensuring that the rule of law is sufficiently strong to defend the new state against inevitable challenges (including challenges posed by the competitive character of democracy and capitalism themselves) require a more interventionist and long-term approach to peacebuilding than that which has been practiced to date. They require international peacebuilders to take on the role of nation builders – to serve as surrogate governing authorities for as long as it takes to implement the liberalizing reforms that the peacebuilders themselves prescribe for war-shattered states.

The direct international administration of war-torn territories is warranted where no functioning governmental institutions exist and have to be created from scratch, and where institutions do exist but have been co-opted and corrupted by one of the political factions that fought the war, such as in Cambodia.[87] International administration is the key to creating a competent, professional, law-abiding bureaucracy. This entails staffing governmental institutions with international personnel, and then gradually replacing these officials with adequately trained and politically nonpartisan locals. Particular attention needs to be paid to the justice and security sectors. In circumstances where local judges are nonexistent, incompetent, corrupt, or lacking independence, courts should be operated by international jurists and lawyers while a new cadre of local judges is being trained. If there is no criminal and civil law in existence, peacebuilders should create suitable legislation and promulgate it. If, at the outset of a mission, serious and widespread violence is occurring in the absence of a working justice system, peacebuilders should be prepared to temporarily impose martial law – as they are permitted to do under international law.[88] The core function of

---

[87] Henry Kamm (1998, p. 252), a longtime observer of Southeast Asia, argues, for example, that Cambodia's state and society are still so dysfunctional that the international community should go back into Cambodia, directly administer the country, and "gradually hand it back to a new generation of Cambodians, who will have matured with respect for their own people and will be ready to take responsibility for them."

[88] Article 4 of the International Covenant on Civil and Political Rights permits certain civil rights to be suspended during a "time of public emergency which threatens the life of the nation and the existence of which is officially proclaimed." See O'Neill 2002, p. 96, n 1.

any state is, as Max Weber put it, the monopoly over the legitimate use of physical force within a particular territory. The first task of peacebuilding is to restore this monopoly as a foundation and precondition for all further institution-building efforts. As the early liberals recognized, a peaceful and limited state presupposes an effective state that can, at a minimum, ensure public security.

Finally, adopting the IBL strategy would require peacebuilding missions to remain in place for a longer period than was typical for operations conducted between 1989 and 1998. Most of these operations lasted from one to three years – the sole exception being the Bosnia mission, which was initially deployed for one year, but whose mandate was subsequently extended when it became obvious that fighting would likely resume if peacebuilders departed. Ideally, no time limits should be placed on peacebuilding missions; they should remain in place until governmental institutions have been constructed and the process of democratization and marketization is well under way. Translating the terms of a democratic settlement into institutional roles and routines is, in the words of Larry Diamond, "gradual, messy, fitful, and slow."[89] The formal U.S. occupation of Germany and Japan after World War II lasted four years and seven years, respectively, during which time the institutional structures of democracy and capitalism were built, but informally, the presence of U.S. troops in these countries continued to exert a stabilizing influence for several decades after the war was over. The challenges of peacebuilding are in some respects even greater: Instead of facing a defeated enemy, peacebuilders must typically deal with formerly warring parties that may still be politically and militarily intact. Most missions should be planned for at least five years, with the expectation that they may last longer. Peacebuilding agencies and their sponsors should not fool themselves into believing that holding hasty elections, particularly in the conflict-prone and underinstitutionalized conditions of most war-shattered states, will create the necessary conditions for self-sustaining peace.

Possible Criticisms of IBL

Having set out the main elements of the IBL strategy, the remainder of this chapter considers a number of critiques that might be leveled against the strategy. In particular, some observers might argue 1) that peacebuilders who follow the IBL approach will become bogged down in endless missions; 2) that direct international administration of war-shattered states will create a "culture of dependency" among local people, who might come to rely on international officials and lose interest in governing themselves; and 3) that

---

[89] Diamond, cited in Decalo 1992, p. 35.

the IBL strategy would be too costly and is therefore impracticable.⁹⁰ I respond to each of these concerns below.

The Endless-Mission Critique

Could the emphasis on institution building and gradual liberalization result in operations that effectively never end? This danger certainly exists. Any postconflict operation runs the risk of prolonged deployment if it encounters problems that impede the fulfillment of its mandate; and when peacebuilding mandates become more complex, the potential obstacles to their realization increase correspondingly. Because IBL calls upon peacebuilders to begin the construction of domestic institutions before launching full-scale political and economic liberalization, the danger of getting bogged down is probably higher for missions that pursue the IBL strategy than it is for "quick and dirty" missions that emphasize rapid liberalization and speedy withdrawal.

There are two responses to this concern. First and most important, the "quick and dirty" approach to peacebuilding is fundamentally flawed, as I have argued. It is less likely to achieve the central goal of peacebuilding – the creation of a stable and lasting peace – than the IBL strategy. Indeed, international agencies in Bosnia discovered this lesson the hard way: They began under the assumption that the mission could be accomplished in one year, but soon realized that their departure would likely result in a resumption of fighting and decided to extend the mission. But in the meantime, they pressed forward with premature elections that reinforced the power of the least conciliatory elements in the society, which ultimately increased the difficulty of establishing an effective Bosnian state. If the operation had started with the goal of reconstructing the country's political and economic institutions and promoting the growth of cross-cutting civil-society organizations *before* holding elections, the task of building a functioning Bosnian state might be further along than it is today – even though, paradoxically, pursuing the IBL strategy would have entailed a more open-ended commitment to peacebuilding in Bosnia than the international community was willing to make at the time. The danger of prolonged deployment is one that must be faced and accepted if the goal of peacebuilding is to foster a stable and lasting peace, since the alternative – starting a mission with the intention of completing it within a year or two – creates incentives to rush liberalization and to terminate peacebuilding prematurely.

Second, the IBL strategy does not preclude the judicious use of timetables to maintain the forward momentum of a peacebuilding mission. Targets

---

⁹⁰ Two additional concerns are addressed in Chapter 11: that IBL presupposes an unrealistically high degree of coordination among peacebuilding agencies, and that it requires more "political will" than currently exists within the international community to implement the strategy.

for political and economic reforms should be established (subject to revision, if necessary), and international officials should report regularly on their progress, explaining failures to meet these targets. Yet such schedules should be based primarily on the requirements of institutionalization before liberalization, rather than on unrealistic demands for the speedy termination of an operation.

The Culture-of-Dependency Critique

David Chandler has written extensively on the danger of fostering a "culture of dependency" in populations under international administration.[91] He argues that international authorities in Bosnia, in particular, have limited the development of indigenous democracy by suppressing local involvement in policymaking decisions and by creating the expectation within parts of the indigenous population that international officials will continue to manage their affairs for them. Chandler believes that this approach, which he views as unduly paternalistic and authoritarian, will ultimately "make it more difficult for the international community to exit from Bosnia" because it is paradoxically blocking the development of local capacities for self-government.[92]

Chandler's critique is biting, and it fundamentally challenges the IBL strategy set out in this chapter. It *is* paradoxical, and in some respects unfortunate, that international officials must suppress certain forms of political expression in order to build the foundations for a stable and peaceful democracy. But the problem with Chandler's analysis is that he does not explain how else to reach the end point of stable and lasting peace *without* managing and controlling the destabilizing effects of political and economic liberalization in the short run. I have argued that international peacebuilders have little choice but to act "illiberally" in the earliest phases of a postconflict transition for precisely this reason, and that the IBL strategy is more likely to produce a durable peace – and a stable democracy – than a strategy that promotes political and economic competition in the immediate aftermath of civil war.

Encouraging maximum freedom in the short term may be philosophically more comfortable for peacebuilding agencies and for Chandler, but it ignores the "Hobbesian problem" of building effective institutions to contain free competition within peaceful bounds – just as scholars of the liberal peace thesis have taken the existence of such institutions largely for granted. This is the uncomfortable reality that peacebuilding agencies (and the states that sponsor these agencies) must embrace if they wish to prevent the pathologies of rapid liberalization from recurring in future operations.

That said, the IBL strategy does not preclude local involvement in the international administration of a war-torn territory. Indeed, peacebuilders

---

[91] Chandler 1999a, 1999b, and 2001.   [92] Chandler 1999a, p. 65.

could go considerably further than they have in previous missions to incorporate local consultation mechanisms into the apparatus of governance. In both Bosnia and East Timor, for example, international officials created unnecessarily opaque governance structures that permitted too little indigenous involvement,[93] yet there is room for much greater consultation and for experimentation with different forms of local participation in international administration,[94] which would help to diminish the reality and the perception of dependency. Furthermore, as noted, decisionmaking authority should be transferred to indigenous institutions as quickly as possible, and locals should be trained in public administration and prepared to take over the management of governmental agencies immediately. In the end, however, the most sweeping demands for immediate democratization can only be partially addressed, since gradual and phased liberalization in war-torn states seems better suited to the establishment of a stable market democracy in the long run.

The Excessive-Costs Critique

Many commentators point to the problem of "donor fatigue," or the limited willingness of states to contribute resources to peace operations and humanitarian endeavors, as a restraining factor in the international community's ability to conduct such operations.[95] One could argue that IBL's demand for longer-lasting and more extensive forms of peacebuilding would be too costly to be practicable, given this problem of donor fatigue. But, in fact, IBL would be a more economical investment of scarce resources than missions that appear cheaper but allow civil violence to rekindle. Scrimping on peacebuilding offers false economies if operations fail to create the conditions for durable peace. Whether the states and agencies that sponsor peacebuilding can be convinced of the need for the up-front investment in IBL is a different question, and one that I cannot answer, although one of the purposes of this book has been to make precisely this case.

In addition to highlighting that IBL would, in the long run, be less expensive than the "quick and dirty" approach – both in terms of human lives and money – it is worth noting that peacebuilding missions to date, including the lengthier and more complex missions, have cost only a tiny fraction of the money spent on national armed forces during the same time. By one calculation, the total UN expenditure for all of the peace operations in the 1990s (including not only peacebuilding missions but those launched during ongoing hostilities) was $19.9 billion, while world military expenditures

[93] For example, Chandler 1999b; and Chopra 2000 and 2002.
[94] See Beauvais 2001; Chopra 2002; and Hohe 2002a and 2002b. See also Korhonen 2001 on the importance of involving indigenous populations in transitional administrations as a means of enhancing the perceived legitimacy of these arrangements.
[95] For example, Kapp 2001.

during the same period was an estimated $6.9 trillion.[96] For the United States alone, total federal budget outlays for national defense between 1991 and 1999 was approximately $2.5 trillion, or 125 times greater than the total UN peace operations budget, to which the United States contributes 25 percent.[97] Given the additional costs to the United States of increasing "homeland defense" in the wake of the September 2001 terrorist attacks, and the fact (as acknowledged by the U.S. government) that states suffering from chronic civil violence have become safe harbors for transnational terrorist groups, investing in more effective peacebuilding would make sense even from the purely self-interested standpoint of American national security, while it would also enhance regional security and address one of the principal causes of humanitarian crises in the world: pervasive civil conflict.

Conclusion

The IBL strategy represents an improvement over the pursuit of rapid liberalization, an approach that dominated peacebuilding missions in the 1990s. Unlike the alternatives of authoritarianism or partition, IBL does not reject the goals of Wilsonianism. Rather, it seeks to achieve these goals through different means: gradual and controlled liberalization, combined with the immediate construction of domestic institutions that are capable of managing the destabilizing effects of democratization and marketization.

But what has happened with regard to peacebuilding since 1998? Thus far, I have deferred discussion of operations in Kosovo, East Timor, and Sierra Leone, all of which were launched in 1999, because their recentness made the outcomes of these operations more difficult to evaluate than previous missions. As we shall see in the next chapter, however, these operations have embraced a few of the elements of the IBL strategy.

[96] Hentges and Coicaud 2002.   [97] Ibid.

Lessons Learned and Not Learned

Kosovo, East Timor, Sierra Leone, and Beyond

The peacebuilding operations launched after 1998 in Kosovo, East Timor, and Sierra Leone have moved gradually in the direction of the IBL strategy: They have devoted more attention and resources to the construction of effective institutions and managed the liberalization process more gradually and deliberately than in previous missions.[1] In Kosovo and East Timor, in particular, peacebuilders have served as "transitional authorities" governing these territories while indigenous institutions are being erected.

But while this shift toward IBL is welcome, it has not gone far enough. Peacebuilders in these more recent operations have remained reluctant to commit themselves to the arduous, open-ended, and inevitably slow task of transforming war-shattered states into stable societies, and have continued to place too much emphasis on rapid liberalization at the expense of adequate institutionalization. As a result, many of the problems experienced in earlier missions have recurred in the post-1998 operations.

As this book went to press, two new postconflict operations were attracting worldwide attention – in Afghanistan and Iraq, whose governments were deposed in U.S.-led military operations in 2001 and 2003, respectively. Both of these operations fall outside the focus of this book, not only because of their recentness, but also because they followed foreign invasions rather than civil wars. The challenges of peacebuilding after conquest (and of peacebuilding conducted by the conqueror) are quite different from those of the missions examined in this book. However, because Afghanistan had been suffering from its own civil war prior to the American intervention, I will briefly discuss the early results of peacebuilding in that country.

Finally, I shall explore some of the challenges of implementing the IBL strategy in future missions, which will require not only better coordination of the international organizations that take part in peacebuilding but also a

---

[1] A fourth operation was authorized for the Democratic Republic of Congo in 1999 but involved only a handful of personnel until the summer of 2001.

strong political commitment from the states and organizations that sponsor these operations.

Kosovo

Kosovo is a province of Serbia, one of two territories that now comprise the Federal Republic of Yugoslavia. The population is more than 90 percent ethnic Albanian and Muslim. The government of Serbia recognized Kosovo as a largely autonomous region in 1974, an arrangement that allowed ethnic Albanians special rights, including their own school system and religious observances, but these rights were withdrawn in 1989.

Following the secession of Slovenia, Croatia, and Bosnia from the Yugoslav federation, an armed separatist group known as the Kosovo Liberation Army (KLA), comprised primarily of ethnic Albanians, began a guerrilla campaign in favor of independence. In the fall of 1998, the Yugoslav army countered with an offensive that forced both the guerrillas and Albanian civilians into the remote mountains of Kosovo. With winter approaching and the civilians in danger of freezing, NATO threatened attacks against Serb forces unless ordinary people were allowed to return to their homes unmolested. Serbian leaders relented and drew back their forces, but in March 1999 they launched yet another military campaign in defiance of international warnings. Once again, Albanian Kosovars fled the assault, this time in even greater numbers; thousands of refugees crossed into neighboring countries, recounting stories of summary executions and forced expulsions by Serbian forces. NATO responded by bombing Serbian targets for eleven consecutive weeks until the government of Yugoslavia finally accepted peace terms, which included the withdrawal of Serbian forces and the deployment of "international civil and security presences" to the province. Soon after, the UN Security Council authorized the creation of a new peace-building mission for Kosovo. The military dimension of the mission (which became known as the Kosovo Force, or KFOR) would be organized by NATO, while the civilian aspects (known as the UN Mission in Kosovo, or UNMIK) would be supervised by the UN in collaboration with the OSCE and EU.

Since their deployment, KFOR and UNMIK have been considerably more assertive and interventionist in constructing functioning governmental institutions, and in managing the liberalization process, than earlier peacebuilding missions – with substantial success. International officials took over key administrative functions, from taxation to garbage collection, in what amounted to the creation of a UN protectorate. Indeed, no previous operation of this kind had exercised such extensive and direct administrative control over a territory. The special representative of the Secretary-General (SRSG) assumed "all...executive authority with respect to Kosovo," including the right to appoint "any person to perform functions in the civil administration of Kosovo, including the judiciary," or to dismiss people from these posts.[2] Under the SRSG's supervision, the UN assumed jurisdiction over public administration, police, and judicial affairs; the OSCE was tasked with building new political institutions, training local administrators, and organizing elections; while the EU undertook to reconstruct physical infrastructure and develop a market-based economy, including a banking system.

In addition to taking direct responsibility for the reconstruction of governmental institutions, peacebuilders in Kosovo also promoted a more controlled process of political liberalization than in earlier operations. Strict media policies required broadcasters and print journalists to comply with codes of conduct that banned the dissemination of material that "denigrates an ethnic or religious group or implies that an ethnic or religious group is responsible for criminal activity."[3] In addition, newspapers, radio, and television broadcasters were prohibited from producing material "that encourages crime or criminal activities or which carries imminent risk of causing harm, such harm being defined as death, or injury, or damage to property or other violence."[4] An internationally staffed Media Hearing Board was established to handle complaints against particular media outlets and empowered to impose sanctions, ranging from a warning to the forcible suspension of the outlet's operations (subject to the right of appeal to a Media Appeals Board). At the same time, the OSCE also promoted the development of a professional and responsible media by offering technical assistance and training opportunities for local journalists. These initiatives appear to have supported the growth of a moderate but still largely free press.

Similarly, in the area of democratization, peacebuilders in Kosovo were more conscious of limiting the excesses of local actors than in previous missions. Preparations for elections included the drafting of a code of conduct that not only prohibited political parties and candidates from using language or symbols "likely to incite hatred towards others" but also imposed a positive requirement on parties and candidates to "be publicly outspoken in the condemnation of violence, threats of violence or intimidation, during the electoral process."[5] Moreover, political parties, coalitions and independent candidates were allowed to participate in elections only after being certified by the internationally run Central Election Commission as complying with the code of conduct.[6] The powers of the territory's elected Assembly were limited and subject to the oversight of the SRSG, who retained the right to dissolve the assembly, call for new elections, and veto any measure passed by the Assembly that violated the purposes of the peacebuilding operation.[7] The

---

[2] UNMIK Regulation 1999/1 (July 25, 1999), http://www.unmikonline.org/regulations/1999/reg01-99.htm, accessed in July 2002.
[3] Temporary Media Commissioner for Kosovo 2000a (section 2.2) and 2000b (section 2.2).
[4] Ibid., section 2.1 of both codes of conduct.   [5] OSCE 2002a.   [6] OSCE 2002b.
[7] UNMIK 2001, chap. 8.

SRSG exercised his veto power almost immediately, annulling a resolution passed by the Assembly in May 2002 that would have supported Kosovo's becoming a sovereign state rather than remaining part of Serbia – an issue that the Assembly was explicitly prohibited from addressing due to its highly controversial nature, given that the government of Yugoslavia had agreed to the deployment of UNMIK on the understanding that the mission would not facilitate Kosovo's secession.

At the same time, peacebuilders have been training local Kosovars to serve in the internationally run administration of the territory in the hope of eventually producing an entirely indigenous, professionalized, and independent bureaucracy to support the territorial government, which will in turn gain more powers.[8] Taken as a whole, the willingness of international authorities to assume full responsibility for the governance of the territory, then hand over political authority to local elected leaders and trained administrators in a gradual and controlled manner, represents a departure from the hastier and less interventionist approach to democratization that was practiced in earlier peacebuilding missions. To date, this approach seems to have limited the potentially destabilizing effects of liberalization that affected many previous missions.

However, the significant progress that peacebuilders have made in Kosovo has been diminished by their apparent unwillingness to embrace the IBL strategy more fully. At the outset of the operation, in particular, international officials were reluctant to assert their powers over the political and judicial affairs of the province, which ultimately made it more difficult to end violence and revenge attacks against the minority population of ethnic Serbs, to promote peaceful coexistence between the Serbian and Albanian communities, to remove extremist groups and individuals from positions of responsibility, and to establish a neutral and effective international administration over the territory. The period immediately following the termination of Yugoslav military operations in Kosovo was filled with revenge attacks upon Serb civilians perpetrated by extremist elements in the KLA, who intimidated Albanian moderates and extended their control of a pervasive black market economy transshipping drugs to Western Europe, and who also began to establish their own local governments in violation of the peace agreement.[9] Peacebuilders were initially hesitant to suppress the violence and remove these illegal governance structures for fear of being perceived as "overly colonial."[10] As a result, these bodies became harder to dislodge and impeded efforts to establish the rule of law and human rights.[11] By mid-2002, illegal political structures continued to exist (particularly within

---

[8] See the website of the Institute for Civil Administration: http://www.osce.org/kosovo/democratization/ica, accessed in July 2002.
[9] O'Neill 2002.   [10] Rhode 2000.   [11] O'Neill 2002, p. 38.

Serbian sections of Kosovo) and to block UNMIK from exercising its governing authority throughout the province.[12]

Tentativeness also marred efforts to establish the rule of law in Kosovo. UNMIK officials were at first disinclined to impose an internationally staffed justice system on the province and refused calls for an internationalization of the judiciary, even in the face of "overwhelming" evidence of intimidation and ethnic bias among local judges and prosecutors.[13] Under these circumstances, attacks upon Serb civilians continued with relative impunity, diminishing the prospects of promoting peaceful relations between Serbian and Albanian communities. It was not until 2000 that UNMIK finally realized its mistake and began to appoint international judges and lawyers, but by then much harm had been done to the peace process. As William O'Neill argues, if UNMIK and KFOR had immediately declared the equivalent of martial law in Kosovo and established an effective international justice system, hard-liners in both the Serb and Albanian communities might have recognized that violent attacks would not be tolerated, and fewer minorities might have been forced to flee their homes.[14]

Moreover, while the democratization process has been handled more effectively in Kosovo than in many previous missions, UNMIK may have moved too quickly to hold elections, reinforcing the power of those politicians who are committed to Kosovo's separation from Yugoslavia. The November 2001 territorial elections were praised internationally on the grounds that they represented a "clear victory for political moderates," as the *Washington Post* wrote in an editorial, which also noted that Ibrahim Rugova, a longtime proponent of achieving Kosovar independence through nonviolent means, had won the largest number of votes.[15] But political moderation in Kosovo is a relative concept: Most of the province's politicians, including Rugova, reject any option short of full independence for Kosovo. In the long term, the election of these politicians to public office poses a problem for peacebuilders, in that they are likely to press for outright secession, which is precisely the scenario that UNMIK and the UN Security Council would like to avoid. International officials fear that a declaration of independence by the Kosovo Assembly could spark renewed conflict not only in Yugoslavia, whose central government in Belgrade is fiercely opposed to the province's secession, but perhaps also in neighboring states, including Macedonia, where there is a significant Albanian minority. Furthermore, the November 2001 elections registered modest gains for parties that are political successors of the KLA, and which have not clearly rejected the use of violence to achieve independence.[16]

In sum, it is difficult to understand how the empowerment of Kosovo separatists through democratic elections serves the interests of achieving a

---

[12] Wood 2002.   [13] Ibid., p. 89.   [14] Ibid., pp. 75–76 and 138.
[15] *Washington Post* 2001 (November 23).
[16] Dempsey 2001; International Crisis Group 2002, pp. 10–11.

long-term peaceful solution to the Kosovo problem. The fact that UNMIK pushed for rapid elections that bolstered the power of secessionists is even more puzzling in the light of UN Secretary-General Kofi Annan's statement in 1999 that he did not wish to repeat in Kosovo the "mistakes" of elections in Bosnia, which according to Annan "legitimized those who caused the war."[17]

There was never much danger that elections would incite violent rebellion by Serb communities in Kosovo because more than two-thirds of the Serb population had fled the province during the NATO offensive of 1999 and before, leaving only a rump community of approximately eighty to a hundred thousand, and this remnant population no longer enjoyed the military support of the Yugoslav government. For these reasons, the danger that democratization would spark renewed civil war in Kosovo was not high, just as it was not high in Croatia or Namibia: One party to the preceding conflict had effectively abandoned the territory. Nevertheless, relations between the remaining Serb community and Albanian majority remained tense and violent, and encouraging peaceful coexistence was one of the central objectives of the peacebuilding mission. Elections have not furthered this objective because most Serbs have refused to participate in a procedure they have viewed as illegitimate.[18] Under pressure from the SRSG, Rugova did include a Kosovo Serb in his cabinet in March 2002, but this gesture did little to diminish the widespread Serb belief that elections serve merely to further the goals of Albanian separatists – a view that has some basis in fact.[19]

Finally, there have been disturbing signals that UNMIK may be using rapid democratization as a means of extracting itself from Kosovo prematurely. When Michael Steiner was appointed as the new SRSG in February 2002, he announced that his top goal was to transfer administrative powers to Kosovo's elected leaders as quickly as possible, although it was far from clear how doing this would advance the goal of resolving the dispute over Kosovo's status within Yugoslavia.[20] Although Steiner emphasized that final status negotiations should not commence until Kosovo has fully functioning governmental institutions, he and other UNMIK officials have hinted that they believe that they are in a "race against time" to complete the peacebuilding mission.[21] "We're not going to be here much longer," said the spokesman for Kosovo's UN police in March 2002, who went on to note that the American government is skeptical of long-term peacekeeping deployments

---

[17] Quoted in Perlez 1999.

[18] More Serbs participated in the November 2001 elections than in previous votes, but the vast majority of the Serb population refused to participate (International Crisis Group 2002, p. i).

[19] Indeed, this was also the prevailing view in Albania proper, where most commentators celebrated the November 2001 election as a major step toward Kosovar independence. See Mici 2001.

[20] Arieff 2002.   [21] UNMIK 2002.

and that the British government is pushing for greater attention to Africa's problems.[22]

As we have seen in the case of many of the missions that preceded UNMIK, speedy democratization is one way of creating the appearance of a peacebuilding "success" without resolving difficult issues and underlying sources of conflict. It is essential that the Kosovo mission, which has largely recognized the need for effective institutionalization and managed liberalization, not squander its substantial accomplishments by pushing democratization before the territory's status – and its capability to manage its internal and external affairs peacefully – is fully secured.

East Timor

The operation in East Timor also illustrates the increased willingness of peacebuilders to focus on institutional reconstruction and move in the direction of the IBL strategy. East Timor had been a subject of concern to the United Nations since the 1960s, when the territory (which is located at the eastern end of the Indonesian archipelago, just north of Australia) was still administered by Portugal. In 1974 Portugal attempted to establish a provisional government that would determine the status of East Timor, but civil war erupted between those who favored independence and those who advocated integration with Indonesia, and when Portugal withdrew, Indonesian military units intervened and annexed East Timor. It was not until 1999 that Jakarta agreed to hold a "popular consultation" under UN auspices to determine whether the people of East Timor were willing to approve a special autonomy arrangement for the territory within Indonesia. In August of that year, the East Timorese voted overwhelmingly (78.5 percent) against autonomy, a result that was correctly interpreted as an expression of support for independence. Immediately, anti-independence militias in East Timor, some of which were reportedly controlled by the Indonesian armed forces, began a campaign of violence and intimidation that resulted in the deaths of approximately two thousand people and the displacement of hundreds of thousands of civilians, many of whom fled the territory.

In response, the UN authorized the creation of an Australian-led military force to restore order in East Timor, which it quickly accomplished, but only after fighting had destroyed much of the territory's physical infrastructure along with the civil administration and judicial systems. In September 1999, Indonesia agreed to transfer political authority over East Timor to the United Nations, pending the territory's transition to sovereign independence and self-rule. The Security Council consequently empowered a new peacebuilding operation – the UN Transitional Administration in East Timor

---

[22] Quoted in Holley 2002.

(UNTAET) – to assume "overall responsibility for the administration of East Timor" and "to exercise all legislative and executive authority, including the administration of justice."[23] UNTAET was instructed to establish an "effective administration" over the territory and to support "capacity-building for self-government."[24] In August 2001, more than 91 percent of East Timor's eligible voters went to the polls once again, this time to elect a Constituent Assembly that would draw up plans for future elections and the transition to full independence. With international guidance, the Constituent Assembly signed into force the territory's first Constitution in March 2002, and the following month presidential elections were held. More than 80 percent of voters selected Xanana Gusmão, a former guerrilla leader who had fought against Indonesian rule, as the country's first president. Gusmão was sworn in and East Timor became an independent nation on May 20, 2002.

While the UN's experience in East Timor from 1998 to 2002 showed how much international peacebuilders can accomplish when they commit themselves to the task of reconstructing the governmental institutions of war-torn territories, the early phases of UN involvement actually highlighted the dangers of precipitous and ill-prepared liberalization. Many international observers had predicted that the 1999 referendum would end in bloodshed, and that anti-independence gangs supported by the Indonesian army would not allow East Timor to secede without a fight.[25] Even pro-independence campaigners, including Gusmão himself, said that they preferred several years of quasi autonomy to prepare for the referendum, rather than moving ahead immediately.[26] Nevertheless, the UN proceeded with the vote, deploying only a small number of observers and security forces (three hundred soldiers and four hundred police) into a highly unstable environment, leaving the primary responsibility for security during and after the referendum in the suspect hands of the Indonesian armed forces. As widely expected, violence erupted and thousands of civilians were killed or driven from their homes. Many criticized the UN for lack of foresight and preparation, including the editorial writers for *Le Monde,* France's newspaper of record: "By taking on the organization of the referendum, the UN implicitly guaranteed not only the security of the voting operation, but that of the voters in the aftermath of the poll. It has betrayed their trust; it has abandoned them without defense."[27] Furthermore, the United Nations did not authorize the deployment of a multinational force to restore peace and security in East Timor until two weeks after the vote, and foreign troops only started arriving in large numbers at the end of September.[28]

---

[23] UN Security Council Resolution 1272 (October 25, 1999).   [24] Ibid.
[25] For example, Knox 1999; and *Le Monde* 1999b.   [26] Shukman 1999.
[27] *Le Monde* 1999a.
[28] For a glimpse into the UN's complete lack of preparation for this scenario, see Martin 2001, chap. 7.

Why the UN failed to foresee this outcome, even after the organization's experience with abortive elections in other deeply divided societies, remains unclear. According to Secretary-General Annan, "Nobody in his wildest dreams thought that what we are witnessing could have happened."[29] Yet the peacebuilding record to date should have provided Annan with sufficient grounds to anticipate the problems that surrounded East Timor's 1999 referendum.

The UN was able to recover from this setback. UNTAET soon assumed greater governing powers over East Timor than international agencies had exercised in any previous peacebuilding mission, including Kosovo, and quickly began the process of reconstituting a functioning governmental administration for the territory.[30] As in Kosovo, the Secretary-General's special representative was granted extraordinary powers to enact new laws and regulations and to amend or repeal existing ones – powers that he immediately used to create a central fiscal authority, courts and police system, defense force, and even traffic rules. International military contingents were given robust rules of engagement and permitted to pursue and fire on anti-independence militiamen who infiltrated the territory from neighboring West Timor.[31] Under direct international governance, the rule of law was largely restored, roads and schools rebuilt, health systems reestablished, and training programs begun in order to prepare the East Timorese for their gradual assumption of positions of responsibility within the administration. The April 2002 presidential election and the campaign that preceded it were well regulated, peaceful, and orderly, proceeding "without significant incidents."[32] As Jose Ramos-Horta, the Nobel peace laureate who became the country's first foreign minister, commented after the election, "[The UN mission to East Timor] has been a tremendous, dramatic accomplishment."[33]

The success of the East Timor mission to date is a testament to the willingness of peacebuilders to assume full responsibility for the reconstruction of a functioning state apparatus. Yet without diminishing these real accomplishments, it is also true that in East Timor the immediate postconflict period was less fragile, less susceptible to a resurgence of violence, and less vulnerable to the disruptive effects of liberalization than in most other countries that have hosted peacebuilding operations. After the defeat and departure of anti-independence militias from the territory in 1999, there were effectively no "formerly warring parties" in East Timor. Rather, they were individuals who had been more or less affiliated with the Indonesian regime. The elite of the society was broadly united, and "no significant group [felt] marginalized

---

[29] Quoted in Thoenes and Vo 1999, p. 1.   [30] Suhrke 2001.   [31] Smith with Doe 2003.
[32] "Report of the Secretary-General on the United Nations Transitional Administration in East Timor," UN document S/2002/432 (April 17, 2002), para. 7.
[33] Quoted in Chandrasekaran 2002.

or tempted to start a civil war."[34] As in Namibia, the roots of the conflict were more those of foreign occupation than indigenous civil war.[35] When the foreign presence departed, the task of promoting reconciliation was greatly eased – although some divisions (including those caused by the residual effects of Indonesian occupation) continue to exist in East Timorese society.

Nonetheless, the East Timor model of assertive peacebuilding, with an emphasis on institution building and managed liberalization, represents an improvement upon the quick-and-dirty style of peacebuilding that prevailed for much of the 1990s. Indeed, one of the distinguishing features of the East Timor mission has been the willingness of the UN and other international agencies to maintain a major presence in the country even after the territory became formally independent. Both the SRSG for East Timor and the Secretary-General himself, along with President Gusmão, have emphasized the importance of continuing international institution-building efforts into the postindependence period.[36] Much work was required in the area of training indigenous bureaucrats and further developing the courts and police system.[37] Accordingly, in May 2002 the Security Council authorized the continued deployment of 5,000 UN troops to maintain security, 1,250 police officers to preserve law enforcement, and more than 100 civilian UN personnel to serve directly in the newly independent national government.[38] In the words of the SRSG, "we can't just let them [the East Timorese] fend for themselves."[39] The process of handing over responsibility for judicial and security affairs was scheduled to continue, gradually and deliberately, as local capacities for peaceful and effective self-governance increased.

The territory will continue to face challenges in the coming years, including more traditional problems of economic development: When East Timor gained independence, it instantly became the poorest country in Asia. But the record of peacebuilding in East Timor to date illustrates how much can be accomplished (albeit under relatively favorable circumstances) when international agencies devote time and resources to rebuilding institutional structures in war-torn lands and carefully manage the movement toward democratization.

---

[34] Steele 2002, p. 86.

[35] Meden 2002. As John Sanderson (2001, p. 159) writes: "[T]he situation in East Timor lends itself to political experimentation in a way that would be very difficult and costly in most other places."

[36] "Report of the Secretary-General on the United Nations Transitional Administration in East Timor," UN document S/2002/432 (April 17, 2002); Holloway 2002; and Annan 2002.

[37] On the need for more extensive and coordinated training of local judges and lawyers, for example, see Pritchard 2001.

[38] UN Security Council Resolution 1410 (May 17, 2002).

[39] Quoted in Chandrasekaran 2002.

Sierra Leone

Sierra Leone is a West African country that gained its independence from Britain in 1961. Its civil conflict began in March 1991 when a guerrilla group, the Revolutionary United Front (RUF), launched a military campaign from the eastern part of the country, near the border with Liberia, aimed at overthrowing the government. In 1992, in the midst of the war, junior officers in the Sierra Leone army staged a coup, claiming that the government was not providing sufficient support to front-line soldiers. Initial support for the coup from ordinary citizens soon dissipated as it became clear that the new regime was no less corrupt or brutal in its treatment of the civilian population than its predecessor had been.[40] In response to international pressure, the military government agreed to hold multiparty elections in February 1996 – the country's first free vote since 1967 – which resulted in victory for Ahmed Tejan Kabbah. But Kabbah was soon overthrown in another military coup, whose leaders immediately suspended the country's short-lived democratic constitution.

Kabbah fled to neighboring Guinea, where he mobilized international support. With the assistance of a large Nigerian-led military force, which was officially sponsored by the Economic Community of West African States, Kabbah was restored to power in the spring of 1998. Thereafter, the ECOWAS force took a leading role in fighting the RUF guerrillas on behalf of the Kabbah government. The RUF continued to battle for control of the countryside and the capital, Freetown. After several stillborn efforts to negotiate an end to the conflict, the parties finally reached an agreement in July 1999, which included the demobilization of the RUF and a power-sharing arrangement between the Kabbah government and the RUF rebels during a transitional period leading up to new elections, all of which would be supervised by the UN Mission in Sierra Leone (UNAMSIL).

However, fighting soon resumed, and when rebels took more than five hundred UN troops hostage in May 2000, the future of UNAMSIL appeared to be in doubt. The arrival of a British military task force later that month stabilized the deteriorating situation by securing Freetown and neighboring areas and by undertaking to retrain the disorganized Sierra Leone army. The Security Council also responded by increasing the size of the military contingent attached to UNAMSIL (from an initial deployment of 6,000 soldiers to 17,500 in March 2001) and by expanding the mandate of the mission to permit UN troops to fight the rebels directly. Elections were postponed from November 2001 to May 2002. During this period, the RUF ceased hostilities and largely abided by the cease-fire, UNAMSIL and the Sierra Leone army gained control of most of the country, the RUF began to transform itself into a political party (as required under the 1999 peace agreement), and

---

[40] Laggah, Allie, and Wright 1999, p. 184.

UN personnel supervised the disarming and demobilization of tens of thousands of rebel troops. Elections took place on May 14, 2002, in relatively peaceful conditions, with President Kabbah taking over 70 percent of the vote. It was, as the International Crisis Group pointed out, "the first truly non-violent vote in the country's history."[41]

The record of peacebuilding in Sierra Leone to date supports a number of provisional observations. First, the key difference between the failed elections of 1996 and the apparently successful elections of 2002 was that no internationally sponsored demobilization or institution building took place preceding the 1996 election, whereas the 2002 vote followed several months during which international actors rebuilt the Sierra Leone army and disarmed antigovernment rebels. Between June 2000 and September 2001, the British retrained no fewer than eighty-five hundred members of the Sierra Leone army.[42] Moreover, the national army was reinforced by a large contingent of UN troops, who effectively fought on behalf of the government, and – most importantly – by an elite British military task force. British intervention was "decisive" in overcoming the RUF on the battlefield and in convincing rebels to abide by the 1999 peace agreement.[43] British forces routed RUF fighters near Freetown and went on to capture the group's leader, Foday Sankoh, incarcerating him on murder charges. What peacebuilders did, in effect, was to focus on one vital institution of the Sierra Leone government – the army – and make it more effective in order to deter and suppress violent challenges to the electoral process or its results. In this way, the peacebuilding mission pursued one element of the IBL strategy.

However, peacebuilders did little to establish functioning governmental institutions in Sierra Leone prior to the elections – and this seems likely to become a source of problems in the future. As of mid-2002, the country still lacked an effective police and courts system. Although the UN and Commonwealth have provided some police training, and Britain and the UNDP have provided some equipment, the capacity of the Sierra Leone police to perform basic law enforcement is very limited. At the heart of the problem is a lack of resources and training. Most districts are understaffed; some lack even such vital equipment as vehicles and radios, and few police personnel have managerial skills or the capacity to train new recruits.[44] The judiciary barely functions: Only five of the fourteen magistrate courts in the country are operational, and even these courts have "very limited capacity in terms of trained personnel and logistics."[45] Furthermore, governmental bureaucracies at both the national and local levels are rife with corruption and incompetence. In spite of the efforts of the internationally sponsored Anti-Corruption

[41] International Crisis Group 2002, p. i.   [42] Chege 2002, p. 155.   [43] Tran 2002.
[44] International Crisis Group 2002, pp. 12–13.
[45] "Fourteenth Report of the Secretary-General on the United Nations Mission in Sierra Leone," UN document S/2002/679 (June 19, 2002), para. 24.

Commission to root out government officials who misappropriate funds, the problems of corruption and the lack of trained administrators are so profound that some international officials have privately expressed doubt that measurable progress has been made in professionalizing the Sierra Leone bureaucracy.[46] Without an effective police and courts system, and a minimally competent and efficient bureaucracy, the new government – faced with popular demands for peace, justice, public services, and economic reform – risks collapse.

Furthermore, few institutional mechanisms have been established to ensure that the newly elected government will uphold its constitutional commitments to preserve democracy. Like the experience of its neighbor Liberia, Sierra Leone's history of political instability and violence is a story of rival factions competing for total power in a system of "winner-take-all" politics, where ruling groups use their control of the state to enrich themselves and their associates while brutally suppressing their opponents.[47] This style of politics has resulted in a vicious cycle of violent uprisings and coups, followed by repression and embezzlement, which give rise to new uprisings and new coups. If democratization is to provide Sierra Leone with an escape from this cycle of violence, such mechanisms as an effective constitutional court are needed to prevent the new Kabbah government from reverting to one-party rule. In the aftermath of the May 2002 elections, there were already signs of possible backsliding: Despite international entreaties to create a broad-based cabinet, President Kabbah appointed only loyalists affiliated with his own party. Further, his party's overwhelming domination of parliament has diminished hopes that an effective "loyal opposition" will emerge. Failure to guard against an unconstitutional usurpation of power may result in a tragic and wasteful loss of the real, but fragile, accomplishments of peacebuilding in Sierra Leone.

In hindsight, it might have been preferable for peacebuilders to assume more direct responsibility for the administration of the country before holding national elections. In Kosovo and East Timor, by contrast, international governance has built a preliminary foundation not only for more effective and professional administration but also for a politically neutral bureaucracy. Peacebuilders should remain in Sierra Leone for an extended period in order to preserve what is still a tenuous peace. They should redouble their efforts to build effective state institutions, not only to help the new government meet the challenges of postwar reconstruction and reconciliation but also to protect the country against possible governmental excesses.

---

[46] International Crisis Group 2002, pp. 15–16. Hirsch (2001) suggests that leadership positions in the bureaucracy could be staffed, at least initially, by professionals recruited from the large diaspora community of educated Sierra Leoneans who fled the country during the preceding two decades.

[47] Bøås 2001; and Kandeh 2002.

Although UN officials have publicly called for a continuation of the peace-building mission beyond 2002, the countries supporting this mission and the Secretary-General himself actually seem to be preparing to scale back the operation. In June 2002, Annan reported that "planning for the drawdown of UNAMSIL" was under way;[48] and in July the British government withdrew two hundred of the three hundred military officers who had been retraining the Sierra Leone army,[49] a decision that caused anxiety among observers in Sierra Leone, who fear that the national army still lacks the skill and cohesion to operate independently.[50] Sierra Leone has emerged from a period of appalling brutality, and an opportunity now exists to set the country on a path toward stable and lasting peace. The international community should resist the temptation to declare the peacebuilding mission a completed "success" on grounds that Sierra Leone is now a "democracy."

Backsliding in Afghanistan

Recent missions in Kosovo, East Timor, and Sierra Leone suggest that international agencies have begun to embrace longer-term, more interventionist forms of postconflict peacebuilding that place greater emphasis on institutional reconstruction and on more gradual and controlled approaches to liberalization. But these developments have been modest in comparison to the Institutionalization Before Liberalization strategy set out in Chapter 10. Furthermore, this budding trend toward more assertive and gradual peacebuilding was partly reversed in 2001 with the deployment of a postconflict mission to Afghanistan – a mission that has suffered from a lack of international commitment to rebuild effective governmental structures in the country.

Following the September 2001 terrorist attacks on New York and Washington, D.C., the United States launched a military operation in Afghanistan to destroy members of the Al Qaeda organization and to overthrow Afghanistan's ruling Taliban regime. The fighting was largely over by mid-December, at which point the UN Security Council voted to authorize the deployment of a multinational security force to maintain order in the country's capital city, Kabul, and immediate environs. The decision to create the security force had been made a few days earlier at a meeting in Bonn, Germany, which brought together Afghan leaders, UN officials, American diplomats, and representatives of other interested states. Participants at the Bonn meeting also set out the framework for postwar transitional arrangements in Afghanistan, including the rapid creation of a new government for the country. Although a new civilian UN mission was to be created for

---

[48] "Fourteenth Report of the Secretary-General on the United Nations Mission in Sierra Leone," UN document S/2002/679 (June 19, 2002), para. 42.
[49] Hall 2002.   [50] Fofana 2002.

Afghanistan, its role was limited to providing technical, humanitarian, and financial assistance to the newly formed indigenous government, and no UN or international administrative power was envisaged. On the contrary, the United Nations emphasized that its presence would be "based on the concept of having a 'small footprint' in the country."[51]

In many respects, the postwar mission in Afghanistan is unlike those studied in this book: It followed the conquest of the country by the United States and its allies, rather than a negotiated settlement to a civil war. Nevertheless, the country was (and remains) deeply divided along ethnic and tribal lines, and it was engaged in a civil war for more than a decade prior to the American intervention. So the conditions in postwar Afghanistan bear some resemblance to the states that hosted peacebuilding missions in the 1990s.

One of the interesting features of the postconflict mission in Afghanistan is the relatively modest role that international agencies have assumed, in comparison to the more extensive functions performed in Kosovo and East Timor, in particular. The apparent "reversal of the increasingly intrusive trend in transitional administration"[52] raises an important question that is directly relevant to this study: Has the "light footprint" model of international peacebuilding in Afghanistan proven effective to date?

The answer appears to be no. At the time of this writing, the international security force continues to be limited to Kabul. Feuding warlords remain in control of most of the country, including local police and security forces, while the new Afghan government barely exercises its writ beyond the suburbs of the capital. The Taliban seems to have been destroyed and members of Al Qaeda largely expelled from the country, but conditions that fueled the earlier civil war in Afghanistan are still very much present: most importantly, the absence of an effective central state and the continued fragmentation of political authority among adversarial, local warlords.[53] The light-footprint approach to peacebuilding in Afghanistan seems, by its very nature, to be incapable of addressing this problem. Providing "technical advice" to a fragile and weak Afghan government will not, by itself, create an effective state. Internationally sponsored efforts to retrain a national army, which might be used to counteract the power of the warlords, have been underfunded and painfully slow.[54] Meanwhile, American troops in the country (who are not part of the international security force in Kabul) have focused on hunting down remaining pockets of suspected terrorists and are not available for peacekeeping work.

Without a more extensive international commitment to rebuilding a stable and effective central government, the prognosis for peace in Afghanistan is not encouraging; nor are the prospects that the country will break out of

[51] United Nations 2002, p. 11. See also Chesterman 2002.
[52] Their and Chopra 2002, p. 894.   [53] Goodhand 2002.   [54] Sedra 2003.

its cycle of state failure and violence.[55] Even the U.S. military commander in the country, Lt. Gen. Dan McNeill, expressed his frustration in March 2003 that the international community had "not made a more bold step" to rebuild an effective government for Afghanistan.[56] Observers report that conditions outside Kabul are reverting to the anarchy of the previous years.[57] As Kimberly Zisk Marten writes, "Creating new security institutions that will be fully operational only after several years' time is not an adequate response to these dangers. To get itself on its feet and prove itself to the population, the central government needs security support throughout the country now, not later."[58]

Without effective central institutions, moreover, there is a danger that democratic elections (currently scheduled for 2004) will act as a stimulus for destructive competition among the country's major factional leaders. The Bonn Agreement explicitly required elections to be held within two years of the formation of the Afghan transitional administration. By emphasizing time limits rather than setting out substantive preconditions for successful elections, the Bonn Agreement repeated the errors of the quick-and-dirty approach to liberalization that, I have argued, diminished the effectiveness of earlier peacebuilding missions. Pressing forward with elections without having first begun the process of building these institutional foundations – including a central government with authority beyond Kabul, agreement on the detailed provisions of a new constitution, an independent judicial mechanism to interpret the constitution and uphold electoral laws, and an effective and neutral security apparatus – is a recipe for continued instability in a country that has no experience with democracy and a long history of violent, zero-sum competition among regional warlords.

The Challenges Ahead

Given the continued problem of civil violence in many parts of the world, the demand for new peacebuilding operations is unlikely to diminish in the coming years. The best hope for future progress toward more realistic and effective forms of postconflict intervention is to build upon the achievements of the Kosovo and East Timor operations and to embrace the IBL strategy in its entirety as the guiding doctrine for peacebuilding. The effective implementation of the IBL strategy, however, will ultimately require more than just a commitment to the specific policies outlined in Chapter 10. In order to accomplish these policies, international peacebuilders will also need 1) to coordinate their activities much more closely, and 2) to rely on strong support from the principal states that sponsor and fund peacebuilding missions. I address each of these issues in turn.

[55] Goodson 2003. [56] Quoted in Reeves 2003. [57] Gall 2003; Bar'el 2003.
[58] Marten 2002/03, p. 39.

Better Coordination of Peacebuilding Agencies

IBL presupposes the ability to manage different elements of peacebuilding in a carefully coordinated manner – elements that include the construction of political and economic institutions, the development of "good" civil society and independent media, the design and implementation of market-oriented economic reforms, and planning for democratic reforms including elections. The decentralized and jumbled structure of peacebuilding operations has been a common criticism of past missions,[59] but lack of coordination among international agencies would be even more problematic under the IBL strategy, which calls for a more controlled and phased approach to liberalization than has been the practice to date.

Institutional turf battles among peacebuilding agencies are common, with individual organizations sometimes working at cross-purposes in vital policy areas. In El Salvador, Mozambique, and Cambodia, for example, the UN urged the governments of these war-shattered states to increase spending on peacebuilding-related programs, while the IMF pushed in the opposite direction, demanding fiscal restraint.[60] Attempts in more recent operations to achieve greater coordination among peacebuilding agencies have been only partly successful. In Kosovo, for example, peacebuilders devised an explicit division of labor that gave specific agencies the primary responsibility for different tasks under the overall supervisory authority of the SRSG, who was empowered to "coordinate the activities of all United Nations agencies and other international organizations" in Kosovo.[61] In practice, however, the mission continued to suffer from significant overlaps and conflicts in the activities of these agencies – a problem that numerous observers noted.[62] Similar criticisms were also leveled against the Bosnia operation, where the "United Nations did not respond as a system but rather as a series of separate and largely autonomous agencies. Each had its own institutional dynamics, formulated its own priorities, and moved according to a timetable of its own devising."[63]

The lack of a clear institutional center for peacebuilding also makes it difficult to accumulate expertise and experience from one mission to the next. Because none of the agencies engaged in these operations views peacebuilding as its *primary* task, the personnel, resources, and knowledge necessary for peacebuilding must be cobbled together every time. This problem was evident in the planning for the East Timor operation.[64] Before the violence

---

[59] For example, Jones 2002; and Fleitz 2002, chap. 5.

[60] On El Salvador see de Soto and del Castillo 1994; on Mozambique see Willet 1995; on Cambodia see UNRISD 1993. For other examples of coordination problems, see Jones 2002; and Fleitz 2002, chap. 5.

[61] "Report of the Secretary-General Pursuant to Paragraph 10 of Security Council Resolution 1244 (1999)," UN document S/1999/672 (June 12, 1999), paras. 2–3.

[62] For example, Erlanger 1999; Rueb 1999; and Wilkinson 2000.   [63] Minear et al. 1994.

[64] This example is drawn from Suhrke 2001.

of 1999, the UN's Department of Political Affairs (DPA) had been the principal unit in the Secretariat to handle East Timor, and it had developed considerable knowledge about local conditions in the territory. But when preparations for a major peacebuilding mission began in the wake of the violence, responsibility for the operation was transferred to the Department of Peacekeeping Operations (DPKO), the unit normally tasked with running military operations. Not only did DPKO lack DPA's local knowledge of East Timor, but it also had little expertise in direct governmental administration, which was a central feature of the mission.[65] Secretary-General Annan himself acknowledged that the mission lacked "important expertise in a number of fields."[66]

The improvised character of peacebuilding can also lead to damaging delays in the deployment of operations to the field. The task of establishing the rule of law, in particular, becomes more complicated when the arrival of peacebuilders is postponed during the vital first weeks of a mission. The Kosovo operation, like others, had to be patched together largely from scratch, thereby slowing the deployment of security and judicial personnel and making it more difficult for UNMIK to perform its governance functions at the outset of the operation. Instead of a strong international presence, a de facto institutional vacuum existed for several weeks, permitting the spread of retributive violence and illegal governance structures – problems that the mission is still struggling to manage.[67]

These and other difficulties that arise from the ad hoc nature of peacebuilding operations have not gone unnoticed within the UN. A high-profile panel report, commissioned by the secretary-general and chaired by former Algerian foreign minister Lakhdar Brahimi, offered the following observations and recommendations in August 2000:

Effective peacebuilding also requires a focal point to coordinate the many different activities that building peace entails. In the view of the Panel, the United Nations should be considered the focal point for peacebuilding activities by the donor community. To that end, there is great merit in creating a consolidated and permanent institutional capacity within the United Nations system.[68]

While the implementation of this proposal might help to resolve some of the organizational problems within the UN itself, it does not address the challenge of coordinating the activities of *non*-UN agencies that are major players in peacebuilding. Tinkering with the UN's internal organizational chart is not enough. What is needed, in the words of the British ambassador

---

[65] Suhrke 2001.
[66] "Report of the Secretary-General on the United Nations Transitional Administration in East Timor (for the period January 27–July 26, 2000)," UN document S/2000/738 (July 26), para 64.
[67] Strauss 1999; USGAO 2002, p. 2.
[68] Panel on United Nations Peace Operations 2000, para. 44.

to the UN, is a "paradigm shift to a more integrated approach among the international institutions" engaged in peacebuilding.[69] The problem is systemic in the sense that it extends across all of the agencies that conduct peacebuilding, and it therefore requires a systemic remedy.

One possible solution is the creation of a new central international agency (either inside or outside the existing structure of the UN) that would be dedicated to postconflict peacebuilding.[70] This agency could be equipped with a permanent staff of experts on international governance and postconflict rehabilitation, some of whom might be rapidly deployed to establish the leadership component of new peacebuilding missions. For the bulk of the civilian personnel and equipment required for each operation, the agency could rely on prenegotiated agreements with other international organizations (including regional organizations, such as the OSCE and EU, and UN agencies), which would pledge in advance to provide staff and resources directly to the central peacebuilding agency for the duration of the mission. In this way, peacebuilding personnel would be responsible to a single entity, not to a hodgepodge of independent agencies. On the military side, the new body could continue to rely on the UN Security Council to authorize either UN-run "blue helmet" forces or non-UN "coalitions of the willing." But these forces, once created, should be placed under the direct authority of the peacebuilding agency, acting on behalf of the Security Council. The ultimate disposition of military forces – including the power to terminate the military dimension of operations – should remain under the jurisdiction of the Security Council, but the day-to-day management of military forces should be fully delegated to the peacebuilding organization.

Because political control of this peacebuilding body would be a sensitive issue, a new political council should be created with the sole purpose of overseeing the agency's activities. The council's composition might be designed to reflect the constellation of actors that have the most direct interest in postconflict peacebuilding, including national governments and major international and nongovernmental organizations that are deeply involved. State membership might be determined by the Security Council, perhaps on a system of rotating regional representation, reserving a certain number of seats for states that have contributed the most resources to previous missions.

---

[69] "Statement to the Security Council by Sir Jeremy Greenstock, Permanent Representative of the United Kingdom, February 5, 2001," reproduced on the website of the United Kingdom Mission to the United Nations, http://www.ukun.org/xq/asp/SarticleType.17/Article_ID.207/qx/articles_show.htm, accessed in August 2002.

[70] If the new agency is established within the UN framework, it should be conceived as an entirely new body, not a reconstituted version of the UN Trusteeship Council. Reviving the Trusteeship Council would be legally difficult (Gordon 1995) and might unnecessarily taint the new peacebuilding agency with the Trusteeship Council's historical connections to colonialism (Langford 1999).

Major international and nongovernmental organizations could also serve on a rotating basis.

Some might oppose the creation of a centralized peacebuilding organization on the grounds that it would represent a revival of colonialism. In particular, comparisons might be drawn between the new body and the League of Nations' mandates system or the United Nations' trusteeship system, which served the quasi-colonial function of legitimizing the continuation of direct foreign rule by certain "advanced" states over a number of "non-self-governing territories," most of which were former European colonies.[71] Yet there would be vital differences between those older mechanisms and the proposed new peacebuilding agency: Countries placed under the authority of the new agency would be administered not by a single state, as in the mandates and trusteeship systems, but by a multilateral organization comprised of several states, along with international and nongovernmental organizations. The decisions of this new entity would be subject to the approval of the agency's political council, and ultimately to the oversight of the UN Security Council. Local parties in the host state would also be provided with an opportunity to address the political council and with the right to appeal its decisions. Most importantly, the new agency would not serve as a "cover" for the continuation of colonialism, as the mandates and trusteeship systems largely did,[72] but would seek instead to restore the effective sovereignty of war-shattered states by working to create conditions under which such states could govern themselves independently and peacefully.[73]

---

[71] After World War I, the League of Nations established a mandates system to oversee the administration of colonies that had been stripped from Germany and Turkey as a result of their defeat in the war, and it assigned responsibility to particular states – most notably, Britain and France – to administer the dependent territories directly, under the general supervision of the League's Mandates Council (see Wright 1930; and Hall 1948). The administering states were required to provide for the "welfare and development" of their dependent territories and to help them develop the capacity to eventually "stand by themselves under the strenuous conditions of the modern world" (Article 22 of the League Covenant). But in practice, the Mandates Council imposed few practical constraints on the behavior of the administering states themselves, which tended to treat these territories as colonial holdings of their own. After World War II, the mandates system was incorporated into the UN's new Trusteeship Council, which again assigned administrative responsibilities to particular states, mostly former colonial powers (Article 73 of the UN Charter). With the rise of the decolonization movement in the 1950s and 1960s, however, most trust territories moved quickly to independence.

[72] Haas 1952 and 1953.

[73] That said, peacebuilding does represent a form of international control over territories that have proven incapable of self-government, and in this sense may be viewed as a type of trusteeship, but one that is essential in order to prevent the recurrence of civil wars that have devastated civilian populations and threatened regional and international security. For an elaboration of this argument, including a discussion of the similarities and differences between peacebuilding and colonialism, see Paris 2002a.

There may be other ways – apart from creating a new, central peace-building agency – to address the problem of insufficient coordination among peacebuilding agencies. But whatever solutions are considered, the broader point is that current arrangements are not well suited to the implementation of the relatively demanding policies of the IBL strategy. Indeed, unless the coordination problem is remedied, the IBL strategy may be too difficult to implement in practice.

The Requirement of Political Support

In addition to establishing mechanisms aimed at centralizing the manage-ment of peacebuilding, implementing the IBL strategy will also demand ex-tensive political and financial support from the states and international orga-nizations that fund and administer peacebuilding operations. Critics might argue that the international community currently lacks the political will to implement the IBL strategy – and they might be right. The minimalist char-acter of the peacebuilding mission in Afghanistan seems to have been driven, in part, by the hope of accomplishing the goals of postconflict reconstruc-tion "on the cheap." One of the functions of this book, however, has been to highlight the inadequacy of half-hearted and hurried approaches to peace-building, and to make the case for a more sustained and serious response to the problem of consolidating peace in war-shattered states.

Faced with the challenges of postconflict reconstruction, the international community has three basic options. First, it can choose to ignore these chal-lenges by allowing war-torn states to sort out their own problems without international involvement. This, I would argue, is the worst possible course of action. Chronic civil violence poses a threat most directly to people living within affected states, whose suffering cannot be ignored, particularly when it becomes so acute that it attracts the attention of international media. Even if we were to disregard this suffering, the problems of state failure and civil conflict can rarely be contained within the borders of a single state, or even a single region. As one World Bank study has shown, intrastate wars tend to destabilize neighboring countries, produce the world's largest refugee flows, spread infectious diseases like malaria and HIV, facilitate the production and international trafficking of illegal narcotics, and attract international criminal syndicates and terrorist groups.[74] Thus, allowing conflict-ridden countries to fester in violence is "not just heartless, it is foolish."[75] Such arguments may be gaining ground, particularly since the terrorist attacks of September 11, 2001, which prompted policymakers in many countries to acknowledge that global security depends, in part, on establishing effective governments within failed states.

The second option for the international community is to maintain the sta-tus quo and launch new peacebuilding missions on the same faulty and overly

[74] Collier et al. 2003, chap. 2.   [75] Ibid., p. 11.

optimistic premises that governed the design and conduct of missions in the 1990s: that war-torn states can be transformed into stable market democracies without investing the time and effort in establishing the institutional conditions for successful democratization and marketization. For reasons I have already described in detail, this approach is not likely to provide a sustainable or effective response to the problem of civil violence.

The third option is to rethink the basic assumptions, strategies, and tools of peacebuilding. Chapter 10 identified guidelines for a new Institutionalization Before Liberalization strategy, derived from the preceding analysis of the flawed assumptions of recent peacebuilding missions. Although IBL is just one possible alternative to the status quo, any new approaches should be based on the understanding that rapid democratization and marketization do not provide an easy cure for civil violence.

Conclusion

The record of peacebuilding in Kosovo, East Timor, Sierra Leone, and Afghanistan offers cause for both hope and concern over the prospects of implementing the IBL strategy. In Kosovo and East Timor, peacebuilding agencies appear to have learned from previous experience that rapid liberalization without adequate attention to the construction of effective institutions is a risky strategy for rehabilitating war-shattered states. But the new emphasis on more assertive and longer-lasting peacebuilding operations, focusing more directly on the task of institutionalization, has been tentative and incomplete, even in East Timor and Kosovo. Furthermore, the peacebuilding experience in Sierra Leone and Afghanistan, where efforts to rebuild domestic institutions have been relatively insubstantial, suggests that the lessons highlighted in this book remain largely unlearned, with potentially grave consequences for both of these countries.

Conclusion

Peacebuilders in the 1990s placed their faith in rapid democratization and marketization as a means of consolidating peace in countries that were just emerging from civil wars. As it turned out, however, immediate liberalization generated a number of destabilizing side effects that endangered the very peace that such policies were intended to strengthen. This conclusion has cast doubt on the prevailing methods of peacebuilding. It has also exposed a blind spot in the existing literature on the "liberal peace thesis," which has paid relatively little attention to the war-proneness of states that are undergoing the transition to market democracy, particularly those with a recent history of civil conflict.

A central dilemma for peacebuilders, I have argued, is to devise methods of avoiding the pathologies of liberalization, while placing war-shattered states on a long-term path to democracy and market-oriented economics. The first step in resolving this dilemma is to recognize that democratization and marketization are inherently tumultuous and conflict-promoting processes, and that postconflict states are poorly equipped to manage these disruptions. By constructing the foundations of effective political and economic institutions prior to implementing extensive liberalizing reforms, peacebuilders should be able to bolster the "conflict dampening" qualities of societies that host these missions, and in so doing, increase the likelihood of a successful, gradual, and peaceful transition to stable market democracy over the longer term. Classical liberal theorists understood the importance of effective state institutions as a prerequisite for domestic peace, and their insights should now be reincorporated into the scholarship on the liberal peace and into the practice of peacebuilding itself.

The effectiveness of future peacebuilding operations has implications that reach far beyond the borders of the states hosting such operations. One of the principal problems facing the world in the early years of the twenty-first century is the prevalence of internal war and state failure. Chronic civil violence cannot be ignored, for it directly endangers millions of innocent civilians; threatens the stability of neighboring states; impedes efforts to control the spread of disease, famine and crime; and provides refuge to transnational terrorist organizations. Unless the international community improves its techniques for preventing hostilities from reigniting after a cease-fire, attempts to terminate ongoing conflicts will have little prospect of achieving durable and self-sustaining, stable peace. Making peacebuilding more effective is, therefore, an essential first step in countering the broader problem of civil conflict in the post–Cold War era.

Bibliography

Abi-Saab, Georges. 1978. *The United Nations Operation in the Congo, 1960–1964.* Oxford: Oxford University Press.

Abrahamsen, Rita. 1997. "The Victory of Popular Forces or Passive Revolution? A Neo-Gramscian Perspective on Democratization." *Journal of Modern African Studies* 35:1 (March), pp. 129–152.

Abrahamsson, Hans, and Anders Nilsson. 1995. *Mozambique: The Troubled Transition.* Translated by Mary Dally. London: Zed.

Acevedo, Carlos. 1996. "The Historical Background to the Conflict," in James K. Boyce, ed., *Economic Policy for Building Peace.* Boulder, Colo.: Lynne Rienner, pp. 19–30.

Acevedo, Domingo E., and Claudio Grossman. 1996. "The Organization of American States and the Protection of Democracy," in Tom Farer, ed., *Beyond Sovereignty: Collectively Defending Democracy in the Americas.* Baltimore: Johns Hopkins University Press, pp. 132–149.

Adebajo, Adekeye. 2002. "Liberia: A Warlord's Peace," in Stephen John Stedman, Donald Rothchild, and Elizabeth M. Cousens, eds., *Ending Civil Wars: The Implementation of Peace Agreements.* Boulder, Colo.: Lynne Rienner, pp. 599–630.

Adekanye, J. 'Bayo. 1995. "Structural Adjustment, Democratization and Rising Ethnic Tensions in Africa." *Development and Change* 26:2 (April), pp. 355–374.

Adelman, Howard, and Astri Suhrke, with Bruce Jones. 1996. *The International Response to Conflict and Genocide: Lessons From the Rwandan Experience,* Study 2: *Early Warning and Conflict Management.* Copenhagen: Joint Evaluation of Emergency Assistance to Rwanda, Foreign Ministry of Denmark.

Africa Watch. 1992. *Accountability in Namibia: Human Rights and the Transition to Democracy.* Washington, D.C.: Africa Watch/Human Rights Watch.

Akashi, Yasushi. 1994. "The Challenge of Peacekeeping in Cambodia." *International Peacekeeping* 1:2 (Summer), pp. 204–215.

Ake, Claude. 1967. *A Theory of Political Integration.* Homewood, Ill.: Dorsey.

Ake, Claude. 1974. "Modernization and Political Instability: A Theoretical Exploration." *World Politics* 26:4 (July), pp. 576–591.

Ake, Claude. 1996. *Democracy and Development in Africa.* Washington, D.C.: Brookings Institution.

Alao, Abiodun. 1998. *The Burden of Collective Goodwill: The International Involvement in the Liberian Civil War.* Aldershot, U.K.: Ashgate.

Alao, Abiodun, John Mackinlay, and Funmi Olonisakin. 1999. *Peacekeepers, Politicians, and Warlords: The Liberian Peace Process.* Tokyo: United Nations University Press.

Alden, Chris. 1996. "Political Violence in Mozambique: Past, Present, and Future." *Terrorism and Political Violence* 8:4 (Winter), pp. 40–57.

Alden, Chris. 2001. *Mozambique and the Construction of the New African State: From Negotiations to Nation Building.* London: Palgrave.

Alden, Chris, and Mark Simpson. 1993. "Mozambique: A Delicate Peace." *Journal of Modern African Studies* 31:1 (March), pp. 109–130.

Amnesty International. 1998. "Mozambique: Human Rights and the Police." Document no. AFR 41/01/98 (April 1).

Amnesty International. 2002. "Liberia: State of Emergency Signifies a Greater Need for International Involvement in Human Rights Protection." Document no. AFR 34/004/2002 (April 9).

Anderson, Leslie, and Lawrence C. Dodd. 2002. "Nicaragua Votes: The Elections of 2001." *Journal of Democracy* 13:3 (July), pp. 80–94.

Annan, Kofi. 1997. "Good Governance Essential to Development, Prosperity, Peace, Secretary-General Tells International Conference." UN press release SG/SM/6291 DEV/2166 (July 28).

Annan, Kofi. 1998. "The Causes of Conflict and the Promotion of Durable Peace and Sustainable Development in Africa." Report of the Secretary-General to the Security Council, UN document no. S/1998/318 (April 13).

Annan, Kofi. 1999a. "Peace and Development – One Struggle, Two Fronts." Address to the staff of the World Bank (October 19), http://www.worldbank.org/html/extdr/extme/kasp101999.htm, accessed in March 2002.

Annan, Kofi. 1999b. "Report of the Secretary-General on the Work of the Organization." UN document no. A/51/4 (August 31).

Annan, Kofi. 2000. UN Secretary General Kofi Annan's Closing Remarks to the Ministerial Meeting, "Towards A Community of Democracies" conference. Reproduced on the website of the United States delegation to the conference, http://www.democracyconference.org/kofiannan.html, accessed in March 2002.

Annan, Kofi. 2001. "War Less Likely Between Mature Democracies." Speech at Oxford University, UN document no. SG/SM/7850 (June 19).

Annan, Kofi. 2002. "Celebrating the Birth of a Nation." *Christian Science Monitor* (May 7).

Anstee, Margaret Joan. 1996. *Orphan of the Cold War: The Inside Story of the Collapse of the Angolan Peace Process, 1992–93.* New York: St. Martin's.

Apter, David. 1970. "Political Systems and Developmental Change," in Robert T. Holt and John E. Turner, eds., *The Methodology of Comparative Research.* New York: Free Press, pp. 151–171.

Arana, Mario. 1997. "General Economic Policy," in Thomas W. Walker, ed., *Nicaragua Without Illusions: Regime Transition and Structural Adjustment in the 1990s.* Wilmington, Del.: Scholarly Resources, pp. 81–96.

Aravena, Oscar Catalán. 1996. "Controlling Hyperinflation and Structural Adjustment in Nicaragua," in Alex E. Fernández Jilberto and André Mommen, eds., *Liberalization in the Developing World: Institutional and Economic Changes in Latin America, Africa and Asia.* New York: Routledge, pp. 122–137.

Arfi, Badredine. 1998. "Democratization and Communal Politics." *Democratization* 5:1 (Spring), pp. 42–63.

Arias, Oscar. 1997. "Ten Years After Esquipulas: Looking Toward the Future." Speech delivered at the tenth annual meeting of the Academic Council on the United Nations System, San José, Costa Rica (June 25), Academic Council on the United Nations System Reports and Papers no. 4. Providence, R.I.: Academic Council on the United Nations System.

Arieff, Irwin. 2002. "Kosovo Governor Keen to Cede UN Power." Reuters (February 11).

Armijo, Leslie Elliot, Thomas J. Biersteker, and Abraham F. Lowenthal. 1994. "The Problems of Simultaneous Transitions." *Journal of Democracy* 5:4 (October), pp. 161–175.

Armony, Ariel C. 1997. "The Former Contras," in Thomas W. Walker, ed., *Nicaragua Without Illusions: Regime Transition and Structural Adjustment in the 1990s.* Wilmington, Del.: Scholarly Resources, pp. 203–218.

Article Nineteen. 1995. *Broadcasting Genocide: Censorship, Propaganda and State-Sponsored Violence in Rwanda, 1990–1994.* London: Article Nineteen.

Associated Press. 1997. "El Salvador's Ex-Rebels Gaining Some Political Clout." *Miami Herald* (March 18).

Associated Press. 1998. "Cambodian Forces Battle Near Thai Border." *New York Times* (January 18).

Austin, Dennis. 1994. *Democracy and Violence in India and Sri Lanka.* London: Royal Institute of International Affairs.

Ayoob, Mohammed. 1995. *The Third World Security Predicament: State Making, Regional Conflict, and the International System.* Boulder, Colo.: Lynne Rienner.

Babst, D. V. 1972. "A Force for Peace." *Industrial Research* 14 (April), pp. 55–58.

Baloyra, Enrique A. 1982. *El Salvador in Transition.* Chapel Hill: University of North Carolina Press.

Barclay, Anthony. 1999. "Consolidating Peace Through Governance and Regional Cooperation: The Liberian Experience," in Adebayo Adedeji, ed., *Comprehending and Mastering African Conflict: The Search for Sustainable Peace and Good Governance.* London: Zed, pp. 297–316.

Bar'el, Zvi. 2003. "Flaws in the Afghan Model." *Haaretz* (March 14).

Barkan, Joel D. 1997. "Can Established Democracies Nurture Democracy Abroad? Lessons from Africa," in Axel Hadenius, ed., *Democracy's Victory and Crisis.* Cambridge: Cambridge University Press, pp. 371–403.

Barnett, Michael. 1995. "The New United Nations Politics of Peace: From Juridical Sovereignty to Empirical Sovereignty." *Global Governance* 1:1 (January–March), pp. 79–97.

Barnett, Michael. 1997. "Bringing In the New World Order: Liberalism, Legitimacy, and the United Nations." *World Politics* 49:4 (July), pp. 526–551.

Barrett, John. 1996. "NATO Reform: Alliance Policy and Cooperative Security," in Ingo Peters, ed., *New Security Challenges: The Adaptation of International Institutions.* New York: St. Martin's, pp. 123–151.

Bartlett, Will, and Višnja Samardžija. 2000. "The Reconstruction of South East Europe, the Stability Pact and the Role of the EU: An Overview." *Moct-Most: Economic Journal on Eastern Europe and the Soviet Union* 10:2, pp. 245–263.

Bauer, Gretchen. 1999. "Challenges to Democratic Consolidation in Namibia," in Richard Joseph, ed., *State, Conflict, and Democracy in Africa.* Boulder, Colo.: Lynne Rienner, pp. 429–448.

Baylies, Carolyn. 1995. "'Political Conditionality' and Democratization." *Review of African Political Economy* 65:22 (September), pp. 321–337.

Beauvais, Joel C. 2001. "Benevolent Despotism: A Critique of UN State-Building in East Timor." *New York University Journal of International Law and Politics* 33:4 (Summer), pp. 1101–1178.

Beitz, Charles R. 1981. "Democracy in Developing Societies." in Peter G. Brown and Henry Shue, eds., *Boundaries: National Autonomy and Its Limits.* Totowa, N.J.: Rowman and Littlefield, pp. 177–208.

Belloni, Roberto. 2001. "Civil Society and Peacebuilding in Bosnia and Herzegovina." *Journal of Peace Research* 38:2 (March), pp. 163–180.

Benería, Lourdes, and Breny Mendoza. 1995. "Structural Adjustment and Social Emergency Funds: The Cases of Honduras, Mexico and Nicaragua." *European Journal of Development Research* 7:1 (June), pp. 53–76.

Berdal, Mats, and Michael Leifer. 1996. "Cambodia." in James Mayall, ed., *The New Interventionism 1991–1994: United Nations Experience in Cambodia, Former Yugoslavia, and Somalia.* Cambridge: Cambridge University Press, pp. 25–58.

Berman, Sheri. 1997. "Civil Society and the Collapse of the Weimar Republic." *World Politics* 49:3 (April), pp. 401–429.

Berns, Laurence. 1987. "Thomas Hobbes," in Leo Strauss and Joseph Cropsey, eds., *History of Political Philosophy*, 3d ed. Chicago: University of Chicago Press, pp. 396–420.

Bertram, Eva. 1995. "Reinventing Governments: The Promise and Perils of United Nations Peace Building." *Journal of Conflict Resolution* 39:3 (September), pp. 387–418.

Bhattacharya, Rina. 1997. "Pace, Sequencing and Credibility of Structural Reforms." *World Development* 25:7 (July), pp. 1045–1061.

Bird, Graham, and Ann Helwege. 1997. "Can Neoliberalism Survive in Latin America?" *Millennium* 26:1, pp. 31–56.

Birdsall, Nancy, and Frederick Jaspersen, eds. 1997. *Pathways to Growth: Comparing East Asia and Latin America.* Washington, D.C.: Inter-American Development Bank.

Bjornlund, Eric. 2001. "Democracy Inc." *Wilson Quarterly* (Summer), pp. 18–24.

Black, James. 1998. "Scorched Earth in a Time of Peace." *NACLA Report on the Americas* 32:1 (July–August), pp. 11–15.

Blair, Harry. 1997. "Donors, Democratization and Civil Society: Relating Theory to Practice," in David Hulme and Michael Edwards, eds., *NGOs, States and Donors: Too Close for Comfort?* New York: St. Martin's, pp. 23–42.

Bliss, Harry, and Bruce Russett. 1998. "Democratic Trading Partners: The Liberal Connection." *Journal of Politics* 60:4 (November), pp. 1126–1147.

Bøås, Morten. 2001. "Liberia and Sierra Leone – Dead Ringers? The Logic of Neopatrimonial Rule." *Third World Quarterly* 22:5 (October), pp. 697–723.

Boli, John, and George M. Thomas. 1997. "World Culture in the World Polity: A Century of International Non-Governmental Organization." *American Sociological Review* 62:2 (April), pp. 171–190.

Boli, John, and George M. Thomas, eds. 1999. *Constructing World Culture: International Nongovernmental Organizations Since 1875*. Stanford, Calif.: Stanford University Press.

Boniface, Dexter S. 2002. "Is There a Democratic Norm in the Americas? An Analysis of the Organization of American States." *Global Governance* 8:3 (July–September), pp. 365–381.

Booth, John A., and Thomas W. Walker. 1999. *Understanding Central America*, 3d ed. Boulder, Colo.: Westview.

Borden, Anthony, Slavenka Drakulic, and George Kenny. 1996. "Bosnia's Democratic Charade." *The Nation* 263:8 (September 23), pp. 14–20.

Boutros-Ghali, Boutros. 1992. *An Agenda for Peace: Preventive Diplomacy, Peacemaking and Peace-keeping*. New York: United Nations.

Boutros-Ghali, Boutros. 1994. *An Agenda for Development*. New York: United Nations.

Boutros-Ghali, Boutros. 1995. "Supplement to An Agenda for Peace." UN document no. A/50/60-S/1995/1 (January 3).

Boutros-Ghali, Boutros. 1996. *An Agenda for Democratization*. New York: United Nations.

Boyce, James K. 1995. "Adjustment Toward Peace: An Introduction." *World Development* 23:12 (December), pp. 2067–2077.

Boyce, James K. 2002. *Investing in Peace: Aid and Conditionality After Civil Wars*. Adelphi Paper no. 351. London: International Institute for Strategic Studies.

Boyce, James K., and Manuel Pastor, Jr. 1997. "Macroeconomic Policy and Peace Building in El Salvador," in Krishna Kumar, ed., *Rebuilding Societies After Civil War: Critical Roles for International Assistance*. Boulder, Colo.: Lynne Rienner, pp. 287–314.

Boyd, Charles G. 1998. "Making Bosnia Work." *Foreign Affairs* 77:1 (January/February), pp. 42–55.

Brass, Paul R. 1974. *Language, Religion and Politics in North India*. Cambridge: Cambridge University Press.

Brautigam, Deborah. 1996. "State Capacity and Effective Governance," in Benno Ndulu et al., *Agenda for Africa's Economic Renewal*. New Brunswick, N.J.: Transaction Publishers, pp. 81–108.

Brittain, Victoria. 1998. *Death of Dignity: Angola's Civil War*. London: Pluto.

Bryant, Christopher G. A. 1993. "Social Self-Organization, Civility, and Sociology: A Comment on Kumar's 'Civil Society.'" *British Journal of Sociology* 44:3 (September), pp. 397–401.

Buckley, Stephen. 1998. "Mass Slaughter Was Avoidable, General Says." *Washington Post* (February 26).

Burkhalter, Holly J. 1994/95. "The Question of Genocide: The Clinton Administration and Rwanda." *World Policy Journal* 11:4 (Winter), pp. 44–54.

Business Week. 2000. "Guatemala on Three Dollars a Day" (November 6).

Byman, Daniel, and Stephen Van Evera. 1998. "Why They Fight: Hypotheses on the Causes of Contemporary Deadly Conflict." *Security Studies* 7:3 (Spring), pp. 1–50.

Cahen, Michel. 1993. "Check on Socialism in Mozambique – What Check? What Socialism?" *Review of African Political Economy* 20:57 (July), pp. 46–59.

Callaghy, Thomas R. 1993. "Vision and Politics in the Transformation of Global Political Economy: Lessons from the Second and Third Worlds," in Robert O. Slater, Barry M. Schutz, and Steven R. Dorr, eds., *Global Transformation and the Third World*. Boulder, Colo.: Lynne Rienner, pp. 161–257.

Campbell, David. 1998. *National Deconstruction: Violence, Identity, and Justice in Bosnia*. Minneapolis: University of Minnesota Press.

Canas, Antonio, and Hector Dada. 1999. "Political Transition and Institutionalization in El Salvador," in Cynthia J. Arnson, ed., *Comparative Peace Processes in Latin America*. Stanford, Calif.: Stanford University Press, pp. 69–95.

Caplan, Richard. 2002. *A New Trusteeship? The International Administration of War-Torn Territories*. Adelphi Paper no. 341. New York: Oxford University Press.

Carothers, Thomas. 1994. "Democracy and Human Rights: Policy Allies or Rivals?" *Washington Quarterly* 17:3 (Summer), pp. 109–120.

Carothers, Thomas. 1999. *Aiding Democracy Abroad: The Learning Curve*. Washington, D.C.: Carnegie Endowment for International Peace.

Carothers, Thomas. 2000. "The Clinton Record on Democracy Promotion." Carnegie Endowment for International Peace Working Paper no. 16 (September).

Carothers, Thomas. 2002. "The End of the Transition Paradigm." *Journal of Democracy* 13:1 (January), pp. 5–21.

Caufield, Catherine. 1996. *Masters of Illusion: The World Bank and the Poverty of Nations*. New York: Henry Holt.

CBC [Canadian Broadcasting Corporation]. 1995. "Rwanda: Autopsy of a Genocide." *Prime Time News* (July 5).

Chambers, Simone, and Jeffrey Kopstein. 2001. "Bad Civil Society." *Political Theory* 29:6 (December), pp. 837–865.

Chan, Steve. 1997. "In Search of Democratic Peace: Problems and Promise." *Mershon International Studies Review* 41 (supp. 1), pp. 59–91.

Chandler, David. 1999a. *Bosnia: Faking Democracy After Dayton*. London: Pluto.

Chandler, David. 1999b. "The Limits of Peacebuilding: International Regulation and Civil Society Development in Bosnia." *International Peacekeeping* 6:1 (Spring), pp. 109–125.

Chandler, David. 2001. "Bosnia: The Democracy Paradox." *Current History* 100:644 (March), pp. 114–119.

Chandrasekaran, Rajiv. 2002. "Saved From Ruin: The Reincarnation of East Timor." *Christian Science Monitor* (May 19).

Cheema, Shabbir. 1999. "Opening Remarks." Conference on Electoral Management Bodies as Institutions of Governance, Mexico City, Mexico (May 26–29), http://magnet.undp.org/Docs/electoral/opening_remarks.htm, accessed in March 2002.

Chege, Michael. 1996/97. "Africa's Murderous Professors." *National Interest* 46 (Winter), pp. 32–40.

Chege, Michael. 2002. "Sierra Leone: The State That Came Back from the Dead." *Washington Quarterly* 25:3 (Summer), pp. 147–160.

Chernick, Marc W. 1996. "Peacemaking and Violence in Latin America." in Michael E. Brown, ed., *The International Dimensions of Internal Conflict*. Cambridge, Mass.: MIT Press, pp. 267–307.

Chesterman, Simon. 2002. "Walking Softly in Afghanistan: The Future of UN State-Building." *Survival* 44:3 (Autumn), pp. 37–46.

Child, Jack. 1992. *The Central American Peace Process, 1983–1991: Sheathing Swords, Building Confidence.* Boulder, Colo.: Lynne Rienner.

Child, Jack. 2000. "External Actors: The United Nations and the Organization of American States," in Thomas W. Walker and Ariel C. Armony, eds., *Repression, Resistance, and Democratic Transition in Central America.* Wilmington, Del.: Scholarly Resources, pp. 165–185.

Chiriyankandath, James. 1991. "The 1986 Elections: Tradition, Ideology and Ethnicity," in Peter Woodward, ed., *Sudan After Nimeiri.* New York: Routledge, pp. 76–91.

Chopra, Jarat. 1994. *United Nations Authority in Cambodia.* Thomas J. Watson Jr. Institute for International Studies Occasional Paper no. 15. Providence, R.I.: Watson Institute, Brown University.

Chopra, Jarat. 2000. "The UN's Kingdom in East Timor." *Survival* 42:3 (Autumn), pp. 27–39.

Chopra, Jarat. 2002. "Building State Failure in East Timor." *Development and Change* 33:5 (November), pp. 979–1000.

Chossudovsky, Michel. 1997. *The Globalization of Poverty: Impacts of the IMF and World Bank Reform.* London: Zed Books.

Cigar, Norman. 1995. *Genocide in Bosnia: The Policy of "Ethnic Cleansing."* College Station: Texas A&M University Press.

CIIR [Catholic Institute for International Relations]. 1993. *El Salvador: Wager for Peace.* London: CIIR.

Ciment, James. 1997. *Angola and Mozambique: Postcolonial Wars in Southern Africa.* New York: Facts on File.

Clapham, Christopher. 1998. "Rwanda: The Perils of Peacemaking." *Journal of Peace Research* 35:2 (March), pp. 193–210.

Clark, Elizabeth Spiro. 2000. "Why Elections Matter." *Washington Quarterly* 23:3 (Summer), pp. 27–40.

Clerc, Valérie. 2000. "The Reconstruction of War-Torn Societies: A Bibliography." Centre for Applied Studies in International Negotiations (CASIN), Geneva, http://www.casin.ch/pdf/bibliography.pdf, accessed in August 2002.

Cliffe, Lionel, with Ray Bush, Jenny Lindsay, Brian Mokopakgosi, Donna Pankhurst, and Balefi Tsie. 1994. *The Transition to Independence in Namibia.* Boulder, Colo.: Lynne Rienner.

Cockell, John G. 2000. "Conceptualizing Peacebuilding: Human Security and Sustainable Peace," in Michael Pugh, ed., *Regeneration of War-Torn Societies.* London: Macmillan, pp. 15–34.

Cohen, Lenard J. 1993. *Broken Bonds: The Disintegration of Yugoslavia.* Boulder, Colo.: Westview.

Collier, Paul, Lani Elliot, Håvard Hegre, Anke Hoeffler, Marta Reynal-Querol, and Nicholas Sambanis. 2003. *Breaking the Conflict Trap: Civil War and Development Policy.* Washington, D.C., and New York: World Bank and Oxford University Press.

Collier, Paul, and Anke Hoeffler. 2002. "Aid, Policy and Growth in Post-Conflict Societies." World Bank Policy Research Working Paper no. 2902 (October).

Collier, Paul, and Nicholas Sambanis. 2002. "Understanding Civil War: A New Agenda." *Journal of Conflict Resolution* 46:1 (February), pp. 3–12.

Commins, Stephen. 1997. "World Vision International and Donors: Too Close for Comfort?" in David Hulme and Michael Edwards, eds., *NGOs, States and Donors: Too Close for Comfort?* New York: St. Martin's, pp. 140–155.

Connor, Walker. 1972. "Nation-Building or Nation-Destroying?" *World Politics* 24:3 (April), pp. 319–355.

Constantine, Gus. 1996. "Namibia Stands as UN Success Story in Africa." *Washington Times* (June 13).

Conteh, Al-Hassan, Joseph S, Guannu, Hal Badio, and Claneh W. Bruce. 1999. "Liberia," in Adebayo Adedeji, ed., *Comprehending and Mastering African Conflict: The Search for Sustainable Peace and Good Governance*. New York: Zed Books, pp. 104–140.

Cornia, Giovanni Andrea, Richard Jolly, and Frances Stewart, eds. 1987. *Adjustment with a Human Face*. Oxford: Clarendon Press.

Coser, Lewis A. 1956. *The Functions of Social Conflict*. Glencoe, Ill.: Free Press.

Cousens, Elizabeth. 1997. "Making Peace in Bosnia Work." *Cornell International Law Journal* 30:3, pp. 769–818.

Cousens, Elizabeth M. 2001. "Introduction," in Elizabeth M. Cousens and Chetan Kumar, eds., *Peacebuilding As Politics: Cultivating Peace in Fragile Societies*. Boulder, Colo.: Lynne Rienner, pp. 1–20.

Cousens, Elizabeth M., and Chetan Kumar, eds. 2001. *Peacebuilding As Politics: Cultivating Peace in Fragile Societies*. Boulder, Colo.: Lynne Rienner.

Cox, Marcus. 2001. "State Building and Post Conflict Reconstruction: Lessons from Bosnia." Geneva: Centre for Applied Studies in International Negotiations.

Cropsey, Joseph. 1957. *Polity and Economy: An Interpretation of the Principles of Adam Smith*. The Hague: Martinus Nijhoff.

CSCE [Conference on Security and Cooperation in Europe]. 1990. "Document of the Copenhagen Meeting of the Conference on the Human Dimension, June 29, 1990," http://www.osce.org/docs/english/1990-1999/hd/cope90e.htm, accessed in May 2003.

Daalder, Ivo H. 1996. "Fear and Loathing in the Former Yugoslavia," in Michael E. Brown, ed., *The International Dimensions of Internal Conflict*. Cambridge, Mass.: MIT Press, pp. 35–67.

Dahl, Robert A. 1971. *Polyarchy: Participation and Opposition*. New Haven, Conn.: Yale University Press.

Dahl, Robert A. 1982. *Dilemmas of Pluralist Democracy: Autonomy vs. Control*. New Haven, Conn.: Yale University Press.

Dahl, Robert A. 1986. *Democracy, Liberty, and Equality*. Oslo: Norwegian University Press.

Dahrendorf, Nicola, and Hrair Balian. 1999. *The Limits and Scope for the Use of Development Assistance Incentives and Disincentives for Influencing Conflict Situations: Case Study – Bosnia and Herzegovina*. Paris: Organization for Economic Cooperation and Development, Development Assistance Committee, Informal Task Force on Conflict, Peace and Development Cooperation.

Daley, Suzanne. 1996. "In Mozambique, Guns for Plowshares and Bicycles." *New York Times* (March 2).

Dalton, George. 1965. "History, Politics, and Economic Development in Liberia." *Journal of Economic History* 25:4 (December), pp. 569–591.

Dalton, Juan Jose. 1996. "El Salvador: The Ideology of Fear." Inter Press Service (November 12).

Debrix, François. 1999. *Re-Envisioning Peacekeeping: The United Nations and the Mobilization of Ideology*. Minneapolis: University of Minnesota Press.

Decalo, Samuel. 1992. "The Process, Prospects and Constraints of Democratization in Africa." *African Affairs* 91:362 (January), pp. 7–35.

del Castillo, Graciana. 2001. "Post-Conflict Reconstruction and the Challenge to International Organizations: The Case of El Salvador." *World Development* 29:12 (December), pp. 1967–1985.

Dempsey, Gary. 2001. "Kosovo's Contradictory Elections." Washington, D.C.: CATO Institute, http://www.cato.org/dailys/12-07-01.html, accessed in July 2002.

Deng, Francis M. 1995. *War of Visions: Conflict of Identities in the Sudan*. Washington, D.C.: Brookings Institution.

Denitch, Bogdan. 1996. *Ethnic Nationalism: The Tragic Death of Yugoslavia*, 2d ed. Minneapolis: University of Minnesota Press.

Denitch, Bogdan. 2000. "Democratic Breakthrough in Croatia." *Dissent* 47:2 (Spring), pp. 34–36.

Denmark, Government of. 1995. *Structural Adjustment in Africa: A Survey of the Experience*. Copenhagen: Centre for Development Research, Ministry of Foreign Affairs.

de Soto, Alvaro, and Graciana del Castillo. 1994. "Obstacles to Peacebuilding." *Foreign Policy* 94 (Spring), pp. 69–83.

de Soto, Alvaro, and Graciana del Castillo. 1995. "Implementation of Comprehensive Peace Agreements: Staying the Course in El Salvador." *Global Governance* 1:2 (May–August), pp. 189–203.

de Sousa, Clara. 2003. "Rebuilding Rural Livelihoods and Social Capital in Mozambique," in Tony Addison, ed., *From Conflict to Recovery in Africa*. New York: Oxford University Press, pp. 51–72.

Destexhe, Alain. 1995. *Rwanda and Genocide in the Twentieth Century*. New York: New York University Press.

de Tocqueville, Alexis. 1988. *Democracy in America*. Translated by George Lawrence. Edited by J. P. Mayer. New York: HarperPerennial.

Deutsch, Karl W. 1953. *Nationalism and Social Communication: An Inquiry into the Foundations of Nationality*. New York: John Wiley and Sons.

Deutsch, Karl W. 1961. "Social Mobilization and Political Development." *American Political Science Review* 40:3 (September), pp. 493–514.

Deutsch, Karl W., et al. 1957. *Community and the North Atlantic Area: International Organization in the Light of Historical Experience*. Princeton, N.J.: Princeton University Press.

DeVotta, Neil. 2002. "Illiberalism and Ethnic Conflict in Sri Lanka." *Journal of Democracy* 13:1 (January), 84–98.

de Wall, Alex. 1997. "Democratizing the Aid Encounter in Africa." *International Affairs* 73:4 (October), pp. 623–639.

de Waal, Alex, and Rakiya Omaar. 1995. "The Genocide in Rwanda and the International Response." *Current History* 94:591 (April), pp. 156–161.

DGAP [Development Group for Alternative Policies]. 1995. *Structural Adjustment and the Spreading Crisis in Latin America.* Washington, D.C.: DGAP.

Diamond, Larry. 1995. *Promoting Democracy in the 1990s: Actors and Instruments, Issues and Imperatives.* Report to the Carnegie Commission on Preventing Deadly Violence. New York: Carnegie Corporation.

Diamond, Larry. 1996. "Is the Third Wave Over?" *Journal of Democracy* 7:3 (July), pp. 20–37.

Diamond, Larry. 1997. "Introduction: In Search of Consolidation," in Larry Diamond, Marc F. Plattner, Yun-han Chu, and Hung-mao Tien, eds., *Consolidating Third Wave Democracies.* Baltimore: Johns Hopkins University Press.

Diamond, Larry. 2001. "How People View Democracy: Findings from Public Opinion Surveys in Four Regions." Paper presented to the Stanford Seminar on Democratization (January 11).

Diamond, Larry, Juan J. Linz, and Seymour Martin Lipset, eds. 1990. *Politics in Developing Countries: Comparing Experiences with Democracy.* Boulder, Colo.: Lynne Rienner.

Diamond, Larry, and Marc F. Plattner. 1996. "Introduction," in Larry Diamond and Marc F. Plattner, eds., *The Global Resurgence of Democracy,* 2d ed. Baltimore: Johns Hopkins University Press, pp. ix–xxxii.

Díaz, Alvaro. 1997. "New Developments in Economic and Social Restructuring in Latin America," in William C. Smith and Roberto Patricio Kornzeniewicz, eds., *Politics, Social Change, and Economic Restructuring in Latin America.* Miami: North-South Center, pp. 37–52.

Dinmore, Guy. 1999. "Serbs Take Tough Line over Kosovo." *Financial Times* (March 11).

Dinnen, Sinclair. 1996. "Violence, Security and the 1992 Elections," in Yaw Saffu, ed., *The 1992 Papua New Guinea Elections: Change and Continuity in Electoral Politics.* Canberra: Hyland Press/Research School of Pacific and Asian Studies, Australian National University, pp. 77–104.

Dique, Jorge. 1996. "Mozambique: Crime on the Rise." Inter Press Service (October 25).

Dobell, Lauren. 1995. "SWAPO in Office," in Colin Leys and John S. Saul, eds., *Namibia's Liberation Struggle: The Two-Edged Sword.* Athens, Ohio: Ohio University Press, pp. 171–195.

Dolan, Chris, and Jessica Schafer. 1997. *The Reintegration of Ex-Combatants in Mozambique.* Oxford: Refugee Studies Programme, Queen Elizabeth House, Oxford University.

Dolo, Emmanuel. 1996. *Democracy Versus Dictatorship: The Quest for Freedom and Justice in Africa's Oldest Republic – Liberia.* New York: University Press of America.

Donais, Timothy. 2002. "The Politics of Privatization in Post-Dayton Bosnia." *Southeast European Politics* 3:1 (June), pp. 3–19.

Downs, George, and Stephen John Stedman. 2002. "Evaluation Issues in Peace Implementation," in Stephen Stedman, Donald Rothchild, and Elizabeth M. Cousens, eds., *Ending Civil Wars : The Implementation of Peace Agreements.* Boulder, Colo.: Lynne Rienner, pp. 43–69.

Doyle, Michael W. 1983. "Kant, Liberal Legacies, and Foreign Affairs," Parts 1 and 2. *Philosophy and Public Affairs* 12:3–4 (Summer and Fall), pp. 205–254 and 323–353.

Doyle, Michael W. 1986. "Liberalism and World Politics." *American Political Science Review* 80:4 (December), pp. 1151–1169.

Doyle, Michael W. 1995a. "Liberalism and World Politics Revisited," in Charles W. Kegley, Jr., ed., *Controversies in International Relations Theory: Realism and the Neoliberal Challenge*. New York: St. Martin's, pp. 83–106.

Doyle, Michael W. 1995b. *UN Peacekeeping in Cambodia. UNTAC's Civil Mandate*. Boulder, Colo.: Lynne Rienner.

Doyle, Michael W. 1996a. "Peacebuilding in Cambodia," *IPA Policy Briefing Series*. New York: International Peace Academy.

Doyle, Michael W. 1996b. "Strategies of Enhanced Consent," in Abram Chayes and Antonia Handler Chayes, eds., *Preventing Conflict in the Post-Communist World: Mobilizing International and Regional Organizations*. Washington, D.C.: Brookings Institution, pp. 483–505.

Doyle, Michael W. 2001. "Peacebuilding in Cambodia: Legitimacy and Power," in Elizabeth M. Cousens and Chetan Kumar, eds., *Peacebuilding as Politics: Cultivating Peace in Fragile Societies*. Boulder, Colo.: Lynne Rienner, pp. 89–111.

Doyle, Michael W., and Nicholas Sambanis. 2000. "International Peacebuilding: A Theoretical and Quantitative Analysis." *American Political Science Review* 94:4 (December), pp. 779–801.

Dravis, Michael. 2000. "Burundi in the 1990s: From Democratization to Communal War," in Ted Robert Gurr, ed., *Peoples Versus States: Minorities at Risk in the New Century*. Washington, D.C.: United States Institute of Peace Press.

Dunkerly, James. 1994. *The Pacification of Central America: Political Change in the Isthmus, 1987–1993*. New York: Verso.

Dye, David R., Judy Butler, Deena Abu-Lughod, Jack Spence, and George Vickers. 1995. *Contesting Everything, Winning Nothing: The Search for Consensus in Nicaragua, 1990–1995*. Cambridge, Mass.: Hemisphere Initiatives.

Easterly, William. 2001. "IMF and World Bank Structural Adjustment Programs and Poverty." World Bank working paper, http://www.nber.org/~confer/2001/ccdf/easterly.pdf, accessed in May 2002.

Easton, David. 1965. *A Systems Analysis of Political Life*. New York: John Wiley.

Eckstein, Harry. 1975. "Case Study and Theory in Political Science," in Fred I. Greenstein and Nelson W. Polsby, eds., *Handbook of Political Science*. Reading, Mass.: Addison-Wesley, pp. 79–138.

Economist. 1992. "Angola: Close Call" (October 17).

Economist. 1996. "All Free Traders Now?" (December 7).

Economist. 1997a. "Cambodia's Bitter Partnership" (February 1).

Economist. 1997b. "Mozambique: Bending the Rules" (June 28).

Economist. 2001. "The Boggy Road to Peace: Guatemala" (February 24).

Economist. 2002. "Winning Ways" (February 9).

EIU [Economist Intelligence Unit]. 1996a. *Country Report: Guatemala, El Salvador*. Fourth Quarter. London: EIU.

EIU [Economist Intelligence Unit]. 1996b. *Country Report: Nicaragua, Honduras*. Fourth Quarter. London: EIU.

EIU [Economist Intelligence Unit]. 1997a. *Country Profile: Bosnia and Herzegovina, 1997–98*. London: EIU.

EIU [Economist Intelligence Unit]. 1997b. *Country Profile: El Salvador, 1997–98*. London: EIU.

EIU [Economist Intelligence Unit]. 1997c. *Country Profile: Nicaragua, 1997–98.* London: EIU.

EIU [Economist Intelligence Unit]. 1997d. *Country Report: Mozambique, Malawi.* Fourth Quarter. London: EIU.

EIU [Economist Intelligence Unit]. 1999a. *Country Profile: Guatemala, El Salvador, 1999–2000.* London: EIU.

EIU [Economist Intelligence Unit]. 1999b. *Country Profile: Nicaragua, Honduras, 1999–2000.* London: Economist Intelligence Unit.

Eller, Jack David, and Reed M. Coughlan. 1993. "The Poverty of Primordialism: The Demystification of Ethnic Attachments." *Ethnic and Racial Studies* 16:2 (April), pp. 183–201.

Engberg-Pedersen, Poul, et al., eds. 1996. *Limits of Adjustment in Africa: The Effects of Economic Liberalization, 1986–94.* Portsmouth, N.H.: Heinemann.

Envío. 1997a. "The United Nations Hits the Nail on the Head," 16:197 (December), pp. 3–10.

Envío. 1997b. "Violence: A National Epidemic," 16:196 (November), p. 17.

EPSA [European Parliamentarians for Southern Africa]. 1997. *Mozambique Peace Process Bulletin* 19 (September), http://www.mozambique.mz/awepa/eawp19/eawepa29.htm, accessed in June 2002.

Eriksen, Thomas Hylland. 1993. *Ethnicity and Nationalism: Anthropological Perspectives.* London: Pluto Press.

Erlanger, Steven. 1999. "In Victory's Wake, A Battle of Bureaucrats." *New York Times* (November 28).

Ero, Comfort. 2000. "Dilemmas of Accommodation and Reconstruction: Liberia," in Michael Pugh, ed., *Regeneration of War-Torn Societies.* New York: St. Martin's, pp. 195–213.

Esman, Milton. 1990. "Political and Psychological Factors in Ethnic Conflict," in Joseph V. Montville, ed., *Conflict and Peacemaking in Multiethnic Societies.* Lexington, Mass.: Lexington Books, pp. 53–64.

Esman, Milton J. 1994. *Ethnic Politics.* Ithaca, N.Y.: Cornell University Press.

EURODAD [European Network on Debt and Development]. 1998. *Third World Debt in the 1990s* 21 (March), reproduced on http://www.oneworld.org/eurodad/21e_2.htm, accessed in January 2000.

European Union. 2000a. *Bosnia and Herzegovina: A Future With Europe.* [February], http://www.seerecon.org/Bosnia/Bosnia-DonorPrograms/Bosnia-Donors-EC/Future-with-Europe/contents.htm, accessed in May 2003.

European Union. 2000b. *Kosovo: The European Contribution,* 2d ed. [November], http://europa.eu.int/comm/external_relations/see/fry/kosovo/assist_kosovo.pdf, accessed in May 2003.

European Union. 2001. *Bosnia and Herzegovina: The European Contribution,* rev. ed. [June], http://europa.eu.int/comm/external_relations/see/bosnie_herze/bh2001.pdf, accessed in May 2003.

Evans, Ernest H. 1998. "The El Salvadoran Peace Process Five Years On: An Assessment." *Studies in Conflict and Terrorism* 21:2 (April–June), pp. 171–179.

Evans, Peter B., Dietrich Rueschemeyer, and Theda Skocpol, eds. 1985. *Bringing the State Back In.* New York: Cambridge University Press.

Everingham, Mark. 1998. "Neoliberalism in a New Democracy: Elite Politics and State Reform in Nicaragua." *Journal of Developing Areas* 32:2 (Winter), pp. 237–264.

Fagan, Patricia Weiss. 1996. "Lessons in Peace Consolidation," in Tom Farer, ed., *Beyond Sovereignty: Collectively Defending Democracy in the Americas*. Baltimore: Johns Hopkins University Press, pp. 213–237.

Farah, Douglas. 1996. "Killing in Salvadoran Crime Wave Outpaces Deaths During Civil War." *Washington Post* (March 16).

Farah, Douglas. 2001a. "Liberia's Diverted Dreams." *Washington Post* (January 31).

Farah, Douglas. 2001b. "Taylor Puts Liberia on War Footing." *Washington Post* (April 25).

Faruqee, Rashid, and Ishrat Husain, eds. 1994. *Adjustment in Africa: Lessons from Country Case Studies*. Washington, D.C.: World Bank.

Fearon, James D., and David D. Laitin. 2003. "Ethnicity, Insurgency, and Civil War." *American Political Science Review* 97:1 (February), pp. 75–90.

Feinberg, Richard. 1988. "The Changing Relationship Between the World Bank and the International Monetary Fund." *International Organization* 42:3 (Summer), pp. 545–560.

Fernando, Jude L., and Alan W. Heston. 1997. "Introduction: NGOs Between States, Markets, and Civil Society." *The Annals of the American Academy of Political and Social Science* 554 (November), pp. 8–21.

Finnegan, William. 1992. *A Complicated War: The Harrowing of Mozambique*. Berkeley: University of California Press.

Fishel, Kimbra L. 1998. "From Peace Making to Peace Building in Central America: The Illusion Versus the Reality of Peace." *Small Wars and Insurgencies* 9:1 (Spring), pp. 32–49.

Fitzpatrick, Mary. 1997. "Liberia's Tenuous Election." *Christian Science Monitor* (August 1).

Fleitz, Frederick H., Jr. 2002. *Peacekeeping Fiascoes of the 1990s: Causes, Solutions, and U.S. Interests*. Westport, Conn.: Praeger.

Fofana, Lansana. 2002. "Pullout of British Troops Causes Concern." Inter Press Service (August 1).

Forrest, Joshua Bernard. 1994. "Namibia – The First Postapartheid Democracy." *Journal of Democracy* 5:3 (July), pp. 88–100.

Forrest, Joshua Bernard. 2000. "Democracy and Development in Post-Independence Namibia," in York Bradshaw and Stephen N. Ndegwa, eds., *The Uncertain Promise of Southern Africa*. Bloomington: Indiana University Press, pp. 94–114.

Forsythe, David P. 1996. "The United Nations, Democracy, and the Americas," in Tom Farer, ed., *Beyond Sovereignty: Collectively Defending Democracy in the Americas*. Baltimore: Johns Hopkins University Press, pp. 107–131.

Fortna, Virginia Page. 1993a. "United Nations Angola Verification Mission I," in William J. Durch, ed., *The Evolution of UN Peacekeeping: Case Studies and Comparative Analysis*. New York: St. Martin's, pp. 376–387.

Fortna, Virginia Page. 1993b. "United Nations Angola Verification Mission II," in William J. Durch, ed., *The Evolution of UN Peacekeeping: Case Studies and Comparative Analysis*. New York: St. Martin's, pp. 388–405.

Fortna, Virginia Page. 1993c. "United Nations Transition Assistance Group," in William J. Durch, ed., *The Evolution of UN Peacekeeping: Case Studies and Comparative Analysis* New York: St. Martin's, pp. 353–375.

Fortna, Virginia Page. 1995. "Success and Failure in Southern Africa: Peacekeeping in Namibia and Angola," in Donald C. F. Daniel and Bradd C. Hayes, eds., *Beyond Traditional Peacekeeping*. New York: St. Martin's Press, pp. 282–299.

Fortna, Virginia Page. 2002. "Does Peacekeeping Keep Peace? And If So, How?" Paper prepared for the Workshop on Peacekeeping and Politics, Columbia University, New York (October 18).

Franck, Thomas M. 1992. "The Emerging Right to Democratic Governance." *American Journal of International Law* 86:1 (January), pp. 46–91.

Franck, Thomas M. 2000. "Legitimacy and Democratic Entitlement," in Gregory H. Fox and Brad R. Roth, eds., *Democratic Governance and International Law*. New York: Cambridge University Press, pp. 25–47.

Fukuyama, Francis. 1989. "The End of History?" *National Interest* 16 (Summer), pp. 3–18.

Gall, Carlotta. 2003. "In Warlord Land, Democracy Tries Baby Steps." *New York Times* (June 11).

Galtung, John. 1969. "Violence, Peace, and Peace Research." *Journal of Peace Research* 6:3, pp. 167–191.

Ganguly, Sumit. 1996. "Explaining the Kashmir Insurgency: Political Mobilization and Institutional Decay." *International Security* 21:2 (Fall), pp. 76–107.

Garcia, Edmundo. 1989. "Resolution of Internal Armed Conflict in the Philippines," in Edmundo Garcia and Carol Hernandez, eds., *Waging Peace in the Philippines*. Quezon City, Philippines: Ateneo Center for Social Policy and Public Affairs.

Gayi, Samuel K. 1995. "Adjusting to the Social Costs of Adjustment in Ghana: Problems and Prospects." *European Journal of Development Research* 7:1 (June), pp. 77–100.

Gellner, Ernest. 1991. "Civil Society in Historical Context." *International Social Science Journal* 43:129 (August), pp. 495–510.

George, Alexander. 1979. "Case Studies and Theory Development: The Method of Structured, Focused Comparison," in Paul Gordon Lauren, ed., *Diplomacy: New Approaches in History, Theory, and Policy*. New York: Free Press, pp. 43–68.

Gershman, Carl. 1990. "The United States and the World Democratic Revolution," in Brad Roberts, ed., *The New Democracies: Global Change and U.S. Policy*. Cambridge, Mass.: MIT Press, pp. 3–15.

Gershman, Carl. 1993. "The United Nations and the New World Order." *Journal of Democracy* 4:3 (July), pp. 5–16.

Gibson, Bill. 1993. "Nicaragua," in Lance Taylor, ed., *The Rocky Road to Reform: Adjustment, Income Distribution, and Growth in the Developing World*. Cambridge: Cambridge University Press, pp. 431–456.

Gillies, David. 1996. "Human Rights, Democracy, and Good Governance: Stretching the World Bank's Policy Frontiers," in Jo Marie Gresgaber and Bernhard G. Gunter, eds., *The World Bank: Lending on a Global Scale*. London: Pluto, pp. 101–141.

Gilpin, Robert. 2000. *The Challenge of Global Capitalism: The World Economy in the 21st Century*. Princeton, N.J.: Princeton University Press.

Glaessner, Philip J., Key Woo Lee, Anna Maria Sant'Anna, and Jean-Jacques de St. Antoine. 1994. *Poverty Alleviation and Social Investment Funds: The Latin American Experience*. World Bank Discussion Paper no. 261. Washington, D.C.: World Bank.

Glaser, Barney G., and Anselm L. Strauss. 1967. *The Discovery of Grounded Theory: Strategies for Qualitative Research*. Chicago: Aldine.

Gleditsch, Kristian S., and Michael D. Ward. 2000. "War and Peace in Space and Time: The Role of Democratization." *International Studies Quarterly* 44:1 (March), pp. 1–29.

Gleditsch, Nils Petter, and Håvard Hegre. 1997. "Peace and Democracy: Three Levels of Analysis." *Journal of Conflict Resolution* 41:2 (April), pp. 283–310.

Glickman, Harvey. 1995. "Issues in the Analysis of Ethnic Conflict and Democratization Processes in Africa Today," in Harvey Glickman, ed., *Ethnic Conflict and Democratization in Africa*. Atlanta: African Studies Association, pp. 1–31.

Glickman, Maynard. 1996/97. "US Policy In Bosnia: Rethinking a Flawed Approach. *Survival* 38:4 (Winter), pp. 66–83.

Goldwin, Robert A. 1987. "John Locke," in Leo Strauss and Joseph Cropsey, eds., *History of Political Philosophy*, 3d ed. Chicago: University of Chicago Press, pp. 476–512.

Goodhand, Jonathan. 2002. "Aiding Violence or Building Peace? The Role of International Aid in Afghanistan." *Third World Quarterly* 23:5 (October), pp. 837–859.

Goodson, Larry. 2003. "Afghanistan's Long Road to Reconstruction." *Journal of Democracy* 14:1 (January), pp. 82–99.

Gordon, Ruth. 1995. "Some Legal Problems With Trusteeship." *Cornell International Law Journal* 28:2, pp. 301–347.

Gould, Carol C. 1988. *Rethinking Democracy: Freedom and Social Cooperation in Politics, Economy and Society*. New York: Cambridge University Press.

Graham, Carol. 1994. *Safety Nets, Politics, and the Poor: Transitions to Market Economies*. Washington, D.C.: Brookings Institution.

Graham, Carol. 1995. "The Politics of Safety Nets." *Journal of Democracy* 6:2 (April), pp. 142–156.

Gurr, Ted Robert. 1970. *Why Men Rebel*. Princeton, N.J.: Princeton University Press.

Gurr, Ted Robert. 1993. *Minorities at Risk: A Global View of Ethnopolitical Conflict*. Washington, D.C.: United States Institute of Peace Press.

Gwartney, Jim, and Robert Lawson, with Dexter Samida. *Economic Freedom of the World: 2000 Annual Report*. Vancouver, B.C.: The Fraser Institute, 2000.

Haas, Ernst B. 1952. "The Reconciliation of Conflicting Colonial Policy Aims: Acceptance of the League of Nations Mandate System." *International Organization* 6:4 (November), pp. 521–536.

Haas, Ernst B. 1953. "The Attempt to Terminate Colonialism: Acceptance of the United Nations Trusteeship System." *International Organization* 7:1 (February), pp. 1–21.

Haggard, Stephan, and Robert R. Kaufman. 1992. "Economic Adjustment and the Prospects for Democracy," in Stephen Haggard and Robert R. Kaufman, eds., *The Politics of Economic Adjustment: International Constraints, Distributive Conflicts, and the State*. Princeton, N.J.: Princeton University Press, pp. 319–350.

Haggard, Stephan, and Robert R. Kaufman. 1995. *The Political Economy of Democratic Transitions*. Princeton, N.J.: Princeton University Press.

Hall, H. Duncan. 1948. *Mandates, Dependencies and Trusteeship*. Washington, D.C.: Carnegie Endowment for International Peace.

Hall, John A. 1987. *Liberalism: Politics, Ideology and the Market*. Chapel Hill: University of North Carolina Press.

Hall, John A., ed. 1995. *Civil Society: Theory, History, Comparison*. Cambridge, U.K.: Polity.

Hall, Macer. 2002. "Army Leaves Just 100 Men Behind in Sierra Leone." *Daily Telegraph* (July 29).

Halperin, Morton H. 1993. "Guaranteeing Democracy." *Foreign Policy* 91 (Summer), pp. 105–123.

Hamilton, Alexander, James Madison, and John Jay. 1992 [1788]. *The Federalist.* London: J. M. Dent.

Hampson, Fen Osler. 1996. *Nurturing Peace: Why Peace Settlements Succeed or Fail.* Washington, D.C.: United States Institute of Peace Press.

Hanlon, Joseph. 1996. "Strangling Mozambique: International Monetary Fund 'Stabilization' in the World's Poorest Country." *Multinational Monitor* 17:7–8 (July/August), pp. 17–21.

Hanlon, Joseph. 2000. "Mozambique: Will Growing Economic Divisions Provoke Violence in Mozambique?" Bern, Switzerland: Swiss Peace Foundation, http://www.isn.ethz.ch/publihouse/fast/crp/hanlon_oo.htm, accessed in May 2003.

Harbeson, John W. 1994. "Civil Society and Political Renaissance in Africa," in John W. Harbeson, Donald Rothchild, and Naomi Chazan, eds., *Civil Society and the State in Africa.* Boulder, Colo.: Lynne Rienner, pp. 1–29.

Hardgrave, Robert L., Jr. 1994. "India: Dilemmas of Diversity," in Larry Diamond and Marc F. Plattner, eds., *Nationalism, Ethnic Conflict, and Democracy.* Baltimore: Johns Hopkins University Press, pp. 71–85.

Hare, Paul. 1998. *Angola's Last Best Chance for Peace.* Washington, D.C.: United States Institute of Peace Press.

Harris, David. 1999. "From 'Warlord' to 'Democratic' President: How Charles Taylor Won the 1997 Liberian Elections." *Journal of Modern African Studies* 37:3 (September), pp. 431–455.

Harrison, Graham. 1996. "Democracy in Mozambique: The Significance of Multi-Party Elections." *Review of African Political Economy* 67:23 (March), pp. 19–35.

Hayek, Friedrich A. 1944. *The Road to Serfdom.* Chicago: University of Chicago Press.

Hedges, Chris. 1996. "Bosnia's Nationalist Parties Dominate Election Results." *New York Times* (September 22).

Hedges, Chris. 1997. "NATO Troops in Bosnia Silence Karadzic's Television Station." *New York Times* (October 2).

Hedges, Chris. 1998a. "A Light at the End of Bosnia's Tunnel?" *International Herald Tribune* (January 29).

Hedges, Chris. 1998b. "With West's Help, Bosnian Serb President May Form Cabinet." *New York Times* (January 13).

Hedges, Chris. 1999. "Leaders in Bosnia Are Said to Steal up to $1 Billion." *New York Times* (August 17).

Hegre, Håvard, Tanja Ellingsen, Scott Gates, and Nils Petter Gleditsch. 2001. "Toward a Democratic Civil Peace? Democracy, Political Change, and Civil War, 1816–1992." *American Political Science Review* 95:1 (March), pp. 33–48.

Heininger, Janet E. 1994. *Peacekeeping in Transition: The United Nations in Cambodia.* New York: Twentieth Century Fund.

Held, David. 1998. "Democracy and Globalization," in Daniele Archibugi, David Held, and Martin Köhler, eds., *Re-Imagining Political Community: Studies in Cosmopolitan Democracy.* Stanford, Calif.: Stanford University Press, pp. 11–27.

Helman, Gerald B., and Steven R. Ratner. 1992/93. "Saving Failed States." *Foreign Policy* 89 (Winter), pp. 3–20.

Hentges, Harriet, and Jean-Marc Coucaud. 2002. "Dividends of Peace: The Economics of Peacekeeping." *Journal of International Affairs* 55:2 (Spring), pp. 351–368.

Heredia, Blanca. 1997. "Prosper or Perish? Development in the Age of Global Capital." *Current History* 96:613 (November), pp. 383–388.

Herz, John. 1950. "Idealist Internationalism and the Security Dilemma. *World Politics* 2:2 (January), pp. 157–180.

Heywood, Linda. 2000. *Contested Power in Angola, 1840s to the Present.* Rochester, N.Y.: University of Rochester Press.

Hibou, Béatrice. 2002. "The World Bank: Missionary Deeds (and Misdeeds)," in Peter J. Schraeder, ed., *Exporting Democracy: Rhetoric Vs. Reality.* Boulder, Colo.: Lynne Rienner, pp. 173–191.

Hilderbrand, Mary E., and Merilee S. Grindle. 1997. "Building Sustainable Capacity in the Public Sector: What Can Be Done?" in Merilee S. Grindle, ed., *Getting Good Government: Capacity Building in the Public Sectors of Developing Countries.* Cambridge, Mass.: Harvard University Press, pp. 31–61.

Hirsch, John L. 2001. "War in Sierra Leone." *Survival* 43:3 (Autumn), pp. 145–162.

Hobbes, Thomas. 1968 [1651]. *Leviathan,* edited by C. B. MacPherson. New York: Penguin Books.

Hodges, Tony. 2001. *Angola: From Afro-Stalinism to Petro-Diamond Capitalism.* Bloomington: Indiana University Press.

Hofstadter, Richard. 1948. *The American Political Tradition.* New York: Vintage.

Hohe, Tanja. 2002a. "The Clash of Paradigms: International Administration and Local Political Legitimacy in East Timor." *Contemporary Southeast Asia* 24:3 (December), pp. 569–589.

Hohe, Tanja. 2002b. "Totem Polls: Indigenous Concepts and 'Free and Fair' Elections in East Timor." *International Peacekeeping* 9:4 (Winter), pp. 69–88.

Holbrooke, Richard. 1998. *To End a War.* New York: Random House.

Holiday, David. 1997. "Guatemala's Long Road to Peace." *Current History* 96:607 (February), pp. 68–74.

Holiday, David. 2000. "Guatemala's Precarious Peace." *Current History* 99:634 (February), pp. 78–84.

Holler, Manfred J. 1987. "The Logic of Multiparty Systems: An Overview of Theoretical and Empirical Problems and Results," in Manfred J. Holler, ed., *The Logic of Multiparty Systems.* Boston: Kluwer, pp. 13–48.

Holley, David. 2002. "Kosovo Serbs Fear the Day They'll Have to Walk Alone." *Los Angeles Times* (March 24).

Holloway, Robert. 2002. "Gusmao Urges UN to Remain Closely Involved in Independent East Timor." Agence France Presse (April 26).

Horowitz, Donald L. 1985. *Ethnic Groups in Conflict.* Berkeley: University of California Press.

Horowitz, Donald L. 1990a. "Ethnic Conflict Management for Policymakers," in Joseph V. Montville, ed., *Conflict and Peacemaking in Multiethnic Societies.* Toronto: Lexington Books, pp. 115–132.

Horowitz, Donald L. 1990b. "Making Moderation Pay: The Comparative Politics of Ethnic Conflict Management," in Joseph V. Montville, ed., *Conflict and Peacemaking in Multiethnic Societies.* Toronto: Lexington Books, pp. 451–475.

Horowitz, Donald L. 1991. *A Democratic South Africa? Constitutional Engineering in a Divided Society*. Berkeley: University of California Press.

Howard, Lise Morjé. 2002. "UN Peacekeeping in Civil Wars: Success, Failure, and Organizational Learning." Paper prepared for the Workshop on Peacekeeping and Politics, Columbia University, New York (October 18).

Howard, Ross. 2001. "Media and Peacebuilding: Mapping the Possibilities." *Activate: Journal of the Institute for Media, Policy and Civil Society* (Winter), pp. 12–13.

Human Rights Watch. 1994. *El Salvador: Darkening Horizons: Human Rights on the Eve of the March 1994 Elections*. New York: Human Rights Watch.

Human Rights Watch. 1995. *Playing the Communal Card: Communal Violence and Human Rights*. New York: Human Rights Watch.

Human Rights Watch. 1999. *Leave None to Tell the Story: Genocide in Rwanda*. New York and Paris: Human Rights Watch and the International Federation of Human Rights.

Human Rights Watch. 2002. *World Report 2002: Liberia*. New York: Human Rights Watch.

Human Rights Watch/Helsinki. 1996. "Bosnia-Hercegovina: A Failure in the Making: Human Rights and the Dayton Agreement." *Human Rights Watch/Helsinki Report* 8:8 (June).

Hume, Cameron. 1994. *Ending Mozambique's War: The Role of Mediation and Good Offices*. Washington, D.C.: United States Institute of Peace Press.

Huntington, Samuel P. 1968. *Political Order in Changing Societies*. New Haven, Conn.: Yale University Press.

Hutchinson, Kay Bailey. 1997. "The Bosnia Puzzle Needs a New Solution." *New York Times* (September 11).

Hyland, James L. 1995. *Democratic Theory: The Philosophical Foundations*. New York: Manchester University Press.

IADB [Inter-American Development Bank]. 2001a. "Basic Socio-Economic Data [on Nicaragua] for 21 December 2000," http://www.iadb.org/int/sta/ENGLISH/brptnet/english/nicbrpt.htm, accessed in May 2001.

IADB [Inter-American Development Bank]. 2001b. "Country Economic Assessment Report [El Salvador]," http://www.iadb.org/regions/re2/sep/es-sep.htm, accessed in May 2001.

IADB [Inter-American Development Bank]. 2001c. "Country Economic Assessment Report [Guatemala]," http://www.iadb.org/regions/re2/sep/gu-sep.htm, accessed in May 2001.

Ignatieff, Michael. 1997. *The Warrior's Honor: Ethnic War and the Modern Conscience*. New York: Henry Holt.

Ihonvbere, Julius O. 1996a. "Are Things Falling Apart? The Military and the Crisis of Democratization in Nigeria." *Journal of Modern African Studies* 34:2 (June), pp. 193–225.

Ihonvbere, Julius O. 1996b. "Where Is the Third Wave? A Critical Evaluation of Africa's Non-Transition to Democracy." *Africa Today* 43:4 (October–December), pp. 343–368.

ILO [International Labor Organization]. 2002. *Key Indicators of the Labour Market, 2001–2002*. Geneva: ILO.

IMF [International Monetary Fund]. 1995. "Social Safety Nets for Economic Transition: Options and Recent Experiences," Paper on Policy Analysis and Assessment. Washington, D.C.: IMF Fiscal Affairs Department, Expenditure Policy Division.

IMF [International Monetary Fund]. 1997. *Good Governance: The IMF's Role.* Washington, D.C.. IMF.

IMF [International Monetary Fund]. 1998. *IMF Survey* 27:11 (June 8).

IMF [International Monetary Fund]. 2001. "IMF Concludes Article IV Consultation with Guatemala." Public Information Notice no. 01/56 (May 25).

IMF [International Monetary Fund] and World Bank. 2001. "Assistance to Post-Conflict Countries and the HIPC Framework." Policy statement prepared jointly by the staffs of the World Bank Resource Mobilization Department and the IMF Policy Development and Review and Treasurer's Department (April 20), http://www.imf.org/external/np/hipc/2001/pc/042001.pdf, accessed in August 2002.

International Centre for Human Rights and Democratic Development. 2000. *Annual Report 1999–2000.* Montreal: International Centre for Human Rights and Democratic Development.

International Commission on the Balkans. 1996. *Unfinished Peace: Report of the International Commission on the Balkans.* Washington, D.C. and Berlin: Carnegie Endowment for International Peace and The Aspen Institute.

International Crisis Group. 1997. *Dayton: Two Years On – A Review of Progress in Implementing the Dayton Peace Accords in Bosnia.* Bosnia Project Report no. 27 (November 19).

International Crisis Group. 2002. "Sierra Leone After the Elections: Politics As Usual?" Africa Report no. 49 (July 12).

International Crisis Group. 2003. "Tackling Liberia: The Eye of the Regional Storm." Africa Report no. 62 (April 30).

Interpol. 2003. International Crime Statistics Database, http://www.interpol.int/Public/Statistics/ICS/Default.asp, accessed in May 2003.

Irvin, George. 1993. "Cambodia: Why Recovery Is Unlikely in the Short Term." *European Journal of Development Research* 5:2 (December), pp. 123–141.

Isbester, Katherine. 1996. "Understanding State Disintegration: The Case of Nicaragua." *Journal of Social, Political and Economic Studies* 21:4 (Winter), pp. 455–476.

Islam, Nasir, and David R. Morrison. 1996. "Introduction: Governance, Democracy and Human Rights." *Canadian Journal of Development Studies* (special issue), pp. 4–18.

Jackson, Robert H., and Carl G. Rosberg. 1982. "Why Africa's Weak States Persist: The Empirical and the Juridical in Statehood." *World Politics* 35:1 (October), pp. 1–24.

Jakobsen, Peter Viggo. 1996. "National Interest, Humanitarianism, or CNN: What Triggers UN Peace Enforcement After the Cold War?" *Journal of Peace Research* 33:2 (May), pp. 205–215.

Jakobsen, Peter Viggo. 2002. "The Transformation of United Nations Peace Operations in the 1990s: Adding Globalization to the Conventional 'End of the Cold War Explanation.'" *Cooperation and Conflict* 37:3 (September), pp. 267–282.

Jakobson, Max. 1993. *The United Nations in the 1990s: A Second Chance?* New York: Twentieth Century Fund.

James, Harold. 1998. "From Grandmotherliness to Governance: The Evolution of IMF Conditionality." *Finance and Development* 35:4 (December), pp. 44–47.

Jayarajah, Carl, William Branson, and Binayak Sen. 1996. *Social Dimensions of Adjustment: World Bank Experience, 1980–93.* Washington, D.C.: World Bank.

Jeffries, Richard. 1993. "The State, Structural Adjustment and Good Government in Africa." *Journal of Commonwealth and Comparative Politics* 31:1 (March), pp. 20–35.

Jeldres, Julio A. 1997. "Cambodia: Anatomy of a Coup." *Bangkok Post* (September 7).

Jennar, Raoul M. 1994. "UNTAC: 'International Triumph' in Cambodia?" *Security Dialogue* 25:2 (June), pp. 145–156.

Jeong, Ho-Won. 1996. "Managing Structural Adjustment." *SAIS Review* 16:2 (Fall–Summer), pp. 155–167.

Jett, Dennis Coleman. 1995. "Cementing Democracy: Institution-Building in Mozambique." *Harvard International Review* 17:4 (Fall), pp. 22–25 and 81.

Johnstone, Ian. 1995. *Rights and Reconciliation: UN Strategies in El Salvador.* Boulder, Colo.: Lynne Rienner.

Jonakin, Jon. 1997. "Agrarian Policy," in Thomas W. Walker, ed., *Nicaragua Without Illusions: Regime Transition and Structural Adjustment in the 1990s.* Wilmington, Del.: Scholarly Resources, pp. 97–113.

Jonas, Susanne. 1997. "The Peace Accords: An End and a Beginning." *NACLA Report on the Americas* 30:6 (May–June), pp. 6–10.

Jonas, Susanne. 1998. "Democratization of Guatemala Through the Peace Process." Paper presented to the conference on "Guatemalan Development and Democracy: Proactive Responses to Globalization," Universidad del Valle, Guatemala (March 26–28).

Jonas, Susanne. 2000. *Of Centaurs and Doves: Guatemala's Peace Process.* Boulder, Colo.: Westview.

Jones, Bruce D. 1995. "Humanitarian Intervention in Rwanda, 1990–94." *Journal of International Studies* 24:2 (Summer), pp. 225–249.

Jones, Bruce D. 2001. *Peacemaking in Rwanda: The Dynamics of Failure.* Boulder, Colo.: Lynne Rienner.

Jones, Bruce. 2002. "The Challenges of Strategic Coordination," in Stephen John Stedman, Donald Rothchild, and Elizabeth M. Cousens, eds., *Ending Civil Wars: The Implementation of Peace Agreements* Boulder, Colo.: Lynne Rienner, pp. 89–115.

Journal of Conflict Resolution. 2002. Special issue on "Understanding Civil War," edited by Paul Collier and Nicholas Sambanis, 46:1 (February).

Judah, Tim. 2000. "Croatia Reborn." *New York Review of Books* (August 10).

Kaela, Laurent C. W. 1996. *The Question of Namibia.* New York: St. Martin's.

Kaiser, Paul J. 1996. "Structural Adjustment and the Fragile Nation: The Demise of Social Unity in Tanzania." *Journal of Modern African Studies* 34:2 (June), pp. 227–237.

Kaldor, Mary. 1999. *New and Old Wars: Organized Violence in a Global Era.* Stanford, Calif.: Stanford University Press.

Kamm, Henry. 1998. "The Cambodian Calamity." *New York Review of Books* (August 13).

Kandeh, Jimmy D. 2002. "Subaltern Terror in Sierra Leone," in Tunde Zack-Williams, Diane Frost, and Alex Thompson, eds., *Africa in Crisis: New Challenges and Possibilities*. London: Pluto, pp. 179–195.

Kane, Hal. 1995. *The Hour of Departure: Forces That Create Refugees and Migrants*. Worldwatch Paper no. 125. Washington, D.C.: Worldwatch Institute.

Kane, Hal. 1996. "Refugees on the Rise Again," in Lester R. Brown, Christopher Flavin, and Hal Kane, eds., *Vital Signs 1996*. New York: W. W. Norton, pp. 96–97.

Kant, Immanuel. 1991 [1784]. "Idea for a Universal History With a Cosmopolitan Purpose," reprinted in Hans Reiss, ed., *Kant: Political Writings*. New York: Cambridge University Press, pp. 41–53.

Kaplan, Robert. 1996. *The Ends of the Earth: A Journey at the Dawn of the 21st Century*. New York: Random House.

Kaplan, Robert D. 1997. "Was Democracy Just a Moment?" *Atlantic Monthly* (December), http://www.theatlantic.com/issues/97dec/democ.htm, accessed in May 2003.

Kapp, Clare. 2001. "Funding Squeeze Forces UNHCR Cutbacks," *The Lancet* 358 (October 6), p. 1177.

Karl, Terry Lynn. 1992. "El Salvador's Negotiated Transition." *Foreign Affairs* 71:2 (Spring), pp. 147–164.

Karl, Terry Lynn. 1995. "The Hybrid Regimes of Central America." *Journal of Democracy* 6:3 (July), pp. 72–86.

Karl, Terry Lynn. 2000. "Electoralism," in Richard Rose, ed., *International Encyclopedia of Elections*. Washington, D.C.: C.Q. Press, pp. 95–96.

Karniol, Robert. 1997. "A Divided Coalition Collapses as Unrest Returns to Cambodia." *Jane's Defence Weekly* 28:3 (July 23), p. 19.

Kaufman, Joyce P. 2002. *NATO and the Former Yugoslavia: Crisis, Conflict, and the Atlantic Alliance*. New York: Rowman & Littlefield.

Kaufman, Stuart J. 1996. "Spiraling to Ethnic War: Elites, Masses, and Moscow in Moldova's Civil War." *International Security* 21:2 (Fall), pp. 108–138.

Kaufmann, Chaim D. 1996a. "Intervention in Ethnic and Ideological Civil Wars: Why One Can Be Done and the Other Can't." *Security Studies* 6:1 (Autumn), pp. 62–100.

Kaufmann, Chaim D. 1996b. "Possible and Impossible Solutions to Ethnic Civil Wars." *International Security* 20:4 (Spring), pp. 136–175.

Kaufmann, Chaim D. 1998. "When All Else Fails: Ethnic Population Transfers and Partitions in the Twentieth Century." *International Security* 23:2 (Fall), pp. 120–156.

Kay, Christóbol. 2001. "Reflections on Rural Violence in Latin America." *Third World Quarterly* 22:5 (October), pp. 741–775.

Kelly, Michael. 1998. "Bosnia Finds Peace." *New York Post* (January 21).

Knock, Thomas J. 1992. *To End All Wars: Woodrow Wilson and the Quest for a New World Order*. Princeton, N.J.: Princeton University Press.

Knox, Paul. 1999. "UN Shortcomings Thrown Into Spotlight: Earlier Action Could Have Averted Bloodbath, UNAMET Official Says." *Globe and Mail* (September 14).

Knudsen, Christine M., with I. William Zartman. 1995. "The Large Small War in Angola," in William J. Olson, ed., *Small Wars. Annals of the American Academy of Political and Social Science* 541 (September), pp. 130–143.

Kochanowicz, Jacek. 1994. "Reforming Weak States and Deficient Bureaucracies," in Joan M. Nelson et al., *Intricate Links: Democratization and Market Reforms in Latin America and Eastern Europe*. New Brunswick, N.J.: Transaction, pp. 195–225.

Köhler, Gernot, and Norman Alcock. 1976. "An Empirical Table of Structural Violence." *Journal of Peace Research* 13:4 (July), pp. 343–356.

Kolodko, Grzegorz W. 2000. *From Shock to Therapy: The Political Economy of Postsocial Transformation*. Oxford: Oxford University Press.

Kondo, Seiichi [OECD Deputy Secretary-General]. 1999. "Good Governance for the 21st Century." Address to Pacific Economic Co-operation Council 13th General Assembly, Manila, Philippines (October 21), http://www.oecd.org/media/release/kondomanilaoct99.htm, accessed in October 2000.

Kopstein, Jeffrey S., and David A. Reilly. 2000. "Geographical Diffusion and the Transformation of the Postcommunist World." *World Politics* 53:1 (October), pp. 1–37.

Korhonen, Outi. 2001. "International Governance in Post-Conflict Situations." *Leiden Journal of International Law* 14:3, pp. 495–529.

Kovaleski, Serge F. 1997. "Murders Soar in El Salvador Since Devastating War's End; Some Jobless Ex-Combatants Turn to Life of Crime." *Washington Post* (October 1).

Krain, Matthew, and Marissa Edson Myers. 1997. "Democracy and Civil War: A Note on the Democratic Peace Proposition." *International Interactions* 23:1 (June), pp. 109–118.

Krauthammer, Charles. 1989. "Democracy Has Won." *Washington Post* (March 24).

Kriegsberg, Louis. 1973. *The Sociology of Social Conflicts*. Englewood Cliffs, N.J.: Prentice-Hall.

Kriegsberg, Louis. 1998. *Constructive Conflicts: From Escalation to Resolution*. New York: Rowman and Littlefield.

Kritz, Neil J. 1993. "The CSCE in the New Era." *Journal of Democracy* 4:3 (July), pp. 17–28.

Krška, Vladimír. 1997. "Peacekeeping in Angola (UNAVEM I and II)." *International Peacekeeping* 4:1 (Spring), pp. 75–97.

Krueger, Anne O. 1998. "Whither the World Bank and the IMF?" *Journal of Economic Literature* 36:4 (December), pp. 1983–2020.

Kubicek, Paul. 2002. "The European Union and Democracy Promotion." Paper presented at the annual meeting of the Southern Political Science Association, Savannah, Georgia (November 8).

Kumar, Krishna. 1993. "Civil Society: An Inquiry into the Usefulness of an Historical Term." *British Journal of Sociology* 44:3 (September), pp. 375–396.

Kumar, Radha. 2000. "The Partition Debate: Colonialism Revisited or New Policies?" *Brown Journal of World Affairs* 7:1 (Winter/Spring), pp. 3–11.

Laggah, John Bobor, Joe A.D. Allie, and Roland S. V. Wright. 1999. "Sierra Leone," in Adebayo Adedeji, ed., *Comprehending and Mastering African Conflicts: The Search for Sustainable Peace and Good Governance*. New York: Zed Books, pp. 174–188.

Lake, David A., and Donald Rothchild. 1996. "Containing Fear: Origins and Management of Ethnic Conflict." *International Security* 21:2 (Fall), pp. 41–75.

Lakoff, Sanford. 1996. *Democracy: History, Theory, Practice*. Boulder, Colo.: Westview.

Langford, Tonya. 1999. "Things Fall Apart: State Failure and the Politics of Intervention," *International Studies Review* 1:1 (Spring), pp. 59–79.

Laponce, J. A. 1957. "The Protection of Minorities by the Electoral System." *Western Political Quarterly* 10:2 (June), pp. 318–339.

Lasswell, Harold D. 1935. *World Politics and Personal Insecurity*. New York: McGraw-Hill.

Leatherman, Janie, William DeMars, Patrick D. Gaffney, and Raimo Väyrynen. 1999. *Breaking Cycles of Violence: Conflict Prevention in Intrastate Crises*. West Hartford, Conn.: Kumarian.

Ledeen, Michael A. 1996. *Freedom Betrayed: How America Led a Global Democratic Revolution, Won the Cold War, and Walked Away*. Washington, D.C.: American Enterprise Institute Press.

Lederer, Edith M. 1999. "Bosnia Close to Sustaining Peace." *Associated Press* (February 23).

Leftwich, Adrian. 1993. "Governance, Democracy and Development in the Third World." *Third World Quarterly* 14:3 (September), pp. 605–625.

Lehmann, Ingrid A. 1999. *Peacekeeping and Public Information: Caught in the Crossfire*. London: Frank Cass.

Le Monde. 1999a. "L'ONU Defiée" (September 9).

Le Monde. 1999b. "Timor-Oriental: L'ONU Savait" (September 14).

Levy, Jack S. 1988. "Domestic Politics and War." *Journal of Interdisciplinary History* 18:4 (Spring), pp. 653–673.

Lichtberg, Judith, ed. 1990. *Democracy and the Mass Media: A Collection of Essays*. Cambridge: Cambridge University Press.

Lijphart, Arend. 1969. "Consociational Democracy." *World Politics* 21:2 (January), pp. 207–225.

Lijphart, Arend. 1977. *Democracy in Plural Societies: A Comparative Exploration*. New Haven, Conn.: Yale University Press.

Linz, Juan J. 1988. "Legitimacy of Democracy and the Socioeconomic System," in Mattei Dogan, ed., *Comparing Pluralist Democracies: Strains on Legitimacy*. Boulder, Colo.: Westview, pp. 65–113.

Linz, Juan J., and Alfred Stepan. 1996. "Towards Consolidated Democracies." *Journal of Democracy* 7:2 (April), pp. 14–33.

Lipset, Seymour Martin. 1981. *Political Man: The Social Bases of Politics*. Baltimore: Johns Hopkins University Press.

Lipset, Seymour Martin. 1993. "Concluding Reflections," in Larry Diamond and Marc F. Plattner, eds., *Capitalism, Socialism, and Democracy Revisited*. Baltimore: Johns Hopkins University Press, pp. 119–131.

Lipset, Seymour Martin. 1994. "The Social Requisites of Democracy Revisited." *American Sociological Review* 59:1 (February), pp. 1–22.

Lipson, Michael. 2002. "Peacekeeping: Organized Hypocrisy?" Paper prepared for the Workshop on Peacekeeping and Politics, Columbia University, New York (October 18).

Little, David. 1994. *Sri Lanka: The Invention of Enmity*. Washington, D.C.: United States Institute of Peace Press.

Lloyd, Robert B. 1995. "Mozambique: The Terror of War, the Tensions of Peace." *Current History* 94:591 (April), pp. 152–155.

Locke, John. 1963 [1698]. *Two Treatises of Government*. New York: Cambridge University Press.

Lodico, Yvonne C. 1996. "The Peace That Fell Apart: The United Nations and the War in Angola," in William J. Durch, ed., *UN Peacekeeping, American Politics, and the Uncivil Wars of the 1990s*. New York: St. Martin's, pp. 103–133.

Longman, Timothy. 1997. "Rwanda: Democratization and Disorder – Political Transformation and Social Deterioration," in John F. Clark and David E. Gardinier, eds., *Political Reform in Francophone Africa*. Boulder, Colo.: Westview, pp. 287–306.

Louise, Christopher. 1997. "MINUGUA's Peacebuilding Mandate in Western Guatemala." *International Peacekeeping* 4:2 (Summer), pp. 50–73.

Lowi, Theodore J. 1969. *The End of Liberalism: Ideology, Policy, and the Crisis of Public Authority*. New York: W. W. Norton.

Lumsden, Malvern. 1997. "Breaking the Cycle of Violence." *Journal of Peace Research* 34:4 (November), pp. 377–383.

Lyons, Terrence. 1999. *Voting for Peace: Postconflict Elections in Liberia*. Washington, D.C.: Brookings Institution Press.

Mabbett, Ian, and David Chandler. 1995. *The Khmers*. Cambridge, Mass.: Blackwell.

MacDonald, Christine. 1998. "Nicaragua Is Taking Steps to Join the Global Economy – But Road Is Long." *Boston Globe* (August 9).

MacDonald, Christine. 2001. "In Guatemala, Activists Again Targets of Violence." *Boston Globe* (May 13).

MacFarquhar, Roderick. 1997. "India: The Imprint of Empire." *New York Review of Books* (October 23), pp. 26–32.

Makinda, Samuel M. 1996. "Democracy and Multi-Party Politics in Africa." *Journal of Modern African Studies* 34:4 (December), pp. 555–573.

Malaquias, Assis. 1996. "The UN in Mozambique and Angola: Lessons Learned." *International Peacekeeping* 3:2 (Summer), pp. 87–103.

Mallett, Victor. 1998. "Nujoma's Third Term Makes Namibia's Democracy Look Third Rate." *Financial Times* (December 1).

Mann, Michael. 2001. "Democracy and Ethnic War," in Jarak Barkawi and Mark Laffey, eds., *Democracy, Liberalism, and War: Rethinking the Democratic Peace Debate*. Boulder, Colo.: Lynne Rienner, pp. 67–85.

Mansfield, Edward D., and Jack Snyder. 1995a. "Democratization and War." *Foreign Affairs* 74:3 (May–June), pp. 79–97.

Mansfield, Edward D., and Jack Snyder. 1995b. "Democratization and the Danger of War." *International Security* 20:1 (Summer), pp. 5–38.

Marcum, John A. 1993. "Angola: War Again." *Current History* 92:574 (May), pp. 218–223.

Marten, Kimberly Zisk. 2002-03. "Defending Against Anarchy: From War to Peacekeeping in Afghanistan." *Washington Quarterly* 26:1 (Winter), pp. 35–52.

Martin, Ian. 2001. *Self-Determination in East Timor: The United Nations, the Ballot, and International Intervention*. Boulder, Colo.: Lynne Rienner.

Matloff, Judith. 1997. "Southern Africa's Other Story: Economies Roar." *Christian Science Monitor* (August 7).

Maynard, Kimberly A. 1997. "Rebuilding Community: Psychosocial Healing, Reintegration, and Reconciliation at the Grassroots Level," in Krishna Kumar, ed.,

Rebuilding Societies After Civil War: Critical Roles for International Assistance. Boulder, Colo.: Lynne Rienner, pp. 203–226.

McCleary, Rachel M. 1999. "Postconflict Political Economy of Central America," in Cynthia J. Arnson, ed., *Comparative Peace Processes in Latin America.* Stanford, Calif.: Stanford University Press, pp. 417–435.

McClelland, J. S. 1996. *A History of Western Political Thought.* New York: Routledge.

McCormick, Shawn H. 1991. "Angola: The Road to Peace." *CSIS Africa Notes* 125 (June 1991).

McCrae, Kenneth, ed. 1974. *Consociational Democracy: Political Accommodation in Segmented Societies.* Toronto: McClelland and Stewart.

McLean, Lyndall. 1994. "Civil Administration in Transition: Public Information and the Neutral Political/Electoral Environment," in Hugh Smith, ed., *International Peacekeeping: Building on the Cambodian Experience.* Canberra: Australian Defence Studies Centre, pp. 32–64.

McMahon, Colin. 1996. "Contra War is Over, But Nicaragua Still Troubled; Joblessness, Crime Plague the Peace." *Chicago Tribune* (March 22).

McNeely, Connie L. 1995. *Constructing the Nation-State: International Organization and Prescriptive Action.* Westport, Conn.: Greenwood.

McNeil, Donald G., Jr. 1997. "Free Namibia Stumps the Naysayers." *New York Times* (November 16).

Mearsheimer, John J. 1997. "The Only Exit from Bosnia." *New York Times* (October 7).

Mearsheimer, John J., and Stephen Van Evera. 1996. "Hateful Neighbors." *New York Times* (September 24).

Mearsheimer, John J., and Stephen Van Evera. 1999. "Redraw the Map, Stop the Killing." *New York Times* (April 19).

Meden, Natacha. 2002. "From Resistance to Nation Building: The Changing Role of Civil Society in East Timor," *Development Outreach* (Winter), http://www1.worldbank.org/devoutreach/winter02/article.asp?id=141, accessed in May 2003.

Meldrum, Andrew. 1993a. "Lessons From Angola." *Africa Report* 38:1 (January–February), pp. 22–24.

Meldrum, Andrew. 1993b. "Two Steps Back." *Africa Report* 38:2 (March–April), pp. 44–46.

Metzl, Jamie F. 1997. "Information Intervention: When Switching Channels Isn't Enough." *Foreign Affairs* 76:6 (November–December), pp. 15–20.

Meyer, John W. 1980. "The World Polity and the Authority of the Nation-State," in Albert Bergesen, ed., *Studies of the Modern World-System.* New York: Academic, pp. 109–137.

Meyer, John W. 1999. "The Changing Cultural Content of the Nation-State: A World Society Perspective," in George Steinmetz, ed., *State/Culture: State-Formation After the Cultural Turn.* Ithaca, N.Y.: Cornell University Press, pp. 123–143.

Meyer, John W., John Boli, George M. Thomas, and Francisco O. Ramirez. 1997. "World Society and the Nation-State." *American Journal of Sociology* 103:1 (July), pp. 144–181.

Meyer, John W., and Michael T. Hannan. 1979. *National Development and the World System: Educational, Economic, and Political Change, 1950–1970.* Chicago: University of Chicago Press.

Mici, Sokol. 2001. "Albanians See Kosovo Elections As First Step Toward Independence." *World Press Review* (November 28).

Milanovic, Branko. 1999. "Explaining the Increase in Inequality During Transition." World Bank working paper, http://www.worldbank.org/research/transition/pdf/employ2.pdf, accessed in May 2002.

Milward, Bob. 2000a. "The Macro-Economic Impacts of Structural Adjustment Lending," in Giles Mohan, Ed Brown, Bob Milward, and Alfred B. Zack-Williams, *Structural Adjustment: Theory, Practice and Impacts*. London: Routledge, pp. 41–58.

Milward, Bob. 2000b. "What Is Structural Adjustment," in Giles Mohan, Ed Brown, Bob Milward, and Alfred B. Zack-Williams, *Structural Adjustment: Theory, Practice and Impacts*. London: Routledge, pp. 24–38.

Minear, L., J. Clark, R. Cohen, D. Gallagher, I. Guest, and T. Weiss. 1994. "Humanitarian Action in the Former Yugoslavia: The UN's Role, 1991–1993." Occasional Paper no. 18. Providence, R.I.: Watson Institute, Brown University.

Montgomery, Tommie Sue. 1995. *Revolution in El Salvador: From Civil Strife to Civil Peace*. Boulder, Colo.: Westview.

Montgomery, Tommie Sue. 1997. "Constructing Democracy in El Salvador." *Current History* 96:607 (February), pp. 61–67.

Moore, Mick, and Mark Robinson. 1995. "Can Foreign Aid Be Used to Promote Good Government in Developing Countries?" in Joel H. Rosenthal, ed., *Ethics and International Affairs: A Reader*. Washington, D.C.: Georgetown University Press, pp. 285–303.

Moreno, Dario. 1994. *The Struggle for Peace in Central America*. Miami: University of Florida Press.

Morley, Samuel A. 1995a. *Poverty and Inequality in Latin America: The Impact of Adjustment and Recovery in the 1980s*. Baltimore: Johns Hopkins University Press.

Morley, Samuel A. 1995b. "Structural Adjustment and the Determinants of Poverty in Latin America," in Nora Lustig, ed., *Coping With Austerity: Poverty and Inequality in Latin America*. Washington, D.C.: Brookings Institution, pp. 42–67.

Morris-Hale, Walter. 1996. *Conflict and Harmony in Multiethnic Societies: An International Perspective*. New York: Peter Lang.

Moser, Cathy, and Caroline Moser. 2000. *Violence in a Post-Conflict Context: Urban Poor Perceptions from Guatemala*. Washington, D.C.: World Bank.

Moynihan, Daniel P. 1975. "The American Experiment." *Public Interest* 41 (Fall), pp. 4–8.

Muller, Edward N. 1988. "Democracy, Economic Development, and Income Inequality." *American Sociological Review* 53:1 (February), pp. 50–68.

Muller, Edward N. 1995. "Economic Determinants of Democracy." *American Sociological Review* 60:6 (December), pp. 966–982.

Muller, Edward N., and Mitchell A. Seligson. 1994. "Civic Culture and Democracy: The Question of Causal Relationships." *American Political Science Review* 88:3 (September), pp. 635–652.

Muoz, Nfer. 2000. "Central America: The Most Violent Area in the Americas." Inter Press Service (July 31).

Muravchik, Joshua. 1996. "Promoting Peace Through Democracy," in Chester A. Crocker and Fen Osler Hampsen, with Pamela Aall, eds., *Managing Global*

Chaos: Sources of and Responses to International Conflict. Washington, D.C.: United States Institute of Peace Press, pp. 573–585.

Murray, Roger. 1992. *Namibia Through the 1990s: Turning Rich Resources Into Growth*. London: Economist Intelligence Unit.

Mydans, Seth. 1997a. "Faction Surrenders in Cambodia, But Renewed Fighting Is Predicted." *New York Times* (July 7).

Mydans, Seth. 1997b. "Fighting Erupts Between Rivals Ruling Cambodia." *New York Times* (July 6).

Nagel, Joane. 1994. "Constructing Ethnicity: Creating and Recreating Ethnic Identity and Culture." *Social Problems* 41:1 (February), pp. 152–176.

NATO [North Atlantic Treaty Organization]. 1994. "Partnership for Peace: Framework Document Issued by the Heads of State and Government Participating in the Meeting of the North Atlantic Council" (Brussels, January 10, 1994), http://www.nato.int/docu/basictxt/b940110b.htm, accessed in August 2000.

NATO [North Atlantic Treaty Organization]. 1999. "The Alliance's Strategic Concept, Approved by the Heads of State and Government Participating in the Meeting of the North Atlantic Council in Washington D.C. on 23rd and 24th April 1999," http://www.nato.int/docu/pr/1999/p99-065e.htm, accessed in August 2000.

N'Diaye, Boubacar. 2001. "Mauritania's Stalled Democratization." *Journal of Democracy* 12:3 (July), pp. 88–95.

NDIIA and AAI [National Democratic Institute for International Affairs and the African-American Institute]. 1992. *An Evaluation of the June 21, 1992 Elections in Ethiopia*. Washington, D.C. and New York: NDIIA and AAI.

Neier, Aryeh. 1993. "Asia's Unacceptable Standard." *Foreign Policy* 92 (Fall), pp. 42–51.

Neira, Oscar. 1999. "The IMF and Financial Sector Reform in Nicaragua," in *The All-Too-Visible Hand: A Five-Country Look at the Long and Destructive Reach of the IMF*. Washington, D.C.: Development Group for Alternative Policies.

Nellis, John. 1999. "Time to Rethink Privatization in Transition Economies?" International Finance Corporation Discussion Paper no. 38. Washington, D.C.: World Bank.

Nelson, Joan M. 1994. "How Market Reforms and Democratic Consolidation Affect Each Other," in Joan M. Nelson, Jacek Kochanowicz, Kálmán Mizsei, and Oscar Muñoz, eds., *Intricate Links: Democratization and Market Reforms in Latin America and Eastern Europe*. New Brunswick, N.J.: Transaction, pp. 1–36.

Nelson, Joan M., and Stephanie J. Eglinton. 1996. "Conditioned Aid and the Promotion and Defense of Democracy," in Tom Farer, ed., *Beyond Sovereignty: Collectively Defending Democracy in the Americas*. Baltimore: Johns Hopkins University Press, pp. 169–186.

Nelson, Joan M., with Stephanie J. Eglinton. 1992. *Encouraging Democracy: What Role For Conditioned Aid?* Washington, D.C.: Overseas Development Council.

Newitt, Malyn. 1995. *A History of Mozambique*. Indianapolis: Indiana University Press.

Newshour. 1997. "Cambodian Analysis." Transcript of a discussion with Richard Solomon and Richard Walden, moderated by Margaret Warner, PBS television network (July 14).

New York Times. 1999. "Peace and Poverty in Central America," unsigned editorial (March 11).

Nmona, Veronica. 1995. "Ethnic Conflict, Constitutional Engineering and Democracy in Nigeria," in Harvey Glickman, eds., *Ethnic Conflict and Democratization in Africa.* Atlanta: African Studies Association Press, pp. 311–350.

Noble, Kenneth B. 1992. "Angola to Vote, Unsure About West's Democracy." *New York Times* (September 26).

Nonneman, Gerd, ed. 1996. *Political and Economic Liberalization.* Boulder, Colo.: Lynne Rienner.

Notter, Harley. 1965. *The Origins of the Foreign Policy of Woodrow Wilson.* New York: Russell & Russell.

Novak, Robert D. 1997. "Sen. Hutchinson's Way Out." *Washington Post* (September 11).

OAS [Organization of American States]. 2000. "Quarterly Report of the OAS General Secretariat on the Activities of the Unit for the Promotion of Democracy (UPD)." OAS document OEA/Ser.G CP/doc.3284/00 rev. 1 (March 20), http://www.upd.oas.org/documents/cp06881e07.doc, accessed in August 2000.

O'Connor, Mike. 1998. "West Seeing Payoff From Its Support for Flexible Leaders in Bosnia." *New York Times* (January 24).

O'Driscoll, Gerald P., Jr., Kim R. Holmes, and Mary Anastasia O'Grady, eds. 2001. *2002 Index of Economic Freedom.* Washington, D.C.: Heritage Foundation.

OECD [Organization for Economic Cooperation and Development]. 1996. "Shaping the 21st Century: The Contribution of Development Cooperation." Report adopted by the Development Assistance Committee in May 1996, http://www.oecd.org/dac/htm/stc.htm, accessed in October 2000.

OECD [Organization for Economic Cooperation and Development]. 2002. *African Economic Outlook.* Paris: OECD.

Ohlson, Thomas, and Stephen John Stedman, with Robert Davies. 1994. *The New Is Not Yet Born: Conflict Resolution in Southern Africa.* Washington, D.C.: Brookings Institution.

Öjendal, Joakim. 1996. "Democracy Lost? The Fate of the UN-Implanted Democracy in Cambodia." *Contemporary Southeast Asia* 18:2 (September), pp. 193–218.

Olsen, Gorm Rye. 2002. "The European Union: An Ad Hoc Policy with a Low Priority," in Peter J. Schraeder, ed., *Exporting Democracy: Rhetoric Vs. Reality.* Boulder, Colo.: Lynne Rienner, pp. 131–145.

Oneal, John R., and Bruce Russett. 1997. "The Classical Liberals Were Right: Democracy, Interdependence, and Conflict, 1950–1985." *International Studies Quarterly* 41:2 (June), pp. 267–294.

Oneal, John R., and Bruce Russett. 1999a. "Assessing the Liberal Peace with Alternative Specifications: Trade Still Reduces Conflict." *Journal of Peace Research* 36:4 (July), pp. 423–432.

Oneal, John R., and Bruce Russett. 1999b. "Is the Liberal Peace Just an Artifact of Cold War Interests: Assessing Recent Critiques." *International Interactions* 25:3 (September), pp. 1–29.

Oneal, John R., and Bruce Russett. 1999c. "The Kantian Peace: The Pacific Benefits of Democracy, Interdependence, and International Organizations, 1885–1992." *World Politics* 52:1 (October), pp. 1–37.

Oneal, John R., and Bruce Russett. 2001. "Clear and Clean: The Fixed Effects of Democracy and Economic Interdependence." *International Organization* 55:2 (June), pp. 469–485.

O'Neill, William G. 2002. *Kosovo: An Unfinished Peace.* Boulder, Colo.: Lynne Rienner.

Orford, Anne. 1997. "Locating the International: Military and Monetary Interventions After the Cold War." *Harvard Journal of International Law* 38:2 (Spring), pp. 443–485.

OSCE [Organization for Security and Cooperation in Europe]. 2002a. "The Code of Conduct for Political Parties, Coalitions, Citizens' Initiatives, Independent Candidates, Their Supporters and Candidates." Electoral Rule 1/2002 (March), http://www.osce.org/kosovo/documents/electoral_rules/electoral_rule_1_2002.pdf, accessed in July 2002.

OSCE [Organization for Security and Cooperation in Europe]. 2002b. "Certification of Political Parties, Coalitions, Independent Candidates, and Citizens' Initiatives." Electoral Rule 4/2002 (April), http://www.osce.org/kosovo/documents/electoral_rules/electoral_rule_4_2002.pdf, accessed in July 2002.

Ott, Marvin C. 1997. "Cambodia: Between Hope and Despair." *Current History* 96:614 (December), pp. 431–436.

Ottaway, Marina. 1994. *Democratization and Ethnic Nationalism: African and Eastern European Experiences.* Washington, D.C.: Overseas Development Council.

Ottaway, Marina. 1995. "Democratization in Collapsed States," in I. William Zartman, ed., *Collapsed States: The Disintegration and Restoration of Legitimate Authority.* Boulder, Colo.: Lynne Rienner, pp. 235–249.

Oxfam. 1995. *The Oxfam Poverty Report.* Oxford: Oxfam.

Packenham, Robert A. 1973. *Liberal America and the Third World: Political Development Ideas in Foreign Aid and Social Science.* Princeton, N.J.: Princeton University Press.

Palley, Claire. 1978. *Constitutional Law for Minorities.* London: Minority Rights Group.

Panel on United Nations Peace Operations. 2000. "Report of the Panel on United Nations Peace Operations" [Brahimi Report]. UN document no. A/55/305-S/2000/809 (August 21), http://www.fas.org/man/dod-101/ops/war/2000/08/brahimi-full_report.htm, accessed in July 2002.

Pape, Robert A. 1997. "Partition: An Exit Strategy for Bosnia." *Survival* 39:4 (Winter), pp. 25–28.

Papp, Daniel S. 1993. "The Angolan Civil War and Namibia: The Role of External Intervention," in David R. Smock, ed., *Making War and Waging Peace: Foreign Intervention in Africa.* Washington, D.C.: United States Institute of Peace Press, pp. 161–196.

Paris, Roland. 2000. "Broadening the Study of Peace Operations." *International Studies Review* 2:3 (Fall), pp. 27–44.

Paris, Roland. 2001. "Human Security: Paradigm Shift or Hot Air?" *International Security* 26:2 (Fall), pp. 87–102.

Paris, Roland. 2002a. "International Peacebuilding and the 'Mission Civilisatrice.'" *Review of International Studies* 28:4 (October), pp. 637–656.

Paris, Roland. 2002b. "Peacebuilding in Central America: Reproducing the Sources of Conflict?" *International Peacekeeping* 9:4 (Winter), pp. 39–68.

Paris, Roland. 2003. "Peacekeeping and the Constraints of Global Culture." *European Journal of International Relations* 9:3 (September), pp. 441–473.

Parish, Randall, and Mark Peceny. 2002. "Kantian Liberalism and the Collective Defense of Democracy in Latin America." *Journal of Peace Research* 39:2 (March), pp. 229–250.

Pastor, Manuel, Jr., and Michael E. Conroy. 1996. "Distributional Implications for Macroeconomic Policy: Theory and Applications to El Salvador," in James K. Boyce, ed., *Economic Policy for Building Peace*. Boulder, Colo.: Lynne Rienner, pp. 155–176.

Pastor, Robert A. 1998. "Mediating Elections." *Journal of Democracy* 9:1 (January), pp. 154–163.

Pearce, Jenny. 1998. "From Civil War to 'Civil Society': Has the End of the Cold War Brought Peace to Central America?" *International Affairs* 74:3 (July), pp. 587–615.

Peeler, John. 1998. *Building Democracy in Latin America*. Boulder, Colo.: Lynne Rienner.

Peou, Sorpong. 2000. *Intervention and Change in Cambodia: Towards Democracy?* New York: St. Martin's.

Pereira, Anthony W. 1994. "The Neglected Tragedy: The Return to War in Angola, 1992–3." *Journal of Modern African Studies* 32:1 (March), pp. 1–28.

Perez-Brignoli, Hector. 1989. *A Brief History of Central America*. Translated by Ricardo B. Sawrey and Susana Stettri de Sawrey. Berkeley: University of California Press.

Perlez, Jane. 1999. "Annan Says Quick Elections in Kosovo May Not Help Tensions." *New York Times* (October 20).

Phillips, Michael M. 1999. "IMF Makes a Push for Good Government." *Wall Street Journal* (March 19).

Pitcher, M. Anne. 2000. "Celebration and Confrontation, Resolution and Restructuring: Mozambique from Independence to the Millennium," in York Bradshaw and Stephen N. Ndegwa, eds., *The Uncertain Promise of Southern Africa*. Bloomington: Indiana University Press, pp. 188–212.

Plank, David N. 1993. "Aid, Debt, and the End of Sovereignty: Mozambique and Its Donors." *Journal of Modern African Studies* 31:3 (September), pp. 407–430.

Plunkett, Mark. 1994. "The Establishment of the Rule of Law in Post-Conflict Peacekeeping," in Hugh Smith, ed., *International Peacekeeping: Building on the Cambodian Experience*. Canberra: Australian Defence Studies Centre, pp. 65–78.

Polak, Jacques. 1997. "The World Bank and the IMF: A Changing Relationship," in Devesh Kapur, John P. Lewis, and Richard Webb, eds., *The World Bank: Its First Half Century*, Vol. 2: *Perspectives*. Washington, D.C.: Brookings Institution, pp. 473–521.

Pomerance, Michla. 1976. "The United States and Self-Determination: Perspectives on the Wilsonian Conception." *American Journal of International Law* 70:1 (January), pp. 1–27.

Pomfret, John. 1996. "U.S. Diplomat Delays Local Voting in Bosnia." *Washington Post* (August 27).

Posen, Barry R. 1993. "The Security Dilemma and Ethnic Conflict." *Survival* 35:1 (Spring), pp. 27–47.

Prasso, Sherri. 1995. "Cambodia: A $3 Billion Boondoggle." *Bulletin of the Atomic Scientists* 51:2 (March–April), pp. 36–40.

Prendergast, John, and Emily Plumb. 2002. "Building Local Capacity: From Implementation to Peacebuilding," in Stephen John Stedman, Donald Rothchild, and Elizabeth M. Cousens, eds., *Ending Civil Wars: The Implementation of Peace Agreements.* Boulder, Colo.: Lynne Rienner, pp. 327–349.

Preti, Alessandro. 2002. "Guatemala: Violence in Peacetime – A Critical Analysis of the Armed Conflict and the Peace Process." *Disasters* 26:2 (June), pp. 99–119.

Pritchard, Sarah. 2001. "United Nations Involvement in Post-Conflict Reconstruction Efforts: New and Continuing Challenges in the Case of East Timor." *University of New South Wales Law Journal* 24:1, pp. 183–190.

Prunier, Gérard. 1995. *The Rwanda Crisis: History of a Genocide.* New York: Columbia University Press.

Przeworski, Adam. 1993. "The Neoliberal Fallacy," in Larry Diamond and Marc F. Plattner, eds., *Capitalism, Socialism, and Democracy Revisited.* Baltimore: Johns Hopkins University Press, pp. 39–53.

Pugh, Michael. 2000a. "Protectorates and the Spoils of Peace: Intermestic Manipulations of Political Economy in South-East Europe." Copenhagen Peace Research Institute (COPRI) Working Paper no. 36. Copenhagen: COPRI.

Pugh, Michael. 2000b. "'Protectorate Democracy' in South-East Europe." Copenhagen Peace Research Institute, http://www.ciaonet.org/wps/pum01/, accessed in July 2002.

Putnam, Robert D. 1993. *Making Democracy Work: Civic Traditions in Modern Italy.* Princeton, N.J.: Princeton University Press.

Putnam, Robert D. 1995. "Bowling Alone: America's Declining Social Capital." *Journal of Democracy* 6:1 (January), pp. 65–78.

Pye, Lucien W. 1963. *Politics, Personality and Nation Building: Burma's Search for Identity.* New Haven, Conn.: Yale University Press.

Rabushka, Alvin, and Kenneth A. Shepsle. 1972. *Politics in Plural Societies: A Theory of Democratic Instability.* Columbus, Ohio: Charles E. Merill.

Rader, Steven R. 1996. "NATO," in Trevor Findlay, ed., *Challenges for New Peacekeepers.* New York: Oxford University Press, pp. 142–158.

Rae, Douglas W. 1967. *The Political Consequences of Electoral Laws.* New Haven, Conn.: Yale University Press.

Raman, A. S. 2000. "Politics in India." *Contemporary Review* 276:1610 (March), pp. 135–140.

Raplcy, John. 1996. *Understanding Development: Theory and Practice in the Third World.* Boulder, Colo.: Lynne Rienner.

Ray, James Lee. 1998. "Does Democracy Cause Peace?" *Annual Review of Political Science* 1, pp. 27–46.

Reding, Andrew. 2000. *Guatemala: Hardship Considerations.* Washington, D.C.: United States Immigration and Naturalization Service.

Reed, Pamela L. 1996. "The Politics of Reconciliation: The United Nations Operation in Mozambique," in William J. Durch, ed., *UN Peacekeeping, American Politics, and the Uncivil Wars of the 1990s.* New York: St. Martin's, pp. 275–310.

Reeves, Phil. 2003. "US General: 'West is Failing Afghans.'" *The Independent* (March 23).

Reilly, Benjamin. 2001. *Democracy in Divided Societies: Electoral Engineering for Conflict Management.* Cambridge: Cambridge University Press.

Reilly, William M. 2001a. "Annan Asks Year More for Bosnia Mission." United Press International (June 12).

Reilly, William M. 2001b. "Annan: Fund Post-Conflict Activities." United Press International (April 30).

Reinicke, Wolfgang H. 1996. "Can International Financial Institutions Prevent Internal Violence? The Sources of Ethno-National Conflict in Transnational Societies," in Abram Chayes and Antonia Handler Chayes, eds., *Preventing Conflict in the Post-Communist World: Mobilizing International and Regional Organizations*. Washington, D.C.: Brookings Institution, pp. 281–337.

Reporters Sans Frontières. 1995. *Les Médias de la Haine*. Paris: Éditions de la Découverte.

Reuters. 1996. "Youth Gangs Boom in Nicaragua's Peace" (October 8).

Reuters. 1997a. "Cambodia Gives Khmer Rouge Defectors Top Army Posts" (January 10.)

Reuters. 1997b. "Nicaraguan Army Chief Gives Gangs Ultimatum" (January 28).

Reuters. 1998. "UN Lists Political Killings in Cambodia" (April 7).

Reuters. 2002. "Liberia Rounds Up Youths" (February 12).

Reychler, Luc, and Thania Paffenholz. 2001. *Peace-Building: A Field Guide*. Boulder, Colo.: Lynne Rienner.

Rhode, David. 2000. "Kosovo Seething." *Foreign Affairs* 79:3 (May–June), pp. 65–79.

Richards, Alan, and John Waterbury. 1990. *The Political Economy of the Middle East*. Boulder, Colo.: Westview.

Riggs, Fred W. 1995. "Ethnonational Relations and Viable Constitutionalism." *International Political Science Review* 16:4 (October), pp. 375–404.

Rivera Cámpos, Roberto. 2000. *La Economía Salvadoreña al Final del Siglo: Desafíos*. San Salvador: Facultad Latinoamericana de Ciencias Sociales.

Roberts, Adam. 1994. "Ethnic Conflict: Threat and Challenge to the UN," in Anthony McDermott, ed., *Ethnic Conflict and International Security*. Oslo: Norwegian Institute of International Affairs, pp. 5–36.

Roberts, Brad. 1990. "Introduction," in Brad Roberts, ed., *The New Democracies: Global Change and U.S. Policy*. Cambridge, Mass.: MIT Press, pp. ix–xiii.

Roberts, David W. 2001. *Political Transition in Cambodia, 1991–99*. New York: St. Martin's.

Robinson, Mark. 1993. "Aid, Democracy and Political Conditionality in Sub-Saharan Africa." *European Journal of Development Research* 5:1 (June), pp. 85–99.

Robinson, William I. 1996. *Promoting Polyarchy: Globalization, U.S. Intervention, and Hegemony*. New York: Cambridge University Press.

Robinson, William I. 1997. "Nicaragua and the World: A Globalization Perspective," in Thomas W. Walker, ed., *Nicaragua Without Illusions: Regime Transition and Structural Adjustment in the 1990s*. Wilmington, Del.: Scholarly Resources, pp. 23–42.

Robinson, William I. 2000. "Neoliberalism, the Global Elite, and the Guatemalan Transition: A Critical Macrosocial Analysis." *Journal of Interamerican Studies and World Affair* 42:4 (Winter), pp. 89–108.

Rodgers, Dennis. 2002. "'We Live in a State of Seige': Violence, Crime, and Gangs in Post-Conflict Urban Nicaragua." Development Studies Institute, London School of Economics, Working Paper no. 02-36 (September).

Roeder, Philip G. 1998. "Liberalization and Ethnic Entrepreneurs in the Soviet Successor States," in Beverly Crawford and Ronnie D. Lipschutz, eds., *The Myth of "Ethnic Conflict": Politics, Economics, and "Cultural" Violence.* Berkeley: International and Area Studies, University of California at Berkeley, pp. 78–107.

Roemer, Michael, and Steven C. Radelet. 1991. "Macroeconomic Reform in Developing Countries," in Dwight H. Perkins and Michael Roemer, eds., *Reforming Economic Systems in Developing Countries.* Cambridge, Mass.: Harvard University Press, pp. 56–80.

Rogers, Tim. 2001. "Silent War in Nicaragua." *NACLA Report on the Americas* 34:4 (January), pp. 11–15.

Rose, Richard, and Don Chull Shin. 2001. "Democratization Backwards: The Problem of Third-Wave Democracies." *British Journal of Political Science* 31:2 (April), pp. 299–322.

Rosenau, James N. 1995. "Organizational Proliferation in a Changing World," in *Issues in International Law.* London: Kluwer Law, pp. 371–403.

Rosenberg, Tina. 2001. "The Erosion of Political Reform in Guatemala." *New York Times* (June 3).

Rosenblum, Mort. 1997. "Mozambique Now Free-Market Example for Africa." *Chicago Tribune* (December 30).

Ross, Marc Howard. 1993. *The Culture of Conflict: Interpretations and Interests in Comparative Perspective.* New Haven, Conn.: Yale University Press.

Rothchild, Donald. 1997. *Managing Ethnic Conflict in Africa: Pressures and Incentives for Cooperation.* Washington, D.C.: Brookings Institution.

Rueb, Matthias. 1999. "Reconstructing Kosovo: On the Right Track – But Where Does It Lead?" *NATO Review* 47:3 (Autumn), pp. 20–23.

Rummel, R. J. 1979. *Understanding Conflict and War,* Vol. 4: *War, Power, Peace.* Beverly Hills, Calif.: Sage.

Rummel, R. J. 1995. "Democracy, Power, Genocide, and Mass Murder." *Journal of Conflict Resolution* 39:1 (March), pp. 3–26.

Rummel, R. J. 1997. *Power Kills: Democracy as a Method of Nonviolence.* New Brunswick, N.J.: Transaction.

Rupiya, Martin. 1998. "Historical Context: War and Peace in Mozambique," in *Accord: The Mozambican Peace Process in Perspective.* London: Conciliation Resources.

Russett, Bruce, and John R. Oneal. 2001. *Triangulating Peace: Democracy, Interdependence, and International Organizations.* New York: W. W. Norton.

Russett, Bruce, John R. Oneal, and David Davis. 1998. "The Third Leg of the Kantian Tripod for Peace: International Organizations and Militarized Disputes, 1950–1985." *International Organization* 52:3 (Summer), pp. 441–448.

Russett, Bruce, and Harvey Starr. 2000. "From Democratic Peace to Kantian Peace: Democracy and Conflict in the International System," in Manus Midlarsky, ed., *Handbook of War Studies,* 2d ed. Ann Arbor: University of Michigan Press.

Ruthrauff, John. 1998. "The Guatemalan Peace Process and the Role of the World Bank and Inter-American Development Bank." Paper presented to the conference on "Guatemalan Development and Democracy: Proactive Responses to Globalization," Universidad del Valle, Guatemala (March 26–28).

Sachs, Jeffrey D. 1994. "Life in the Economic Emergency Room," in John Williamson, ed., *The Political Economy of Policy Reform*. Washington, D.C.: Institute for International Economics, pp. 503–523.

Sachs, Jeffrey D. 1999. "Twentieth-Century Political Economy: A Brief History of Global Capitalism." *Oxford Review of Economic Policy* 15:4 (Winter), pp. 90–101.

Salih, Kamal Osman. 1991. "The Sudan, 1985–9: The Fading Democracy," in Peter Woodward, ed., *Sudan After Nimeiri*. New York: Routledge, pp. 45–75.

Salmi, Jamil. 1993. *Violence and Democratic Society*. London: Zed Books.

Sambanis, Nicholas. 2000. "Partition as a Solution to Ethnic War: An Empirical Critique of the Theoretical Literature." *World Politics* 52:4 (July), pp. 437–483.

Sambanis, Nicholas. 2002. "A Review of Recent Advances and Future Directions in the Quantitative Literature on Civil War." *Defense and Peace Economics* 13:2 (June), pp. 215–243.

Sandbrook, Richard. 1996. "Transitions Without Consolidation: Democratization in Six African Cases." *Third World Quarterly* 17:1 (March), pp. 69–87.

Sandbrook, Richard. 1997. "Economic Liberalization Versus Political Democratization: A Socio-Democratic Approach?" *Canadian Journal of African Studies* 31:3, pp. 482–516.

Sanderson, John M. 2001. "The Cambodian Experience: A Success Story Still?" in Ramesh Thakur and Albrecht Schnabel, eds., *United Nations Peacekeeping Operations: Ad Hoc Missions, Permanent Engagement*. New York: United Nations University Press, pp. 155–166.

Sanderson, John M., and Michael Maley. 1998. "Elections and Liberal Democracy in Cambodia." *Australian Journal of International Affairs* 52:3 (November), pp. 241–253.

Santiso, Carlos. 2002. "Promoting Democratic Governance and Preventing the Recurrence of Conflict: The Role of the United Nations Development Programme in Post-Conflict Peace-Building." *Journal of Latin American Studies* 34:3 (August), pp. 555–586.

Saul, John S. 1993. *Recolonization and Resistance: Southern Africa in the 1990s*. Trenton, N.J.: Africa World Press.

Saunders, Harold H. 1999. *A Public Peace Process: Sustained Dialogue to Transform Racial and Ethnic Conflicts*. New York: Palgrave.

Schaffer, Teresita, and Hemani Saigal-Arora. 1999. "India: A Fragmented Democracy." *Washington Quarterly* 22:4 (Autumn), pp. 143–150.

Schattschneider, E. E. 1973. *The Semisovereign People: A Realist's View of Democracy in America*. Hinsdale, Ill.: Dryden Press.

Schear, James A. 1996. "Riding the Tiger: The United Nations and Cambodia's Struggle for Peace," in William J. Durch, ed., *UN Peacekeeping, American Politics, and the Uncivil Wars of the 1990s*. New York: St. Martin's, pp. 135–191.

Schedler, Andreas. 2002. "The Menu of Manipulation." *Journal of Democracy* 13:2 (April), pp. 36–50.

Schmitter, Philippe C., and Terry Lynn Karl. 1991. "What Democracy Is . . . And Is Not." *Journal of Democracy* 2:3 (Summer), pp. 75–88.

Schnably, Stephen J. 2000. "Constitutionalism and Democratic Government in the Inter-American System," in Gregory H. Fox and Brad R. Roth, eds., *Democratic Governance and International Law*. New York: Cambridge University Press, pp. 155–198.

Sedra, Mark. 2003. "Lessons From Afghanistan." Foreign Policy in Focus (March), http://www.foreignpolicy-infocus.org/pdf/reports/PRiraqrebuild2003.pdf, accessed in April 2003.

Selbervik, Hilde. 1997. *Aid as a Tool for the Promotion of Human Rights and Democracy: What Can Norway Do?* Oslo: Royal Ministry of Foreign Affairs.

Seliger, M. 1968. *The Liberal Politics of John Locke.* New York: Praeger.

Sellström, Tor, and Lennart Wohlgemuth. 1996. *The International Response to Conflict and Genocide: Lessons From the Rwandan Experience,* Study 1: *Historical Perspective: Some Explanatory Factors.* Copenhagen: Joint Evaluation of Emergency Assistance to Rwanda, Foreign Ministry of Denmark.

Sesay, Max Ahmadu. 1996. "Bringing Peace to Liberia," in *Accord: The Liberian Peace Process, 1990–1996.* London: Conciliation Resources.

Sharpe, Wayne. 2001. "Cambodia: Working With Radio Journalists to Support a Fragile Democracy." *Activate: Journal of the Institute for Media, Policy and Civil Society* (Winter), pp. 4–5.

Shaw, Timothy M. 1996. "Beyond Post-Conflict Peacebuilding: What Links to Sustainable Development and Human Security?" *International Peacekeeping* 2:3 (Summer), 36–48.

Shawcross, William. 1994. *Cambodia's New Deal.* Washington, D.C.: Carnegie Endowment for International Peace.

Shils, Edward. 1991. "The Virtue of Civil Society." *Government and Opposition* 26:1 (Winter), pp. 3–20.

Shukman, David. 1999. "The Agony of East Timor." *National Review* (October 11).

Siekmann, Robert C. R. 1989. *Basic Documents on the United Nations and Related Peace-Keeping Forces.* London: Martinus Nijhoff.

Silber, Laura, and Allan Little. 1996. *Yugoslavia: Death of a Nation.* New York: T. V. Books.

Simmel, Georg. 1956. *Conflict and the Web of Group Affiliations.* Glencoe, Ill.: Free Press.

Šimunović, Pjer. 1999. "A Framework for Success: Contextual Factors in the UNTAES Operation in Eastern Slavonia." *International Peacekeeping* 6:1 (Spring), pp. 126–142.

Singer, Peter W. 2000. "Bosnia 2000: Phoenix or Flames?" *World Policy Journal* 17:1 (Spring), pp. 31–37.

Sisk, Timothy D. 1995. *Democratization in South Africa: The Elusive Social Contract.* Princeton, N.J.: Princeton University Press.

Sisk, Timothy D., and Andrew Reynolds, eds. 1998. *Elections and Conflict Management in Africa.* Washington, D.C.: United States Institute of Peace.

Skogly, Sigrun I. 1993. "Structural Adjustment and Development: Human Rights – An Agenda for Change." *Human Rights Quarterly* 15:4 (November), pp. 751–778.

Slaughter, Anne-Marie. 1998. "Pushing the Limits of the Liberal Peace: Ethnic Conflict and the 'Ideal Polity,'" in David Wippman, ed., *International Law and Ethnic Conflict.* Ithaca, N.Y.: Cornell University Press, pp. 128–144.

Slim, Randa M., and Harold H. Saunders. 1996. "Managing Conflict in Divided Societies: Lessons from Tajikistan." *Negotiation Journal* 12:1 (January), pp. 31–46.

Smith, Adam. 1976 [1776]. *An Inquiry Into the Nature and Causes of the Wealth of Nations.* Oxford: Clarendon Press.

Smith, Brian D., and William J. Durch. 1993. "UN Observer Group in Central America," in William J. Durch, ed., *The Evolution of UN Peacekeeping: Case Studies and Comparative Analysis*. New York: St. Martin's, pp. 436–462.

Smith, Michael G., with Moreen Dee. 2003. *Peacekeeping in East Timor: The Path to Independence*. Boulder, Colo.: Lynne Rienner.

Smith, R. Jeffrey. 1998. "Local Government Hits Snag in Bosnia: Refusal to Share Power With Minorities Leads to Boycotts, Violence." *Washington Post* (January 29).

Smith, R. Jeffrey. 1999. "Firing of Bosnian Serb President Fuels Tension." *Washington Post* (March 6).

Smith, Tony. 1994. *America's Mission: The United States and the Worldwide Struggle for Democracy in the 20th Century*. Princeton, N.J.: Princeton University Press.

Smock, David R., and Audrey C. Smock. 1975. *The Politics of Pluralism*. New York: Elsevier.

Snow, Donald M. 1996. *Uncivil Wars: International Security and the New Internal Conflicts*. Boulder, Colo.: Lynne Rienner.

Snyder, Jack. 2000. *From Voting to Violence: Democratization and Nationalist Conflict*. New York: W. W. Norton.

Snyder, Jack, and Karen Ballentine. 1996. "Nationalism and the Marketplace of Ideas." *International Security* 21:2 (Fall), pp. 5–40.

Snyder, Jack, and Robert Jervis. 1999. "Civil War and the Security Dilemma," in Barbara F. Walter and Jack Snyder, eds., *Civil Wars, Insecurity, and Intervention*. New York: Columbia University Press, pp. 15–37.

So, Alvin Y. 1990. *Social Change and Development: Modernization, Dependency, and World-System Theories*. London: Sage.

Soloway, Colin. 1996. "Bosnia's Freely Elected Fanatics: And the Winner Is . . . Ethnic Hatred." *US News and World Report* 121:13 (September 30), p. 48.

Spalding, Rose J. 1996. "Nicaragua: Poverty, Politics, and Polarization," in Jorge I. Dominguez and Abraham F. Lowenthal, eds., *Constructing Democratic Governance: Mexico, Central America, and the Caribbean in the 1990s*. Baltimore: Johns Hopkins University Press, pp. 3–25.

Spence, Jack, David R. Dye, Mike Lanchin, and Geoff Thale, with George Vickers. 1997. *Chapultepec: Five Years Later: El Salvador's Political Reality and Uncertain Future*. Cambridge, Mass.: Hemisphere Initiatives.

Standish, Bill. 1996. "Elections in Simbu: Towards Gunpoint Democracy?" in Yaw Saffu, ed., *The 1992 Papua New Guinea Elections: Change and Continuity in Electoral Politics*. Canberra: Hyland Press / Research School of Pacific and Asian Studies, Australian National University, pp. 277–322.

Stanley, William. 1996. *Protectors or Perpetrators? The Institutional Crisis of the Salvadoran Civilian Police*. Edited by George Vickers and Jack Spence. Washington, D.C., and Cambridge, Mass.: Washington Office on Latin America and Hemisphere Initiatives.

Stanley, William, and David Holiday. 2002. "Broad Participation, Diffuse Responsibility: Peace Implementation in Guatemala," in Stephen John Stedman, Donald Rothchild, and Elizabeth M. Cousens, eds., *Ending Civil Wars: The Implementation of Peace Agreements*. Boulder, Colo.: Lynne Rienner, pp. 421–462.

Stanley, William, and Robert Loosle. 1998. "El Salvador: The Civilian Police Component of Peace Operations," in Robert B. Oakley, Michael J. Dziedzic, and Eliot M. Goldberg, eds., *Policing the New World Disorder: Peace Operations and Public Security*. Washington, D.C.: National Defense University Press.

Stanley, William, and Mark Peceny. 2001. "Liberal Social Reconstruction and the Resolution of Civil Wars in Central America. *International Organization* 55:1 (Winter), pp. 149–182.

Staub, Ervin. 1989. *The Roots of Evil: The Origins of Genocide and Other Group Violence*. New York: Cambridge University Press.

Stedman, Stephen John. 1997. "Spoiler Problems in Peace Processes." *International Security* 22:2 (Fall), pp. 5–53.

Stedman, Stephen John. 2002. "Introduction," in Stephen John Stedman, Donald Rothchild, and Elizabeth M. Cousens, eds., *Ending Civil Wars: The Implementation of Peace Agreements*. Boulder, Colo.: Lynne Rienner, pp. 1–40.

Stedman, Stephen John, Donald Rothchild, and Elizabeth M. Cousens, eds. 2002. *Ending Civil Wars: The Implementation of Peace Agreements*. Boulder, Colo.: Lynne Rienner.

Steele, Jonathan. 2002. "Nation Building in East Timor." *World Policy Journal* 14:2 (Summer), pp. 76–87.

Steinberg, James B. 1993. "International Involvement in the Yugoslavia Conflict," in Lori Fisler Damrosch, ed., *Enforcing Restraint: Collective Intervention in Internal Conflicts*. New York: Council on Foreign Relations, pp. 27–75.

Stokke, Olav, ed. 1995. *Aid and Political Conditionality*. London: Frank Cass.

Strand, Per. 1991. *SWAPO and Nation Building in Namibia: Transfer of Power in the Post-Communist Era*. Windhoek, Namibia: Namibian Institute for Social and Economic Research.

Strathearn, Andrew. 1993. "Violence and Political Change in Papua New Guinea." *Pacific Studies* 16:4 (December), pp. 41–60.

Straus, Scott. 1998. "UN Ignored My Pleas: Dallaire." *Globe and Mail* (February 26).

Strauss, Julius. 1999. "UN Squanders NATO's Kosovo Victory." *Daily Telegraph* (November 16).

Strobel, Warren P. 2000. "New Times, Old Scores." *U.S. News & World Report* 128:16 (April 24), p. 39.

Studemeister, Margarita S., ed. 2001. *El Salvador: Implementation of the Peace Accords*. Washington, D.C.: United States Institute of Peace.

Suhrke, Astri. 2001. "Peace-Keepers as Nation-Builders: Dilemmas of the UN in East Timor." *International Peacekeeping* 8:4 (Winter), pp. 1–20.

Sullivan, Kevin. 1999. "Decisions Affecting Serb Republic Dismay Local Leaders." *Christian Science Monitor* (March 12).

Swarns, Rachel L. 2001. "Namibia: President Chooses Not To Run." *New York Times* (November 27).

Székely, Miguel, and Marianne Hilgert. 1999. *The 1990s in Latin America: Another Decade of Persistent Inequality*. Inter-American Development Bank Working Paper no. 410. Washington, D.C.: Inter-American Development Bank.

Takeyh, Ray, and Nikolas K. Gvosdev. 2002. "Do Terrorist Networks Need a Home?" *Washington Quarterly* 25:3 (Summer), pp. 97–108.

Talbott, Strobe. 1997. "Democracy and the International Interest." Remarks to the Denver Summit of the Eight, October 11, 1997, U.S. Department of State website, http://www.state.gov/www/policy_remarks/971001_talbott_democracy.html, accessed in March 2002.

Tanner, Victor. 1998. "Liberia: Railroading Peace." *Review of African Political Economy* 75:25 (March), pp. 133–147.

Taylor, Christopher C. 1999. *Sacrifice as Terror: The Rwandan Genocide of 1994.* New York: Berg.

Taylor, Lance. 1993. "Stabilization, Adjustment, and Reform," in Lance Taylor, ed., *The Rocky Road to Reform: Adjustment, Income Distribution, and Growth in the Developing World.* Cambridge: Cambridge University Press, pp. 39–94.

Taylor, Lance. 1997. "The Revival of the Liberal Creed – The IMF and the World Bank in a Globalized Economy." *World Development* 25:2 (February), pp. 145–152.

Temporary Media Commissioner for Kosovo. 2000a. "Code of Conduct for Broadcast Media," http://www.osce.org/kosovo/bodies/tmc/bcoc.php3?lg=e, accessed in July 2002.

Temporary Media Commissioner for Kosovo. 2000b. "Temporary Code of Conduct for the Print Media in Kosovo," http://www.osce.org/kosovo/bodies/tmc/pcoc.php3?lg=e, accessed in July 2002.

Their, Alexander, and Jarat Chopra. 2002. "The Road Ahead: Political and Institutional Reconstruction in Afghanistan." *Third World Quarterly* 23:5 (October), pp. 893–907.

Thoenes, Sander, and Minh Vo. 1999. "Peacekeepers Were Finally Invited to East Timor Sunday; But Has the UN Been Naïve." *Christian Science Monitor* (September 13).

Thomas, George M., John W. Meyer, Francisco O. Ramirez, and John Boli. 1987. *Institutional Structure: Constituting State, Society, and the Individual.* London: Sage.

Thomas, J. J. 1993. *The Links Between Structural Adjustment and Poverty: Causal or Remedial.* Santiago, Chile: Progama Regional del Empleo para America Latina y Caribe.

Thusi, Thokazani. 2001. "Mission Impossible? Assessing Attempts at Linking Humanitarian Assistance with Development Aid in Mozambique's Transition from War to Peace," in Lisa Thompson and Scarlett Conelissen, eds., *Humanitarian Aid and Development Aid in Southern Africa: Clash or Continuum?* Belleville, South Africa: Centre for Southern African Studies, University of the Western Cape, pp. 25–69.

Tracey, Terry. 1995. "Death Squads Reemerge in El Salvador." *NACLA Report on the Americas* 29:3 (November–December), pp. 2 and 42.

Tran, Mark. 2002. "New Imperialism in Sierra Leone." *Guardian* (May 14).

Tvedten, Inge. 1997. *Angola: Struggle for Peace and Reconstruction.* Boulder, Colo.: Westview.

UNDP [United Nations Development Programme]. 1997. *Governance for Sustainable Human Development: A UNDP Policy Document.* New York: UNDP.

UNDP [United Nations Development Programme]. 1999a. *Estado de la Nación en Desarrollo Humano, 1999.* San Salvador: UNDP.

UNDP [United Nations Development Programme]. 1999b. *Guatemala: El Rostro Rural del Desarrollo Humano.* Guatemala: UNDP.

UNDP [United Nations Development Programme]. 2000a. *Compendium of On-going Interventions,* "Table 14: Regular Resources: Commitments by Sub-Focus Areas, 1997–2000," http://stone.undp.org/eis3/compendium/comp98/TABLE14. PDF, accessed in October 2000.

UNDP [United Nations Development Programme]. 2000b. *El Desarrollo Humano en Nicaragua 2000.* Managua: UNDP.

UNDP [United Nations Development Programme]. 2000c. *Poverty Report 2000: Overcoming Human Poverty.* New York: UNDP.

UNDP [United Nations Development Programme]. 2002. *Human Development Report 2002.* New York: Oxford University Press.

UNHCR [United Nations High Commissioner for Refugees]. 2001. *Provisional Statistics on Refugees and Others of Concern to UNHCR for the Year 2000.* Geneva: UNHCR.

United Nations. 1992. *Yearbook of the United Nations 1991.* Boston: Martinus Nijhoff.

United Nations. 1994. *The United Nations and the Situation in Rwanda.* UN document no. DPI/1484/AFR/PKO Aug. 1994. New York: United Nations.

United Nations. 1995. *The United Nations and Cambodia, 1991–1995.* New York: United Nations.

United Nations. 1996a. *An Inventory of Post-Conflict Peace-Building Activities.* New York: United Nations.

United Nations. 1996b. *The Blue Helmets: A Review of United Nations Peacekeeping,* 3d ed. New York: United Nations.

United Nations. 1996c. *World Economic and Social Survey 1996.* New York: United Nations.

United Nations. 2002. *Immediate and Transitional Assistance Programme for the Afghan People 2002.* New York: United Nations.

United States Army. 1994. *Peace Operations.* Field Manual 100–23.

United States Department of State. 2002. *Liberia: Country Reports on Human Rights Practices, 2001.* Washington, D.C.: Department of State.

UNMIK [United Nations Mission in Kosovo]. 2001. "Constitutional Framework for Provisional Self-Government." UNMIK Regulation 2001/9 (May), http://www.unmikonline.org/constframework.htm, accessed in July 2002.

UNMIK [United Nations Mission in Kosovo]. 2002. "Address to Kosovo Assembly by SRSG Michael Steiner." UNMIK Press Release 732 (May 9), http://www.unmikonline.org/press/2002/pressr/pr732.htm, accessed in July 2002.

UNRISD [United Nations Research Institute for Social Development]. 1993. *Rebuilding Wartorn Societies.* Report of the Workshops on the Challenge of Rebuilding Wartorn Societies and the Social Consequences of the Peace Process in Cambodia, held in Geneva on April 27–30, 1993. Geneva: UNRISD.

Urquhart, Brian. 1972. *Hammarskjöld.* New York: Harper Colophon.

USGAO [United States General Accounting Office]. 1993. *UN Peacekeeping: Lessons Learned in Managing Recent Missions.* Document no. GAO/NSIAD-94-9 (December).

USGAO [United States General Accounting Office]. 1997a. *Bosnia Peace Operation: Progress Toward Achieving the Dayton Agreement's Goals.* Document no. GAO/NSIAD-97-132 (May).

USGAO [United States General Accounting Office]. 1997b. *Bosnia Peace Operation: Progress Toward Achieving the Dayton Agreement's Goals – An Update.* Document no. GAO/T-NSIAD-97-216 (July).

USGAO [United States General Accounting Office]. 2002. "Issues in Implementing International Peace Operations." Document no. GAO-02-707R (May 24), http://www.gao.gov/new.items/d02707r.pdf, accessed in July 2002.

USIP [United States Institute of Peace]. 1996. *Special Report on Angola*. Washington, D.C.: USIP.

USIP [United States Institute of Peace]. 2000. *Bosnia's Next Five Years: Dayton and Beyond*. USIP Special Report no. 83. Washington, D.C.: USIP.

Uvin, Peter. 1993. "'Do As I Say, Not As I Do': The Limits of Political Conditionality." *European Journal of Development Research* 5:1 (June), pp. 63–84.

Uvin, Peter. 1998. *Aiding Violence: The Development Enterprise in Rwanda*. West Hartford, Conn.: Kumarian.

Vaccaro, Matthew J. 1996. "The Politics of Genocide: Peacekeeping and Disaster Relief in Rwanda," in William J. Durch, ed., *UN Peacekeeping, American Politics, and the Uncivil Wars of the 1990s*. New York: St. Martin's, pp. 367–407.

van de Walle, Nicolas. 1997. "Economic Reform and the Consolidation of Democracy," in Marina Ottaway, eds., *Democracy in Africa: The Hard Road Ahead*. Boulder, Colo.: Lynne Rienner, pp. 15–41.

VeneKlasen, Lisa. 1996. "The Challenge of Democracy-Building: Practical Lessons on NGO Advocacy and Political Change," in Andrew Clayton, ed., *NGOs, Civil Society and the State: Building Democracy in Transitional Societies*. Oxford: International Non-Governmental Organisation Training and Research Centre, pp. 219–240.

Vickers, George. 1995. "Keeping the Peace: The History and Challenges of the Accords." *Harvard International Review* 17:2 (Spring), pp. 8–11 and 56–58.

Vilas, Carlos M. 1995a. "A Painful Peace: El Salvador After the Accords." *NACLA Report on the Americas* 28:6 (May–June), pp. 6–11.

Vilas, Carlos M. 1995b. *Between Earthquakes and Volcanoes: Market, State, and the Revolutions in Central America*. Translated by Ted Kuster. New York: Monthly Review Press.

Vilas, Carlos M. 1996. "Prospects for Democratization in a Post-Revolutionary Setting: Central America." *Journal of Latin American Studies* 28 (May), pp. 461–503.

Vilas, Carlos M. 2000. "Neoliberalism in Central America," in Thomas W. Walker and Ariel C. Armony, eds., *Repression, Resistance, and Democratic Transition in Central America*. Wilmington, Del.: Scholarly Resources, pp. 211–231.

Vines, Alex. 1995. *Angola and Mozambique: The Aftermath of Conflict*. Conflict Studies Series no. 200. London: Research Institute for the Study of Conflict and Terrorism.

Vivian, Jessica, ed. 1995. *Adjustment and Social Sector Restructuring*. Geneva: United Nations Research Institute for Social Development.

Walker, Thomas W. 1991. *Nicaragua: The Land of Sandino*, 3d ed. Boulder, Colo.: Westview.

Walker, Thomas W. 1997. "Introduction: Historical Setting and Important Issues," in Thomas W. Walker, ed., *Nicaragua Without Illusions: Regime Transition and Structural Adjustment in the 1990s*. Wilmington, Del.: Scholarly Resources, pp. 1–19.

Walker, Thomas W., and Ariel C. Armony, eds. 2000. *Repression, Resistance, and Democratic Transition in Central America*. Wilmington, Del.: Scholarly Resources.

Wallensteen, Peter, and Margareta Sollenberg. 2001. "Armed Conflict, 1989–2000." *Journal of Peace Research* 38:5 (September), pp. 629–644.

Walter, Barbara. 1994. "The Resolution of Civil Wars: Why Negotiations Fail," Ph.D. diss., University of Chicago.

Walton, John, and David Seddon. 1994. *Free Markets and Food Riots: The Politics of Global Adjustment.* Cambridge, Mass.: Blackwell.

Walzer, Michael. 1991. "The Idea of Civil Society." *Dissent* 38 (Spring), pp. 293–304.

Walzer, Michael. 1996. "The Hard Questions: Vote Early." *New Republic* 215:18 (October 28), p. 29.

Washington Post. 2001. "The Kosovo Formula," unsigned editorial (November 23).

Washington Post. 2002. "Losing Liberty in Liberia," unsigned editorial (February 14).

Watson, Paul. 1999. "In Bosnia, Tide Turns Against Hard-Line Serbs." *Los Angeles Times* (March 6).

Weaver, James H. 1995. "What Is Structural Adjustment?" in Daniel M. Schydlowsky, ed., *Structural Adjustment: Retrospect and Prospect.* Westport, Conn.: Praeger, pp. 3–17.

Weinstein, Jeremy M. 2002. "Mozambique: A Fading U.N. Success Story." *Journal of Democracy* 13:1 (January), pp. 141–156.

Weiss, Thomas. 2000. "Governance, Good Governance, and Global Governance: Conceptual and Actual Challenges." *Third World Quarterly* 21:5 (October), pp. 795–814.

Wesley, Michael. 1997. *Casualties of the New World Order: The Causes of Failure of UN Missions to Civil Wars.* New York: St. Martin's.

Wilkinson, Philip. 2000. "Enhancing EU Civil-Military Cohesion and Cooperation," in "Enhancing the EU's Response to Violent Conflict: Moving Beyond Reaction to Preventive Action: Conference Report and Policy Recommendations." International Security Information Service, Brussels, http://www.isis-europe.org/isiseu/conference/conference_3/part_2a_cohesion.html, accessed in August 2002.

Wilkinson, Tracy. 1998. "Slowly, Factions Forming Fragile Peace in Bosnia." *Dallas Morning News* (January 25).

Will, Gerhard. 1993. "The Elections in Cambodia: Taking Stock of a UN Mission." *Aussenpolitik* (English edition) 44:4, pp. 393–402.

Willett, Susan. 1995. "Ostriches, Wise Old Elephants and Economic Reconstruction in Mozambique." *International Peacekeeping* 2:1 (Spring), pp. 34–55.

Williams, David, and Tom Young. 1994. "Governance, the World Bank and Liberal Theory." *Policy Studies* 42:1 (March), pp. 84–100.

Williams, Philip J. 1990. "Elections and Democratization in Nicaragua: The 1990 Elections in Perspective." *Journal of Interamerican Studies and World Affairs* 32:4 (Winter), pp. 13–34.

Williamson, John. 1989. "What Washington Means By Policy Reform," in John Williamson, ed., *Latin American Adjustment: How Much Has Happened?* Washington, D.C.: Institute for International Economics.

Wilson, Woodrow. 1901. *The State: Elements of Historical and Practical Politics.* Boston: Heath.

Wilson, Woodrow. 1965. *The Political Thought of Woodrow Wilson.* Edited by E. David Cronon. New York: Bobbs-Merrill.

Wilson, Woodrow. 1968. "The Modern Democratic State," in Arthur S. Link, ed., *The Papers of Woodrow Wilson,* vol. 5. Princeton, N.J.: Princeton University Press.

Wood, Elisabeth. 1996. "The Peace Accords and Postwar Reconstruction," in James K. Boyce, ed., *Economic Policy for Building Peace.* Boulder, Colo.: Lynne Rienner, pp. 73–105.

Wood, Elisabeth, and Alexander Segovia. 1995. "Macroeconomic Policy and the Salvadoran Peace Accords." *World Development* 23:12 (December), pp. 2079–2099.

Wood, Nicholas. 2002. "Division and Disorder Still Tearing at Kosovo." *Washington Post* (June 22).

Woodard, Colin. 2000. "Bosnia: Stillborn." *Bulletin of the Atomic Scientists* 56:4 (July–August), pp. 17–19.

Woodward, Susan. 1995. *Balkan Tragedy: Chaos and Dissolution After the Cold War.* Washington, D.C.: Brookings Institution.

Woodward, Susan. 1997. "Bosnia After Dayton: Year Two." *Current History* 96:608 (March), pp. 97–103.

Woodward, Susan. 1999. "Transitional Elections and the Dilemmas of International Assistance to Bosnia and Herzegovina," in Steven M. Riskin, ed., *Three Dimensions of Peacebuilding in Bosnia: Findings from USIP-Sponsored Research and Field Projects.* Washington, D.C.: United States Institute of Peace, pp. 5–9.

World Bank. 1992. *Governance and Development.* Washington, D.C.: World Bank.

World Bank. 1994. *Governance: The World Bank's Experience.* Washington, D.C.: World Bank.

World Bank. 1995. *Advancing Social Development: A World Bank Contribution to the Social Summit.* Washington, D.C.: World Bank.

World Bank. 1996a. *Bosnia and Herzegovina: From Recovery to Sustainable Growth.* Washington, D.C.: World Bank.

World Bank. 1996b. *El Salvador: Meeting the Challenge of Globalization.* Washington, D.C.: World Bank.

World Bank. 1997. *The State in a Changing World.* New York: Oxford University Press.

World Bank. 1998. *Post-Conflict Reconstruction: The Role of the World Bank.* Washington, D.C.: World Bank.

World Health Organization. 2003. WHO Mortality Database. February 25, 2003, update, http://www.who.int/en/index.html, accessed in May 2003.

Wright, Quincy. 1930. *Mandates Under the League of Nations.* Chicago: University of Chicago Press.

Wright, Robin. 1997. "Democracy: Challenges and Innovations in the 1990s." *Washington Quarterly* 20:3 (Summer), pp. 23–36.

Wuyts, Marc. 2001. "The Agrarian Question in Mozambique's Transition and Reconstruction." World Institute for Development Economics Research, Discussion Paper no. 2001/14. Tokyo: United Nations University.

Wuyts, Marc. 2003. "The Agrarian Question in Mozambique's Transition and Reconstruction," in Tony Addison, ed., *From Conflict to Recovery in Africa.* New York: Oxford University Press, pp. 141–159.

Young, Tom. 1994. "From the MNR to RENAMO: Making Sense of an African Counter-Revolutionary Insurgency," in Paul B. Rich, ed., *The Dynamics of Change in Southern Africa*. New York: St. Martin's.

Youngs, Richard. 2001a. "Democracy Promotion: The Case of European Union Strategy." Centre for European Policy Studies, Working Document no. 167 (October).

Youngs, Richard. 2001b. *The European Union and the Promotion of Democracy*. New York: Oxford University Press.

Zakaria, Fareed. 1997. "The Rise of Illiberal Democracy." *Foreign Affairs* 76:6 (November–December), pp. 22–43.

Zakaria, Fareed. 2003. *The Future of Freedom: Illiberal Democracy at Home and Abroad*. New York: W. W. Norton.

Zartman, I. William. 1993. "Changing Forms of Conflict Mitigation," in Robert O. Slater, Barry M. Schutz, and Steven R. Dorr, eds., *Global Transformation in the Third World*. Boulder, Colo.: Lynne Rienner, pp. 325–338.

Zimmermann, Warren. 1996. *Origins of a Catastrophe: Yugoslavia and Its Destroyers – America's Last Ambassador Tells What Happened and Why*. New York: Random House.

Index